Collins

Handy Home Tips

First published in 2005 by HarperCollins*Publishers*
77–85 Fulham Palace Road, London, W6 8JB

The Collins website address is:
www.collins.co.uk

Based on material from Collins *Ultimate Home Solutions*

The majority of the photographs in this book were taken by Focus Publishing (see p448 for other acknowledgements)

Edited and designed by: Focus Publishing,
11a St Botolph's Road, Sevenoaks, Kent, TN13 3AJ
Project manager: Guy Croton
Editor: Vanessa Townsend
Designer: David Etherington

For HarperCollins
Senior managing editor: Angela Newton
Design manager: Luke Griffin
Editor: Alastair Laing
Production controller: Chris Gurney

A CIP catalogue record for this book is available from the British Library

ISBN 0 00 719173 1

Colour reproduction in Singapore by Colourscan
Printed and bound by Printing Express Ltd, Hong Kong

Contents

How To Use This Book

***Handy Home Tips* is a uniquely user-friendly guide to most aspects of home living. The pocket-sized format makes it quick and easy to refer to. The chapters are each colour-coded and contain handy tips boxes in the same colour.**

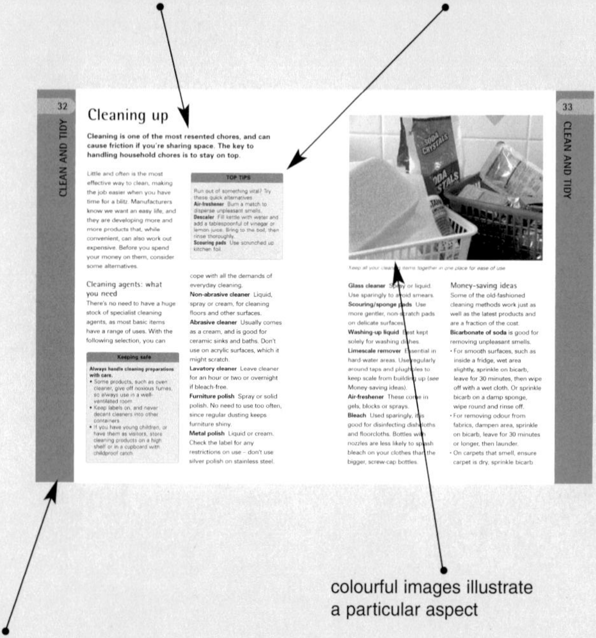
a brief introduction clearly summarises each section
top tip boxes highlight useful advice
colourful images illustrate a particular aspect
colour-coded margins for each section

32 CLEAN AND TIDY

Cleaning up

Cleaning is one of the most resented chores, and can cause friction if you're sharing space. The key to handling household chores is to stay on top.

Little and often is the most effective way to clean, making the job easier when you have time for a blitz. Manufacturers know we want an easy life, and they are developing more and more products that, while convenient, can also work out expensive. Before you spend your money on them, consider some alternatives.

TOP TIPS

Run out of something vital? Try these quick alternatives.
Air-freshener Burn a match to disperse unpleasant smells.
Descaler Fill kettle with water and add a tablespoonful of vinegar or lemon juice. Bring to the boil, then rinse thoroughly.
Scouring pads Use scrunched up kitchen foil.

Cleaning agents: what you need

There's no need to have a huge stock of specialist cleaning agents, as most basic items have a range of uses. With the following selection, you can cope with all the demands of everyday cleaning.

Keeping safe

Always handle cleaning preparations with care.
- Some products, such as oven cleaner, give off noxious fumes, so always use in a well-ventilated room.
- Keep labels on, and never decant cleaners into other containers.
- If you have young children, or have them as visitors, store cleaning products on a high shelf or in a cupboard with childproof catch.

Non-abrasive cleaner Liquid, spray or cream, for cleaning floors and other surfaces.
Abrasive cleaner Usually comes as a cream, and is good for ceramic sinks and baths. Don't use on acrylic surfaces, which it might scratch.
Lavatory cleaner Leave cleaner for an hour or two or overnight if bleach-free.
Furniture polish Spray or solid polish. No need to use too often, since regular dusting keeps furniture shiny.
Metal polish Liquid or cream. Check the label for any restrictions on use – don't use silver polish on stainless steel.

33 CLEAN AND TIDY

Keep all your cleaning items together in one place for ease of use

Glass cleaner Spray or liquid. Use sparingly to avoid smears.
Scouring/sponge pads Use more gentler, non-scratch pads on delicate surfaces.
Washing-up liquid Best kept solely for washing dishes.
Limescale remover Essential in hard-water areas. Use regularly around taps and plugholes to keep scale from building up (*see* Money-saving ideas).
Air-freshener These come in gels, blocks or sprays.
Bleach Used sparingly, it is good for disinfecting dishcloths and floorcloths. Bottles with nozzles are less likely to splash bleach on your clothes than the bigger, screw-cap bottles.

Money-saving ideas

Some of the old-fashioned cleaning methods work just as well as the latest products and are a fraction of the cost.

Bicarbonate of soda is good for removing unpleasant smells.
- For smooth surfaces, such as inside a fridge, wet area slightly, sprinkle on bicarb, leave for 30 minutes, then wipe off with a wet cloth. Or sprinkle bicarb on a damp sponge, wipe round and rinse off.
- For removing odour from fabrics, dampen area, sprinkle on bicarb, leave for 30 minutes or longer, then launder.
- On carpets that smell, ensure carpet is dry, sprinkle bicarb

Introduction

Our home should be where we are most at ease with ourselves. However, running a home is one of the biggest challenges we face in life and most of us tackle it mainly through trial and error, not knowing where to start with the tricky business of home management.

How much are we told about even the basics of home living? For example, renting, buying or selling a home; getting connected to utilities such as water, gas and electricity; and paying regular bills such as water rates and Council Tax. And what about simply cleaning and maintaining your living space? Most of us know how to go round with a duster and vacuum cleaner, but what about really stubborn stains or accidental spills on the carpet or clothes?

Handy Home Tips is a practical, straightforward guide to advise not only the novice, but also those who wish to make their living space work better for them. Each chapter deals with a different aspect of home living, whether you rent or own your own place or whether you live in a flat or a house.

From getting your home thoroughly organised in the first instance, through to cleaning, maintaining and improving it, other chapters cover finding professional help for renovation or home improvements, using your home as a work place and guiding you through the minefield that is buying and selling property.

Handy Home Tips is designed for dipping in and out of rather than reading from cover to cover. The chapters are divided in sections, with an introduction at the start of each subsection within the chapter, clearly summarising what the main idea of the section is about. Coloured boxes contain quick tips and ideas that will really help in the particular area you are looking in.

Whether you have owned your own home for years or are looking for a place to live for the first time, *Handy Home Tips* will prove to be an invaluable source of advice, useful information – and, especially, inspiration.

6:
7:

Getting Organised

If you are aiming to run a smooth, efficient and successful household, the first thing to do is to get the basic compartments of your life in and around the home sorted out and organised.

When routine, day-to-day household tasks are arranged in a manageable way, then it follows that other projects can then be organised and planned without causing too much disruption or difficulty. Time management, keeping on top of bills and correspondence, and storage around the house are among the most important basic household aspects to get straight from the beginning. You will often find that if you take care of the basics, you will also save yourself time and money in the long run.

Time management

Many of us spend so much time dealing with work priorities, that we have too little time left to devote to things that are personally meaningful.

To get out of this rut, step back and think about what's really important to you and have the courage to make this a priority in your life. Check that you're using time productively, so that you can quickly switch into 'efficient mode' when you need to. Decide which techniques here could work for you.

Value your time

Books on time management proliferate, but most carry the same fundamental message – work out what's truly important to you. Think about where you want to be with each of your aims, big and small, in one year, two years and five years. Then work out steps to move you gradually in the right direction, and keep these in your mind as a priority. With very simple time-management techniques, you can win a few minutes here, a few minutes there – and minutes soon add up to hours. Spend these furthering your aims, whatever they are, and you will get a sense of taking charge of your life.

Lists and diaries

- Use the same diary for home and work commitments to avoid confusion.
- Using weekly and yearly planners can help map progress on long-term goals.

'To-do' lists

Some time-management specialists advocate using two 'to-do' lists – a master list, plus a daily one that is updated each night. Others say the more complicated your system, the less likely you are to use it, so one list is all you need. Either way, categorise listed items in order of importance, using labels such as 'must do', 'want to do'. Bear in mind that the most urgent may not be the most important. If you routinely do trivial but urgent jobs first, you may have less quality time for important things.

Decide how to tackle each task by applying the 'four Ds' principle:

Ditch it Put the task on trial: does it really need to be done?

Delegate it Am I the best person to do this task?
Delay it Would it be better to do this when I am less tired, or after I've finished more important tasks?
Do it Prioritise, following these criteria:

- Do the worst job first.
- Schedule the most demanding job for your best time of day.
- Actually doing something, like ringing the plumber, can be quicker than writing it on a list for the fifth time.
- Make big jobs, such as redecorating, less daunting by breaking them down into manageable segments.
- Alternate dull tasks with interesting ones and physical activities with mental ones.
- Performing routine tasks, such as tidying, is effective in short, intense bursts.

What the experts say

Mark Forster, author of *Get Everything Done – And Still Have Time to Play*:
'If we do not find time to play our work suffers, and correspondingly our personal lives are enriched by work well done. Working in a concentrated and purposeful way is less stressful than working in a distracted or unfocused way ... we can do more and better work when we limit our working hours.'

Nicky Singer and Kim Pickin, authors of *The Tiny Book of Time*:
'You can regain control over your life not by cramming more in, but by changing the way you think. Work up a sweat putting weedkiller on the lawn or lie in a deckchair and admire the daisies – it's mind over matter.'

Dr David Lewis, psychologist specialising in stress:
'Without specific and well-defined life goals, you will never really know how best to invest your time. Goals help you to focus your efforts, clarify your thoughts, establish priorities, and improve your motivation.'

Organise your time by writing down what you need to get done

Running the household

- Don't try to clean the whole house in one go. Tackle one room at a time, or one aspect of one room, such as kitchen drawers. Be systematic, and jobs will get done.
- Know when to stop. Spend a set amount of time on cleaning, then move on to something else.
- Wipe down baths and sinks immediately after use.
- Keep a small squeegee in the shower to wipe down walls and door after each use.
- Put a waste bin in every room.
- Keep cleaning materials together in a box or bucket to carry where they're needed.
- Store laundered bedclothes in sets, with a bottom sheet folded round the duvet cover and pillowcases.
- When visitors come, don't rush to complete all preparations before they arrive – let them join in and help you create the occasion.

Food shopping

- Examine your food shopping routine. Most of us shop on the run, making an average of three 30-minute supermarket dashes each week. Consider using local shops to top up rather than driving to a supermarket every time. Reduced toll on your nerves and time makes up for smaller choice and higher prices. Or order via the Internet, and have the goods delivered.
- Bulk-buy staple dry goods – pasta, rice, noodles.
- Divide shopping lists into sections according to the layout of stores, such as fresh produce, refrigerated goods, and the rest. Pack the bags at the till bearing in mind where things will be put at home.
- If you're planning to cook something versatile like bolognese sauce or ratatouille, buy and cook double the amount and freeze the extra portion.
- Put used dishes and utensils straight into the dishwasher.

Time for yourself

- Add time for yourself into your daily and weekly plans, and value this as much as other tasks.
- Give yourself regular time every day to exercise and relax, and to get in touch with things you really care about.
- Be selective when catching up on chores. Are they all essential?
- Aim to leave work behind when you finish for the day –

find absorbing interests that take over from stress.

- Just because a request is reasonable doesn't mean you have to comply with it. Saying yes to others means saying no to yourself.
- You don't need to know everything about everything. Give yourself a break from the news and do something you enjoy more.
- If you're not already doing so, make time for fun: films you want to see, new restaurants to try, interesting books and CDs to buy or borrow, places to go.
- Regularly use quiet time alone to think about your goals.
- Enjoy the moment. Don't waste time hankering after the next house, job, or holiday. Look at the things and people around you and enjoy their presence.
- Don't forget how to be spontaneous.

Technology and time

Technology that is designed to make life easier also increases the pressure to be in touch and react. Hands-free sets mean we can talk on the phone while driving or jogging. Work-related calls come on the mobile at home, at the weekend, on the train. E-mails can be picked up anywhere.

The answer is to **turn off your mobile and pager** when travelling or at home. Don't take them, or your laptop, on holiday. Maintain the distinction between work and leisure, and your health will benefit as you regain a sense of balance.

Don't forget to give yourself time off for pastimes you enjoy

Keeping on top of admin

As e-mail and land addresses are increasingly traded between companies, unsolicited offers and catalogues threaten to swamp the items we genuinely want to read or keep – and they eat into our time.

You may not want your home to feel like an office, but you can still usefully apply business systems to incoming mail and accumulated paperwork: make a firm decision on every item as soon as you can, store only what you have good reason to keep, and be ruthless in what you throw away.

Copies of out-of-date newspapers should be consigned to recycling bins

Sorting mail

- Accept that this takes a little time and don't put it off.
- Open post near the bin and throw away unwanted items immediately. Sort post into stacking trays labelled 'respond now', 'needs action before responding', 'for reading' and 'for filing'.
- As you read post, annotate it – 'book tickets', 'check with S before accepting' – to avoid re-reading.
- Tackle the 'respond now' tray daily and empty it.
- Before keeping any communication, ask yourself whether you really need it. Is there any real likelihood of you going to the event or buying the item on offer? Could you get the information elsewhere if you did need it?
- To make retrieving important e-mails easier, and free up valuable memory space, create folders in your e-mail inbox and file there only what you really need to keep. Set your computer to empty

your 'delete' file every time you log off.

Responding to mail

- When calling service centres, choose off-peak times to cut costs and time spent in a telephone queuing system.
- Keep a stock of plain postcards headed with your address near where you open the post and use them for instant replies. Buy books of postage stamps so you always have some on hand.
- Stockpile items that can wait a while and deal with them every weekend.
- After answering invitations, clip them to your calendar or put in your diary so that you can find them on the day.
- Note non-confidential details that you may need when filling in forms – such as National Insurance number and doctor's address – in your diary or personal information manager.

Getting informed

- Keep things you intend to read in one place. If items are still unopened after a set time – two days, two weeks, two months – throw them out.
- Always carry reading material with you and use every opportunity to catch up.
- When reading, practise following the printed line with your finger to keep the eye from being distracted and increase speed.
- If you're job hunting, check whether newspapers or magazines covering your field offer an online career manager service, which will e-mail job ads to you automatically.
- If you end up throwing out newspapers unread, get a quick news fix from online news sources or from weekly digests (produced as supplements by some newspapers).

What to keep

- Since taxation self-assessment was introduced in 1996, it's been a legal requirement that you **keep records of income and expenditure relating to work** for at least two years after the year to which they apply, and for six years if you are self-employed. If you are in any doubt, check with the Inland Revenue before disposing of financial records.
- Sort carefully any correspondence relating to past events such as house purchases and job searches, and **don't throw out any contractual documents**.
- If you can't bear to throw out **personal letters** and old greeting cards, pack them in a box out of sight so you can enjoy rediscovering them another time.

A filing cabinet is useful; having a decent filing system is even better...

Start a filing system

A small filing cabinet is good for organising household papers, but a portable file box may be all you need. Put papers into plastic or card folders labelled by subject, so that you can take out everything to do with a particular subject in one go.

Named files might include: bank and credit cards (keep bank statements in ring binders of the correct size, available from your bank); clubs/societies; employment; financial planning; garden maintenance and equipment; holidays; household equipment (keep receipts, warranties and the instruction book together); household repairs and maintenance; utilities; insurances; investments; loans; medical/dental records; mortgage; pensions; personal documents such as birth and exam certificates; pet records; receipts for smaller purchases (in case you have a credit card query or need to take something back); savings; subscriptions; tax.

- Stick a list on the front of the file box or, in the case of a filing cabinet, each drawer, indicating files inside.
- File papers as soon as they are dealt with. Do not put them back in the in-tray.
- Before filing, write a 'destroy' date on each piece. Purge your files every time you go to them or once a month.
- Start a new file rather than putting an item in a file that only approximates its subject, where you will have difficulty finding it.
- Tackle a filing backlog for ten minutes at a time. If you get bored, you'll be more likely to stuff papers in the wrong files, just to get them out the way.

Essential security

- Note bank account and credit card numbers, photocopy driving licence and other vital documents, and keep them locked away together with a list of phone numbers to ring in case of loss. Join a credit card protection scheme if you want one organisation to notify all your card issuers of card loss, to save time.
- Keep important documents such as house deeds, wills, share certificates and passports in a secure, fireproof container.
- Whenever your credit or bank card expires, don't just bin it – take a pair of scissors and cut into small pieces. Put the pieces in various bins to thwart any reconstruction efforts.

Junk mail

- **Get your name removed from direct mailing lists** by writing, telephoning, or e-mailing the Mailing Preference Service. It may take three months for your request to be implemented, and may not prevent all unwanted mail, as the system depends on the cooperation of the companies sending material.
- Check any document that asks for mail details and **tick the box requesting that you do not receive further mailings**. Read the text next to the box carefully – some wily companies require you to tick if you *do* want mailings.
- **Use prepaid reply envelopes** to send back requests to be taken off the mailing list.
- When you receive mail from a source that doesn't interest you, take a minute to **send a postcard, headed with your address**, asking to be taken off their list.

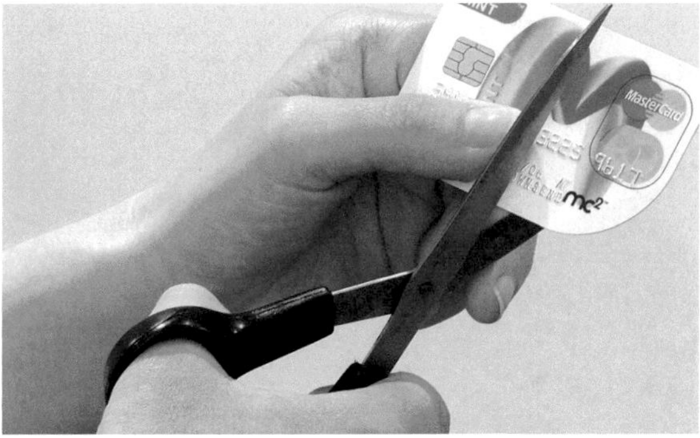

Always cut up old credit cards

Box files or document wallets are ideal for sorting paperwork into categories

Storing other items

- Do not buy tons of storage containers unless you are clear about how you plan to use them – otherwise they will merely create more clutter around the house.
- **Magazines, mail-order catalogues** Keep in cardboard holders, which sit on a shelf. Throw out a magazine whenever you put a new one in.
- **Items needed occasionally** Pin details of sports clubs, medical/dental surgery hours, takeaway menus and so on to a small noticeboard or put together in bulldog clips and hang from hooks under a shelf.
- **Coupons, special offers, affinity card discounts** Clip together and keep in your wallet, so they don't get left behind.
- **Addresses and phone numbers** Even if you store addresses electronically, you might find it useful to have a card index box or small indexed ring binder of contact details near the phone. List emergency numbers – plumber, vehicle rescue, family contacts – on

the front, in case someone else has to phone.

- **Storing items in drawers** Drawers can be extremely useful places for hiding away clutter. However, do not just throw items into them willy-nilly. Have one drawer for a specific purpose, such as a medicines drawer. Divide space inside the drawer to help you see at a glance what's in there. Do not put too much inside that you can't see what's in there. Every few months, clean the drawer out and get rid of accumulated rubbish.

Using technology

- **Manage your bank accounts online** with an Internet banking facility – you can pay bills and make transfers between accounts from your desk. A quick daily check of your balance keeps you in control.
- There are plenty of **money management software packages**, if you can face inputting the figures or make yourself a budget planner (*see* p251).
- **Personal information managers (PIMs)** are powerful organising tools. Everything you enter can be downloaded on to your computer. As well as storing phone numbers, appointments and things to do, a PIM can keep track of budgets, timesheets and expenses on spreadsheets.

Storage containers are only worthwhile if you actually make use of them

SODA CRYSTALS
STAIN
EMOVER
PRE-WASH
Removes:
GREASE
CRAYON
COFFEE

Clean and Tidy

There are some people who have let their homes get out of control and live surrounded by mess, with paperwork everywhere and layers of dust. However, you needn't let cleaning become a chore.

The first step is to make your home as clutter-free as possible, which means sifting through your things and throwing out the junk. Storage is the next stage. Consider as many space saving solutions as you can to make storage as efficient as possible. Only then can you get down to giving your home a proper clean. In this chapter you'll discover some great cleaning and stain removing ideas using cheap, household products, rather than the often more expensive proprietary makes.

Clutter solutions

We have more possessions than any previous generation, yet the stuff we devote so much time and energy to accumulating can become a source of underlying annoyance when the home silts up with piles of items that we don't fundamentally need or want.

'Dejunking' has become almost a spiritual movement in the USA, and the same looks set to happen in the UK. The process uses commonsense techniques, but also seems to have a positive effect psychologically, creating a sense of freedom and renewed energy.

Why dejunk?

Clutter takes up valuable space

Get rid of clutter before you start to think of reorganising your storage.

Clutter needs cleaning

American dejunking guru Don Aslett reckons 40% of time spent cleaning actually goes into shifting clutter, plus cleaning things that you really don't use.

Clutter is distracting

Too much clutter can distract you from what you really want to do, and indecision and fear of regret can get in the way of tackling the junk.

You want to move forward

Work out what you hope to gain from clearing out your junk. What are you making the space for? Identify the things that make you feel relaxed and happy about your home, and use these as a guide to what to get rid of and what to keep.

What is junk?

Rubbish is junk. Most of the stuff piled on kitchen tables is simply rubbish that hasn't been thrown away yet. Likewise dried-up shoe polish, shampoo dregs in the bathroom and odd earrings.
Broken gadgets are junk. So are things with bits missing or that were never quite right.
Miscellaneous jumble is junk. Odds and ends left on a shelf will only gather dust. Separate unrelated items and put them in the right place or chuck them out.
Ancient history is junk. Not just yesterday's phone messages and last year's calendar, but unwanted gifts, too.
Half-finished stuff is junk. Will you ever really finish making that picture-frame?

Recognising junk is an important first step to clearing it out.

The living room should have enough storage to keep items neat and tidy

Cutting clutter

- Treat shopping for goods as passé. Spend the money on eating out, going to the theatre, holidays. Every time you do succumb to a new purchase, throw out a similar, old item. One pair of shoes in, one pair out.
- Have a ten-minute tidy every night before you go to bed. Throw out newspapers, magazines, unwanted mail. Don't let clutter reaccumulate.
- Gather together old packs of photographs. Pick the best from each batch and make them into framed collages, or put into albums. Throw the rest away.
- It is said that 80% of people wear only 20% of their wardrobe. Examine your clothes with a ruthless eye. Part company with items that haven't been worn for over a year, including jewellery. Put clothes that no longer fit into a bag and label with a date six months away. Still not fitting after six months? Take the bag to a charity shop. After that, keep a 'chuck bag' permanently in the wardrobe to fill with things for the charity shop.
- Avoid accumulating a pile of clothes on the bedroom chair. Put your clothes on your bed as you undress every night, then put them away or into the laundry basket before you get into bed.
- If you feel totally overwhelmed by the amount of junk you need to clear, consider calling in a decluttering expert, who may charge an hourly or daily rate to help you with the clear-out. Try the National Association of Professional Organisers.

Six steps to getting rid of clutter

1 Start by equipping yourself with four boxes: one for items to throw away, one for stuff to recycle, one for things you want to keep but that are in the wrong place, and a 'maybe' box for those difficult objects whose fate is undecided.

2 Go round each room, systematically looking in every drawer and cupboard, clearing every surface and shelf. Take it slowly – an hour at a time is enough. Maybe put on a CD to time yourself (when the music stops, so do you). Give yourself one day off every week, and allow yourself a treat when you've sorted out a particularly daunting area.

3 Make 'a place for everything, and everything in its place' your mantra. Put items you want to keep straight back where you found them or in the box for sorting and re-homing. Set up demarcation zones – a place for eating, a place for working, a place for relaxing – and store close at hand the things you use most frequently in each place. Then decide on just one place to keep the most commonly used items – notepads, pens, scissors, sticky tape, writing paper, envelopes, and stamps.

4 You will need to get into the habit of regularly throwing things away – and for a lifelong clutter freak, this is really hard. Ease yourself in gently – start off by chucking out a couple of bags of things you've been meaning to get rid of for ages. Take the process seriously. Don't keep pens that leak, a dodgy watch, a ten-year-old guidebook. If it's ugly or broken, bin it.

5 Deal with the 'maybe' box. It's almost inevitable that the

A place for everything, and everything in its place – keep books on a shelf

thought of throwing out some things will be quite difficult. Many of us find it hard to let go of the past. But you don't have to throw everything away immediately. Put items you're unsure about into the 'maybe' box, seal it up, and label it with a date six months away. On that date, reconsider. If you haven't thought about the items in the box since you put them away, you're ready to get rid of them. Don't even let yourself open the box. If the idea of losing those items still upsets you, put them away for another six months and check how you feel then.

6 Find a creative way to deal with items you've been keeping for sentimental reasons. Look at each piece individually and think about why you want to keep it. Don't keep anything that doesn't make you smile. One way to move forward is to mount and frame part of whatever it is you're holding on to – a few scraps from a dress, one or two letters – then throw the rest away. Or take and frame a photo of a special item before you part company with it. This can be useful for anything large, such as a piece of inherited furniture that doesn't fit into your life as it is today.

What the experts say about junk

- **Mess therapist Yvonne Surrey:** 'Ask yourself, what is the clutter doing to you personally? Is it affecting your creativity, exhausting you, making you depressed, causing rows?'
- **Elizabeth Hilliard, interior design specialist and author of** *Perfect Order: 101 Simple Storage Solutions,* **says decluttering is** 'a good way to cleanse the mind and soul, and very cathartic. It's not just about shelves and files, it's a whole new attitude to life. Rid yourself of the burden of unwanted possessions.'
- **Psychologist Oliver James agrees.** 'We have many times more possessions than our parents' generation, yet rate ourselves as being less satisfied with our lives.'
- **Dejunking guru Don Aslett explains why this is.** He believes that we can become addicted to our belongings, believing that they represent love or security. 'In childhood we think that objects, like teddies, can make us happy. In adulthood, the message becomes: if one little thing makes us feel secure, surely more things increase our pleasure. We look for ways to make ourselves more impressive to other people, and that includes getting and keeping more stuff.'
- **Aslett sees getting rid of clutter as crucial to well-being.** 'Junk is everywhere. It's on us, in us and around us, and we have to take back our control of it. When you get all the junk out of your life, everything improves – mentally, physically and emotionally.'

Storage and saving space

Despite trends towards minimalism, most of us have more possessions than we have space to store them. New houses often have limited storage areas, while older properties may have awkward spaces that don't lend themselves to straightforward solutions.

If you want to impose more order on your belongings, first assess your current and future needs realistically, then search out suitable products, rather than buy items on impulse. Creative use of dead space, such as above a kitchen door or under the stairs, can increase available storage without creating clutter.

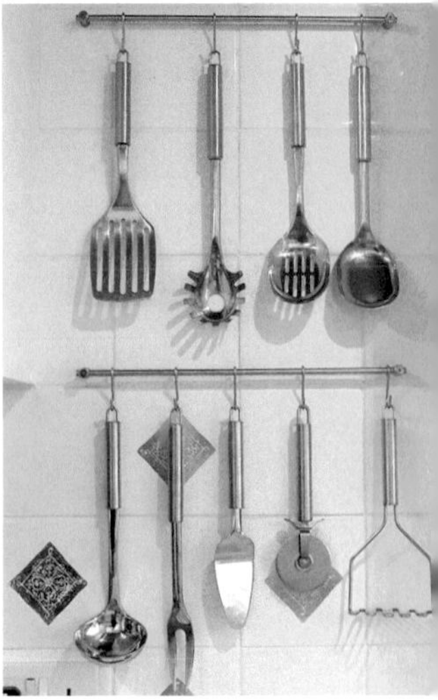

Make the most of wall space by hanging utensils from a row of hooks

Room by room ideas

The kitchen

- The storage space you need depends partly on your shopping routine. If you rely on daily shopping at local or convenience stores, you'll need less space than if you buy a trolley-load of groceries once a month. How heavily do you depend on frozen foods? Can you manage with a small freezer compartment above the fridge or can you justify a more substantial freezer?
- Make the most of wall space by fitting a wire storage-grid, peg rail, or row of hooks for frequently used utensils. Position within easy reach, but far enough away from the hob to avoid grease splashes – unless, of course, you have a hob cover which lifts up to protect them. A wall-mounted wooden or metal plate rack

provides permanent storage for crockery. Ceiling racks can hold colanders, jugs, ladles and even pans, though be sure to leave enough headroom.

- Make use of kitchen unit add-ons. Possibilities include adjustable shelves for cupboards, clip-on baskets, and trays for pan lids. Many items fit any standard unit. Also look for drawer dividers to sort cutlery and utensils; covered tidies for cleaning materials; tiered racks and carousels for pans, lids, crockery, baking tins and groceries. Augment existing kitchen units with free-standing cupboards, extra shelves or a drop-leaf table that could act as a food preparation area.
- A kitchen trolley on castors can simply be parked under a table when not in use. For extra flexibility choose one with a butcher's block on top and drawers or shelves below. Folding bar stools provide breakfast seating that can be stashed away.
- Regularly consign newspapers, bottles, and cans destined for recycling to the garage, shed, or cellar, if you can. Avoid storing in thin plastic carriers, which tend to split. Instead, use stackable plastic crates or baskets, or, if floor space is at a premium, hang plastic laundry

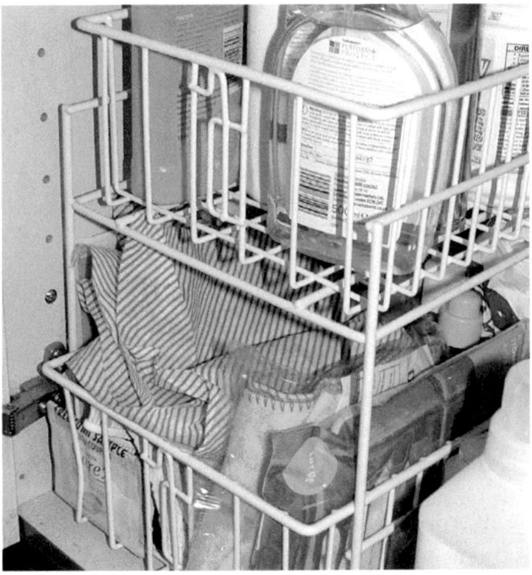

Wire trays or compartments are ideal for storing cleaning equipment so you can see exactly where everything is

A bed with drawers underneath is an excellent solution to storage problems

bags or canvas holdalls from hooks, and sort your papers and rinsed bottles and cans as you discard them.

The bedroom

Bedrooms are often home not just to clothes and associated accessories, but to sports equipment, extra bed linen, luggage and ironing equipment. Ease the pressure by utilising other spaces. A boxroom, wide landing or understairs alcove could accommodate, for example, a trunk, cupboard or chest of drawers.

- Buy a bed with drawers underneath. Failing that, fill the space under the bed with zipped, breathable duvet and blanket bags or else plastic boxes and crates with lids. Vacuum storage packs fit into small spaces. Fill with clothes or bedding, then shrink down using suction from a vacuum cleaner.
- If you're short of wardrobe space, sort clothes by season, and store those not currently in use in breathable bags under the bed. Hang clothes of the same length together. Many items – jackets, shirts, short skirts, folded trousers – only use half the height of a standard hanging-rail, allowing you to fit a second half-height rail below the original one. Add a shelf at the top for luggage and bags. Hang ties and belts on the inside of the wardrobe door.

- Short of drawers? Canvas hanging-holders, divided into generous slots for T-shirts or sweaters, use only 30cm (12in) of wardrobe width. Pocketed organisers are useful in shallow drawers to segregate underwear and other small items.
- Get shoes off the floor and on to racks or in to narrow, purpose-built cupboards. Hanging pockets that hook over the top of a door are a cheap solution for shoe storage and hung inside a wardrobe can be used for scarves, socks or underwear.

Where to buy

Mail order companies specialise in storage items. Check catalogues and web sites for trunks, boxes and baskets; CD, video and magazine racks; units specially designed for computers, TVs and video recorders; corner desks, nesting tables and trolleys. Some companies are dedicated to kitchen storage. Before ordering, work out where you would put each item and measure available space to be sure of fit.

Hardware shops are a good source to buy small storage items. **Superstores and department stores** sell a wide range of storage solutions from shelving and cupboards down to inexpensive fitments that organise the interiors of drawers and cupboards.

Mail order companies or department stores specialise in storage solutions

A wire tray is a useful addition in the bathroom and stops shampoo and shower gel bottles from being scattered around the bath

The living room

You may have books, newspapers, magazines, TV, videos, remotes, sound system, CDs and hobby paraphernalia. If your living room doubles as an eating area, you'll also have dining essentials to accommodate. If space permits, invest in built-in or free-standing storage units.

- Don't have too many shelves in the living room. Necessary for books and good for displaying decorative items, they can also act like a magnet to assorted clutter. Better to add some concealed storage, such as drawers and chests, where unattractive or rarely used items can be kept.
- A small wire-mesh trolley is useful for cutlery, table mats and so on, and can be moved to wherever it's needed.
- Mini chests of drawers are good for keys, stamps and other small items.

The bathroom

- Plastic or stainless steel wire baskets that hang from shower attachments or stand in the corner of the bath get bottles off the edge of the bath.
- Bathroom cabinets are useful for storing medicines and cosmetics but can be very expensive. Buy a plain cupboard, have a mirror cut to fit and screw it into the doors for a cheaper solution.

- Attach a wire grid to the wall and hang wire baskets on it for bottles, face cloths and towels. Or hang string bags on hooks.

Extra storage ideas

- Open shelving is relatively cheap to install. Check the weight of the items to be shelved and buy the correct thickness of wood to avoid bowing. Look to fit shelving where you have unused space. A deep shelf above the kitchen door, for instance, is good for bulky but infrequently used equipment. Buy a small set of steps so that you can reach things safely. Put corners to good use with triangular shelves for cookery books. Mount a glass shelf above or across a window for trailing house plants.
- Hooks that hang over doors need no permanent fixings and provide a place for umbrellas, tools or bags. For outdoor clothes, add a second row of coat hooks at waist height to accommodate jackets.
- Cast an eye over existing furniture to see where it could work harder. Swapping a side table for a low cupboard, for instance, retains a useful flat surface while adding storage space.

Built-in or free-standing?

Whichever type of storage you go for, be generous and allow space to store items you might acquire in future, as well as those you already own.

Built-in storage furniture

- Built to fit it looks neat and makes maximum use of floor space.
- If custom-made by a joiner, it can fit your exact requirements and match your decor.
- Wardrobes need a minimum depth of 60cm (24in) to allow clothes to hang freely.
- Off-the-peg ranges come in a wide choice of styles and prices.
- Cheaper built-in furniture can be updated by adding new handles and painting over a melamine finish – wet first and rub down lightly (just enough to roughen the surface without penetrating the melamine) with fine, waterproof glasspaper, before applying vinyl silk or matt paint.
- Built-in storage can add to the value of your home, but is probably only worth the outlay if you plan to stay for several years.

Free-standing storage furniture

- Individual pieces or sets give a warmer, more furnished look than built-in units, and are particularly appropriate in period properties.
- Free-standing furniture is usually less expensive than built-in, particularly if you buy second-hand and revamp it.
- Individual items can be made to fit in with existing built-in furniture by filling gaps at sides and above with fascia-boards.
- You can take it with you when you move – though there is a risk that it will not fit the style or available spaces in your next home.

Cleaning up

Cleaning is one of the most resented chores, and can cause friction if you're sharing space. The key to handling household chores is to stay on top.

Little and often is the most effective way to clean, making the job easier when you have time for a blitz. Manufacturers know we want an easy life, and they are developing more and more products that, while convenient, can also work out expensive. Before you spend your money on them, consider some alternatives.

> **TOP TIPS**
>
> Run out of something vital? Try these quick alternatives.
> **Air-freshener** Burn a match to disperse unpleasant smells.
> **Descaler** Fill kettle with water and add a tablespoonful of vinegar or lemon juice. Bring to the boil, then rinse thoroughly.
> **Scouring pads** Use scrunched up kitchen foil.

Cleaning agents: what you need

There's no need to have a huge stock of specialist cleaning agents, as most basic items have a range of uses. With the following selection, you can cope with all the demands of everyday cleaning.

> **Keeping safe**
>
> **Always handle cleaning preparations with care.**
>
> - Some products, such as oven cleaner, give off noxious fumes, so always use in a well-ventilated room.
> - Keep labels on, and never decant cleaners into other containers.
> - If you have young children, or have them as visitors, store cleaning products on a high shelf or in a cupboard with childproof catch.

Non-abrasive cleaner Liquid, spray or cream, for cleaning floors and other surfaces.

Abrasive cleaner Usually comes as a cream, and is good for ceramic sinks and baths. Don't use on acrylic surfaces, which it might scratch.

Lavatory cleaner Leave cleaner for an hour or two or overnight if bleach-free.

Furniture polish Spray or solid polish. No need to use too often, since regular dusting keeps furniture shiny.

Metal polish Liquid or cream. Check the label for any restrictions on use – don't use silver polish on stainless steel.

Keep all your cleaning items together in one place for ease of use

Glass cleaner Spray or liquid. Use sparingly to avoid smears.
Scouring/sponge pads Use more gentler, non-scratch pads on delicate surfaces.
Washing-up liquid Best kept solely for washing dishes.
Limescale remover Essential in hard-water areas. Use regularly around taps and plugholes to keep scale from building up (*see* Money-saving ideas).
Air-freshener These come in gels, blocks or sprays.
Bleach Used sparingly, it is good for disinfecting dishcloths and floorcloths. Bottles with nozzles are less likely to splash bleach on your clothes than the bigger, screw-cap bottles.

Money-saving ideas

Some of the old-fashioned cleaning methods work just as well as the latest products and are a fraction of the cost.
Bicarbonate of soda is good for removing unpleasant smells.

- For smooth surfaces, such as inside a fridge, wet area slightly, sprinkle on bicarb, leave for 30 minutes, then wipe off with a wet cloth. Or sprinkle bicarb on a damp sponge, wipe round and rinse off.
- For removing odour from fabrics, dampen area, sprinkle on bicarb, leave for 30 minutes or longer, then launder.
- On carpets that smell, ensure carpet is dry, sprinkle bicarb

generously and leave for at least 30 minutes (overnight in bad cases) before vacuuming off.

Salt can prove very handy.

- To get rid of black stains left by eggs on cutlery, rub the area with a damp cloth sprinkled with salt.
- Revive dingy carpets by sprinkling salt generously, leaving for an hour or two, then vacuuming.
- To unblock drains without using a caustic cleaner, pour in 70g (2½oz) salt and 70g (2½oz) bicarb, followed by 1 litre (2 pints) of boiling water. Leave overnight, then flush thoroughly with water. Alternatively, try 70g (2½oz) bicarb and 100ml (3½fl oz) white vinegar. Cover drain and leave for a few minutes, then pour boiling water down to flush. Don't use either of these remedies if a proprietary drain-cleaner has already been used.

Vinegar is versatile.

- Paint white vinegar onto stubborn price tags on china and glass. Leave to soak in, then rub the tag off.
- Wash dull kitchen floors with a solution of 200ml (7fl oz) vinegar in 2 litre (4pt) water.
- To slow grease build-up, wipe out your oven with a cloth dampened with water and vinegar.
- Cover limescale deposits round taps and plugholes with kitchen roll soaked in vinegar. Leave for an hour, then scrape

Lemon juice can be mixed with vegetable oil for a fragrant furniture polish

off the softened scale using a blunt knife tip. Another method is to use a flour and vinegar paste.
- For streak-free windows, wash with a mixture of equal parts warm water and white vinegar, and dry with a soft cloth. Don't clean windows when the sun is shining on them.
- To unblock a clogged shower head, soak for an hour in a solution of equal parts hot water and white vinegar.

Ice cubes applied to fresh grease spots on a wooden floor will harden the grease, which can then be gently scraped off with a round-edged knife.

Lemon juice and vegetable oil in equal parts is a good mixture for treating furniture scratches. Rub gently into the scratches with a soft cloth. A blend of two parts oil to one part lemon juice makes an effective and fragrant furniture polish.

Methylated spirit removes grease and grime from telephones and piano keys. A little on a damp cloth gives extra shine to mirrors and glass.

Mustard powder and water can deodorise bottles and jars. Just rinse – no need to soak.

Stale bread, rubbed on gently, can clean dirty marks from wallpaper or leather.

Basic cleaning kit

The equipment you can't afford to be without:

Vacuum cleaner Buy the most powerful cleaner you can afford. Cylinder cleaners are good for tackling stairs and tricky corners, while uprights are good for large rooms. Make use of the cleaner's attachments – an upholstery nozzle is small and wedge-shaped with no bristles, good for getting pet hairs or crumbs off dining chairs, sofas and armchairs. The dusting brush has soft bristles and is suitable for curtains and lampshades, as well as window sills, hearths and other smooth surfaces. The crevice nozzle is long and slender, ideal for getting into corners and between sofa cushions.

Long-handled soft and hard brooms Easier to use than a brush and dustpan on large floor areas. Use soft broom on wood, vinyl or tiled floors, hard broom on concrete surfaces or patios.

Sponge mop Choose one that wrings out the sponge.

Bucket Buy a large one, for less-frequent refills. Rectangular buckets are easier to use if you have a wide mop-head than round buckets.

Scrubbing brush Handy for removing ingrained dirt on quarry tiles or other tough surfaces.

Chamois leather Especially good for glass and windows.

Dusters and soft cloths Use old cotton T-shirts – they don't shed fibres.

Dusting brush Good for tackling cobwebs, awkward corners and light-fittings. Choose between a short or long-handled brush, with dusting head made of fleece, feathers or sponge. Antistatic dusters and brushes are designed to repel dust from TV and computer screens.

Cleaning routines around the house

Bathrooms

Baths and basins

- Check labels of proprietary cleaners and stain removers – not all of them are suitable for all materials.
- Wipe round baths, basins, bidets, showers and taps straight after use. Wipe off toothpaste splashes immediately – some brands, particularly those containing fluoride, can harm the glaze on vitreous china. Oily bath additives create rings round the tub – rinse off immediately after emptying bath. Dried-on rings can be removed with a damp sponge sprinkled with bicarbonate of soda or vinegar.
- Use an old toothbrush or even a baby's bottlebrush for cleaning overflows and round plugholes.
- Rinse soap dishes often, to prevent a build-up of hardened soap on basin, bath or shower.
- Treat light scratches on acrylic baths by rubbing gently with metal polish.
- Never leave washing to soak in detergent in an enamelled bath or basin.

Limescale

Take care with limescale removers; check on the pack that they are suitable for the particular surface. Enamel is easily damaged, even by mild solutions. You can use a paste of flour and lemon juice or vinegar, but even these can eat into the surface below the limescale, so check frequently and remove as soon as possible. Once the limescale is softened, wash off completely. Try rubbing stubborn deposits with the flat end of a wooden clothes peg, but go easy to avoid scratches.

Ten ways to a cleaner home

1. Rather than trying to blitz the whole house, do **one room at a time** and do it thoroughly.
2. **Share chores** – get everyone to do the jobs they prefer.
3. When **dusting**, start at the top of the room and work down.
4. When **washing walls**, start at the bottom of the wall and work up, since water trickling onto dry surfaces can create indelible streaks.
5. **Tidy daily** to make cleaning easier
6. **Don't let dirt build up** or splash marks set. Wipe the stove top clean after use.
7. Put a **waste bin** in every room and aim to empty daily.
8. Place a **large doormat** inside every external door.
9. Keep **sets of cleaning equipment** in the bathroom and bedrooms to make spontaneous cleaning simple.
10. To keep rooms smelling fresh, **open windows daily**.

WCs

- Lavatory brushes, when used correctly, are wonderful inventions. Unfortunately, they are often left unwashed, festering away in their containers, breeding untold germs and bacteria. Try replacing your brush with a pair of long rubber gloves – used solely for use down the toilet. If you must use them, wash lavatory brushes in hot, soapy water, then rinse with hot water plus a shot of disinfectant.
- Scrub the toilet bowl daily, including under the rim.
- Wipe around the seat, including the area around the hinges.
- Don't mix different toilet cleaners, and never mix a cleaner with bleach. Don't use bleach if you are also using a cleaner block in the cistern.
- Flush away bleach cleaners after no more than an hour – they can discolour the glaze below the waterline if left for too long.

Taps and showers

- Be gentle with these, as the finishes are easily damaged. Avoid abrasive cleaners – use warm soapy water instead. Dry taps after cleaning and polish with a soft cloth.
- Clean glass shower doors with a damp sponge sprinkled with white vinegar.
- Before hanging it, soak a new shower curtain in a salt water solution to help prevent mildew forming.

Tiling

- Dirt comes off tiles more easily when loosened by steam, so run a hot shower for a few minutes before starting. Open a window when you've finished.
- Wipe tiles with warm soapy water, rinse and dry with a soft cloth. Don't use abrasive cleaners, which might damage the glaze.
- Clean blackened grout with a proprietary antifungal cleaner, or paint carefully with a mild bleach solution, leave for a few minutes, then rinse off. Do not attempt to clean with wire wool, which can produce rust stains. Avoid mould growth by ventilating the bathroom.

Living rooms and bedrooms

Carpets

- Vacuum regularly to remove dirt before it becomes ingrained.
- On smooth, cut-pile carpets, an upright cleaner with a 'beater bar' that raises dust and dirt gives the best results. For loop-pile (such as Berbers) and

Cleaning schedule

Every day
- Tidy all living areas.
- Chuck old newspapers or store for recycling.
- Empty rubbish.
- Wipe sinks, baths and showers.
- Put dirty clothes into laundry basket.
- Hang clothes up.

Every week
- Clean worktops and other surfaces with all-purpose cleaner.
- Dust and polish.
- Vacuum floors.
- Wash kitchen floor.

Every month
- Clean out fridge.
- Wipe kitchen cabinets, inside and out.
- Move furniture and vacuum underneath.
- Dust walls, furniture, light-fittings.

deep-pile carpets, a cylinder suction-cleaner is better.

- If carpets still look grimy after vacuuming, consider deep cleaning with a shampooer or spray extraction-cleaner. Both can be hired or the job can be done professionally.
- Carpets treated with stain repellent, either during manufacture or after laying, are easier to clean.
- Use a stain remover on small spots or try a washing-up liquid solution – often just as effective. Either way, test on a hidden spot first.
- Tackle carpet stains immediately. Don't rub wet stains, but blot them with a white cloth. Rinse thoroughly, as any stain remover left behind can attract more dirt.

Wooden floors

Make up a solution of 120ml (4fl oz) cider vinegar in 4 litres (8pt) warm water. Squeeze out a soft cloth in this solution until just damp, then wipe floor. Dry with another cloth to bring up the shine.

Vinyl floors

- Sweep or vacuum with hard-floor attachment to remove loose debris, then mop with a solution of dishwasher detergent in warm water. Tackle ground-in grime with a white nylon scourer. Polish or wax the surface occasionally to help prevent dirt penetrating.
- Remove heel marks from solid floors with a pencil eraser.

Curtains and blinds

- Use the vacuum cleaner dusting brush to remove dust from curtains and blinds.
- Clean venetian blinds by wiping slats with a damp cloth or using a special brush designed for blinds.

Furniture

- A soft, clean paintbrush is good for winkling dust out of carved or awkward parts of furniture. An old toothbrush gets into really tight corners.

- Regularly move furniture to vacuum underneath.

Cane and wicker

Vacuum with dusting brush. Wash down occasionally using a solution of 30ml (1fl oz) ammonia to 4 litres (8pt) warm water. Wear rubber gloves and rinse well. Leave to dry outside, avoiding direct sunlight.

Dusting

- Speed up by putting an old sock on each hand and dusting with both simultaneously.
- Don't forget the tops of doors and pictures, light fittings, mouldings on doors and skirting boards.
- Remove dust from wallpapered walls by vacuuming lightly with the dusting brush attachment.
- To reduce the static which encourages dust to collect on TV and computer screens, wipe them with a dampened fabric-softener sheet.

Lampshades

- Vacuum fabric and pleated lampshades with the dusting brush. Don't let dirt accumulate as it could stain.
- Plain fabric lampshades can be dunked in warm soapy water, rinsed, and dried. Treat with caution any that are trimmed or edged with a different colour, as the colour may run.

Glass table tops

Rub over glass with lemon juice on a soft cloth; dry, then polish with scrunched newspaper.

Kitchen

Sinks

Stainless-steel sinks and drainers sparkle if wiped with a little vinegar on a cloth.

Worktops

- Remove everything, then sweep up or vacuum crumbs, using crevice nozzle in corners.
- Use an all-surface cleaner in warm water to wash down worktops and tiling, tackling any hard deposits with a white nylon scourer. Dry and polish with an old cotton T-shirt.

Cleaning kitchen equipment

- **Let burnt saucepans stand overnight filled with a strong salt-water solution**, then bring to the boil slowly. The burnt material will come away easily and you can then wash off.
- **Clean the outside of cast iron pans with oven cleaner spray.** To prevent rust, rub vegetable oil on the insides after washing. Remove rust spots with scouring powder.
- After cooking scrambled eggs, immediately **soak the pan for 15 minutes with water plus a dessertspoonful of dishwasher detergent**. Use plain cold water for porridge pans.
- **Rub a chopping board with a cut lemon** or a squirt of lemon juice to kill smells.

Stain removal

Spills and stains on clothes and carpets are best dealt with as quickly as possible. Luckily, many modern fabrics are easy to care for, and there's a wide range of products that deal kindly and effectively with most everyday stains.

For stains that prove to be more stubborn, there are some specialist techniques that you can try.

First response

Using the right technique on a specific stain can make all the difference to your success. If you don't know what caused the stain on a garment, take the item to a dry cleaner's. Be sure to point out the stain, which otherwise might be missed.

For most stains on washable fabrics an overnight soak in cold water can be an effective initial treatment. If this does not clear the stain, use the branded stain remover of your choice and follow, if necessary, with a wash on the correct cycle for the fabric, using biological detergent. Most common stains will respond to this treatment.

For stubborn or tricky stains, try the various techniques and handy hints suggested in the *A–Z of tricky stains* on the following pages. Give a DIY remedy a good chance to work before trying another method. If you use stain-shifters like glycerine or eucalyptus oil, work them well into the stain for maximum effect, but do it gently.

> **TOP TIP**
>
> **Clean and deodorise baby spills or accidents on your carpet** by soaking up as much of the spill as possible. Clean the stain according to the carpet manufacturer's instructions and allow to dry. When the area is dry, sprinkle liberally with baking soda and leave it for 15 minutes before vacuuming it up.

A–Z of tricky stains

Baking trays

Rusting is a common problem with baking trays. To remove rust from tin trays, rub with half a raw potato that has been dipped in scouring powder. Rinse off, then dry in a moderately warm oven. To prevent rusting in the first place, rub the new tray inside

Proprietary stain removers are useful to have among your cleaning equipment

and out with lard and place it in a moderate oven for 45 minutes. Once it has cooled off, wipe with a piece of kitchen towel.

Ballpoint ink

There are quite a few tips for removing ink stains from all types of surfaces. It may be a trial and error process, but eventually you will get there with one of these tips.

Many of the specialist stain removers deal with ballpoint ink. Alternatively, soak a pad of cotton wool in methylated spirits and hold it under the stain. Use dry cotton wool to dab from above in order to draw the meths up through the fibres and shift the stain. A Q-tip or cotton wool bud also works well and is excellent for getting into awkward areas.

Another option is to apply a couple of squirts of hairspray to the stain, then rub gently with a

TOP TIP

To clean the grimy or mouldy bottom of a shower curtain, put the bottom of the shower curtain in a bucket of cold water mixed with two capfuls of bleach. Check every ten minutes to see when it is ready to remove. Empty the bucket and wash off the shower curtain with running water using a hand shower.

Techniques for tackling stains

Act fast – fresh stains are far easier to shift than old, dried ones.

- Never dab at a stain with a coloured cloth or paper – the dye might run and make the problem worse. Use plain white kitchen paper or cloths.
- Carefully scrape off any surface deposit before you start treating the fabric.
- Test any stain-removal product on the least obvious corner of fabrics, to make sure that the colour doesn't run.
- Use mild treatments before moving on to stronger ones.
- Avoid the temptation to rub vigorously at a stain, as you may damage the fibres and leave a permanent mark. Instead, dab carefully, and be prepared to treat the stain several times, until it has completely disappeared.
- Start work at the edge of the stain, moving gradually to the centre.
- For a really bad stain, take the item straight to the cleaner's rather than having a go at it yourself.
- Silk is particularly delicate and is often better treated by a professional, as are velvet and lurex materials.

dry cloth. Either way, launder as usual after treatment.

You can also remove ink stains on coloured fabrics by soaking the the material in milk overnight and then launder as usual.

If your ink stain is on a white material, use a bit of lemon juice and salt made into a paste and then rub the ink stained area. Letting the material hang dry in the sun will leave your white material quite stain free!

To remove ink marks from a wall, apply toothpaste to the marks, wait 30 minutes and then wipe clean.

Baths

A tap that has been left to drip over time can leave unsightly stains in the bath. Try rubbing a paste made from lemon juice and salt onto the stain, then rinse well. If this method does not work, use a toothbrush and rub in a mixture of cream of tartar and peroxide. Rinse off well.

A heavily soiled bath is best dealt with by filling the bath with warm water and adding a few scoops of biological washing powder. Leave the water in the bath to soak overnight, then let the water out and rinse well.

Bath mats

Lots of people have an overhead shower in the bath and use a bath mat or shower slip mat to make it safer when showering. To prevent your slip mat becoming mouldy or mildewy in the first place, wash

Rub at the edge of a stain and move gradually to the centre

the mat on both sides with hot soapy water after use.

However, if the mat has already got signs of mould growing on it, scrub it off using a nailbrush and a mixture of one part bleach and four parts hot water. Wear rubber or latex gloves to do this.

Beer

Beer leaves a brown mark on clothes if left to dry. Sponge gently with vinegar and warm water, then wash as usual. On dried stains, try rubbing gently with methylated spirits.

Bird droppings

Clean washing hanging on the washing line is the usual – and most annoying – victim. Scrape off any deposit and rewash. Berry stains may be stubborn – use a stain remover before washing or soak in a solution of biological washing powder.

Blood

There are various ideas and tips for removing blood stains. Try the various methods and see which steps work best for you.

If the blood stain is fresh and it is possible to soak the

Put together a stain-removal kit

Special stain-removing products for laundry include:

- **branded stain removers in bottles**, usually with a foam applicator or rollerball top
- **pre-wash sprays in guns**
- **soaking solutions**
- **stain-removing powders and liquids** to use with ordinary detergents
- **everyday detergents** with extra stain-removing properties
- **biological detergents** (it's worth having a small quantity in the cupboard, even if you don't normally use one)
- **soap bars** (cheap and often effective).

Some of the treatments in the A–Z in this section involve traditional stain removers, available from pharmacies, such as **methylated spirits, glycerine, eucalyptus oil, bleach** and **borax**.

For stains on carpets or upholstery, specialist **carpet stain removers** are available as sprays or mousses.

After treating blood-stained clothes, spray with a pre-treat product and wash

clothing item or piece of carpet, then do so immediately in cold water and the stain will flow out. Do not use warm or hot water as this will set the blood in the material. If the blood stain is more stubborn, then apply a paste of meat tenderising crystals and cold water to the area, leave for about an hour and rinse in cool water.

Fresh blood stains on clothes are easier to remove when you rub an ice cube over the stained area. Once you see the ice starting to melt, rinse in cold water and launder as usual.

Another tip for removing stubborn blood stains is by applying hydrogen peroxide to the stained area, allowing it to bubble, then keep repeating

TOP TIP

Cover smears of **bicycle or engine oil** on clothes with a generous amount of neat washing-up liquid and work it in well, before wiping off with a clean cloth. Gently rub with warm water, then launder.

the application until stain is gone. Launder as usual. Hydrogen peroxide is the main ingredient in commercial blood stain removers.

You can also get blood stains out of clothing or carpeting using a paste made of corn starch and water. Apply the thick paste to the stained area, then rinse with cool water and blot as needed. After the area has dried, brush off any residue or vacuum up the excess corn starch.

A step-by-step method can work on really stubborn blood stains on clothing:

- Soak in cold milk and rub until nearly gone.
- Immerse and rub in ice cold water that has one tablespoon ammonia in it per cup of water.
- Rub with ordinary hand soap. Add some borax and continue to rub.
- Rinse and rub in ammonia solution. Do this until stain is almost 100% gone. Rinse in clean cold water.
- Spray with hydrogen peroxide, leave for a few minutes then rub until clean.
- Rinse in cold water and spray with pre-treat and wash in washing machine.

TOP TIP

Unfortunately, **pets often have mishaps in the home**. If your pet has cut itself or left a mess on your carpet, you can still get the stain out. Milk poured over a blood stain – fresh or dried – will loosen the blood, allowing you to blot it out of the carpet with paper kitchen towel. Remember, never use warm water.

TOP TIPS

Food stains on clothes are often unavoidable, especially with the younger members of the family. If you tackle them straight away, you'll have a better chance of banishing them completely:

Drinks (including tea, coffee, soft drinks) Sponge or soak the stain promptly in cool water; then leave to soak in biological detergent before washing as normal.

Ketchup Pre-soak in biological detergent overnight, then wash in the hottest temperature for that particular fabric.

Dairy products (including baby food) Pre-soak in biological detergent overnight, then wash in the hottest temperature for that particular fabric. If the stain persists, rewash using a mild bleach for fabrics.

Mustard Soak the stain and while wet, pre-treat with a pre-wash stain remover before washing.

Candle wax

On a hard surface, candle wax is not too tricky to remove. Scrape the wax first with your

Candles create a relaxed atmosphere, but dripped wax can leave stains

finger nail to chip it off or try scraping with a playing card or plastic knife. If wax has dripped on the furniture or carpet, leave until set, then chip and scrape off as much as possible. Next use a medium-to-hot iron, depending on the fabric, over a doubled sheet of white kitchen paper or a single sheet of brown wrapping paper (an

TOP TIP

If you have a **dried, caked-in stain**, you can still work it out. Using a mixture of vinegar, washing up liquid and water, wet your rag or cloth and press into the stained area. Blot the area dry with a clean cloth and repeat until you have lifted the stain. You can get out dried stains like blood, wine, coffee, chocolate, tomato ketchup even tea using this method!

Upholstery nozzle

Dust brush

Crevice nozzle

Cleaning attachments for a vacuum cleaner can help remove dried stains

opened-up brown envelope will do) to remove the remaining wax. You can also sandwich the stain between absorbent paper, then apply the hot iron to the top layer of paper. Any residual stains from coloured wax should respond to stain remover.

Chewing gum

Don't be tempted to pick, as you will end up pressing the gum deeper into the fabric. Rub the area with an ice cube wrapped in a plastic bag to harden the gum, or place the entire garment in a plastic carrier and put it in the freezer overnight, then chip off the frozen gum. Use dry-cleaning fluid to remove residues, then wash as usual.

Chocolate

Scrape off as much as you can. Use a specialist cleaner or apply glycerine to loosen the stain before washing. If you have neither, work neat liquid detergent into the stain, then rinse thoroughly with tepid water. Wash in biological detergent or have non-washables dry-cleaned.

Cleaning dirty ivory

Dirty ivory can be cleaned by soaking the item for a few hours in milk, then washing with warm soapy water. For ivory piano keys, carefully dab the milk on with a cloth, but not so much that the milk runs down the keys and into the piano itself. Leave for a few hours, then gently rub off with a clean, damp cloth, again taking care not to over saturate.

Coffee

Rinse or blot as much as possible. You may need to use a stain remover if milk in the coffee leaves a grease stain. Soak washables in biological

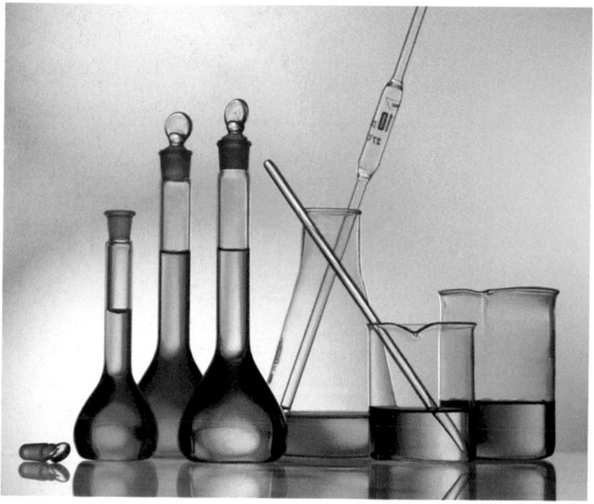

Some of the chemicals used in cleaning products need to be handled with care

detergent solution before laundering.

Soda water is an excellent cleaner for removing coffee spills on carpet, so keep a bottle handy. Pour on to the stain and absorb the moisture by placing white kitchen towel on top and pressing in until nearly dry.

TOP TIP

If you have a **cigarette burn in your carpet**, try this method to lessen the appearance of these burns in your carpeting. Just take a sharp pairs of scissors and snip the burnt edges off the little indentation in the carpet. Use a tiny pair of manicure scissors or a fine pair of sewing scissors so that you do not cut too much of the carpet pile off.

Crayon marks

If you find an artistic, but unwanted, creation in crayon on your radiators, try rubbing with a paper towel soaked in ice-cold milk from the fridge. If the crayon is trodden into a carpet, however, try to remove as much as possible with a knife or old credit card, then place a few layers of paper towel over the mark. Press gently with a warm iron and hopefully the towels will soak up the slightly melted, waxy by-product.

Curry

The combination of turmeric and oil that features in most curries creates a stain that can be very hard to remove. Try to keep the area wet. A speedy application of glycerine can keep the stain from setting. Rinse repeatedly with tepid water, or a mixture of 300ml (½pt) warm water with 10ml (2 tsp) borax.

You can descale a kettle using distilled white vinegar instead of tablets

TOP TIP

Bicarbonate of soda is a great cleaner and should be kept handy for help with stain removing. The gentle abrasive properties helps to cut through grease, so use it as a scrubbing product in baths, basins and sinks. An added advantage is that it is also a natural deodoriser, eliminating unsavoury household smells.

Descaling a kettle

The need to descale or defur a kettle occurs when limescale builds up on the element and around the spout. Distilled white vinegar is an excellent alternative to shop-bought descaling tablets. To prevent the build-up of limescale, fill the kettle with half water, half vinegar, leave to soak for a few hours, then rinse thoroughly. To descale a kettle, pour

TOP TIP

If an area of carpet has been flattened by items of furniture, **restore the carpet pile to life** by placing several layers of damp cloth onto the area. Next, hold a hot iron lightly on top of the cloth. The steam from the iron helps to bring back the bounce to the carpet, which you can then fluff up more effectively using a nail brush.

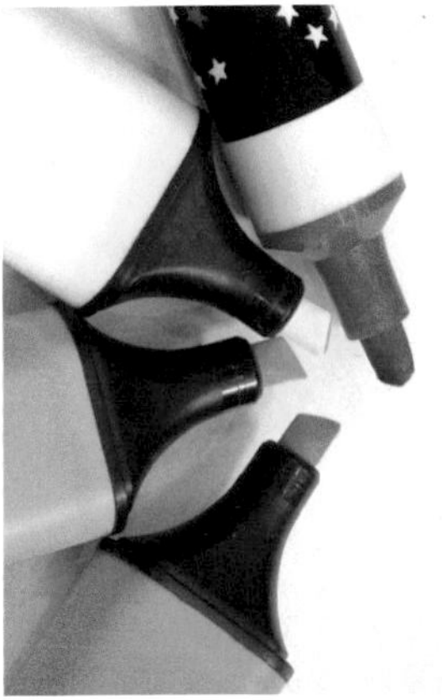

Always replace the lids on felt-tipped pens to avoid stains occurring

in a small amount of vinegar, bring to the boil and swirl it round vigorously. Allow it to cool then rinse out thoroughly. Both these methods may need to be repeated several times.

Another – rather drastic – method of descaling is to fill the kettle with cold water and place it in the freezer. Once frozen, remove from the freezer and when it defrosts, the ice will pull the fur away from the sides of the kettle.

Dye

Red sock syndrome, where one non-fast coloured item sneaks into a load of whites and lightly colours the lot. You might get away with washing everything again immediately, with a generous dose of detergent, before laundry has had a chance to dry. If any colour is still left, you could try a branded run remover – unfortunately these can also affect the original colour of the garment. For whites, wash again with 20ml (4 tsp) bleach in the detergent compartment of the washing machine – check the care label first to make sure the garments can withstand such strong treatment. Never use bleach on acetate, polyester, drip-dry cottons, silk or wool.

Felt-tipped pen

If you're lucky, the ink will be water-soluble and will come out with cold water. If not, try a branded stain remover.

Another tip is to use hair spray over the area and the dab it up with a paper towel. If you still have a slight stain left, you can pour some milk over the area to lift the remaining ink.

TOP TIP

After defrosting and cleaning the freezer, rub the inside with glycerine and the next time you come to defrost, you should find that the ice comes away easily.

TOP TIP

Never throw away your old toothbrushes – just put them to a new use! Toothbrushes are invaluable cleaning tools and are excellent for getting into awkward, tiny gaps and crevices that fingers holding cloths or dusters just cannot reach.

Try this tip if you have ball point ink on your furniture or on the car seats.

Fruit juice

Fruit juices, especially dark-coloured fruits such as red berries and blackcurrants, are extremely hard to shift once dry. For fresh stains, wash through in cold water and treat any remaining stain with methylated spirits or a stain remover. For dried in stains, apply a glycerine solution (equal parts water and glycerine), leave for one hour, then sponge repeatedly with warm soapy water.

Lemon juice is a natural bleaching agent, so try rubbing half a cut lemon onto the fresh fruit juice stain.

Grass

If the fabric will take it, soak in a mild bleach solution (follow directions on the bottle). Alternatively, apply glycerine,

Rugs and carpets often have a protective treatment against stains included

> **TOP TIP**
>
> **Not cleaned the inside of the microwave for a while?** Simply put a few lemon slices into a bowl of water (do not cover) and put the microwave on high for about three minutes. The lemony condensation will loosen any baked on food stains – and the aroma of lemon will freshen up any horrible, lingering smells.

leave for several hours, then sponge well with warm soapy water and launder.

Rubbing half a lemon onto the grass stain is also a tried and tested solution.

Grease

Dab immediately with dry-cleaning fluid on a pad of cotton wool or else sponge well with warm soapy water before laundering.

For colourless grease stains on leather or upholstery, sprinkle on fuller's earth (an earthy powder available from chemists), cover and leave overnight. You may need several applications. Or use a specialist leather cleaner.

Hard water deposits

If you discover hard water deposits in jugs, bottles, vases or glasses, fill with malt vinegar and leave to stand for a few hours. Empty the vinegar and rub away the marks with a fine scouring pad and rinse thoroughly. The vinegar can be poured back into its container and kept to be reused next time you spot any stubborn water marks in your glass objects.

Lipstick

Try dry-cleaning fluid, followed by warm soapy water. Or apply eucalyptus oil, let it soak in and loosen the lipstick, then blot away the stain. Dry clean, or for washable fabrics, sponge with soapy water as hot as the fabric can stand, then launder.

Milk stains

Treat milk spillages as soon as possible, otherwise the lingering smell that is left is virtually impossible to remove. On carpets, sponge with clear, warm water and apply an aerosol cleaner. A professional carpet cleaner may be needed to be used if the stain has been allowed to dry in.

> **TOP TIP**
>
> Wash **dirty mirrors and glass** with kitchen towel dabbed in a solution of water and vinegar. To buff them up, use a coffee filter paper and rub until the moisture is absorbed.

It's so easy to tread mud into the house – your shoes don't have to look like this!

Mud
Leave until completely dry, then brush off and, in the case of clothing, launder. If is a particularly stubborn stain on clothes, dab with methylated spirits. With carpets, vacuum the area once it is dry. If needs be, loosen the dried mud with a stiff brush. Again, if the carpet still shows a mark, dap a little methylated spirit or carpet-spotting treatment onto the stain after vacuuming.

Perspiration stains
Sponge washable clothing (ie. not dry-clean only) with a solution of 1 tsp of ammonia to 1 pint of cold water, then rinse. If the dye has run, sponge off with 1 tbsp distilled white vinegar diluted in 250ml of water.

Pets
Wipe up urine mishaps immediately, mopping up with paper towels to limit absorption. After absorbing as much as possible, wash the area with a tablespoon of vinegar in 500ml (1pt) water. For solid offerings, remove as much as possible from the surface. Wipe off thoroughly with kitchen paper. Sponge the area well with warm water, or use a carpet spot shampoo, testing first. To remove the unmistakable odour left by cat spray, sponge the

Any 'accident' by a loveable pet needs to be cleaned up immediately

area with a mixture of half warm water, half white vinegar.

Biological washing powder contains enzymes which break down the ammonia in pet urine and can neutralise strong odours. Mix in warm water and rub vigorously into the stain. Rinse off with a clean cloth.

If a pet persists in soiling the same area, the smell will linger and this can only mean that the urine has seeped through into the underlay or the floorboards beneath. No amount of deodorising will mask the stench. Unfortunately, the only remedy is to lift up the carpet, cut out the damaged area of underlay and thoroughly scrub the floorboards with a vinegar solution or bicarbonate of soda. You can buy small pieces of underlay from most carpet retailers. Simply cut a piece to fit and place back underneath the carpet. Allow both the treated carpet and floorboards to have a thorough airing before covering.

Hopefully, the carpet will just need repeated treatments of scrubbing with a vinegar or

TOP TIP

If your toilet is particularly stained, pour a **can of cola** into the bowl, leave for a few hours, then flush. The acid in the cola will eat away at the limescale stains.

TOP TIP

An excellent method to make your toilet sparkle is to add a couple of **denture cleaning tablets** into the toilet bowl, leave overnight, then flush in the morning.

bicarbonate of soda solution, rather than replacing. However, in some cases this may be the only solution to completely eradicate the pervading odour.

Scorch marks

Have you ever placed a hot serving bowl or pan onto your dining table or a hot cup onto your tables? You invariably will be left with a white mark. When hot dishes or plates leave a white stain on the dining room table (or any furniture), take a wet sponge and rub dry baking soda (bicarbonate of soda) in circular motions on the mark.

Another method is to dampen a cloth with rubbing alcohol and dab it onto the white scorch. Allow it to dry and wipe clean. You may have to repeat this process several times to completely remove the scorch mark.

Tea

Apply glycerine immediately, then sponge with warm soapy water and launder. For dried stains, leave glycerine on for longer before sponging.

Laundry borax is also good for removing stains on clothes and tea towels. Simply place the item over a bowl or basin, sprinkle borax over the stain and pour a kettleful of hot water onto the area. Repeat the treatment if necessary.

On carpets, blot with kitchen towel to absorb most of the moisture, then sponge with lukewarm water or apply soda water onto the stain.

To get rid of stubborn tea stains from mugs and cups, rub with a piece of kitchen towel and a little salt, borax or bicarbonate of soda. The abrasive action will get rid of any marks.

Tomato ketchup

With ketchup on a carpet, first of all, dab up as much as possible using paper kitchen towels. Spray what remains with shaving foam and wipe off with a damp cloth. The shaving foam will bring away the ketchup from the surface of the carpet.

If the stain is more dried and set in, you can spray the area using a tablespoon of ammonia and a quarter of a cup of cool water. Blot the stain

TOP TIP

Unsightly **black scuff marks** on linoleum floors can be easily removed by rubbing with an everyday pencil rubber (eraser). Add a few drops of paraffin in your water when washing a linoleum floor to really help the floor to shine.

up and repeat as needed to bring the entire stain out. Do not soak the carpet with the ammonia – just keep blotting to bring the stain out. Apply pressure as needed to get the moisture out, but do not rub the carpet.

Vomit

Wearing rubber gloves, remove all the deposit, sponge well with warm soapy water, then launder as usual. On carpet, sponge with a teaspoonful of borax mixed with 500 ml/1 pt warm water. You could also add a few drops of antiseptic, which will also help to neutralise any remaining, unpleasant odours.

Wine

If possible treat the wine stain immediately after the spill or accident. For red wine, quickly pour over some white wine or mineral water, then dab off with a cloth and, with luck, the stain will have disappeared. If not,

There are various methods to use to remove spilt wine from your carpet

apply glycerine to loosen the stain before laundering.

Another method is to sprinkle salt liberally over the stained area to absorb the wine spill. After the salt has absorbed the wine, you can vacuum it up or brush it off the carpet. However, be wary of applying salt to red wine stains – although it works on some fabrics, on others it sets the stain permanently.

If you spill wine on your clothing or on a tablecloth, blot it up immediately with a clean and absorbent cloth or kitchen towels, then sponge the stained area with carbonated

TOP TIP

To clean a **stained thermos flask**, add 3 tbsp of bicarbonate of soda and fill to the top with water. Screw on the lid and shake vigorously. Leave to stand for about an hour, then rinse well and leave to dry. If you will not be using your flask for a while, put two or three sugar lumps into the flask to prevent mouldy smells developing.

soda water. The bubbles in the soda water will lift the stain right out of the material. If red wine is spilled on your carpet, do not panic. Sponge the stained area with carbonated soda water. Blot well, but do not rub, as rubbing pushes the stain in further. Then dab the area with a damp cloth with detergent solution followed by a rinsing with clean water.

If the stain persists you can use a solution of half glycerin and half water diluting the stain. This solution can be left on the stain for up to an hour, then rinsed off with a warm water and blotted well with a clean dry cloth.

Another measure is to try dabbing the area with some hydrogen peroxide and wash as described above.

A spotless room is your reward for removing all those nasty stains

Laundry tips

Ever thought that clothes get a much harder time in the wash than when they're being worn? Some simple routines will limit the damage to garments on their journey from dirty clothes basket to cupboard, not least matching the wash cycle to the fabric.

If you are looking to buy a new washer or dryer, use the following checklists to pinpoint the features that will be genuinely useful for your particular needs.

Choosing laundry equipment

Washing machines

Look for the energy label displayed on every machine, giving a rating for energy consumption ranging from 'A' (the best) to 'G' (very poor). Washing machines are also rated A–G for washing and spinning performance. A good spin rating, A–C, means that tumble-drying will be quicker and cheaper.

Some washing machine features are far more useful than others. Don't be tempted to pay over the odds for an impressive array of programmes if you are not going to use them, for instance – most people stick to the same three or four.

Automatic timer Some machines can be loaded then left to turn themselves on automatically – useful for taking advantage of off-peak electricity, or for getting the washing done while you're out.

Extra rinse Worth considering for anyone whose skin reacts to detergent traces left in clothes.

Fuzzy logic Many machines come equipped with sensors that monitor the wash and alter different aspects of the performance accordingly. A machine with fuzzy logic might adjust the water intake and temperature, add an extra rinse to clear excess foam, and choose the best spin speed for

TOP TIP

After you have bought your **new washing machine**, treat it with care. Like any piece of machinery, it needs to be well maintained. Keep the **drain filter** clear and the machine will work more effectively. Remove traces of powder and fabric softener from the **detergent drawer** on a regular basis – most just pull out.

The latest washing machines are equipped with sensors that can 'read' your wash and alter parts of the programme accordingly, such as using less water for a smaller load

the load. These machines cost more than standard models, but they do make the most economic use of energy and will also save you money if you do more than three full loads each week.

Life expectancy A few machines, made from top-quality materials and using sophisticated electronic technology, claim to have a life of up to 20 years, rather than the 5–10 year life expectancy that is realistic for other machines. These machines are at the top end of the price range, but over time could prove to be worth the extra initial investment.

Machine size Compact machines can squeeze into a small space, but have a smaller capacity and a limited range of

> **TOP TIP**
>
> **Run the machine on empty** every few months – without adding detergent – to give it a good rinse. Adding **descaling tablets** to your wash can help prevent limescale building up, which will help the heating element last longer and maintain a good wash cycle for your clothes.

Three drying tips

1 **Sort clothes for tumble-drying into batches** and dry similar fabrics together, on the correct setting, to avoid shrinkage.

2 **Fresh air is free.** Peg clothes so that they hang the same way as you would wear them – skirts and trousers pegged at the waist, shirts at the shoulders – to reduce creasing.

3 **Lie heavy jumpers flat** on a towel or drying rack so that they don't stretch or lose shape. A short spin first will make the process quicker, but check the care label.

programmes. Top-loaders are not as wide as front-loaders, so are useful if you're short of space. They can be awkward to use, however, if they have to be wheeled out from under a worktop, and they can be noisy. Some standard-sized machines have a large drum that can accommodate 6kg (13lb) of laundry rather than the usual 5kg (11lb). Only useful if you regularly do a large amount of washing.

Quick-wash or economy settings Useful for lightly soiled clothes.

Spin speed Higher spin speeds mean drier washing, so look for a machine that offers a top speed of 1,100 revolutions per minute (rpm) or more. Some machines have variable speeds, so you can give fabrics that crease badly a very slow spin.

Tumble-dryers

The main choice is between air-vented and condenser dryers. Air-vented are cheaper and dry washing faster, but the steam is removed through a broad hose that has to be ducted through an external wall or hung out of a window or open door, restricting where you can put the machine. Condenser dryers are a little more expensive, but you can position them anywhere. They work by condensing the steam back into water, which collects in a built-in container that you empty when necessary. If you can position the dryer near a sink, it can be plumbed in so that the water goes down the drain.

Three ironing tips

1 Check care labels and **sort clothes before ironing**, doing those needing the coolest iron first.

2 **Ironing clothes inside out** means you're less likely to get shiny patches or scorch marks showing.

3 **Never iron over plastic or glittery decorations** – they'll probably melt and be ruined. Turn them inside out or iron over a cloth.

Automatic timer As for washing machines.
Filters All machines have these fluff traps, which need regular cleaning. Choose a machine with a filter that is easy to get at.
Heat settings Most people use just two: a low setting for synthetics, high for cottons. A cool phase at the end of the cycle allows clothes to cool down gradually and helps prevent creasing.
Reservoir warning A light that comes on when the container in a condenser dryer is full. Prevents overflows.
Reverse tumble This fairly standard feature prevents tangling. It may be missing from economy-range compacts.
Size Compact machines are handy if you have limited space, but can handle only 2kg (4½lb) rather than the standard 5kg (11lb) load.
Start button Designed to prevent an automatic start-up when the door is shut, in case children or pets climb into the dryer.

TOP TIP

Never overfill a tumble dryer. They work quickest and at their best when there is enough space for the clothes to move around freely, usually at about half full.

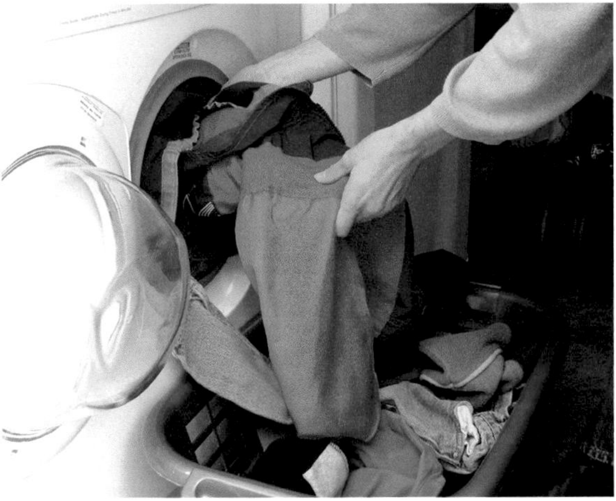

Do not overload your tumble dryer, as clothes will take much longer to dry

What care labels mean

The International Association for Textile Care Labelling (GINETEX) developed a language-independent care-labelling system in 1975. There are five basic symbols for washing, bleaching, ironing, dry-cleaning, and tumble-drying. Symbols refer to the maximum treatment the textile can bear without irreversible damage.

	40°C	Mechanical action normal; rinsing normal; spinning normal
	40°C	Mechanical action reduced; rinsing at gradually decreasing temperature; spinning reduced
	40°C	Mechanical action much reduced; rinsing normal; spinning normal
	40°C	Handwash only
	Do not wash	
	Chlorine-based bleaching in a cold and dilute solution is suitable	
	Iron at a maximum temperature of 200°C	
	Iron at a maximum temperature of 150°C	
	Iron at a maximum temperature of 110°C (steam iron may be risky)	
	Drycleaning in all solvents normally used for dry-cleaning, with normal procedures	
	Drycleaning in all solvents normally used for dry-cleaning, except trichloroethylene, with normal cleaning procedures. Self-service cleaning is possible	
	The bar placed under the circle indicates strict limitations on the addition of water and/or mechanical action and/or temperature during cleaning and/or drying. Self-service cleaning is not recommended	
	Tumble-drying possible at lower temperature setting (60°C maximum) after a washing process	
	No restrictions concerning the temperature of tumble-drying after washing	

Separate your white clothes from the dark ones before washing

Washer-dryers

Two machines in one can be the answer if you are short of space or cash. Drawbacks:

- these machines don't dry as fast or as efficiently as a standard tumble-dryer
- the whole process takes longer, because the dryer can only dry half a normal wash-load at a time. And you have to wait for a wash to finish before you can dry anything.

Getting the best from your washing

Sort washing carefully

- Ideally you should separate your laundry into three groups by colour: whites, light colours and dark colours. This is to ensure the whites stay white, and dark dyes from black and navy garments don't turn paler colours dingy. If you don't have enough for three loads, at least keep whites separate – it's worth doing a half load.

TOP TIP

To check whether you are getting any **colour run** from your clothes, put an old white handkerchief or white piece of cloth in with the suspect wash. This will pick up any loose dye from clothes. Only when it stays white has all the dye eventually run out.

TOP TIP

Your favourite pair of white socks has just been washed in a coloured load by mistake. Not to worry. Simply take an old saucepan, add water and a few slices of lemon, and boil the socks on the hob for five or ten minutes. The lemon acts as a natural bleaching agent to bring back the whiteness of the socks.

- It pays to wash items of certain fabric types together. For example, synthetics need a cool rinse and short spin, whereas heavy cotton items like towels, can take a hotter wash and longer spin.

Loading the machine

- Don't be tempted to overload the drum. Performance will be reduced and your machine will suffer greater wear and tear. The motor might even burn out if you overdo it too often.
- Empty pockets and remove badges, brooches, or any loose buttons before you wash. Small loose items can lodge in the machine and cause considerable and expensive damage.

Improving performance

If your washing machine consistently produces poor

Drying clothes outside is the best way to keep them smelling clean and fresh

results, pour a little bleach into the detergent compartment, then let the machine run empty through a complete warm wash cycle.

The bleach will remove any clogged soap scum in the machine and should improve washing and rinsing.

Detergents and softeners

The first choice is between detergent in powder, tablet or liquid form. Tests carried out by the Consumers' Association found that powders and tablets are more effective at removing stains than liquid detergents. Beyond that, the choice is between different types of product, designed for different uses.

Biological Excellent for stain removal, even at low temperatures.

TOP TIP

Make life easy for yourself by **keeping all your laundry detergent, fabric softener and stain cleaners together**. And don't simply stuff them in the back of a cupboard on the other side of the kitchen or laundry room, just because that's the only space left. Keep them as near as possible to the washing machine or tumble dryer to save any more effort than is necessary. You may even consider building a new shelf or installing a wire rack to make this possible.

Washing detergent comes in tablets, as well as liquid and powder

Non-biological Good for sensitive skins (including babies) – especially for anyone with an allergy to enzyme detergents. May not remove deep staining.

Colour Lower bleach content means colours are less likely to fade.

Wool wash A liquid that's appropriate for delicate fabrics, particularly silk and wool.

Fabric softeners Produce fragrant, soft garments that shed creases more easily and may need less ironing.

Water-softener tablets Stop the limescale build-up that damages the insides of washing machines.

The clean kitchen

Food scares involving salmonella and *E. coli* have highlighted the need to be careful about food and how we store, prepare, and cook it. By making simple hygiene rules a habit, you can reduce the risk of food from your kitchen making you ill.

Preventing food poisoning

There are some 4.5 million cases of food poisoning a year in the UK, partly owing to increased reliance on takeaways and convenience food. The World Health Organisation (WHO) has identified four main causes of food poisoning:

- preparing food several hours before it is needed and leaving it in a warm place
- not cooking or reheating food thoroughly enough
- not having sufficiently high standards of hygiene in handling and preparing food
- cross-contamination between raw and cooked foods.

At home, all of these are easy to avoid, as long as you follow certain food hygiene regimes.

Good food hygiene

- Always buy pasteurised dairy products, such as milk and cheese. Vulnerable groups (the very young, the elderly, pregnant women and anyone who is ill) should also avoid unpasteurised juices.
- Read and follow the storage instructions on products. Avoid food that is past its 'best before' date, especially if it contains meat or fish.
- Before you go on a major food shopping expedition, go through your fridge and remove any out-of-date items, especially any vegetables. Clean the shelves and racks.

Most food and drink products come with a 'best before end' date

- Wash your hands with hot water and soap before preparing food. Wash them again if you stop cooking to change a baby's nappy, use the toilet or if you stroke your pet. Always wash your hands after handling raw meat.
- All animals, including dogs, cats, birds and especially reptiles, can harbour germs which could contaminate food. Keep them away from food preparation areas. If you feed pets in the kitchen, don't leave dirty food dishes out, as these can attract flies and, more alarming, rodents. Keep cat litter trays out of the kitchen. The hall or lobby is a better place.
- Fruits and vegetables that are to be eaten raw should be washed and/or scrubbed well and rinsed under cold, running water.
- Clean the inside of the refrigerator and freezer regularly. Keep worktops scrupulously clean.
- Always cook food thoroughly, especially poultry, meat, and eggs. Check that meat juices run clear and eggs are set. Defrost meat, poultry and fish completely before cooking.
- Eat foods while still piping hot. If allowed to cool to room

Keeping the kitchen clean

Clean worktops frequently by wiping down with an all-surface cleaner that contains bleach, diluted according to directions. Hot, soapy water is also good for cleaning worktops, but may not kill all bacteria. Water on its own removes visible marks, but doesn't affect bacteria.

There is as yet no convincing evidence that **anti-bacterial products** are more effective than standard disinfectants, such as chlorine bleach.

Keep cloths and sponges clean, and replace them often. Wash out frequently in hot, soapy water and hang up where they can dry. If left wet and crumpled they provide an excellent environment for bacteria to grow.

Bits of food can easily become trapped in the plughole and overflow of the kitchen sink, where damp conditions mean they become full of bacteria. Clean the sink daily and pour a solution of one capful of bleach in 1 litre water down the drain once a week.

After washing up, **leave everything to dry in the air** rather than using a cloth, which can harbour germs. If you leave dishes to soak, pour away the water and use fresh, hot water and detergent to wash.

Wipe kitchen drainers and worktops down with an all-surface cleaner

temperature, they provide the perfect environment for bacteria to multiply.

- If you need to cook in advance, or keep leftovers, store the cooked food either above 60°C (140°F) or below 10°C (50°F). This is vital if the food is to be kept for more than four to five hours, because microbes can thrive in warm food over this length of time. Baby food ideally should not be stored at all unless frozen immediately.
- No food, whether perishables, prepared dishes or leftovers, should stay out of the fridge for more than two hours, especially during the summer.
- Cooked foods are easily contaminated by contact with raw meat – keep them separate at all times. Store raw meat at the bottom of the fridge, so that juices can't drip on to cooked foods. Use different chopping boards and knives for raw meat, and wash thoroughly in hot soapy water between uses.
- Store food in closed containers to protect it from contamination by rodents or insects.
- Reheat food thoroughly, until steaming hot right through, and until liquids boil. This is the best protection against food poisoning, since although proper storage slows bacterial growth, only thorough cooking destroys the organisms.

Using the freezer safely

Buying frozen food

- Choose packs that are well below the top line in the shop's freezer.
- Avoid packs of frozen food that are damaged, icy or feel at all soft.
- Check the 'best before' date – some foods have a relatively short freezer life.
- Take a cool box to the supermarket and pack all frozen goods into it together to take home or else buy one of the insulated shopping bags many supermarkets now provide.

Freezing know-how

- Food quality deteriorates if kept frozen for too long. Observe the star ratings on your freezer and always follow recommendations on packs.
- Use frozen foods systematically – first in, first out. Scribble an expiry date on the lid of the container with ink.
- Putting hot food straight into the freezer makes the overall temperature rise, and also affects the flavour and texture of the food. Refrigerate hot food as soon

How long will food keep in the freezer?

Item	Keep for
Pre-packed frozen meals	3–4 months
Home made soups and casseroles	2–3 months
Mince	3–4 months
Bacon	1 month
Sausages	1–2 months
Ham	1–2 months
Beef steaks and joints	6 months to 1 year
Lamb chops and joints	6–9 months
Pork chops and joints	4–6 months
Offal	3–4 months
Leftover cooked meats and meat dishes	2–3 months
Gravies and stock	2–3 months
Poultry: whole	1 year
Poultry: joints	9 months

TOP TIP

Check the **contents of your fridge** every couple of days and throw out anything that is past its best. Keep a particular eye on salad items and vegetables that are kept in the fridge. If you are constantly chucking out soggy lettuce or mushy cucumber, you may be over-stocking. Only buy when you know you are going to use it.

as possible after cooling and freeze after no more than 90 minutes of chilling.

- Never refreeze food, unless it has been cooked in the meantime.
- Don't cram the freezer too full – you will prevent cold air from circulating.
- Defrost food either in the fridge or microwave, or by placing packages of frozen food in cold water.

If the power supply to the freezer stops

- Keep the door closed if the freezer is likely to be on again within 24 hours.

> **TOP TIP**
>
> **The more often you open the door to the freezer**, the more often you will need to defrost it. Every time you rummage in compartments or pull out freezer drawers, the water vapour in the air gets into the freezer and forms ice. Why not put a list of contents on the freezer door – and update it when you stock up – to shorten the time you have the door open?

- Consider removing some food to be thawed, cooked, then refrozen later.
- If you have warning of a power loss, turn your freezer on to fast-freeze – if it has this function, of course – for 30 minutes beforehand.

Do not cram the freezer too full – any drawers should pull out easily

Refrigerator sense

- Get into the habit of using a fridge thermometer to ensure that the temperature remains between 0–5°C (32–41°F). Put a shelf with a built-in thermometer – a useful feature to look for when buying a new fridge – at the top of a larder fridge. Larder fridges tend to be colder at the bottom, while fridges with a built-in ice box have a more even temperature.

How long will food keep in the fridge?

Item	Keep for
Ready-made salads	3–5 days
Ready-made convenience meals	1–2 days
Soups, casseroles	3–4 days
Leftover gravy or stock	1–2 days
Raw pre-stuffed meats, such as chicken breasts	1 day
Raw mince	1–2 days
Raw meats such as steaks, chops, joints	3–5 days
Raw poultry, whole or joints	1–2 days
Offal	1–2 days
Cold cooked meats such as ham	3–4 days
Bacon	1 week
Raw sausages	1–2 days
Leftover cooked meat and meat dishes	3–4 days

A well-stocked fridge needn't be overflowing with foodstuffs. Air needs to be able to circulate around the shelves to keep everything at an optimum temperature

Using eggs

Eggs sometimes contain the ***salmonella* bacteria**, which can cause stomach upsets and can be particularly harmful to pregnant women, babies, elderly people and anyone whose immune system may be weak. The Food Standards Agency (FSA) advises that **eating raw eggs may pose a health risk** and these vulnerable groups should only eat eggs that have been cooked until the whites and yolks are solid. These groups should also avoid foods made with raw eggs, such as home-made mayonnaise and ice-cream.

It's especially important to keep a check if the temperature of your kitchen varies widely through the year or if the fridge door is opened frequently.

- If you buy your vegetables from a supermarket pre-wrapped in packets, they will often come ready washed and some already cut. If this is the case, then the best place to store them is in the refrigerator.
- Keep vegetables in the fridge in plastic bags to keep them for longer. Take out the air from the bag before tying to keep vegetables from getting mouldy.
- Storing potatoes in a bag in the fridge helps them last longer without rooting. This is similar to keeping them in a cool, dark place, such as a larder, where there is no heat.
- Keep celery fresh by wrapping in aluminum foil and storing in the fridge for crisp celery every time!
- To keep cottage cheese, yogurt or sour cream fresh for longer, store them upside down in the refrigerator. This keeps the air from

TOP TIPS

- **Food poisoning** is often caused when harmful bacteria on one type of food are spread by means of hands or kitchen utensils to cross-contaminate other foods. Good hygiene in the kitchen helps prevent this.
- Wash your hands after handling **raw foods** and before touching other foods and utensils.

TOP TIP

Keep raw foods separate from cooked and ready-to-eat food at all times. In particular keep raw meat, fish, poultry and other raw foods away from ready-to-eat foods such as salads, bread and sandwiches. Never put cooked food on a plate which has previously held raw foods until it has been thoroughly washed. Ideally use separate chopping boards for raw and cooked foods.

getting into the container and causing mould to develop.

- Don't put large quantities of hot food into the fridge in one large container. Foods do not cool right through as quickly as they should to prevent bacteria multiplying. Instead, divide the food into smaller, shallow dishes, for faster cooling – and more manageable portions.
- When storing stuffed meats or poultry, remove the stuffing and refrigerate it separately.
- While a well-stocked refrigerator helps to save electricity, don't overfill the fridge – leave enough space for air to circulate freely and keep foodstuffs at the correct temperature.

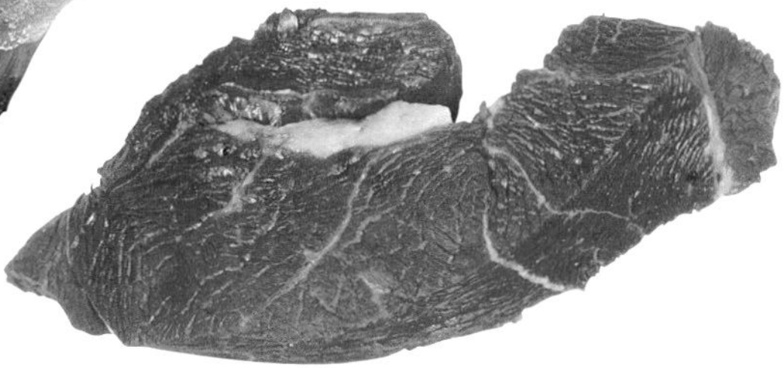

Keep fruit and vegetables in a separate compartment in the fridge. Wrap meat and fish, and also keep separate

Dealing with pests

Some pests are health hazards – rats, mice and cockroaches carry and spread disease. Others inflict painful bites and stings. Many, such as silverfish, are harmless. Any infestation is an unwelcome invasion, but pests can get into the cleanest homes.

There are three options in dealing with pests: DIY treatment, help from the local Environmental Health department or calling in private specialists. However, the best solution is to take precautions to deter pests in the first place (*see* box below).

A–Z of pests

Ants

These will sometimes invade the house in search of food, then establish a trail to the source. Ants are harmless. Store food where they can't get to it. Draw a chalk line across their entrance point to the house to deter them. To exterminate ants, pour boiling water on their nest. If this fails, or the nest is out of sight, use branded chemical treatments, brushing powder into crevices with a small paintbrush.

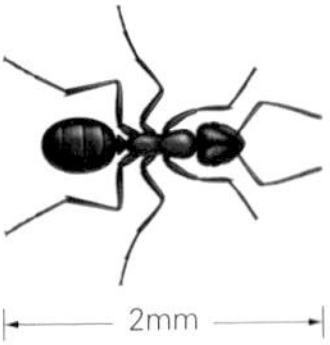

Bedbugs

These insects need warmth, darkness and a supply of blood from humans or animals to survive. They thrive around the buttons of mattresses and in the crevices of sofas and armchairs, and may also nest behind wallpaper. Their bite does not carry disease but can irritate and can cause persistent loss of sleep, resulting in lack of energy, especially in children. Infestations should be treated by a specialist.

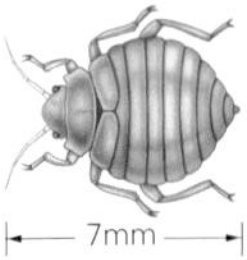

Deterring pests

- **Vacuum** the house thoroughly and regularly.
- **Clear away food** immediately after a meal.
- **Store food** in the fridge or in sealed containers.
- **Empty the kitchen bin** daily.
- Put rubbish out in **sealed bags**.
- Keep the **lid on the dustbin**.
- Put **food for birds** where only birds can get it.
- Clear away leftover **pet food**.
- **Get rid of damp** in the home.
- **Seal cracks** in walls and around skirting boards.

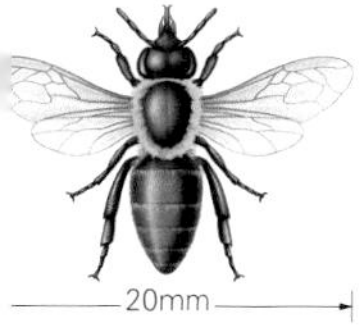

Bees

Never harm a bee – they will not sting unless provoked. Some bees are protected by law – it's illegal to kill them. If a bee is trapped in your house, catch it in a loosely balled tea towel and gently shake free outside or catch it in an upended tumbler and slide a piece of card across the bottom. Rarely, a swarm settles in a garden away from the hive or even enter a house. Keep children and pets away and phone your local authority.

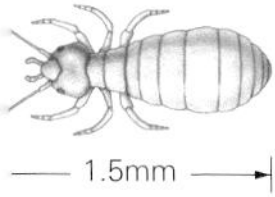

Booklice

These live on moulds, so attack damp plaster and books, but can contaminate dry goods such as flour, chocolate, milk powder and cereals. They are most active between April and November and may come into the house via birds' nests, thatch or firewood. Treat with a branded insecticide. Try to store books in a dry, well-aired room.

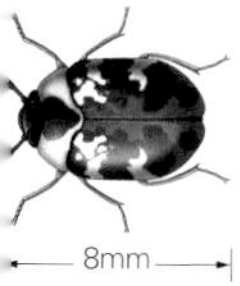

Carpet beetles

These beetles feed on soiled carpet fibres and may also attack wool, silk and leather. They thrive indoors in warm, dry conditions. Their larvae may dig long galleries in

Rats and mice

The dangers Rats thrive in sewers. They pose a serious health risk and may be carriers of Weil's disease, which can cause severe muscle pain and even death. Mice can cause serious food poisoning. Both are attracted to easy food sources and to shelter in which to nest, such as a shed or a pile of old newspapers under the stairs. Rodents can gnaw through cables and pipes. They multiply within weeks of birth, so any infestation needs to be dealt with quickly.

Remedies You can detect the presence of rodents by gnawed material, evidence of droppings and the smell of their urine. Your best option is to call the experts – local authority extermination services are usually free. DIY remedies are humane traps, baited mousetraps and dedicated poisons – rodenticides. Keep children away from the infested area. Protect poison bait from pets and wild animals, placing it, for example, in a length of plastic pipe of a diameter small enough to stop a bird or hedgehog from entering (around 2.5cm/1in). After rodents have been exterminated, clear out all infected materials, wash the area thoroughly with disinfectant and block up entry holes.

Rat

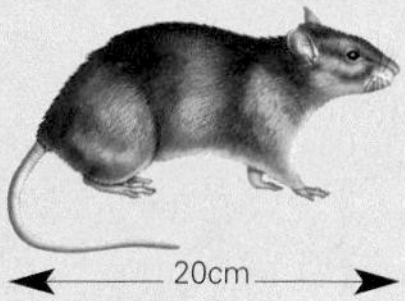

Mouse

wood in which to pupate. Vacuum carpets and the floor beneath, paying attention to cracks, crevices and skirting boards. Spray insecticide into cracks. If the problem persists, call a professional.

Cockroaches

An infestation of cockroaches can be treated with branded cockroach-killer, but is best treated professionally. Several treatments may be necessary, as the eggs are very resilient. They live in warm, dark places, such as behind a stove, and also congregate around drains and toilets. If you see cockroaches regularly, in daylight, the infestation will be severe. Cockroaches need water, which is why you may find them drowned in a toilet bowl or sink. After eradication, seal cracks. Surfaces may need to be left for a week without cleaning, but after that, clean all surfaces near the infestation regularly.

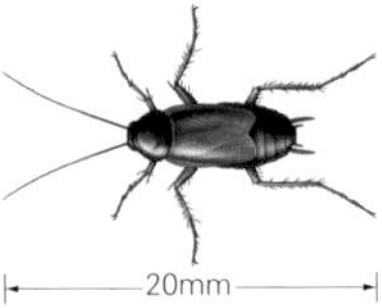

Fleas

Usually brought into the house by cats and dogs, fleas breed fast and their bites can make life a misery for humans. Their eggs, laid in cracks and crevices, are long-lived and difficult to kill. Flea larvae feed on dirt and dust and the adults feed on blood. Fleas sense their victims' approach by vibrations on the floor, and can jump 30cm (12in) to land on them. Among the many flea treatments for pets are powders and sprays, dog shampoos, herbal remedies, combing with a flea comb or using a flea collar. Use in conjunction with regular vacuuming. To treat a serious infestation, call a professional.

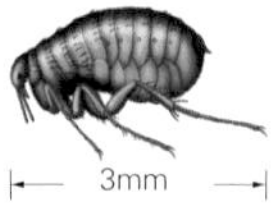

Flies

Houseflies feed indiscriminately on excreta and human food, and can transmit diseases and cause diarrhoea. They emerge in the warmer weather and breed prolifically, laying eggs in foodstuffs, especially on meat. The eggs hatch into maggots and start to feed. Fit fly screens or hang bead or bamboo curtains over open doors. Lace or muslin at open windows will also keep them out. Be scrupulous about food hygiene. Mesh domes used to cover meat are no protection – flies can lay

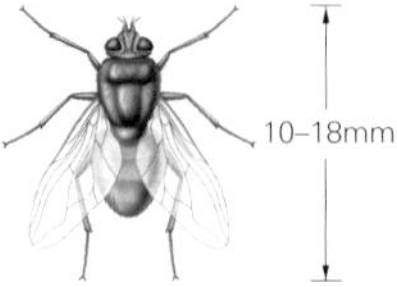

their eggs through the mesh. Uneaten cat- or dog-food is a prime breeding site. Swatting is healthier than fly spray, as is old-fashioned flypaper.

Flour beetles

These beetles are occasionally found in flour, cereals and other dried food stored or bought in unsealed or damaged packaging. Throw out the contaminated food, clean the cupboard thoroughly and start again, storing food in airtight containers.

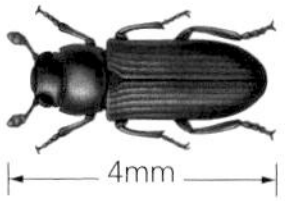

Head lice

An infestation of head lice can spread quickly through a family and through a whole class or school. Head lice live on the scalp, biting it and causing inflammation and itching, and laying their tiny pale eggs (nits) near the roots of the hair and behind the ears. Both lice and eggs will die once deprived of the warmth of the scalp. The whole family of a sufferer should use a nit comb and a dedicated non-toxic shampoo, available from chemists and most health food shops.

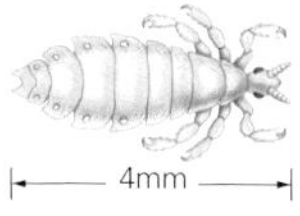

Safety with DIY treatments

- If you use poisons in the home, don't forget that **they can harm or kill other creatures** besides your target pest.
- **Store poisons** in their original containers, away from children and pets.
- **Follow the instructions** scrupulously.
- Wear a **protective mask and rubber gloves**. Keep room well ventilated.
- **Never use sprays near aquarium fish** or near food that is not properly sealed or put away.
- **Keep children and animals away** from the treated area. Allow the poison to do its work, then wash the area and let it dry. Wash fabrics and air upholstery thoroughly. Never spray poisons on beds or bedding – call in the experts.

Mites

Not insects but arachnids (spider family), scabies mites live on blood, burrowing into the skin, usually on the hands. This causes scabies, an extremely itchy rash. Mites are passed on by close contact with a sufferer. Treat with a prescription cream or try tea-tree natural antiseptic oil or ointment. Furniture mites or dust mites, harmless in themselves, live in mattresses

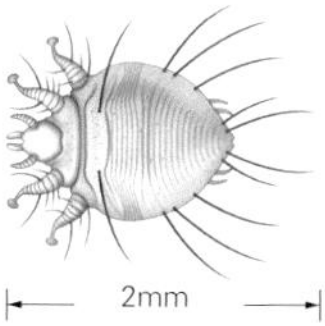

Deterring other people's pets

Keep strange cats out of your home by **installing a cat flap operated by an electronic tag** on your own cat's collar. People who have no pets of their own can deter dogs and cats with an ultrasonic device called a Dazer. It's harmless but annoying to animal pests and doesn't affect birds or fish.

The law says that **dogs must be kept under proper control** by their owners. If a neighbour's dog repeatedly visits your garden and causes a nuisance, and the neighbour does nothing when asked to keep the dog in, call the local police, who will visit the neighbour on your behalf.

and elsewhere in the house on flakes of human skin. Their droppings may exacerbate asthma. Vacuum mattresses and upholstery regularly.

Mosquitoes

Male mosquitoes live on nectar, but the females bite and suck blood from humans and animals. In the tropics, they can transmit malaria and other diseases. In cooler climes, victims may suffer a painful swelling. Mosquitoes are active after sundown, their flight

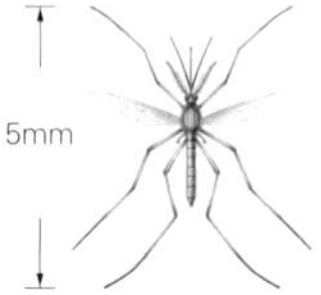

detected by an annoying whine, which stops as they land to feed. Females have lower-pitched whines than males. They lay their eggs on still water. Cover water butts and site ponds away from the house. Burn mosquito coils or use plug-in devices with replaceable deterrents. Sleeping with a mosquito net over the bed is more pleasant than using a repellent on the skin. Consider fly screens at the windows.

Moths

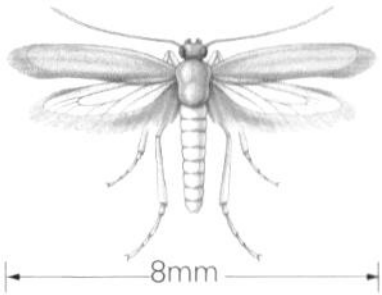

Clothes moths lay eggs on wool, then their larvae hatch out and eat it. They will also attack other natural and mixed fibres, especially when soiled with sweat or food. They can damage carpets, bedding and upholstery and clothes. Brush clothes well to remove eggs and larvae, air in the sun and put them away in sealed bags or a clean cupboard with sachets of lavender, rosemary and bay. Camphor mint is stronger-smelling, but preferable to the smell of mothballs.

Silverfish

These are harmless. They are attracted to damp and can sometimes

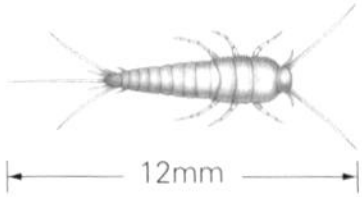

be found in kitchens and bathrooms, where they feed on cereal crumbs and wallpaper paste. Vacuum them up. Keep food sealed and clean out cupboards. Use an insecticide if necessary. Eliminate damp and they will not return.

Ticks

Ticks are arachnid parasites that fasten their mouthparts into the skin of cats, dogs, humans, and other animals. They suck blood and can transmit infections, including Lyme disease, which is rare in the UK, but on the increase. Lyme disease can be

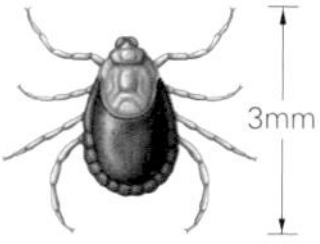

serious and even fatal. A red rash of tiny circles is followed by flu-like symptoms. Treatment is with antibiotics. Cover limbs on country walks, and check children's skin and clothing. To remove a tick, grip it with tweezers at the base and twist as you pull. It's important to remove the mouthparts – the old remedy of burning a tick with a lighted cigarette is not recommended.

Wasps and hornets

Wasps and hornets can give a powerful sting and should be treated with caution, as their behaviour is unpredictable. Remove in the same way as you would for bees (p75). Alternatively, swat or spray individuals and remove them carefully once dead. Hornets are rare and their presence probably indicates a nearby nest. Wasp and hornet nests should be destroyed by professionals – don't attempt this yourself. On picnics, keep fruit and sweet drinks covered. A glass with a little beer or honeyed water makes an effective wasp trap.

Woodworm

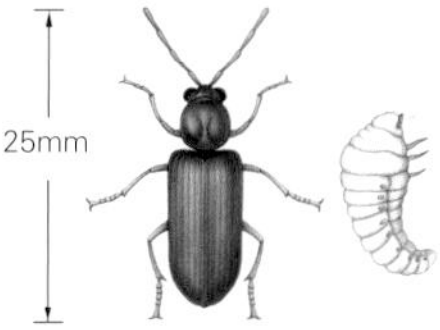

You can spot an attack of woodworm by a peppering of tiny holes on the surface of wood, but only if there is dust around them are there live woodworm inside. Check secondhand furniture before you buy. Treat a small outbreak with dedicated insecticide. Burn an item you're discarding. Call in professionals if the timbers of the house are infected.

Contact details

Useful websites and addresses about the information given in this chapter.

Ariel
www.ariel.co.uk
Website of leading detergent manufacturer. There are lots of laundry hints.

Allergy UK, Deepdene House, 30 Bellgrove Road, Welling, Kent DA16 3PY
Tel: 020 8303 8525
Fax: 020 8303 8792
e-mail: info@allergyuk.org
www.allergyuk.org
Allergy UK gives a seal of approval to products found to be beneficial to allergy sufferers, and offers other information, advice and support.

British Pest Control Association (BPCA), Ground Floor, Gleneagles House, Vernongate, Derby DE1 1UP
Tel: 01332 294 288
Fax: 01332 295 904
e-mail: enquiry@bpca.org.uk
www.bpca.org.uk
A UK trade association representing all those professionally involved with the eradication of public health and nuisance pests. Find a pest controller in your area who is a member of the association on the website.

Food Standards Agency
www.foodstandards.gov.uk
Government-based website offering advice and information on all aspects of food safety and hygiene, including tips on summer eating (especially the dangers of barbecued food), keeping your kitchen safe from harmful germs and bacteria, and advice on food poisoning.

Grandma Knows Best
e-mail: g-k-b@enquire.fsnet.co.uk
www.g-k-b.fsnet.co.uk
Tips on a wide range of domestic subjects.

Hints and things
www.hintsandthings.co.uk
A website devoted to the type of information that used to be passed down from generation to generation on a variety of subjects including basic cooking, knitting, sewing, gardening terms and general advice on cutting costs.

Mailing Preference Service (MPS), DMA House, 70 Margaret Street, London W1W 8SS
Tel: 020 7291 3310
Fax: 020 7323 4226
e-mail: mps@dma.org.uk
www.mpsonline.org.uk
Register free with this organisation to avoid receiving unwanted junk mail. You can also block unwanted telephone, fax and e-mail contact via this route.

myhouseandgarden.com
www.myhouseandgarden.com
A lifestyle website offering household and garden solutions.

National Asthma Campaign, Providence House, Providence Place, London N1 0NT
Helpline: 08457 010 203
Head office: 020 7226 2260
Fax: 020 7704 0740
www.asthma.org.uk
Offers news, research and other information for asthma sufferers.

National Carpet Cleaners Association (NCCA), 62c London Road, Oadby, Leicester LE2 5DH
Tel: 0116 271 9550
Fax: 0116 271 9588
e-mail: info@ncca.co.uk
www.ncca.co.uk
Advice on the cleaning and care of carpets, upholstery and other materials.

Partnership for Food Safety Education
www.fightbac.org
US-based resource for information on food safety and how to prevent harmful bacteria from spreading. Some of the articles on the site are slanted towards the USA, but most of the material is relevant to any food preparation.

Persil
Tel: 0800 776 644
www.persil.co.uk
Website of leading detergent manufacturer. There are lots of laundry hints.

Surf
Tel: 0800 444 200
www.surf.co.uk
Website of leading detergent manufacturer. There are lots of laundry hints.

TipKing.com
www.tipking.com
Over 6,000 tips, snippets of advice and articles on over 2,000 household subjects relating to life around the home that have been passed down through the generations. The site is continually being added to.

50 mm

Home Improvements

Improving our living space can be important, whether we are moving into a new home or simply brightening up a tired and tatty look that we have lived with for many years.

Unfortunately, many of us cannot afford the expertise of an interior designer and so have to make choices of colour, design and style ourselves. This can range from the simple addition of indoor plants or hanging new curtains in a room, giving one room a new coat of paint to the entire home being given a brand new redesign, with new furnishings and furniture throughout. Whatever improvements are made, the planning aspect is crucial.

Colour choice

Magazines and TV programmes revel in completely transforming rooms with colour, which can be both inspiring and daunting when it comes to choosing paint schemes for your own home.

There are some basic factors to take into account, such as the shape and size of the room, features you want to draw attention to or hide, and the effect of natural light. Even subtle variations of shade can have a significant impact on the overall look. There are simple ways to test colours and, even if you get it horribly wrong, it doesn't take long or cost too much to repaint a room.

What to consider when choosing paint

Colour is a background that complements the furniture, pictures, books and accessories that make up your home. Colour can add interest to a room without needing to be outrageously bold. Equally, intense, bright shades can be effective without being overpowering. The key to choosing the right colour for a room is taking into account the various factors that will affect its final appearance.

- Choose colours that match the mood of a room and how and when it's used. Vibrant combinations work best in areas where you don't spend much time – the hallway, for example. Rich red walls may be fine in the evening but could look dark and oppressive by daylight.
- Choose calming colours, even if they're dark, for the bedroom, which is the first and last thing you see each day.
- Bold colours can work well in kitchens and bathrooms, but as these rooms tend to have a lot of visual clutter, a simple overall colour scheme will probably work best.

TIPS OF THE TRADE

If you're buying fabric as well as paint, **create a sample board** of all the room's main areas of colour – walls, floors, curtains, upholstery, woodwork and accessories. Glue fabric swatches onto stiff card and arrange them with your paint samples on the board – flooring at the bottom, ceiling colour at the top. Try to keep the proportions the same as in the room.

Sally Jackson, interior designer

- Natural light affects the appearance of a colour. Whitewashed walls, cool and fresh in Mediterranean light, can look flat and dull in the softer light of northern Europe. Light, ice-blue walls might make a north-facing room look chilly but the same colour in a south-facing room will seem airy and bright.
- Artificial light – especially harsh fluorescent light – can alter colours. Change the lighting or the paint.
- The of the painted area affects colour. A small patch of lemon yellow looks fresh and clean, but the same colour on an entire wall will start to look green.
- Pale colours maximise the amount of light in a room. The commonsense conclusion is that you should use light colours in small, dark, or poorly lit rooms and darker colours only in bigger, lighter rooms. However, sometimes it's better to do the opposite and emphasise a room's character, enhancing a large, sunny room with light, bright colours, and making a small, dark area warm and cosy with strong, deep shades.
- Colour can give a sense of continuity throughout the house. Even if you use different colours to create an individual mood for each room, you could create a visual link by choosing one colour to appear in every room on, say, the skirting boards or even in the furnishings.
- Don't make switches of mood or style too abrupt. Going from Edwardian to Scandinavian to Mediterranean in the same house would make it feel disjointed and small.

Why paint and when?

You may decide to paint because you want to give a room a new look or because the old paint is looking tired, but there are good practical reasons for repainting, too. **Paint is protective**, preserving both the inside and outside of a building from the damaging effects of moisture, pollution, sunlight, and everyday wear and tear.

Paintwork also makes your home easier to keep clean, as it seals dusty walls and creates smooth, wipeable surfaces.

The inside of a house **usually needs repainting at least every seven to ten years**, and the outside every five to seven years, though these times will depend on the property's location, the prevailing weather and the quality of both the materials and work when the house was last painted.

Types of finish

As well as the colour, the type of paint finish affects the impression of light in a room.

- Matt is the most light-absorbent finish, which makes it a good choice for covering minor imperfections in plasterwork.
- Satin gives a degree of reflection and looks livelier than the matt equivalent of the same shades.
- Gloss reflects the most light: it's hard on the eyes if used over a large area, but used on relatively small areas it adds sparkle to the overall scheme. It's also the most durable finish, so it's ideal for surfaces that get heavy wear, like skirting boards, window frames and doors.

Looking at paint charts

All colours are derived from three primary colours: red, yellow and blue. Two primaries mixed in equal proportions create a secondary colour (red plus yellow makes orange; yellow plus blue makes green; blue plus red makes violet). The shades in between – the tertiary colours – are a combination of a primary and a secondary colour.

The colours on the red and yellow side of a colour wheel are often described as 'warm' and those on

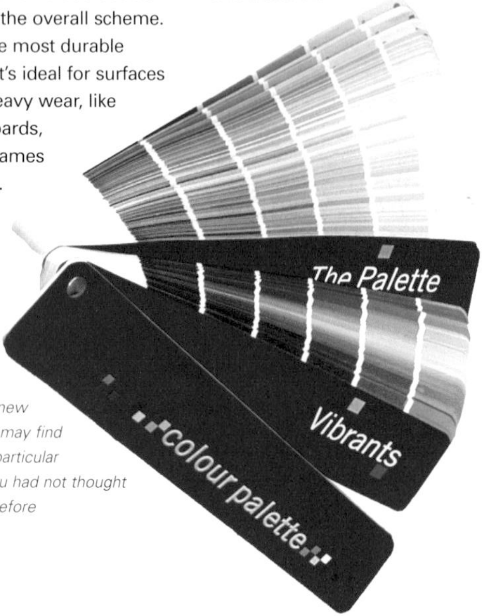

Paint charts can give you new ideas, as you may find a colour in a particular shade that you had not thought about using before

Decorative paint effects can be used to good effect on items of furniture

the blue and green side as 'cool'. With decorating colours, however, the terms 'warm' and 'cool' indicate the amount of red present in various shades of the same colour – so you can have cool and warm versions of all the main colours (*see* below). It's best not to combine warm and cool shades in a colour scheme, as the warm shades can take on a muddy hue, while the cool ones may look thin and harsh. Many paint charts are divided into groups of colours that share similar characteristics of, say, warmth, coolness, depth or intensity, and one of these groups makes a good starting point. The range of colours in each group is wide enough to

Visual tricks

- Choose the colour for the main wall by picking the colour of another **significant feature** in the room. A painting may inspire you or you could use your furniture colour as the main room colour.
- Make a room look **more spacious** by using the same light colour on the walls, ceilings and woodwork – this has the effect of removing visual clutter and making awkward features less noticeable. Make a small house or flat seem bigger by using the same colour scheme throughout.
- Make a **high ceiling appear lower** by painting it a darker colour than the walls or bring the ceiling colour part-way down the walls to an imaginary or actual picture rail. Warm shades on the end walls can shorten a long, narrow room.
- **Bulky items of furniture**, such as wardrobes, look less obtrusive if you paint them the same colour as the walls. The same applies to pipes or radiators: paint them the colour of the skirting board or wall they're against.
- Make pieces of **cheap or secondhand furniture** look co-ordinated by giving them a matching paint treatment.
- Highlight attractive **architectural details**, such as cornices and ceiling roses, with a contrasting colour.
- Use **special-effect paints** to make just about anything look like something else – turn wood into metal, plastic into stone and so on.

allow you to experiment with different effects, but because the shades sit comfortably together there's no risk of visual jarring.

Testing different colours

When choosing a paint colour, the best way to decide what you like and what's suitable for the room is to test a number of different colours.

Test different colours out on a room before buying large tins of paint

- Use 1–2m (3–6ft) lengths of lining paper (plain wallpaper made to be painted over) for each colour. The larger the sample, the better you will be able to judge it.
- Before you apply the paint to the lining paper, write the manufacturer and the name or code number of the colour on the back of the paper.
- Paint the lining paper, taking the colour as close to the edges as possible. Trim off unpainted margins when the paint has dried.
- Stick the samples on the walls and live with them for a while. Look at them in natural light – on both sunny and dull days – and in artificial light, in the darkest corner of the room as well as on the brightest wall. Make sure they work well with the room's carpet, curtains and furniture.

Cool (left) *and warm* (right) *versions of blue, green and yellow. Cool shades recede and generally make rooms look bigger, and sometimes austere, while warm shades appear to come towards you, and will make rooms look smaller and more intimate*

Choosing paint

Paints fall into two types: oil-based (also referred to as solvent-based) and water-based. Recently there's been a swing towards using water-based paints, for health and environmental reasons, and for the home decorator these are much easier to use, especially when cleaning up.

Water-based paints also offer a great deal of choice: the range of colours is vast and there are a variety of finishes for – literally – floor to ceiling. There are still some situations, however, in which an oil-based paint will give the best results.

What's in the can?

All paints are made up of pigments suspended in a medium that, once the paint has been applied, forms a solid film that binds the pigments together and sticks to the painted surface. In oil-based paints, the medium is a mixture of oil and natural or synthetic resins. In water-based paints, the medium is made up of water and synthetic resins.

What determines the final appearance of water-based paints is the proportion of pigment to resin. Matt finishes contain the most pigment and therefore have the greatest covering capacity. Gloss finishes have a higher proportion of resin. Generally, the higher the gloss, the more durable the finish is. Various other additives affect the qualities of paint, such as how quickly it dries, whether it's liquid or non-drip and its shelf-life.

Cheap paints usually contain a lower proportion of pigment and therefore several more coats may be needed – so they don't necessarily save you money and may cost you far more in terms of time.

Which type of paint?

Water-based paints include: matt and silk vinyl emulsions; masonry paints; primers; undercoats; acrylic satin and gloss paints.

- Advantages: quick drying; low odour; clean up with water; less toxic.
- Disadvantages: less durable; more easily marked.

Oil-based paints include: primers; undercoats; satin and gloss paints; masonry paints; metal paints.

- Advantages: hard wearing; gloss retains shine longer; greater resistance to damp.
- Disadvantages: slow drying; strong odour; white spirit or other solvent clean-up.

Paints for walls and ceilings

Previously painted or papered surfaces

These are usually given one of the following finishes:

- **Flat emulsion** (sometimes called flat matt) A non-reflective finish that covers well and hides blemishes. Good for ceilings but marks easily on walls.
- **Matt emulsion** Despite its name, this is sometimes very slightly light-reflective. Good for hiding minor imperfections and suitable for ceilings and for walls in low-traffic areas.
- **Soft-sheen and mid-sheen emulsions** Found in ranges for kitchens and bathrooms, they have more reflective finishes.
- **Silk emulsion** Reflects light, is resistant to scuffs, and can be sponged clean. Suitable for most walls, although imperfections will be more conspicuous.
- **Paints for decorative effects** These are for sponging, ragging, and so on. Some have metallic finishes. Most are two-paint systems (which you buy together) – an undercoat followed by a topcoat. Follow the instructions.
- **Textured finishes** These include masonry paint with sand in it. Good for disguising poor plasterwork. The preparation required is similar to that for other painting tasks but you must remove wallpaper and mask adjacent surfaces, as splashes are hard to remove once they've dried.

It is easier to apply large surface areas using a roller and paint tray

Brand new plasterwork

You can buy paint that's specifically for plaster, which allows the surface to breathe. Don't use standard vinyl emulsion, as it creates a film that prevents the plaster from drying out completely.

Dry, unpainted cement and plaster finishes

These absorbent surfaces can be difficult and expensive to paint – it takes more effort to drag the brush or roller across the surface, and most of the paint will be sucked into the material, rather than form a film on top. Avoid these problems by using a primer sealer or diluting the first coat of emulsion with up to 10% water (follow the manufacturer's recommendations).

A three-stage system for wood and metal

Bare wood and metal are traditionally treated with a three-paint system – of primer, undercoat, and topcoat – which gives maximum adhesion to these constantly expanding and contracting materials. Buy all three paints from the same manufacturer, as they're designed to work together. Properly applied, the paints are able to withstand climatic extremes.

Primer The first layer of protection. You can buy oil-based and water-based primers. Some primers are for a specific type of surface – wood, metal, non-ferrous metal – but if you have a number of small painting tasks to do, it's most economical to buy a multi-purpose primer.

Undercoat Provides a key – a surface to which the topcoat can adhere – and helps build the depth of colour, so always use the colour recommended for your chosen topcoat. Two coats of undercoat will increase the life of the topcoat, especially on exterior surfaces.

Topcoat Provides a decorative finish and a tough skin that resists moisture, mould, ultra-violet rays, and pollution. Because it also provides a smooth surface, dirt is less likely to stick. The following finishes are available:

- **Satin** A mid-sheen finish. Available in oil-based and water-based paints.
- **Eggshell** A slightly glossy finish – the oil-based equivalent of silk emulsion, but more durable. It can also be used on walls.
- **Gloss** A hard-wearing, shiny finish that resists knocks and can be wiped clean. It highlights surface

How much paint?

First **calculate the size of the surfaces** you're going to paint by multiplying the height of the area in metres by the width in metres, to give a figure in square metres (sq m). Most paint labels give a **coverage estimate** in square metres: divide your total area by this figure. The answer is the number of cans you need. The table overleaf shows the covering capacity in square metres of a range of paints and different sizes of can.

Covering capacity			
Volume of paint	Undercoat (sq m)	Gloss (sq m)	Emulsion (sq m)
500 ml	8	8.5	6
1 litre	16	17	12
2.5 litre	40	42	30
5 litre	80	84	60

imperfections. Available in oil-based and water-based paints.

- **Liquid gloss** An oil-based paint that gives the smoothest, shiniest finish. It's the most unforgiving of a less-than-perfect surface and is the most durable finish, so it's suitable for exposed exterior woodwork and metal.

Special-purpose paints

Kitchen and bathroom paints These are designed to resist moisture and condensation. Some contain fungicide to protect against mould growth.

Floor paints Formulated to be tougher than paints for walls. Water-based versions are good for old wooden,

A roller will only take the paint close to the walls. Paint the edges butting up to the ceiling using a brush

concrete or stone floors, but for areas of heavy wear – doorsteps, garage floors, passageways – oil-based products are recommended.

Anti-mould emulsions and gloss paints These contain fungicide. They're designed to block out staining caused by minor mould growth and to deter regrowth. They do not solve the underlying cause of mould.

Anti-damp paints These can be applied to damp surfaces before you redecorate with your chosen colour – but they are of lasting benefit only if the source of damp is cured first.

Anti-burglar or security paint Remains permanently slippery. Use it on drainpipes to deter people from trying to climb up them.

Slip-resistant paints Recommended for doorsteps and concrete floors, but note that they're not non-slip.

Paints for difficult surfaces

Multi-surface primer (as opposed to multi-purpose) Can be used on almost any surface, from MDF (medium-density fibreboard) to melamine, to create a good base for a gloss or satin topcoat.

Paints for outside

Masonry paints are available as:
- smooth water-based paints, which are like exterior-grade emulsions and provide a dirt-resistant finish
- sand-textured water-based paints, which disguise minor imperfections and give a very durable finish
- moisture-permeable, quick-drying, oil-based paints, which can be applied in damp conditions and give a smooth finish.

Woodwork is usually painted with:
- a three-stage system (*see* p91)
- single-coat exterior-grade gloss
- moisture-permeable paints or woodstains (new wood only).

Metal can be painted with:
- a three-stage system (*see* p91)
- single-coat exterior-grade gloss
- three-in-one hammered or smooth-finish paint.

Ceramic tile primer and paint These give greater adhesion than ordinary paints, which means that they are good for painting tiles.

Vinyl floor paint This can be used on vinyl and other soft flooring. It's formulated to stick to and flex with the surface.

Wood-grain effect paint Can be applied to most surfaces. It can give a painted door, for instance, a passably natural-looking finish. Saves the hassle of stripping back to bare wood.

Choosing curtains

When you're doing up a room, curtains represent a considerable part of the expense. Whether you buy curtains ready-made or have them made to fit, you need to measure accurately the window and its surrounds and decide whether to opt for a pole or track.

If you are having curtains made, the amount of fabric required will depend on the style of heading you want (*see* illustrations in this section), but also on the length you choose – you have flexibility here.

Made-to-measure curtains

Whether sewn by you, a friend or a professional curtain-maker, made-to-measure curtains give you the widest choice of fabric and heading. They may be the only option if your windows don't conform to the standard sizes of ready-made curtains.

Choosing fabric

Sheers, voiles and laces are extremely thin fabrics that provide daytime privacy and can also help screen off an ugly outlook.

Medium-weight fabrics, like cotton prints or linen, can offer privacy after dark but, unless they are lined, will not completely keep out the morning light or stop heat loss and draughts.

Heavy fabrics, like velvet, chenille or tapestry, are good for keeping light out and keeping heat in.

Fabric seconds can be great bargains, but find out what the fault is before you buy. A pattern printed just slightly askew will look conspicuously crooked once it's hanging at a window.

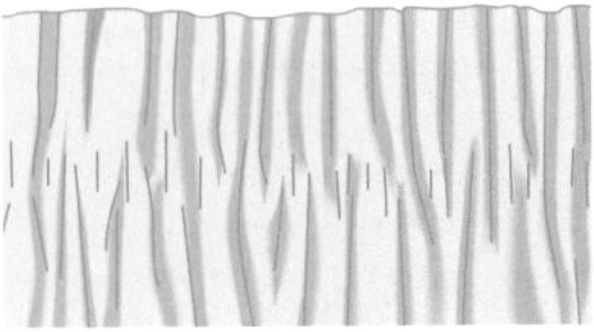

Gathered or standard heading

Pencil pleats

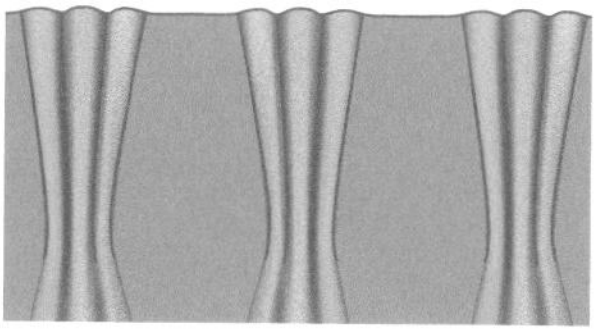

Pinch pleats

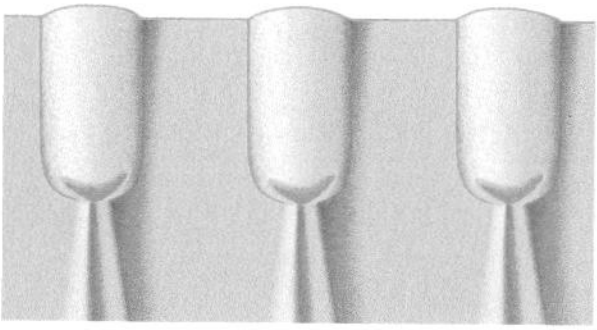

Goblet pleats

Heading tapes

The heading tape hides the edge of the top of the curtain, holds the cords that are used to draw up the curtain fabric to the required width and provides slots to hold the curtain hooks. These are the most popular heading tapes.

Gathered or standard heading Pulls the fabric into an irregular ruffle. Good for unlined, lightweight fabrics. Allow one and a half to three times the width of the pole or track.

Pencil pleats Suitable for all fabrics. Allow twice the width of the pole or track (three times for lightweight fabric).

Pinch pleats This heading tape makes regular and evenly spaced pleats. This means that you cannot always gather the fabric to exactly the right width, so you must err on the generous side when calculating the fabric required or the curtains won't meet in the middle. Pronged hooks, which are more expensive than standard hooks, hold the pleats in place. Allow twice the width of the pole or track.

Goblet pleats An eye-catching heading, especially if each goblet is finished with a fabric-covered button. Like pinch pleats, goblet pleats are evenly spaced. Allow two and a half times the width of the pole or track.

Buying ready-made curtains

Ready-made curtains can be much less expensive than professionally made-to-measure ones.

Fabric Obviously, you have to choose from what's on offer. But there are many companies selling ready-made curtains. Shop around.

Heading tape This is usually pencil pleat because it is easily adjusted for different widths and is suitable for both track and pole.

Ready-made curtains can easily be altered to fit the size of your window

TIPS OF THE TRADE

- If you have to **shorten curtains** – especially if they're lined and have a professionally finished hem – cut off the excess from the top, rather than the bottom, and attach new heading tape.
- When **cutting fabric** for curtains, give yourself an accurate line to cut along by pulling out one or two cross threads between the selvedges (the bound edges of a length of fabric).
- **Weights** stitched into the bottom corners make curtains hang well – leftover foreign coins would do.

Karen Swindon, curtain-maker

Size Don't give up if the available sizes don't suit your windows. Many suppliers offer, for a fee, an alteration service. It is also possible to shorten curtains yourself without too much hassle (*see* Tips of the Trade, left). If your window is wider than the maximum width of curtain available, consider buying two pairs of narrower curtains. A few stitches at the top will join them or you can draw them as four individual curtains.

Hanging curtains

Poles and blinds certainly look contemporary, but if you have a bay window, you may have to choose track. Go for a flexible track with a metal core that can be bent to any shape without springing back. If you have to bend a plastic track, warm it first with a hairdryer.

Choosing poles and tracks

Poles

Curtain poles are sold in lengths of up to 3m (10ft), often with a wide choice of finials – decorative ends that prevent the curtains sliding off. Most poles are supplied as kits with wall fixings. The brackets should be fitted about 10cm (4in) in from either end of the pole.

- To decide what length to cut the curtain pole, hold it above the window with one curtain attached and position it with enough pole protruding beyond the frame to allow the curtain to overlap the wall. Allow at least 20cm (8in), depending on the thickness of the cloth. Pull the curtain into the open position so it draws right back from the window.
- Telescopic poles save the need for cutting to size, but they are not as strong as solid poles. Check that the pole will take the weight of the curtain fabric.
- Poles allow you to hang curtains with rings or tabs of material. Tabs are available in kits that include decorative buttons, clips, pins and iron-on tab templates. Cut leftovers of your curtain material to size and simply iron on the templates to make the tabs.
- Choose slim, lightweight rods for hanging muslin, lace or voile curtains. Make café blinds by fitting a brass rod across the window, and fixing the fabric in place with pincer clips.

Tracks

Curtain tracks are sold in lengths up to 3m (10ft) and come with fixing brackets, slip-on hooks, end stops and instructions for hanging the curtains. If you want a valance to hide the top of the curtains and the track, opt for a combined track and valance rail kit. Check the track packaging to make sure it will support the weight of your curtains, including linings. As with a pole, track should extend beyond the window frame by at least 20cm (8in), depending on the thickness of the curtains.

Fixing the supports

You will need a hammer drill fitted with a masonry bit to make holes in the wall above the window.

Solid brick or block walls

Track kits normally include wall plugs for fixing into solid walls. If not, use plugs at least 50mm (2in) long to give a strong grip for the combined track and curtain weight.

Concrete lintel

Concrete is difficult to drill. Instead of drilling lots of holes for the fixing brackets, fix a 25 x 50mm (1 x 2in) timber batten to the wall with a screw at either end, beyond the lintel ends, and attach the brackets to this.

Woodwork

You can sometimes attach track (but usually not poles) to the architrave of the window.

Safety when drilling

Always wear **eye protection** – drilling can produce a lot of sawdust and may shoot metal shavings and wood chips up into your eyes. **Protective gloves** are also recommended as drill bits rotate at extremely high speeds.

Drill holes for the brackets with a wood bit. Screw the brackets into the highest parts of a decorative architrave so that the track doesn't buckle. Where the architrave of the window is flush with the wall, fix track to the edges of the window reveal. To extend the track on to the walls either side of the window, giving more light when the curtains are open, fix a timber batten over the top of the architrave.

Plasterboard walls

Buy cavity wall fixings with flanges that open out on the inside face of the plasterboard to give a strong grip in plasterboard ceilings or walls. Avoid heavyweight curtains unless you can fix the track or pole to the timber battens behind the plasterboard.

Ceilings

Fitting track to a ceiling can be difficult if the joists behind the ceiling run parallel to the window wall, as the nearest joist may be in the wrong position. In this case, you will need to fix cross battens between the joists so that you have something to screw into. You will need a special ceiling fixing kit to attach to the brackets.

How to fix poles and tracks

1 Decide on the height of the pole or track above the window frame by holding the curtains up to the window. It should be at least 75mm (3in). The curtain should be around 12mm (1⁄2in) above the floor to reduce wear on the hem. For shorter curtains, allow at least 50mm (2in) to drop below the bottom of the window frame, but make sure the fabric does not touch a radiator.

2 Draw a line above the window where the pole or track brackets are to be fixed. Use a spirit level to ensure the line is horizontal. Continue the line beyond each side of the window frame – *see* Choosing poles and tracks.

3 Fit your drill with a masonry bit the same diameter as wall plugs. Wrap tape around the bit to mark the length of the plug. Drill bracket fixing holes along the pencil line, spaced according to the kit instructions. The end brackets should be around 50mm (2in) in from the ends of the pole or track to prevent sagging.

4 Tap wall plugs or cavity fixings into the drilled holes. If plugs protrude, take them out and make the holes deeper.

5 For poles, screw the pair of end brackets to the wall. You may need a central bracket for extra support. Attach the curtains to the pole and slot it through the brackets. The end ring or tab should sit between the bracket and the end of the pole to hold the curtains in place as you draw them. Check that the pole ends overhang the window frame equally. Screw the pole securely to the brackets.

Put the end ring after the bracket and fit the end stop to the pole

6 For tracks, screw the fixing brackets in place, making sure the track clips are all vertical. Clip on the curtain track. Stand back and check that the track ends overhang the window frame equally at either side. Fit the curtains to the track and add any cord fittings or valance rails. If the curtains are hard to pull, apply a light spray of silicone wax polish to the track.

Design and style

With the profusion of style and makeover programmes bombarded at us on the television, it is understandable that many of us are left confused and bewildered at the approach to adopt in our own homes.

Whatever new design or colour scheme you are planning, you should first take into account not only your lifestyle, but also the environment in which you are living. For example, if you live in an urban, one-bedroomed apartment the style of decoration you adopt may be totally different to someone living in a palatial, five-bedroomed, traditional period-style house.

Choosing a style

When you are thinking about a style for a particular room, it is important to consider not only what sort of look you like – for example, modern, traditional, country cottage, ethnic – but also to take into account the function of the room and its size.

> **TOP TIP**
>
> Once you have found an **established style** you like, do not be scared of adapting it to suit your home and your lifestyle. This way you add a touch of individuality to your design.

Look at the room with a critical eye. Consider the following points:

- **Does the room have high or low ceilings?** Light colours tend to add a feeling of spaciousness, whereas a darker colour can make a high ceiling appear lower than it is.
- **How much natural light is there?** This will not only impact on colour choice, but may even mean that you need to consider installing more light points before you undertake any decorating.
- **What about the existing furniture?** This will have a bearing on what your design will be. This is not a problem if you are just changing the colour scheme rather than the overall style (although the choice of colour should obviously sit well with your existing furniture!).

However, if you are going for a new style and cannot afford to discard your existing furniture, then your design choices will be limited. If you are

A plain style can be much easier to work with in a room, as opposed to more ornate designs and colour schemes

splashing out on new furniture – effectively working with a blank canvas – then your style choices will not be so restricted.

- **How large or small is the actual space?** Space may well be at a premium, especially in an urban dwelling, and you may be hampered by existing architectural features. Adapt your scheme accordingly.

Design examples

Modern schemes are invariably characterised by their innovative use of colour, furniture, fabric and material. A room decorated in a modern style may not be the best choice if you have more traditional furniture.

Traditional themes tend to hark back to the classical, Victorian or Edwardian eras and can centre on more ornate decoration and traditional period-style furniture. Older properties tend to lend themselves more to this sort of approach.

Ethnic style designs aim to replicate a flavour of a particular region, such as Mexican, Chinese, Moroccan or Indian. Accessories, fabrics and ethnic ornaments are key to completing this scheme.

TOP TIP

Don't be in too much of a hurry to finish off your newly decorated scheme the moment the main DIY jobs are out of the way. Take your time to collect different ornaments and accessories to add to the overall effect. Once you have lived in the space for a while, you will be more in tune with what goes and what does not. Rushing out and spending a fortune on finishing touches straight after decorating can end up being disastrous.

House plants

A well-chosen and correctly positioned plant can have a stunning impact on the look and feel of a room. Indoor plants can liven up any home and make it feel more lived in and cared for.

Most people view house plants as a bit of a challenge, remembering their failed attempts at keeping a spider plant alive, but if you choose the right plant, understand what type of care it needs and place it in the correct environment, then an indoor plant can enhance the design aspect of any room.

Bathrooms and kitchens

There are particular plants that thrive in the humid conditions and low light levels that these rooms often provide. Ferns tend to thrive in bathrooms and kitchens because the steamy conditions help to maintain humidity around their delicate foliage. However, this environment is obviously not constant and these plants will need misting regularly when the humidity drops. Other plants that enjoy these conditions include Chlorophytum, *Cissus antarctica*, Philodendron and Pilea, which all do well in fairly low light levels.

Indoor plants bring a bit of the outdoors inside

The home office

House plants bring an element of nature into the home and this can be especially useful in an area of the home that has been turned into a work space. If your home office is not used over the weekend, and so you may not go into that room over the weekend, for instance, it might make sense to choose really tough plants that will survive a bit of neglect. Plants to consider include cacti and succulents, Chlorophytum, Dracaena and Monstera.

Make sure that your plants are seated in deep trays to avoid water spillage near computer equipment.

Dining and living rooms

These are the rooms where you can choose plants to make a statement or fit in with the overall design and feel of the room. For example, do you want to create a feature in the room with a large foliage plant or a group of smaller plants? Leaves come in many shapes and sizes of glossy (*Fatsia japonica*), textured (Peperomia) or coloured (Begonia) leaves.

Alternatively, flowering plants can add splashes of colour that will brighten up a dull room, even in winter. Jasmine and Cyclamen provide a welcome burst of colour indoors at the time of year when even the garden looks drab. Try experimenting with placing flowering plants next to different foliage plants. Add your own style to the room with your choice of house plants.

TOP TIP

Decide first where you want to place a plant; then choose a species to **fit the environment** and conditions of this position.

TOP TIP

Flowering plants such as jasmine, hyacinth and gardenia can bring **delicious spring scents** into your home, giving the added benefit of making your house smell fresh and clean, as well as providing a burst of colour to any room.

The hallway

Hallways tend to be quite dull areas and so a hardy plant, such as the Aspidistra, is ideal to cope with fluctuations in temperature, draughts and varying light levels that is often prevalent in the hall. Be careful not to place your plant in a position where it is likely to get brushed into or knocked about. Plants rarely like this sort of treatment and can cause the leaves to brown and wilt.

Buying sofas and beds

We spend over a third of our lives in bed, so a bed that's past its best can seriously affect our quality of sleep. When it comes to buying sofas, it's easy to be swayed by looks, but style and quality are also important if you want to sit in comfort for any time and get the wear you hope for.

Whether you are buying beds or sofas, the choice often comes down to something cheap and cheerful for occasional and short-term use or paying out for quality and durability.

Choosing a sofa

Making the wrong choice when buying upholstered furniture can be an expensive mistake, so think carefully about what you want from your sofa before you buy.

Quality

Cheaper sofas are upholstered with foam or padding. The frames are made of chipboard and the cushions are supported on straps or springs.

More expensive sofas have sturdy, hardwood frames; thickly padded, sprung interiors; and cushions filled with good-quality wadding or feathers. If you treat a good sofa with care you should get ten years of wear, maybe more,

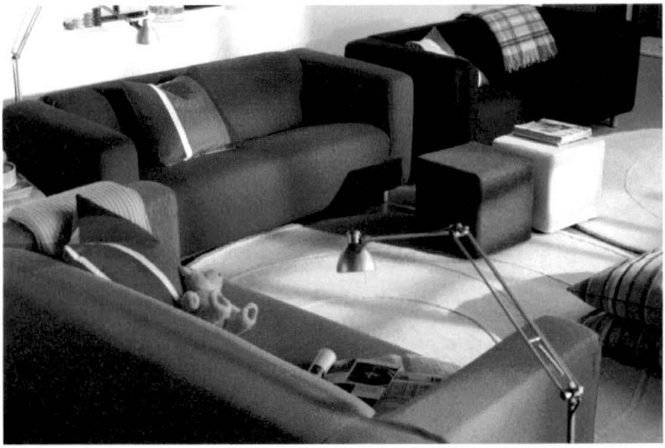

Sofas need to fit in to your house style – and suit the way you sit or lie on them

though you might need to renew the covers.

Covers

Fitted covers are fastened permanently and can't be removed for cleaning. It may be worth having the item treated with stain repellent, although this does add considerably to the cost.

Loose covers are fastened with zips or Velcro for easy removal and cleaning. Buy a second set for a change of colour scheme. More expensive than fitted covers.

Fabrics are usually classified for either light, general, or severe use. Choose leather or synthetic fabrics if your sofa will get a lot of wear.

Buying a sofa

- Think about how you and any other members of the household like to sit. Do you want head support from a high back? Or do you like to put your feet up and sit sideways? If the latter, you'll need arms that are high enough to rest your back on comfortably.
- When working out how many seats you need, bear in mind that a two-seater may actually feel small for two people.
- Sit on the sofa for several minutes. Does it support the small of your back properly? Get someone to sit beside you so you can check whether the cushions tip you into the middle.
- Do you struggle to stand up from the sofa? If so, it may be too low or too soft.
- To ensure that the sofa will fit where you want it, check the dimensions of your hall, doorways and (if relevant) stairs before buying.
- Sofas are often advertised for mail order, but the obvious drawback is that you can't try before you buy. Check that your chosen company offers a trial period – most do – and that, if you reject the sofa for any reason within this time, the company will collect free of charge and give a full refund.

Do you need a new bed?

Beds get a lot of wear and even the best need replacing after ten years. If you can answer 'Yes' to any of the following questions, it's probably time to buy.

- Has the bed become uncomfortable? Don't wait until a saggy mattress starts interfering with your sleep before you make a change.
- Are the castors bent?

- Is the base sagging?
- Does the bed creak when you turn over? Can you feel bulges or ridges in the mattress?
- Are the divan edges frayed?
- Is the mattress covering torn?
- Does your neck or back ache when you wake up in the morning?
- In a double bed, do you roll towards the middle unintentionally?

Caring for beds and sofas

- **Turning over mattresses** evens out wear and prolongs their life. Every six to eight weeks would be ideal, but even twice a year would help.
- Likewise, regularly **turn and reposition the cushions** on sofas and armchairs – it's a good idea to do this every time you vacuum the room.
- **Vacuum sofas and armchairs** using the upholstery attachment every week.
- If you **wash loose cushion covers**, machine wash on a cool setting and stretch them back into shape while still damp. Try washing a single cover first.
- **Read the manufacturer's literature** about caring for new furniture, and follow any cleaning information given on labels.
- **Trim off any loose threads.**
- **Jumping on sofas or beds damages springs** and other support systems.

Choosing a new bed

It's tempting to buy a cheap bed base with an expensive mattress, but this can be a false economy. Always consider the two parts together: a cheap base that wears quickly won't give the support the mattress needs to provide maximum comfort.

Mattresses

Interior-sprung mattresses
Open springs are found in many mattresses. The price of open-sprung mattresses varies widely according to the filling and covering of the mattress. The wire gauge and number of springs determines how firm the centre of an open-sprung mattress is. Continuous springs are softer and springier than open springs, and mould themselves better to your body shape. Pocket springs are housed individually in fabric pockets. This means they can move independently of each other, which enables them to mould themselves to the body. They give even support, no matter how many times you alter position during the night. Pocket-sprung mattresses are usually more expensive than open-sprung mattresses.

Unsprung mattresses Cheaper than sprung mattresses, and

they don't need turning. Made of latex, foam, or fibre. Foam mattresses are hypo-allergenic. When choosing an unsprung mattress, go for a thick, high-quality one.

Mattress coverings

Durability comes from the closeness of the weave and the quality of the fabric. A 'micro-quilted' finish is the most usual, where the mattress covering is stitched on to a backing material. Pocket-sprung mattresses are often 'tufted' (a series of tapes having been passed through the mattress and fastened with tags) to hold the mattress filling in place.

Bed bases

A base may be either a divan, usually on castors, which comes down almost to the floor and may have built-in storage drawers; or a bedstead, which may be of traditional design, with a gap between the framework and the floor.

Boarded bases are the cheapest, made of hardboard or even cardboard. They give a firm feel to the bed, but because the mattress is taking all the wear the mattress springs will start to wear out sooner than they would on a sprung base.

Firm-edge bases are made of wood with a heavy-duty spring unit inside. They give good support, both when sleeping and when sitting on the edge of the bed.

Sprung-edge bases are best for comfort and wear, and have a complete spring unit on top of a wooden frame. This helps the mattress to last longer.

Slatted bases provide firm support, but are not advised with a pocket-sprung mattress, as the springs and pockets may get damaged where they are not supported at the gaps between the slats. The slats should be evenly spaced, no more than 8cm (3in) apart, to provide adequate mattress support.

Buying a bed

- Go to the shop prepared to **lie on each bed for several minutes**.
- Lie as you normally would to sleep and **try turning over**.
- When considering a double bed, **lie on the bed with your partner**, both back to back and facing. Turn over, singly and together. Bigger doubles are significantly more comfortable than the standard width.
- **The firmest mattress may not be the best** for your particular weight and build. Compare several for comfort.
- Buy the best you can afford.

Contact details

Useful websites and addresses about the information given in this chapter.

B&Q
www.diy.com
Click on the How to's button at the top of the page to go through to the DIY Advice section for information on gardening, decorating, building, carpentry, electrical issues and plumbing.

Casa Paint Company
Tel: 01296 770 139
e-mail:
sales@thebluepenguin.com
www.casa.co.uk/casa.htm
Makers of handmade organic paints. Casa Paints are supplied as a concentrate so they can be watered down to achieve a multitude of effects.

Crown Paints, PO Box 37, Crown House, Hollins Road, Darwen, Lancashire BB3 0BG
Tel: 01254 704 951
www.crownpaint.co.uk
Manufacturer of paints.

Cuprinol, Wexham Road, Slough, Berkshire SL2 5DS
Tel: 01753 550 555
www.cuprinol.co.uk
The How To section on the website of this manufacturer of wood treatments has useful practical advice.

Dulux, ICI Paints, Wexham Road, Slough SL2 5DS
Tel: 01753 550 555
www.dulux.co.uk
Manufacturer of paints.

Farrow & Ball Ltd,
Uddens Estate, Wimborne, Dorset BH21 7NL
Tel: 01202 876 141
Fax: 01202 873 793
e-mail: info@farrow-ball.com
www.farrow-ball.com
Manufacturers of traditional papers and paints.

Fired Earth Ltd
Tel: 01295 814 315
e-mail:
enquiries@firedearth.com
www.firedearth.com
Suppliers of interior finishes – the Inspirations section has a number of design ideas.

Forest Stewardship Council (FSC), UK Working Group,

Unit D, Station Buildings,
Llanidloes, Powys SY18 6EB
Tel: 01686 413 916
Fax: 01686 412 176
e-mail: info@fsc-uk.org
www.fsc-uk.info
Contains a database of wood products and suppliers certified by the FSC, which is dedicated to promoting responsible management of the world's forests.

Hammerite Products Ltd,
Prudhoe, Northumberland
NE42 6LP
Tel: 01661 830 000
Fax: 01661 838 200
www.hammerite.com
Makers of specialist metal paints.

International Paints, Plascon International Ltd, Brewery House, High Street, Twyford, Winchester SO21 1RG
Tel: 01962 717 001
Fax: 01962 711 503
e-mail:
international@sis.akzonobel.com
www.international-paints.co.uk
Makers of specialist paints.

National Carpet Cleaners Association (NCCA), 62c London Road, Oadby, Leicester LE2 5DH
Tel: 0116 271 9550
Fax: 0116 271 9588
e-mail: info@ncca.co.uk
www.ncca.co.uk
Advice on the cleaning and care of carpets, upholstery and other materials if you are not looking to buy new, as well as a searchable database to help you to find a local carpet specialist.

Ronseal
Tel: 0114 246 7171
fax: 0114 245 5629
e-mail: enquiry@ronseal.co.uk
www.ronseal.co.uk
Makers of woodcare products.

Sadolin, Akzo Nobel Woodcare, Meadow Lane, St Ives, Cambridgeshire PE27 4UY
Tel: 01480 496 868
www.sadolin.co.uk
Makers of exterior timber treatments.

Sandtex, Akzo Nobel Decorative Coatings Ltd, PO Box 37, Crown House, Hollins Road, Darwen, Lancashire BB3 0BG
Tel: 01254 704 951
www.sandtex.co.uk
Makers of exterior masonry paints.

Sleep Council
Tel: 01756 791 089; e-mail: info@sleepcouncil.org.uk
www.sleepcouncil.org.uk
Advice on buying a bed.

System **Checks**

The components of your home are like the cogs of a machine: if all parts are well oiled, then the machine works well. Similarly, if an area of your home is faulty, the fabric of your home could be affected.

It is important to acquaint yourself – if only superficially – with the essential services of your home, such as electricity, water and gas, as well as the heating and plumbing systems. Checks both inside and out can also highlight minor faults before they become major – possibly expensive – ones. If you are at all unsure or worried about tackling any problems yourself, check out the contact numbers on pp150–1 and get the experts in.

Inside checks

It pays to be vigilant for deterioration in the fabric of your home, and its inside components, before problems become serious. Making the regular checks given here won't take up much time.

Annual checks inside

Central heating boiler

Regular servicing prevents boilers from becoming noisy, inefficient, and dangerous. To reduce noise:

- lower the pump speed by switching its control to a lower setting
- add descaling liquid (from plumbers' merchants) to the feed and expansion tank.

  Call a CORGI-registered gas fitter or your gas supplier if the boiler is constantly switching on and off or, more worryingly, if there is any sign of soot round the flue, which might be a sign of carbon monoxide escaping.

Insulation

Loft insulation keeps houses warm and saves on fuel bills. Insulation on tanks and pipes prevents freezing. Check:

- there are no gaps between lengths of loft insulation and no dampness
- pipe and tank insulation is correctly fitted.

Reposition loft insulation if necessary. Remove any damp insulation first, then lay new insulation.

Small electrical appliances

If these appliances are moved frequently, flexes and plugs may become worn. Check that:

- flex sheaths are undamaged, and that the sheath continues inside plugs and appliances.
- connections to plug terminals are sound
- plugs have the correct fuse ampage for the appliance's wattage rating.

Replace damaged flex, making sure sheath is secured in the flex grip of the plug. Tighten loose plug terminal screws. For appliances under 700W fit a 3 amp plug fuse. Fit a 13 amp fuse in other appliances.

Smoke detectors

Test your smoke detectors regularly and keep them free of dust and cobwebs. Replace batteries annually.

Stopvalves

The stopvalves on your incoming water supply pipe and any other gate valves and servicing valves on your system can jam open if left unused for long periods. This can turn out to be dangerous if there is a leak and you will need to turn the water off or isolate part of the system. Check that:

- the main stopvalve turns off easily – leave it a quarter turn from fully open
- all servicing valves work – leave them fully open.

Apply light machine oil or lubricant spray to the spindles of stiff stopvalves and servicing valves. Get a plumber to replace any that are difficult to turn.

Spring and autumn checks inside

Central heating

A **low or empty feed and expansion tank** is a common problem. Another is corrosion inside the heating system, which causes gases to collect in radiators. Check that:

- the feed and expansion tank is about one-third full when the heating is on
- the ballvalve moves easily
- radiators feel hot all over.

Top up the feed and expansion tank as necessary. Use silicone grease to lubricate the ballvalve so it moves freely. *See* pp114–8 for more on central heating.

Traps

Piping under baths, basins, shower trays and sinks has a water seal to keep out drain smells. Check for:

- blockages caused by soap, hair, or other debris
- evidence of water drips beneath fittings.

Unscrew traps and clear any debris. Replace faulty sealing rings to stop drips.

Lay new loft insulation if the old insulation is damp or has become too worn

Standard central heating

A standard central heating system, which sends heated water from a boiler to radiators and to the hot water cylinder heating coil, has its own small feed and expansion cistern in the loft. This tops up any water losses due to leaks or evaporation and also provides room for the central heating water to expand as it heats up. The cistern is supplied by a branch pipe from the rising main and fills via a float-operated valve in the same way as the main storage cistern. A second open vent pipe looping over the feed and expansion cistern provides an escape route for air or steam should the heating system overheat for any reason.

When boilers fail to light, the problem may be fixed by replacing a fuse or reigniting the pilot light. If these steps fail, then it is probably time to call in the professionals

Problems

Central heating is wonderful when it works, but can be a nightmare if it goes wrong. Many of the problems that arise with central heating can be dealt with relatively simply, but some may call for the services of a professional contractor.

Draining and refilling a heating system

You may need to drain and refill your central heating system if you want to move radiators or replace them with others of a different size, requiring changes to the pipework or if you want to treat corrosion.

A central heating system that uses water – the vast majority – will have at least one drainvalve that allows you to empty out the water. The drainvalve will usually be at the lowest point in the system, possibly under the floorboards, but there may be additional drainvalves by the boiler or where pipes are looped down from the first floor to a ground floor radiator – often the case with kitchen radiators.

Draining the system

1 Switch off the central heating.
2 Close off the water supply to the feed-and-expansion cistern to stop the system re-filling. To do this you can either turn off the water at the main stopvalve or tie up the ballvalve in the feed and expansion cistern – a better option since it allows you to continue using the kitchen cold tap. You can release the ballvalve any time you want to flush the system through with fresh water. You might need to do this after using a cleanser prior to adding corrosion proofer.
3 At each drainvalve – it doesn't matter where you start – attach a hosepipe to the outlet of the valve and lead the hose outside or into a bath.
4 Using a small spanner, unscrew the valve, allowing water to flow out.
5 Unscrew the air bleed valve on every radiator to make sure all the water is removed. You will need to include the air bleed valve on the hot water cylinder. This is usually located on the highest point on the upper of the two pipes that lead from the boiler into the side of the cylinder.

While the system is empty, you might want to remove individual radiators, take them into the garden and flush them through with water from a garden hose.

Refilling the system

1 Again with the heating system turned off, close all the drainvalves and air bleed valves and release the ballvalve in the feed-and-expansion cistern.

2 As the system fills, bleed each radiator in turn, starting with those on the ground floor and working upwards. You may need to go round the whole system twice, not forgetting the air bleed valve on the hot water circuit next to the hot water cylinder. Corrosion proofer is added on the final fill after cleansing and flushing (check instructions supplied with corrosion proofer for details).

3 When the system is full, turn the boiler on and check that there are no leaks from any of the air bleed valves or drainvalves – tighten any that are leaking.

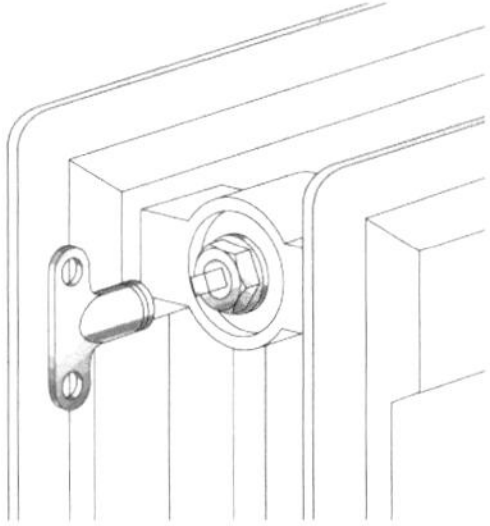

Use a radiator key to open the air-bleed valve

Positioning of radiators

There is a good reason why **radiators are put under windows** – to counteract the draughts and beat the 'cold zone' that would otherwise result, caused by the rate at which heat passes out through the window. But this applies only to single-glazed windows.

If you have **double-glazing** (which for most people means replacement windows), radiators can be put wherever it is most convenient in the room given features and furniture.

Moving a radiator is quite a major job for which you would probably want to employ the skills and services of a plumber. It will certainly mean draining down the system and possibly re-routing some pipes, and you need to know what you are doing to avoid leaks and to avoid leaving air in the system afterwards.

Preventing a freeze-up

In a house that is normally occupied during the winter, there should be no danger of frozen or burst pipes. But if a house is left empty for anything more than a day during a cold snap, there is always the possibility that some pipes will freeze and that some may even burst as they thaw. There are specific precautions you need to take to prevent this, depending on how long you are going to be away.

Away for a weekend

If you are only going to be away from the house for a couple of days, you can either leave the heating on its normal settings and be prepared to pay the fuel bills or, if you want to save money, do the following:

- set the heating programmer to 24-hour ('continuous') operation
- set the room thermostat to a low setting – say 5°C (41°F)
- remove or prop loft hatch fully open.

This will allow the boiler to fire to keep the house (and the loft space) above freezing point.

Away for longer

If you leave the house for more than a few days and want to turn the heating off, you need to drain the hot and cold water systems of all water. If the heating system (which is separate from the hot and cold water systems) has anti-freeze in it, you do not need to drain it.

- Drain down the cold water system entirely – close the main stopvalve, open all cold taps, and flush all WCs.
- Drain down the hot water cylinder fully using a length of hosepipe attached to the drain valve at the base of the hot

How to bleed a radiator

If the tops of the radiators are cold, it is possible that air has collected in the system or that there is corrosion.

Air that regularly collects inside any of the radiators indicates a leak – undetected because it is out of sight and the system is kept topped up by the feed-and-expansion cistern. If there is a leak, you can remove air from a single radiator fairly easily by bleeding it. You will need a small radiator bleed key (available in DIY stores) and a cloth.

1. **Hold the cloth firmly against the radiator just under the air bleed valve** and use the key to unscrew the valve in an anti-clockwise direction.
2. **Stop when you hear a hissing sound** – the air escaping – and wait until the hissing turns first to a dribble and then to a squirt of water.
3. **Close the valve quickly.**

If the hissing never turns to water, there is a **lack of water in the system**, which will almost certainly be because the ballvalve in the feed and expansion cistern up in the loft has become stuck. Because the ballvalve rarely operates in a leak-free system, it may have stuck in the closed position. This leaves the cistern empty because water has evaporated. Ease the ballvalve arm down gently to allow the cistern to re-fill. Don't worry if the level looks low – the cistern should only be around one-third full when cold, to allow space for the water in the system to expand when it is hot.

water cylinder (which needs a small spanner to open); put this into a basin or bath, and open all hot taps.

- When you return, check that all drain valves are closed before opening the mains stopvalve.
- Close taps as water flows from them – the kitchen cold tap first, then all other cold taps, and then all hot taps.

General precautions

Whether you are planning to be away or not, it is sensible to take general precautions against freezing in case you are away during a cold snap and haven't been able to prepare for it beforehand. There are two general ways to prevent freezing:

1 Fit a frost thermostat that brings the boiler on whenever the air temperature drops below a certain level – much lower than the level required to bring the heating on when the house is occupied. This is certainly something you should consider doing if the boiler is situated in the garage or an outhouse that could get seriously cold even if the rest of the house is above freezing.

Take preventative measures if you are away from home during a cold spell

2 Add anti-freeze chemical to the feed and expansion cistern so that it circulates around the central heating system. This chemical is made by specialist firms – and is not the same as the antifreeze used in cars.

Adding anti-freeze to your central heating system or fitting a frost thermostat are useful general precautions against freezing pipes, but you should still take the specific precautions described in the preceding pages if you plan on going away in the winter, in order to prevent the house water pipes freezing.

Outside checks

It is extremely important to check the external structures of your home. If a fault is left and ignored for years, it could be disastrous for the building as a whole. Find those minor faults – before they become major.

Annual checks outside

Gullies

Debris blocks these in-ground collection points for waste pipes and rainwater downpipes. Check that gully gratings are intact and clear of debris and the gully trap itself is clear of debris. Replace missing gratings and clear debris. Flush with water.

Strong winds are quite capable of dislodging TV aerials or satellite dishes

Roofs

Tiles on sloping roofs can be damaged by wind, and heat and frost can damage any roof. Inspect sloping roofs with binoculars and flat roofs from a ladder. Repair damage to felted roofs with bituminous mastic or waterproofer. Call in a roofing contractor to fix a sloping roof.

TV aerial/satellite dish

Use binoculars to check that the dish or aerial:

- is securely fixed to the chimney or wall
- is pointing in the right direction (compare with nearby houses).

Check the downlead is securely attached to the wall. If you have suitable equipment for working at heights, you can carry out any repairs and adjustments yourself. Otherwise call in a specialist.

Spring and autumn checks outside

Airbricks
There should be airbricks (bricks with holes for ventilation) about every 2m (6ft) on external walls.
- are clear of leaves, cobwebs, and other debris
- are clear of soil and not covered by climbing plants.

Replace any damaged airbricks so that mice and other vermin can't get in.

Fences
Water and wind can weaken fence posts. Check that:
- all posts are secure
- struts are securely fixed to posts
- panel fixings are intact
- there is no rot at ground level.

Bolt a concrete fence support, ideally set in concrete, to rotten or loose posts. Use brackets to fix loose or split struts, and C-shaped clips to secure panels. Treat wood with preservative.

Flashing
These metal or mortar strips seal joins on roofs, walls and chimney stacks. Wind and water can affect the seal. Ensure that:
- metal flashings fit closely to roof surfaces and into wall joints
- mortar flashings are intact.

Hammer metal flashings into shape. Replace faulty mortar flashings.

Gutters
Leaves and moss may fall into gutters, resulting in leaks that can cause damp. Using a ladder:
- clear gutters and downpipe inlets
- ensure joints between sections of gutter are not leaking. Reseal leaky plastic gutters. Use bitumen mastic to seal joints on metal ones.

External review every other year

Chimneys

Check the actual structures and have chimneys swept regularly if you burn coal or wood. Using binoculars, look for:
- cracked or leaning pots
- damaged pointing (mortar)
- loose or missing flashings
- any sign of the stack leaning from the vertical.

Use professionals to fix chimney problems. Call a builder to fix masonry and a chimney sweep to clear soot build-up in the flue.

Drains

Underground drains seldom cause problems. Above ground you can check for:
- cracked inspection chamber covers
- debris or standing water over inspection covers.

Remove debris from inspection chamber covers.

Eaves

Eaves woodwork – vertical fascias to which the gutters are fixed and horizontal soffits that fill the space between fascia and wall – is prone to rot. Check that:
- the woodwork and any decorative finish are in good condition

- gutter bracket fixings are secure.

Cut out and replace any rotten woodwork or get a builder to do this. Remove and re-fix gutter brackets if needed.

External walls

Damaged walls allow damp to penetrate, and subsidence can cause problems with the basic structure. Check that:

- brickwork and mortar (pointing) are in good condition
- rendering is not cracked or loose
- mastic round door and window frames is continuous and intact
- soil in flower beds is kept at least 150mm (6in) below the level of the damp-proof course in the house walls, to counter the risk of rising damp
- there are no zigzag cracks in walls.

Repair minor defects and call in a builder for bigger problems. Engage a surveyor to inspect and monitor major cracks.

Paintwork

Disintegrating paint can allow rot and insect attack to develop, especially in outside walls. Check that:

- paint is intact and free from cracks and blisters
- there are no signs of wet rot – wood feels soft and spongy
- putty round windows is intact.

Strip defective paint back to bare wood, then prime and repaint. Cut out and repair areas of rot, using exterior wood filler or replacement sections of wood. Chip out and replace defective putty.

Windows and doors

Windows and doors should open and close easily without sticking. Check that:

- handles and locks engage properly and operate smoothly
- glass is free of cracks.

Plane down, prime and repaint any edges that stick. Tighten loose hinge screws and lubricate hinges. Replace cracked glass.

When brickwork is in this state, get a surveyor in to check what's going on

Electricity in the home

Electricity flows in and out of homes continuously, with appliances picking up whatever current they need to operate. Most of us take this uninterrupted supply for granted – until there's a problem.

Bear in mind that many electrical tasks may require detailed electrical knowledge. Call in a qualified electrician if you are in any doubt.

How electricity is distributed

The service head

The electricity supply reaches your home via an underground or overhead cable. After entering the home, the supply cable is connected to a sealed terminal box called the service head or cut-out. You should never tamper with this.

Service fuse The service head contains the service fuse, which is there to stop appliances from demanding more electricity than the supply cable can safely deliver without overheating. Most modern homes have a service fuse rated at 100 amps, but a 60 or 80 amp fuse is

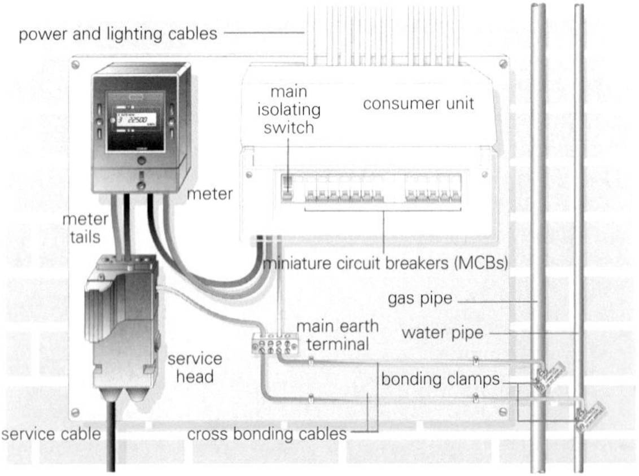

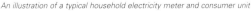

An illustration of a typical household electricity meter and consumer unit

common in older properties. A lower service fuse rating means you can have fewer high-wattage appliances on at once.
Check for overload To work out how many high-wattage appliances your fuse rating can carry at one time, add up the wattages of appliances that you tend to use at the same time (maybe cooker, dishwasher, washing machine, tumble dryer, as well as lights). Divide the total by 230 (the voltage) to get the maximum current flow in amps; check that this does not exceed the service fuse rating.

When to check and replace wiring

Have modern wiring systems checked by a professional **every five years**, and have the wiring checked in any house you buy, unless it is brand new. It may have had amateur work done on it.

Older homes may have several fuse boxes supplying one or two circuits or circuits that supply power points with round holes. Either system should be replaced without delay.

Other **signs of a system in need of modernisation** are lighting circuits with no earth core in their cables, and cables sheathed and insulated in rubber or even, with really old cables, in lead.

The meter

Two cables run from the service head to the electricity meter, which belongs to your electricity supplier and records how much electricity you consume (*see* How much power are you using?, p130). Modern meters are digital and usage is recorded on a row of figures. Older meters have circular dials (*see* Reading meters, p126).

If your home uses cheap night-rate electricity to supply electric storage heaters, you will have a dual-rate meter and a timer instead of a single meter wired in from the service head. The timer switches the supply from one meter to the other at pre-set times to record usage at the two different rates.

Some meters nowadays are in a locked unit on an outside wall. You and your supplier should each have a key to get access to the meter. Ask your supplier if you need a replacement key.

The consumer unit

Two cables called meter tails run from the meter to the centre that distributes power around the home, sometimes referred to as the fuse box but more commonly known nowadays as the consumer unit. This contains the system's main

Key terms

Amps (A), originally **amperes** Units used to measure the rate at which the electrical current flows. A light bulb takes around a quarter of an amp, while a powerful heater may take as much as 12 amps. The supply cable to the house can carry up to 100 amps. Individual circuits in the home carry different amps levels, determined by how much electricity is required.
Circuit A complete and closed path through which a circulating electric current can flow.
Conductor A component, usually a length of wire or cable, along which an electric current can flow.
Overload The drawing of a higher current from a circuit than it is designed to carry.
Short circuit The accidental re-routing of electricity between two points on a circuit. This increases the flow of current and blows a fuse or trips a circuit breaker.
Terminal A point of connection to an electric circuit or appliance.
Trip The automatic disconnection of an electric circuit by a circuit breaker, which happens when an overload or current leak is detected.
Volts (V) Units used to measure the pressure that drives electricity round the circuit. Mains electricity pressure (voltage) is standard in the UK at 230 volts. Low-voltage lighting runs on a voltage of 12 volts and requires a transformer.
Watts (W) Units that measure the rate at which electricity flows through a circuit – for example, lighting a lamp or driving a motor. Watts also indicate the amount of electricity an appliance needs to work – a 100 watt bulb uses more electricity than a 60 watt bulb. The wattage rating of an appliance is shown on the casing or on a silver tag on the flex.

on–off switch. Wiring systems older than about 25 years will have circuit fuses that melt if the circuit is overloaded or short-circuited. More modern systems have a row of switches called **miniature circuit breakers (MCBs)** that switch off automatically if a fault is detected. Each fuse carrier or MCB distributes electricity to an individual circuit in the house and controls the rate of current delivered to each circuit: a maximum of 5–6 amps for each lighting circuit, 30 amps for circuits to power points for portable appliances, and 40 or 45 amps for the big fixed appliances such as cookers, water heaters, and electric showers.

The circuits

All circuits start at a fuse carrier or MCB in the consumer unit.

Ring main circuit In modern wiring systems the circuits that connect power points run in a loop connecting each power point in turn, finally returning to the consumer unit. Electricity flows in both directions round the loop. Each power point on the ring main can have a branch line spur cable connected into its terminals to supply a single or double

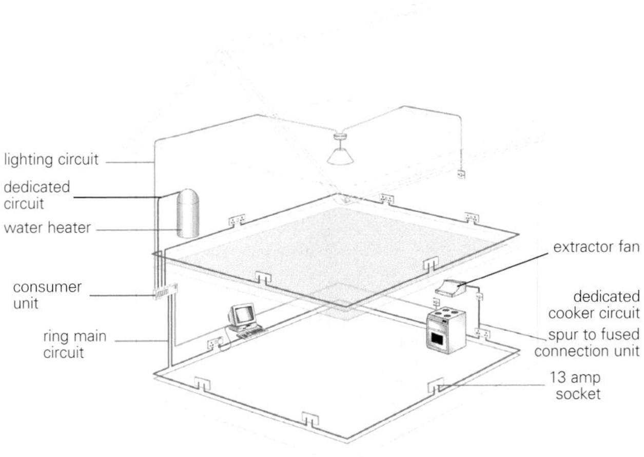

Illustration of the wiring in a modern home

power point at the other end of the cable. This makes it easy to add extra power points, if you need them, with the minimum of rewiring.

Radial circuit In older wiring systems the power point circuit is radial, where the cable delivers electricity to each power point in turn and ends at the last one. Lighting, even in modern systems, runs in radial circuits. Most homes have at least two lighting circuits, since the wattage of all the light bulbs together would overload a single circuit.

Dedicated circuit Large, fixed appliances such as cookers and electric showers always have a dedicated circuit, because the amount of power they use is so great that they would overload a shared circuit.

Electricity supply to flats

Individual flats within a purpose-built or converted building should each have their own fuse board or consumer unit and independent circuits. In some conversions, however, each flat or bedsit may rely on the building's original systems, which will control supplies from just one point, with usage recorded centrally and billed to one address.

Safety features

MCBs

The MCBs (miniature circuit breakers, *see* illustration opposite) in modern consumer units allow you to switch off the power to a specific circuit for repairs or alterations. But they also act as automatic protection in the event of overloading – if you plug in more appliances or use more powerful lights than the circuit is designed to supply. When overloading or a short circuit occurs, the MCB automatically switches itself off,and it cannot be reset to restore power until the fault is corrected.

Wiring systems older than about 25 years and not modernised since installation will have cartridge or rewirable circuit fuses instead of MCBs. These contain a length of special fuse wire that will melt if the circuit is overloaded or short-circuited, cutting off the supply to the circuit (*see* Replacing a circuit fuse, p128).

Reading meters

Digital meters show how many units (1 unit = 1 kilowatt hour, kWh) have been consumed since the meter was installed. To check the cost of recent consumption, subtract the reading on your last bill from that on the meter and multiply by the price per unit, given on your bill.

To read a dial meter, start at the left-hand dial recording 10,000 unit/kWh per division and work across the dials. For each dial, note down the number that the pointer has just passed. If a pointer is directly on a number, you should still record the number below, unless the pointer on the dial to its right is between 0 and 1, in which case note the number the pointer is at. This meter reads 60347.

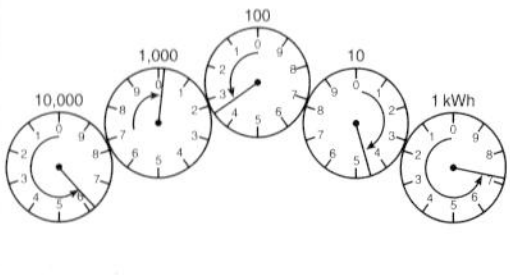

RCDs

Modern consumer units also contain a more general safety feature called a residual current device (RCD) that monitors the flow of electric current through the property. If the RCD detects that current has gone to earth – usually because of a leak caused by broken insulation, or because someone has touched a live wire and received a shock – it switches off the current in a fraction of a second. This is quick enough to prevent a shock from causing heart failure and death.

Because the area outside a house is not protected by the

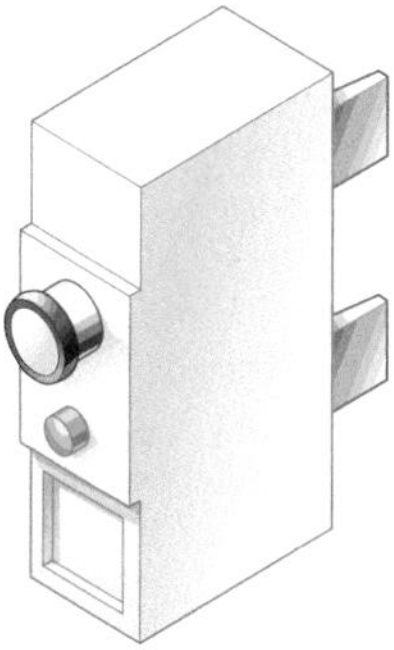

Button-operated miniature circuit breaker (MCB)

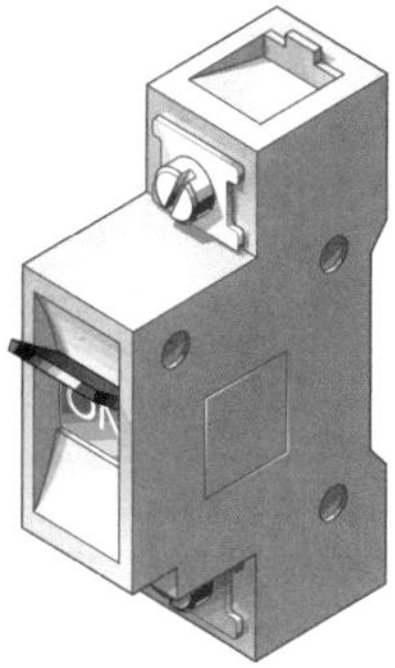

Switch-operated miniature circuit breaker (MCB)

property's earthing system, RCDs are now fitted in new power points intended for appliances being used out of doors, for instance in garages. If you don't have these, you should buy an RCD adaptor to use when you plug an outdoor appliance into an indoor socket.

The importance of earthing
Earthing is one of the most important safety features of your wiring system. It can prevent an electric shock, and makes it much less likely that an electrical fault will develop into a fire.

Earthing provides a safe path for any current that accidentally strays from the circuit wiring because of faulty insulation. The escaped electricity is attracted to earth (the ground) because this is an even better conductor than circuit wiring. Given the chance, electricity will flow to earth by the shortest possible route. If there is no earthing system, this could be through your body.

Every circuit is connected to earth via an earth continuity conductor, which is a wire inside the circuit cable, connected to every lighting point, every socket, and every direct appliance connection point (for instance an immersion heater or electric cooker). All the circuit earth conductors are connected to an earth terminal block in the

Cables and cores

Every cable in your circuits contains wires (also called cores) that are **colour-coded** to indicate which way the current is flowing. The **red-covered live wire** carries the current to where it's needed.

The **black-covered wire** (neutral) carries the current back to where it came from. Both carry electricity at all times.

The bare wire in the cable (covered with a **green-and-yellow outer sheath** when it is exposed at connections) provides a safe path for escaped current, carrying it to earth – *see* The importance of earthing, p127. Cable outer sheath is usually white or grey.

Flex colours

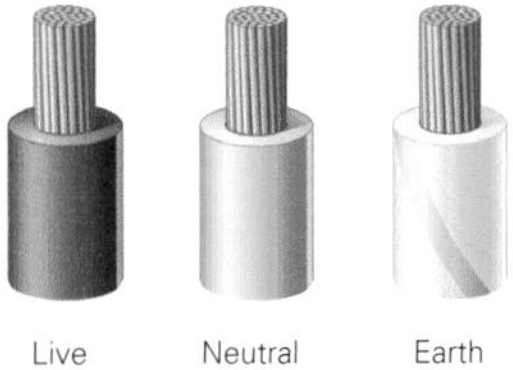

Cable colours

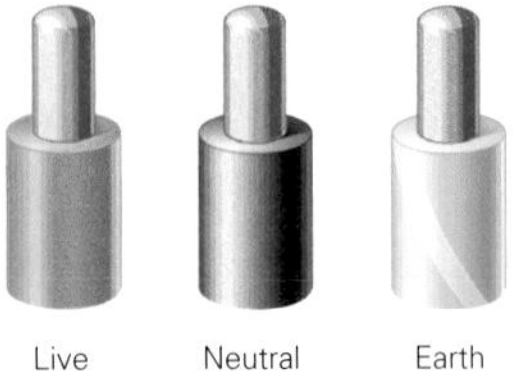

consumer unit or fuse box. This terminal is connected by a cable with green or green-and-yellow insulation, either to a clamp on the sheath of the main supply cable, or to an earth rod driven into the ground beneath or beside the home.

You should also have similar cables connecting metal gas and water pipes, and other exposed metalwork such as sinks and baths, to each other and to the main earth terminal in the consumer unit. These cross-bonding cables ensure that the metalwork is earthed, so that if metalwork comes into contact with a live wire it will not itself become live.

Replacing a circuit fuse

There are two types of circuit fuse found in the home – cartridge and rewirable. **Cartridge fuses** use enclosed fuses – like those in modern fused plugs, but larger – which clip into the fuseholder or are held in place by its pins. To replace a blown cartridge fuse, turn off the power at the main switch, remove the affected fuseholder and insert a replacement fuse of the same rating. Cartridge fuses are colour-coded according to their current rating: white is 5 amps; blue is 15 amps; yellow is 20 amps; red is 30 amps; green is 45 amps. All are different sizes (except the 15- and 20-amp

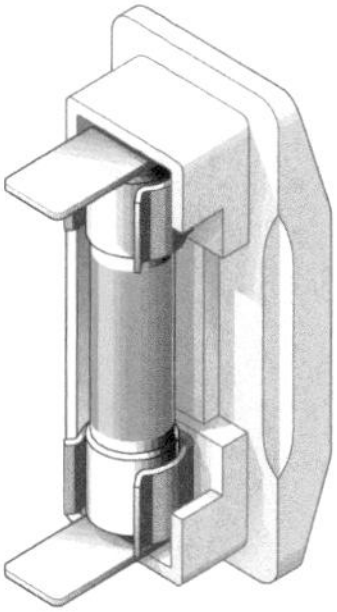

Cartridge fuse carrier

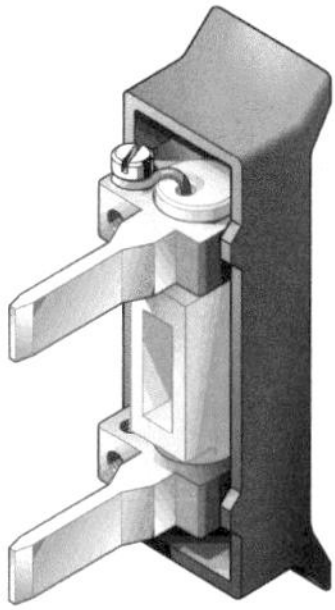

Single-bladed wire fuse carrier

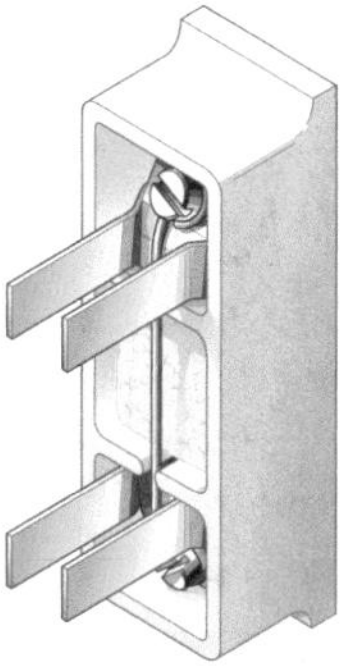

Double-bladed wire fuse carrier

fuses, which are effectively interchangeable), making it impossible to fit the wrong fuse in the fuseholder. Simply replace the fuseholder and restore the power.

Rewirable fuses have a length of wire fitted between two terminals and running across or through a ceramic block inside the fuseholder. In these, the wire itself needs replacing if the fuse is blown. Fuse wire is sold on cards holding wire of three current ratings – 5, 15 and 30 amps – and it's essential to use the correct wire for the circuit concerned. Match the rating stamped on the fuseholder to the size of fuse wire printed on the card it's wrapped around. Loosen the terminals of the fuse so you can release the old fuse wire. Replace it with a new piece of wire, leaving the wire a little slack between the terminals. You will probably need about 50mm (2in) length – the wire has to be long enough to reach from terminal to terminal and to be wrapped around each.

TOP TIP

Always keep **spare fuses, a torch** and **a small electrical screwdriver** in a place close at hand to the consumer unit. It is even more **essential you know where to find them when the lights are out**! Keep spare bulbs and plugs – they are always handy to have in cases of emergency.

How much power are you using?

Appliance	No. of units (kWh)
Computer	0.1 units an hour
Cooker	2.5 units a day
Dishwasher	2 units per load
Electric blanket	1 unit a week
Extractor fan	1 unit a day
Electric fire/ heater (3kW)	3 units an hour
Freezer	1.5 units a day
Fridge	1 unit a day
Fridge/freezer	1.25 units a day
Hair dryer	1 unit an hour
Iron	1 unit an hour
Kettle	0.25 units per fill
Microwave	0.75 units an hour
Shower (8 kW)	1 unit for 7 mins
Television/hi-fi	0.2 units an hour
Tumble drier	2.5 units per load
Vacuum cleaner	1 unit an hour
VCR	0.1 units an hour
Washing machine	2.5 units per load

This is a rough guide to how many units of electricity the most common appliances consume. Check your bill to find out the price you pay per unit. Every appliance and light bulb has its wattage (power rating) recorded somewhere on it. The higher the wattage, the more electricity the appliance uses. To calculate how much an appliance uses that is not listed here, multiply the appliance's rating in kilowatts (1,000 W) by the time in hours that it's on. One unit of electricity (or kilowatt hour – kWh for short) is the amount used by an appliance rated at 1 kilowatt (kW) running for 1 hour. A 3 kW fan heater uses 3 units in an hour, or 1 unit for every 20 minutes. A 100 W (0.1 kW) light bulb uses 1 unit in 10 hours.

All about plugs

Plugs connect electrical appliances to the mains supply at socket outlets. Plugs used on modern wiring systems have three pins with screw-down terminals inside the plug, to which the cores of the appliance flex are connected. The flex is securely held by a clamp where it leaves the plug casing.

Inside a plug

Viewed with the plug top unscrewed and the pins facing away from you:

- the brown (live) core is connected to the bottom right terminal
- the blue (neutral) core is connected to the bottom left terminal
- the earth (green-and-yellow) core is connected to the top terminal; some double-insulated appliances, such as irons, marked with □ on the flex, do not need earthing and have no earth core.

The plug contains a small cartridge fuse next to the live pin. Use a fuse rated at 3 amps (colour-coded red) for appliances rated at up to 700 watts and one rated at 13 amps (colour-coded brown) for more powerful appliances. Use only

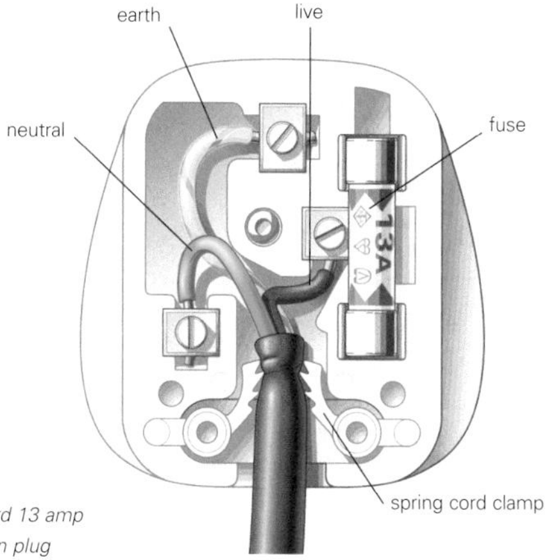

A standard 13 amp square-pin plug

Tips for saving electricity

- **Switch lights off when not needed**, using time delay switches if necessary.
- **Use low-energy light bulbs and low-voltage lighting**, especially for lights that stay on for long periods. Dimmer switches don't save money, and you can't use most low-energy light bulbs with them. Compact fluorescent lamps (CFLs) cost more than ordinary bulbs but their cost is recovered very quickly by the energy they save and their longer life. Replacing bulbs in the lights you use most often with CFLs could save you £50 over the lifetime of the bulbs.
- **New models of big kitchen appliances are much more energy efficient than older models**, especially if you look for one with as high an energy-efficient rating on the label as possible. If your appliances are older than about ten years, replacing them would save you money in the long term.
- **Shut the fridge door promptly.** For every minute your fridge is open, it takes three minutes to regain its temperature. Keep fridges and freezers as full as practicable.
- **Fridge temperature settings should be about 3°C (37°F) and freezers around –18°C (–0°F):** every degree lower than this adds about 5% to running costs.
- **Check fridge and freezer door seals regularly.** Empty the fridge and switch it off before going on holiday.
- **Defrost freezers regularly** – once or twice a year for chest freezers, two or three times a year for uprights – or if buying a new freezer choose one with automatic defrosting. Keep your fridge regularly defrosted.

Tips for saving electricity

- **Microwave ovens** cost up to 70% less to run than conventional ovens and are particularly efficient for reheating food. Fan ovens are 35% cheaper to run and don't need pre-heating. Slow cookers and pressure cookers are also energy-efficient.
- **Hang washing up to dry**, using a tumble drier only when essential. Tumble dry clothes sorted into heavy and lightweight loads. Dry loads consecutively to use residual heat. Check filters regularly.
- A **wash cycle of 40°C** uses a third less electricity than a wash of 60°C. Modern wash powders and detergents are so effective that only very dirty washing needs more than 40°C.
- **Run washing machines and dish-washers less often with full loads**, rather than frequently with part-loads.
- **Turn dishwashers off before the start of the drying cycle** – dishes will dry in the stored heat – or open the door and let them dry naturally.
- **Don't open a heated oven unnecessarily** and close it as quickly as you can. It loses about 15°C (59°F) every time you open the door while it's on.
- **Switch off appliances** such as televisions, hi-fi and computers instead of leaving them on stand-by.
- **Install a timer** so that your immersion heater operates only when it's needed.
- If you have **cheap night-rate electricity** to supply storage heaters, have the immersion heater timed to come on overnight. Avoid using expensive day-time top-ups of storage or immersion heaters.

plugs made to British Standard BS 1363, and fuses made to BS 1362.

All electrical appliances are now sold fitted with a sealed plug. If one gets damaged, cut it off and discard it. Reconnect the flex to a new plug, connecting the cores to the terminals as described above.

All about light bulbs

General lighting service (GLS) lamps may be clear, translucent (pearl), white, or coloured, and have a tungsten wire filament. The standard lamp has a pear, mushroom, or rounded cylinder shape. Other shapes include pointed candle lamps, compact

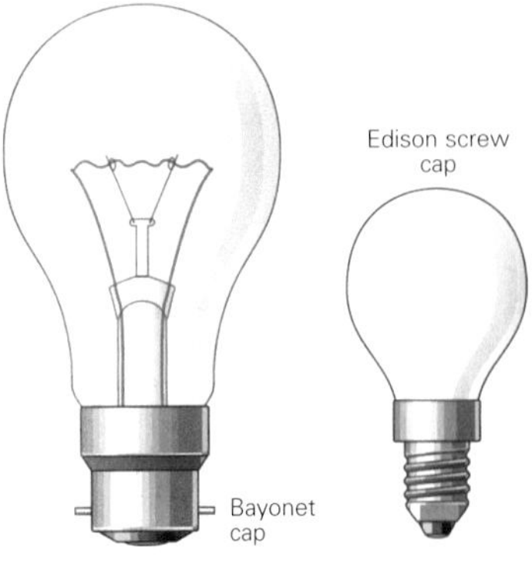

Large clear and small pearl GLS lamps

pygmy lamps, and round golf-ball and globe lamps. Common wattages for GLS lamps are 25, 40, 60 and 100W.

Reflector lamps are used in spotlights. The inside of the glass is silvered to throw light forwards. They come in several sizes, in the same wattages as GLS lamps.

Internal silvered reflector and crown silvered lamps

Compact fluorescent lamps (CFLs) contain small fluorescent tubes instead of a filament, and use much less electricity than a GLS lamp for the same light output. They come in several shapes, with wattages from 3W to 26W (equivalent to GLS lamps rated from 25W to 150W).

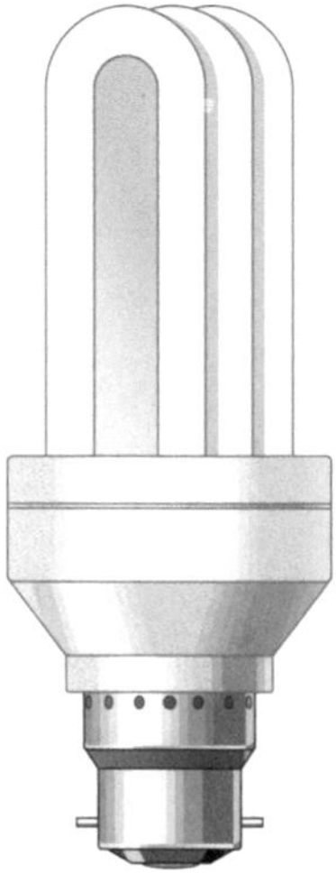

CFL (compact fluorescent lamp) uses much less electricity than a GLS lamp

Halogen lamps are available in mains voltage (230V) and low-

Mains voltage halogen lamp

Electricity faultfinder

This quick checklist will help you trace electrical faults and either fix them – you may need to refer to another page in this book or the manufacturer of an appliance for full instructions – or isolate the cause of the problem if you can't. Don't take on any task if you do not feel fully confident of what you are doing – call a professional if in doubt.

If a light won't work

- Check whether the light bulb works in another lamp; if not, replace.
- Check the circuit fuse or MCB and replace/reset as necessary (*see* Replacing a circuit fuse, pp128–9).
- If the fuse blows or the MCB trips off again immediately, switch off power, open the lampholder covers with the power still off and check for loose connections and damaged wires on the flex. Remake or replace as necessary.

If an appliance won't work

- Unplug it, open its plug and check for loose connections. Remake as necessary, close the plug and test the appliance.
- If it still won't work, unplug again, open the plug and fit a new fuse. Close the plug and test the appliance.
- If it still won't work, unplug it again and open the appliance – if you can – to check connections at the terminal block. Remake as necessary. Replace the flex completely if it is damaged.

If a whole circuit is dead

- Check whether the circuit fuse has blown or the MCB has tripped off. If this has happened, switch off all the lights or unplug all appliances as appropriate and replace the fuse or reset the MCB. Restore the power to the circuit.
- Switch on lights or plug in appliances one by one. If one blows the fuse/trips the MCB again, isolate it for checking as outlined above. Check that the circuit is not being overloaded with too many lights/appliances. *See* Check for overload, p123.
- If you have a split-load unit, supplying electricity at two different costs, check whether the RCD has tripped off. Switch it back on if you can; if you can't, the fault is still present. Locate it if possible by running through the checks above or call in an electrician.

If the whole system is dead

- If your system has a whole-house RCD, check whether it has tripped and reset it if possible. If you cannot, the fault is still present (*see* If a whole circuit is dead, above).
- Check whether there is a local power cut by phoning a neighbour. If there isn't and only your home has no power, call your electricity supplier.

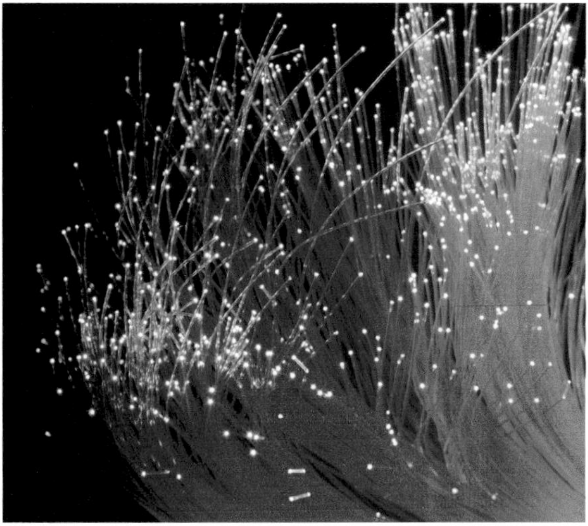

Fibre optic lighting makes an interesting alternative to standard lights in the home

voltage (12V) versions. The latter are powered by a transformer wired into the lighting circuit and come in versions of 20, 35 and 50W.

Tubes may be filament or fluorescent. The former are used for strip lighting, while the latter provide utility lighting to work areas. Filament wattages range from 30W upwards, fluorescent ones from 18 to 58W.

End caps

The brass-coloured end cap, where the light bulbs connect to the fittings, may be the bayonet cap (BC) or Edison screw (ES) type. Some light fittings take lamps with small versions of these end caps, known as SBC and SES.

TOP TIP

If a light bulb breaks inside its fitting when you are trying to unscrew it, make sure that the power is isolated and use something like a carrot or potato to push onto the broken glass. You can then turn the bulb safely. To prevent a light bulb getting stuck in the first place, spray a little lubricating oil around the end cap fitting before installing a new light bulb.

Plumbing matters

Your plumbing system has a number of different parts – the cold and hot water supply, the waste pipes and drains that get rid of the water when you've finished with it, and the heating system, if this relies on hot water to heat the radiators.

Knowing how the plumbing system works not only helps you to use it sensibly; it also means you can track down the cause of any problems and at the very least minimise the mess that a plumbing disaster can cause.

How you pay for water

If your home does not have a water meter, what you pay for your water supply and the disposal of waste water through the local sewer network depends on the chargeable value of your home. This is a figure based on its former rateable value when everyone paid local rates rather than council tax.

Your water company sets a water rate in pence per pound of chargeable value for water supply and waste water disposal, and calculates a supply charge for each service. It then adds a fixed standing charge for each and computes your total annual bill. You will be billed for this in two half-yearly instalments, although those who pay by direct debit also have a choice of paying monthly.

If you have a water meter, you pay a quarterly bill which consists of a standing charge plus an amount for each cubic metre (1,000 litres or 220 gallons) of water you use.

Your cold and hot water supply

Your cold water supply arrives in your home via an underground pipe connected to the water main beneath the road. The pipe is usually buried at a depth of about 750mm (2ft 6in) to protect it from frost, and somewhere between the road and your building there is an underground stopvalve belonging to the water company that allows the home to be shut off from the mains supply. In towns this is probably in a small chamber underneath a hinged cover plate set in the pavement, but in the country it may be found anywhere within the property boundaries – it depends on the siting of the nearest water main. Make sure you know where yours is. You are responsible for the pipe as soon as it leaves the water

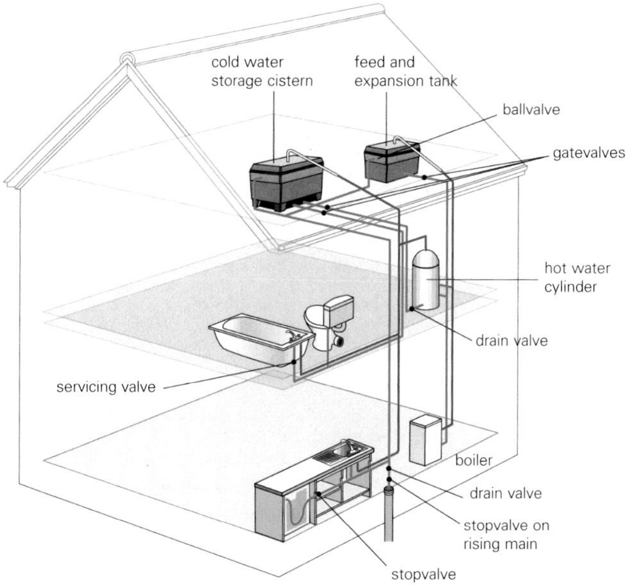

A typical indirect plumbing system (radiator circuit not shown)

company's underground stopvalve.

After the supply pipe enters the home, it will run to another stopvalve. This allows you to cut off the supply within the home in an emergency or to make alterations to the system. Again, find out where yours is, if you don't already know. From here, the route the supply pipe takes depends on whether your home has an indirect or direct plumbing system.

An indirect plumbing system
With this system, found in the majority of homes in the UK, the supply pipe runs up to a cold water storage cistern (tank) in the loft, which fills via a float-operated valve (ballvalve) that shuts off the water flow when the cistern is

Saving water

- A **five-minute shower** uses only a third as much water as a bath.
- **Fix dripping taps.** Each could waste the equivalent of a bathful of water a week.
- Run the **washing machine or dishwasher** only when you have a full load – each full load uses less water than two half-loads.
- **Turn off the tap when cleaning your teeth** – running water can fill a small bath in five minutes.
- **Using the plug every time you run water in a basin or sink** could save £15 a year if you have a water meter. Don't leave the tap running when washing vegetables, and wash dirty mugs and plates in a bowl of water at the end of the day, rather than one by one under a running tap.
- **A third of the average household's water use is flushed down the toilet.** Amazingly, the average household uses the equivalent of two baths a day flushing the toilet. Put a brick in the WC cistern to reduce the volume of water stored. If you have a dual-flush cistern, reduce the flush volume by fitting a conversion cap (supplied with the cistern or available from plumbers' merchants if you have lost yours) into the hole in the side of the special dual-flush siphon unit.
- **Store rainwater in butts** for garden usage and throw away your hosepipe.
- A **garden sprinkler** uses as much water in half an hour as four people use in a day. Use it sparingly, move it often or, better still, get rid of it and use a watering can instead. You must have a water meter installed if you intend to use a garden sprinkler.

full. A branch off this so-called rising main supplies mains-pressure, fresh, cold water direct to the kitchen sink for drinking and cooking. Other branches may also be taken off the rising main to supply a washing machine or dishwasher, a garden tap, or an instantaneous gas or electric shower or water heater. An outlet pipe from the storage cistern supplies all the other cold taps in the home. A second outlet pipe feeds the hot water cylinder, which in turn supplies the hot taps. Each of these two outlet pipes should be fitted with a shut-off valve called a gatevalve.

In an indirect system, the hot water comes from the hot water cylinder. This may be heated by an electric element called an immersion heater, but it is more common for it to be heated by the boiler that operates the central heating system. The cylinder contains a copper coil called a heat exchanger, and this is connected to the boiler by flow-and-return pipes that make up the hot water (primary) circuit for the central heating. This does not mix with the water in the hot water cylinder (secondary circuit).

Gatevalves are on pipes leading from the storage cistern

As hot water from the boiler is pumped through this coil, the coil heats the cold water in the cylinder and the (cooled) water from the coil returns to the boiler to be heated up again. When a hot tap is opened, cold water from

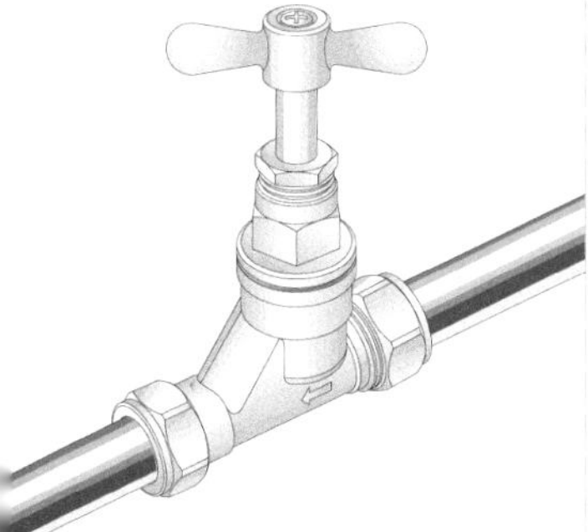
The stopvalve is arguably the most important valve to locate

Getting to know your water system

If your system springs a leak, it's vital that you know where to turn the water off so you can minimise the damage caused. On an ideal system you should be able to isolate every appliance and section of pipe, but in practice you will probably have a limited number of controls available to use.

- The most vital is the **stopvalve** on your rising main. Turning this off stops your cold water storage cistern from filling up and allows you to empty it quickly by turning on all your taps. Give the valve handle a half-turn off and on again every six months or so to make sure it hasn't seized up and will work when you need it.
- Find the orange- or red-handled **gatevalves** on the pipes leading from your storage cistern to the cold taps (usually in the loft) and the hot water cylinder (usually in the airing cupboard). Work out which is which and label them. These allow you to isolate key sections of the system pipework.
- On a modern system you should have small **servicing valves** on pipes to individual taps and WC cisterns, and also to washing machines, dishwashers, and water softeners. These valves usually have a small screw, or a red (hot fill) or blue (cold fill) handle that needs only be turned through 90°.
- You may also have a **drain valve** at the rising main. This looks like a tap without a handle and when opened (for which you'll need a small spanner and a hose), drains off water in the pipes that cannot be drained off via a tap.

the storage cistern in the loft flows into the base of the cylinder, and the pressure drives hot water out of the cylinder via a pipe at the top.

This pipe (from the top of the hot water cylinder) divides into two. One part goes to the hot taps, while the other rises up into the loft and is looped over the main cold water cistern. This pipe – called the open vent pipe – is a safety device and allows air (or steam if the system were to overheat) to escape from the system.

A direct plumbing system

With a direct system, each cold tap and WC is fed directly from the rising main, so there is no main cold water cistern. Hot water may be supplied either from a hot water cylinder with its own small cold water cistern (sometimes on top of the cylinder) or from an instantaneous gas or electric water heater or a 'combination' gas boiler also connected directly to the rising main.

Direct systems using combination boilers are more common in flats and conversions than in houses, although they are increasingly used to replace indirect systems in smaller houses. The advantages are that they require less pipework, do not need space-guzzling cylinders and storage cisterns, the amount of available hot water is not dependent on the amount in the cylinder and they are cheaper to run. Disadvantages are that the boiler itself is more expensive at the outset than the boiler in an indirect system and there is no stored water in reserve if supplies are interrupted for any reason.

Modern water systems have servicing valves on pipes to individual taps and appliances

Your drainage system

When you empty a bath, basin or sink, or flush a WC, the waste water heads for the drains. In a modern home,

Water from basins runs out into a waste pipe that eventually leads to the drains outside the property

each water-connected appliance – including the WC – has a waste pipe that runs directly into a single vertical soil stack, normally sited inside the building. In older properties, sinks, basins and baths empty into ground-level gullies or wall-mounted hoppers, while WC waste is discharged into a separate external soil pipe and the two parts of the system do not merge until they get underground.

The various waste and soil pipes are connected into underground drainpipes that merge in below-ground inspection chambers with metal covers. The drainpipes then run on, via other connecting chambers if necessary, outside towards the nearest sewer.

Rainwater from gutters runs via separate downpipes to

Water consumption	
Washing, drinking, cooking etc	30 litres (6 gall) per person per day
Bathing	80–90 litres (17.5–20 gall) per bath
Showering	30 litres (6 gall) per shower (80 litres [17.5 gall] per power shower)
WC use	9 litres (2 gall) per flush (6 litres [1.3 gall] for WCs fitted after 01.01.2001)
Washing machine	80 litres (17.5 gall) per load
Dishwasher	35 litres (7.7 gall) per load
Hosepipe (garden)	9 litres (2 gall) per minute (540 litres [19 gall] per hour)

Garden sprinklers should only be used on a water meter (see p138)

ground level and then via underground pipes to the surface water drain under the nearest road or to drainage pits called soakaways if no drain is nearby.

Typical water consumption

On p141 are some average consumption figures for the main water-using appliances. To get your annual water usage in cubic metres, add up how many uses you make of each one per week, multiply the total weekly usage by 52 and divide by 1,000, as there are 1,000 litres in a cubic metre.

As a guide, an average household uses about 160cu m (35,000 gall) of water per year. To find out whether you would save money by having a meter, contact your water company and ask for details of their standing charges and costs per cubic metre of water. Work out how much annual water usage would cost on a meter and compare it with current bills.

Most water companies will install a meter free of charge. Bear in mind that your water consumption may rise if your circumstances change – for instance, if you have children.

Gas supply

If your home has a mains gas supply, it will reach the property through an underground pipe from the gas main in the street. Depending on when it was installed, this pipe will be iron, copper or yellow plastic.

How gas enters your home

The pipe runs to the gas meter, which is often under the stairs in older homes, or housed in a special cabinet in an outside wall of more recent buildings.

The flow of gas to the property is controlled by the main on-off lever on the supply pipe immediately before the meter. This lever is fully open when its handle is in line with the pipe, and fully closed when it is at 90° to it. It should be left fully open at all times but it is a sensible precaution to check, at least once a year, that it moves freely, so you are sure it can be operated in an emergency. If the supply pipe is metal, it should be fitted with a metal earth clamp which is connected to the main earthing point on your home's wiring system by a cross-bonding cable covered in green-and-yellow PVC insulation (*see* p127 for why earthing is important).

Iron or copper pipes run from the meter to wherever you need a gas supply within the home. Gas-fired boilers are connected directly to the supply pipework. Cookers are connected to a supply valve with a plug-in bayonet connector or, on older installations, with a screw-on hose fitting. Branch pipes supplying gas fires and room heaters are fitted with a small isolating valve, and a thinner pipe runs on from there to the fire itself.

Most gas meters are under the stairs or housed in a special box outside

Saving on heating

- Check your **loft insulation** and top it up to the level of the joists, if necessary. The recommended minimum thickness is 25cm (10in), for new houses and extensions, though existing joints may not be deep enough for this. Loft insulation can save 20–25% on heating bills.
- Your **central heating thermostat** should be no higher than 18–20°C (64.5–68°F). Turning it down by 1°C (2°F) will make little difference to your comfort and could save £15–20 on a year's heating bill.
- **Cavity wall insulation** is expensive but will more than pay for itself in 3–7 years.
- **Draughts** can lose up to 15% of the heat from your home. Fit draught strips to all external doors and letterboxes, and consider blocking up your chimney flue if you do not use your fireplace.
- Fit a **reflective panel behind radiators** on outside walls to reduce heat loss – you can buy corrugated panels, or use ordinary kitchen foil (much cheaper but not as efficient).
- **Radiators** do not need to be fitted under double-glazed windows. If you are renovating your central heating system, consider moving radiators so that they are back to back on internal walls, which shortens the pipe.
- Make sure your **hot cylinder** is well insulated – a jacket costs about £10 and pays for itself in a few months.

How you're charged for gas

Gas is charged by unit of consumption, with a standing charge on top. You will normally be billed quarterly, for actual or estimated consumption, but you can opt to pay monthly, by direct debit. *See* Choosing utility deals, p268–9.

Using LPG

Around 75,000 homes in the UK use liquefied petroleum gas (LPG) because they have no mains gas supply. LPG is stored in an outside tank (provided and owned by the gas supplier) that is topped up with regular deliveries by road tanker. A gas pipe fitted with a safety valve and pressure regulator runs from the tank to the home. You may have to buy special appliances to run on LPG, though with minor modifications some mains gas appliances can use it. Your gas supplier will advise you. LPG is 50 per cent more expensive than ordinary mains gas, once the annual tank rental is added to the fuel cost. Switching suppliers to save money is more difficult because the supplier owns the tank. You may need planning permission to have an LPG tank, which must be accessible to the delivery tanker.

Home security

Burglary is one of the fastest-growing types of crime. To minimise your risk as a target, check out the security of your building, and examine the security habits (or lack of them) of all the occupants.

Many householders make life easy for the would-be burglar by such simple oversights as leaving windows open and doors unlocked, or by advertising the fact that the house is empty. Don't let your home look a likely bet for the opportunist thief.

What to fit

These practical measures will ensure that your property is secure whether you are at home or not and will satisfy household insurance companies. To improve the security of uPVC windows and doors, seek advice from the manufacturer or a locksmith.

Front doors

These should be fitted with a mortise lock meeting the requirements of British Standard BS 3621. For daytime security when you are in the house – and extra security at

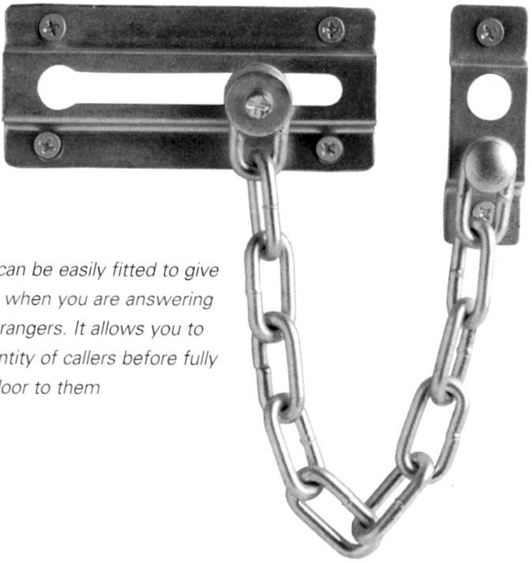

A door chain can be easily fitted to give extra security when you are answering the door to strangers. It allows you to check the identity of callers before fully opening the door to them

Burglary facts

- **Over a million burglaries** are reported to the police every year in England and Wales – almost 2,800 every day or one every 30 seconds – making up around 22% of all reported crime. It is estimated that a further million burglaries go unreported.
- 80% of burglaries occur when the **property is empty**.
- Almost half of all successful burglaries take place in **daylight**.
- 40% of burglaries involve entry via a **front or back door**.
- 33% of burglars get in through a **back window**.
- 20% of burglars don't need to resort to forceful entry – they get in through an **open door or window**.
- Almost 50% of reported burglaries are from **sheds, garages and other outbuildings**, rather than from houses.
- Only 9% of stolen property is ever **recovered**.

all other times – add a cylinder rim lock (also made to BS 3621) with automatic or key-operated deadlocking. Add hinge bolts to the hinged edge to prevent the door being forced. Fit a door viewer (solid doors only), a door chain or a door limiter (all available from hardware stores), so you can check the identity of callers. Fit toughened or laminated glass in place of ordinary glass in all glazed doors and side panes.

Back doors

Fit a mortise sashlock made to BS 3621. This combines the functions of lock and latch, allowing the door to be opened without the need for a key when you're in. Alternatively, fit a latch and separate BS 3621 mortise lock.

Sliding patio doors

Fit key-operated surface-mounted patio door locks to wooden doors at top and bottom, plus an anti-lift device at the top of the frame if the doors were not fitted with one originally.

French doors

Fit a surface-mounted bolt or a concealed mortise rack bolt to the top and bottom of each door so the bolt passes into a hole in the top and bottom of the frame. Fit a mortise sashlock made to BS 3621 to the door that opens first, and add hinge bolts to the hinged edge of each door to prevent a burglar punching out the exposed hinge pins and lifting out the doors.

Windows

A wide range of locks is available for wooden windows and a smaller selection for metal ones. Most are surface-mounted, making them quick and easy to install. Unfortunately, many of these locks are supplied with screws that are too short to make a secure fixing, leaving the window prone to forcing. To tackle this problem, buy the longest possible fixing screws as extras, if necessary.

The best locks for hinged wooden windows lock automatically as the window is closed and need a key to open them. Fit two locks on windows over about 1m (3ft 3in) high. The best locks for sliding sash windows have dual screws, which pass through holes drilled through the top of the lower sash and the bottom of the upper one. Fit two to each window, close to the sides of the sashes.

Keep any keys for window locks nearby the window but invisible from outside the house, so locked windows can be opened quickly, especially in the event of a fire. Make sure everyone sleeping in your home knows where they are kept.

Outbuildings

Sheds, garages, and other outbuildings are likely to contain tools and ladders, which a burglar could use to gain easier entry to the house. They may also contain valuable power tools and garden equipment worth stealing. Strengthen hinged doors with hinge bolts, a surface-mounted

Going on holiday

- Ask a **neighbour** or a nearby friend or relative to keep an eye on the property while you're away, clearing the letter box and checking for unexpected deliveries. If they have a key, ask them to draw curtains and put lights on at night. Otherwise, use automatic time switches to operate lights in the hall or on the landing.
- Cancel **newspaper and milk deliveries.** Do this on the phone, so you're not overheard.
- Leave **small valuables** with friends or relatives or on deposit at your bank. Don't leave larger valuables where they are visible from outside the house.
- Set a **burglar alarm** if you have one and tell the police who your appointed keyholder is. Make sure the keyholder knows how to use the burglar alarm.
- If you are going to be away for **more than a couple of weeks**, arrange for someone to mow the lawn in spring and summer, and sweep up leaves in the autumn.

Security in flats

- The **front door** to an individual flat can be forced if an intruder gains access to the building, so make it as secure as you can.
- In flats with a **communal entrance door**, make sure the door closes properly, preferably on a spring.
- Windows and back doors in basement and garden flats are vulnerable, especially when out of sight of the road. Make sure all possible entry points are locked and **consider installing external grilles** or sliding internal grilles for extra security.

bolt inside the door that closes first, and a five-lever mortise lock to the meeting edge of the doors. Secure up-and-over doors with a floor-mounted ground lock. Fit sheds and greenhouses with a stout hasp, staple and padlock. Replace any vulnerable glass with unbreakable polycarbonate sheeting.

Alarms

Visible burglar alarms make burglars think twice, and even a dummy alarm box may prove an inexpensive deterrent. Check your insurer's preference before deciding between professional or DIY installation and ask whether they stipulate regular servicing. A professionally installed wired system linked to a 24-hour monitoring station is the most secure option, but also the most expensive. It should meet the requirements of British Standard BS 4737. There are two standards for DIY systems – BS 6707 (wired systems) and BS 6799 (wireless systems). Don't install a DIY system unless you have the knowledge and practical skill. If fitted badly, it could trigger endless nuisance alarms.

Extra measures for high-risk areas

Front doors Add door and frame reinforcements to prevent the lock from being forced. These are metal plates that are fixed to both faces of the door over the position of the mortise lock, and metal strips on the frame that prevent the lock keeper from being forced. All these are available from locksmiths.

Back doors Add hinge bolts, security glazing, and door and frame reinforcement. Fit surface-mounted bolts or concealed mortise rack bolts for extra security when you are out and at night.

Sliding patio doors Consider having metal security grilles fitted for these.

Good security habits

Even the best security equipment in the world is no good if you forget to use it. Be security-conscious at all times.

- Close (and lock if you can) all windows including top ventilators when you go out. Shut windows and doors at the front of the house when you are upstairs, in the back garden or out of earshot.
- Lock and bolt side and back doors, and remove the keys from the locks.
- Check that gates are closed and bolted, that outbuildings are secure, and that ladders are under cover or chained up.
- Move tempting portable valuables out of sight and draw the curtains in any room containing valuable home entertainment equipment – which is the favourite target of every burglar.
- Set the burglar alarm if you have one.
- Lock the front door and check that the lock is fully engaged. Make sure keyoperated rim locks are deadlocked.
- Don't leave spare keys hidden anywhere near the front door. Leave spare keys with a neighbour you can trust, but don't put your house name or number on the key tag.
- If you lose your front door key, get the lock changed straight away.
- Identify callers before opening your front door, using a door viewer or door chain and always ask unknown callers to produce identification before letting them in. Don't let small children open the front door.
- If you are going out in the evening, draw curtains and leave lights on and a radio playing, to give the impression that the house is occupied.
- Use a security marker to identify valuable items in the house with your postcode and house number (or the first two letters of its name); take photos of items you cannot mark.

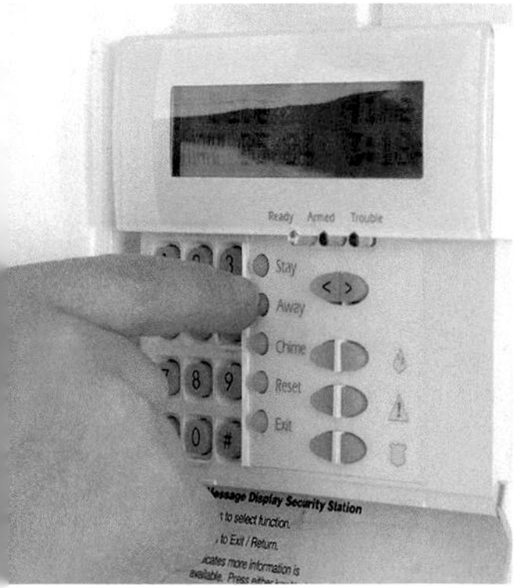

Get into the habit of setting your house alarm whenever you go out

Contact details

Useful websites and addresses about the information given in this chapter.

buy.co.uk, Victoria Station House, 191 Victoria Street, London SW1E 5NE
Tel: 0845 601 2856
Fax: 020 7233 5933
www.buy.co.uk
Save on your household bills by comparing different prices for most consumer services.

CORGI, 1 Elmwood, Chineham Business Park, Crockford Lane, Basingstoke, Hants RG24 8WG
Tel: 01256 372 200
e-mail: enquiries@corgi-gas.com
www.corgi-gas.com
CORGI is the national watchdog for gas safety in the UK. Click on to the consumer website to find a CORGI registered installer in your area.

Discounted Heating, 57 Faringdon Rd, St Judes, Plymouth PL4 9ER
Tel: 01752 301 111
Fax: 01752 515 095
www.discountedheating.co.uk
Buy discounted heating or plumbing products online at this website.

DIY Doctor
e-mail: contact@diydoctor.org.uk
www.diydoctor.org.uk
Home improvement web advice covering every trade.

Gas emergencies
Tel: 0800 111 999
If you smell gas or suspect a gas leak, phone 0800 111 999 anytime. There is no charge for the call-out.

House Contact Centre, PO Box 50, Leeds LS1 1LE
For general enquiries, phone the number on the top of your gas or electricity bill
Fax: 0845 604 0304
e-mail: house@house.co.uk
www.house.co.uk
An online home management service from British Gas, designed to help you run your home more smoothly.

idealhomesecurity.co.uk
Tel: 01442 878 440
www.idealhomesecurity.co.uk
Online shop for safety and security in the home.

Master Locksmiths Association, 5D Great Central Way, Daventry NN11 3PX
Tel: 01327 262 255
Fax: 01327 262 539
e-mail: mla@locksmiths.co.uk
www.locksmiths.co.uk
Find an approved locksmith in your area.

National Insulation Association, PO Box 12, Haslemere, Surrey GU27 3AH
Tel: 01428 654 011
Fax: 01428 651 401
e-mail: insulationassoc@aol.com
www.ncia-ltd.org.uk
Find a registered company for all forms of house insulation.

Northumbria Energy Efficiency Advice Centre (NEEAC)
Tel: 0800 512 012
www.neeac.co.uk
For advice on cutting your bills by using less energy.

Ofgem, 9 Millbank, London SW1P 3GE
Tel: 020 7901 7000
Fax: 020 7901 7066
www.ofgem.gov.uk
The regulator for Britain's gas and electricity industries.

Oftel, 50 Ludgate Hill, London EC4M 7JJ
Tel: 0845 714 5000
Fax: 020 7634 8845
e-mail: advice@oftel.gov.uk
www.oftel.gov.uk
Contact this organisation if you have a complaint which you have not been able to resolve with the phone company concerned.

Royal Society for the Prevention of Accidents (ROSPA), Edgbaston Park, 353 Bristol Road, Edgbaston, Birmingham B5 7ST
Tel: 0121 248 2000
Fax: 0121 248 2001
e-mail: help@rospa.co.uk
www.rospa.com/CMS
Gives general safety advice to prevent DIY accidents.

Unravelit, Xelector House, 76 Talbot Street, Dublin 1, Ireland
Tel: 08451 202 056
e-mail: enquiries@unravelit.com
www.unravelit.com
Helps you to make savings on your household bills.

uSwitch.com, PO Box 33208, London SW1E 5WL
Tel: 0845 601 2856
Fax: 020 7233 5933
e-mail:
customerservices@uswitch.com
www.uswitch.co.uk
Helps you to make savings on your household bills.

Professional Help

Major structural work on a property will inevitably lead to calling in outside help, unless you happen to be in the building trade yourself! This needn't be a daunting prospect if you do your homework first.

This chapter guides you through finding a reputable tradesman or company in the first instance, through all the various stages of the work, including specifications, quotations, agreeing a price, living with the disruption that will more than likely come with the building work and how to avoid problems or getting into disputes. Building regulations and planning permission are also discussed, along with suggestions for possible improvements to consider for your home.

Getting work done

When you own a property, there will be times when you have to pay someone else to work on it. You might need anything from emergency repairs or improvements – perhaps a new kitchen, double glazing or rewiring – to work of a more structural nature.

This section deals with the basic procedures for finding and dealing with contractors, whatever the level of work.

What needs to be done?

There will always be overlaps, but most work is either essential remedial work or home improvement. These deserve more serious consideration than, say, decoration, because they have a lasting impact on the value and saleability of your home.

Essential remedial work

There is nothing glamorous about repairing a roof or curing dampness and rot, but your first priority must always be to make and keep the basic structure of your home sound. Failure to do so jeopardises the tens of thousands of pounds that you've committed to pay for your home (*see* p179 for more on how the main remedial treatments are executed and the upheaval they entail). You may choose to have other work done at the same time, to save disruption later.

Home improvement

The aims of any home improvement should be:

- to improve the quality of your life, giving extra space, light, warmth or convenience
- to add value to your property.

It's important to keep a balance between these two criteria. Don't put in too much capital – it doesn't make sense to install a kitchen that's worth a third of the value of your flat. And beware of devaluing – replacing traditional period windows with aluminium or uPVC frames is a classic mistake.

To avoid these pitfalls:

- look at neighbouring houses to see what changes have been made and whether or not they are successful
- talk to local estate agents about the effect your proposed improvements will have on the

Some professional structural work can cause a great deal of disruption

value of your property. Most agents are happy to give free advice. If not, you need not use them when you come to sell your home.

Prioritising work

If you've bought a renovator's delight that you are not planning to extend, these should be your priorities.

1 Potentially dangerous problems: faulty electrical wiring, old gas appliances, unsafe structures (from staircases to garden walls), loose chimney pots or roof tiles, unstable masonry that could fall and cause injury.

2 The exterior – if this isn't sound, any work you do inside is likely to be spoiled. Carry out repairs to: the roof, cracked or damaged masonry, damaged gutters and downpipes. Repoint brickwork if necessary. Repair damaged drainage systems. Replace or repair rotted window frames – now is the time to decide whether you would benefit from putting in double glazing.

Setting a budget

Many renovations end up **costing twice as much** (and taking twice as long) as originally estimated. The reasons may include appalling weather, problems that become apparent only after work has started or a misunderstanding with the builder. You may even increase the price yourself by deciding on further improvements as you go along. Follow the guidelines on drawing up agreements and don't begin a project unless you have some contingency money available, preferably one-third of the total estimate. If your budget is very tight, check repeatedly that your project is on track financially, and will be completed on time.

What you spend on **renovations and improvements** should be determined by:

- how much you can **afford**
- how much the **value of your home** will increase. This may enable you to extend your mortgage or get a loan to cover the work, but take the repayments into account
- any **grants** for which you may be eligible (*see* p175).

3 Problems that will get worse if left: rising or penetrating damp, dry rot and woodworm.
4 Installing new wiring and new plumbing while floorboards are up and before the walls and ceiling are replastered.
5 Putting in a wired security system if you have decided to do this; it will be more expensive to do later.
6 Roof insulation, one of the most cost-effective home improvements. Do you need any sound insulation, perhaps against a party wall?
7 Making good plaster and floors, which will be durable and provide a firm basis for any fixtures.

Emergency call-outs

Always call the emergency gas line given in the local directory if you suspect a gas leak or have problems with your gas supply. It is actually an offence under the Gas Safety (Installation and Use) Regulations to carry out any work yourself on your gas supply and any appliances connected to it. The work must be done only by a qualified gas fitter or by an installer registered with CORGI (the Council for Registered Gas Installers).

Electricity and water problems may not be so clear cut. The supplier owns piping and fixtures up to a certain point, after which they belong to the householder.

If you need to find professional help quickly, look through your local directory or ask neighbours for their recommendations. Choose contractors who are registered with a professional body.

When you phone:

- describe the problem as best you can
- ask what to do to stabilise the situation until it can be dealt with as a non-emergency
- if the work can't wait, ask what their call-out rate is, what it covers and what additional charges may be incurred – a high hourly rate could kick in after, say, the first 20 minutes
- don't accept the first quote. Say you'll get back to them and make calls to at least two other contractors.

Once contractors arrive:

- ask them to explain what they propose doing and why. If there's a major problem, ask if they can carry out a holding operation until normal working hours. Good contractors will not leave you without mains services unless there is a very convincing reason
- if new parts are fitted, ask to see and keep the old parts. Get them to point out in what way they are worn or faulty
- obtain a fully itemised receipt, which should offer a guarantee of workmanship and materials, and have the contractor's name and contact number. Ask the person who has done the work for you for their name, too, and write it on the receipt.

Four common budget busters

Upping the specification A quote may seem reasonable because it includes such items as ceramic tiles, a bathroom suite and taps selected off the shelf at the local builders' merchant. If you want something more individual, be prepared to pay extra for quality and design. Visit showrooms and suppliers, get catalogues and price lists, and give your builder the make, size, colour, model number and price of the items you require. If you don't want to make up your mind just yet, ask the builder to include a realistic but mid-price cost for these items at the outset. Then you will either pay a bit more or be charged less, depending on the items you choose.

The designer's dream Recreating the latest fashion can run away with the pounds, especially when it comes to kitchen and bathroom fittings. What looks right now may appear dated a few years on, and may even have a negative effect when you want to sell. Go for simplicity rather than gimmicks.

The cost of making good Discuss clearing up with your builders before work starts, or they may leave you with a heap of rubble and fittings that have been ripped out. You may need to spend some money restoring flowerbeds and lawns that have been walked on or used as a store for building materials.

Follow-on expenses You may have a separate budget for major furnishings – curtains, carpets, and furniture – but you should also allow for the smaller, but essential, finishing touches. Light fittings, bathroom cabinets, towel rails, loo roll holders and door hardware are surprisingly pricey and can amount to several hundred pounds.

Specifying the work

A good specification is the foundation of any successful renovation or extension project, and a comparison of contractors' quotations is meaningless unless they have all been prepared against an identical specification.

The first draft of any specification should come from you, the homeowner, though you aren't expected to define thickness of timber or diameter of pipe. It is in your own interests to be clear about what you want – if you don't tell the contractor what you want, you leave the decision to them. You may not like what they choose to use.

The final specification should avoid any misunderstandings about the work to be done, the materials to be used and who is responsible for what.

> **Estimate or quotation?**
>
> According to the Office of Fair Trading, **an estimate is generally a rough price, while a quotation is normally a fixed price**. The price given on a quotation should not be changed at all without your agreement. With an estimate, unless the specification for work has changed or new work has been included, this is approximately what you should expect to pay. Legally there is no difference between a written or verbal quotation, but you will have more difficulty settling a disagreement over a verbal one.
>
> *See* Finding a contractor, pp166–7, for further advice on getting a signed contract.

The basic statement

Before you contact any contractors, draw up a basic statement describing the work you want done. This process will clarify matters in your mind and enable you to prepare a useful brief for potential contractors. It also makes a good starting point if you want to hire an architect. It can be as brief as:

'I have a two-bedroom, first-floor apartment, built in the 1950s, which needs rewiring, new plumbing and central heating installed. Floors and walls will have to be made good afterwards. Do you handle this type of work?'

Your specification document

A specification for quotation purposes needs to be more detailed. It requires you to think

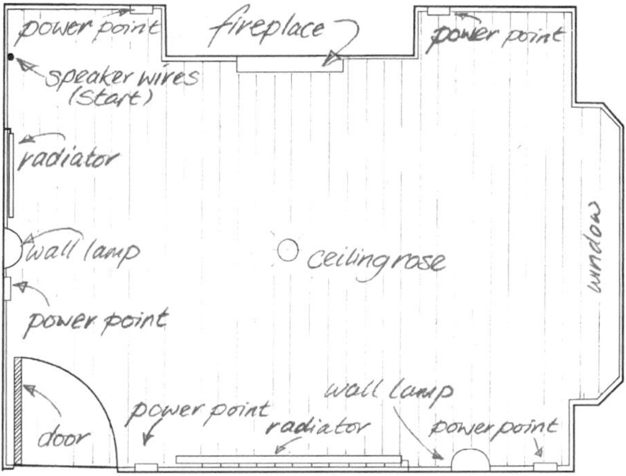

Sample room plan, showing preferred position of new items

about how you will be using each room, and how you would like it to look.

Start by taking a separate piece of paper for every room or area that needs work, label it and list the same headings on every sheet. Writing 'not applicable' is better than forgetting something that needs to be done. Make a plan of each room and mark positions of radiators, power points and so on – see room plan above.

Make several copies of the specification to give to various contractors. Some may be prepared to handle the whole job, others may want you to organise, say, the central heating as a separate job. Ask contractors to indicate which work they are quoting for. Add a clause to the effect that it is the contractor's responsibility to point out errors or omissions in the specification at the time of quoting.

The key headings and issues are:

For interior work

Wiring

The number and position of power sockets and light fittings, including wall lights and under-cupboard lights. Do you want sockets to be mounted on the skirting (cheaper) or set into the wall (neater)? List any permanent electrical appliances, such as cooker and electric fire. Now is the time to consider installing a security system. By planning ahead, you can make sure all wiring is hidden.

Plumbing
Water supply and waste for sink, bath, power shower, bidet, toilet, washing machine, and dishwasher (specify whether cold-fill only or hot and cold for the last two). Do you need an outside tap?

Central heating
Specify type and make, if known, as well as number and position of radiators or hot-air

A sample specification for quotation

Living room	Work required	Responsibility
Wiring	Supply and install 5 x double power sockets as marked on plan Install new wall lamps	Electrical contractor Owner supplies lamps
Plumbing	n/a	n/a
Central heating	Supply and install radiators as marked on plan Contractor to advise on correct sizes	Heating contractor
Gas	Bring supply to fireplace and install fire (owner to specify make and model)	Heating contractor
Floors	Repair and replace floorboards in readiness for sanding Sand and finish floor	Contractor Owner
Walls and ceiling	Make good damaged plaster in readiness for painting Fit new plaster ceiling rose Paint walls and woodwork	Contractor Owner to specify style Owner
Woodwork	Replace damaged skirting to match existing skirting	Contractor
Other	Take speaker wires through to kitchen before floorboards are replaced	Owner

grilles. Do you want individual thermostats on each radiator?

Gas

Supply for cooker, gas fire, hot water or central heating.

Floors

Repair and replace as necessary. The quality of the work you ask for should reflect the finish you want – greater care has to be taken if you want floorboards polished rather than covered with carpet.

Walls and ceilings

Make good as necessary. Even if they are in good condition now, new wiring may have to be channelled in. Do you want coving or a ceiling rose? If you plan to do the decorating yourself, make a note: 'decorating to be done by owner'.

Woodwork

Do the window frames need attention? If you live in a period property, specify that architraves, skirting and doors must match the original.

For exterior work

Draw up lists for each elevation – rear, front, north side, south side – and structures such as conservatory or garage. The headings on each list should cover the roof, woodwork, masonry and gutters.

Specifying materials

Misunderstandings about what materials are to be used are a common cause of controversy between contractors and clients.

- Basic **'trade' materials**, such as electric cable, copper pipe, nails, screws, plaster and timber, don't have to be specified unless you particularly want, say, thicker than normal plasterboard for soundproofing qualities or timber from a sustainable resource. Unless you have knowledge of building materials, you have to trust your contractor to supply goods that comply with regulations and will give you the result you want.
- Generally, **visible materials** – all the things you tend to take for granted, such as electric switch plates, door hardware, skirting boards and architraves – are supplied by the contractor. It is your responsibility to make sure they are what you want. Don't assume that the contractor shares your tastes or automatically uses fittings that are architecturally or environmentally sympathetic.
- For any item where **styling** is important to you, specify make, model, colour and size or undertake to supply the item yourself. Allow plenty of time for your stockist to order goods so that everything is ready for the contractors the moment they require it. Make sure there is provision for this before accepting a quotation.
- Bear in mind that **good-quality fittings** like taps and power showers will function well for years and the installation costs are the same, whatever the price of these items.

Hiring professionals

Depending on the scale of your project, you may well want to pay for some specialist input, whether it's a one-off consultation with a structural engineer about a load-bearing wall or the services of an architect to see through a whole extension from start to finish.

Before you being, you need to know what different professionals do – as well as what to expect if you manage the project yourself.

Draughting technician

A technician who puts plans on to paper, often using computer-aided design. Before you enlist any other professional help, consider commissioning a scale plan of your home in its current format, showing its orientation and its position on the site. Then, with tracing paper, a scale rule and a pencil and rubber, you can experiment with alterations, such as removing a wall to enlarge a kitchen. Ideas generated at this stage make a good basis for an initial consultation with an architect or building surveyor.

Consider whether you need to hire a draughting technician or an architect

What does it cost? To employ a drafting technician to measure up and prepare plans may cost up to £300.

Architect

To trade as an architect, a person must have a degree in architecture and be registered with the Architects' Registration Council. He or she may also be a member of a professional organisation such as the Royal Institute of British Architects.

Architects specialise in different areas (industrial, new building work and so on), so choose one who has experience and an interest in domestic renovations.

An architect can offer different levels of service tailored to your needs and budget. The first stage is a consultation about the feasibility of and options for improving your home. The second involves drawing up plans and obtaining planning permission or building regulations approval. The third is to take complete control, finding builders and overseeing all work and payments.

What does it cost? The initial consultation is often free, but take it seriously and be prepared to discuss your own ideas, sketches, or plans. For drawing up and submitting plans to the council, a flat fee will be based on the amount of time involved. If you would like the architect to handle the entire project, payment is usually calculated as a percentage of the total cost.

Avoiding possible pitfalls

- The last thing you want to feel is that the architect's ideas have been foisted on you. Don't employ anyone who fails to lend a sympathetic ear to your thoughts. At the initial meeting, explain clearly what you want to achieve – such as extra living space or another bedroom – how you envisage the scheme and how much you want to spend. Find out whether your architect usually teams up with a particular builder, so you can ask around about the builder's reputation.
- Architects' fees rank alongside plumbers' charges in horror stories about costs running out of control. If you don't want, or can't afford, to employ an architect to handle the whole job, it's important to agree their level of involvement from the outset. Ask for a clear explanation of their fees and what service you will receive. If you change your mind as work progresses, check how much extra this will cost.

Building surveyor

Surveyors offer the same sort of services as architects, undertaking anything from consultation to total management. Make sure the surveyor you choose has recognised qualifications and relevant experience. Look for one who is a member of the Royal Institution of Chartered Surveyors or another professional body.

What does it cost? Charges are comparable to architects' fees.

Seven ways to find professional help

1 **Personal recommendation.**
2 Professional organisations will supply a **list of members** practising in your area.
3 ***Yellow Pages***. Look under Architects, Architectural services, Architectural technicians, Building consultants, Computer-aided design services, Draughtsmen and Surveyors. Make sure the company deals with your type of work.
4 Check the **Internet** for professionals in your area. Some have websites with descriptions of recent work.
5 **Local newspapers** often carry small advertisements for architectural consultants, draughtsmen and specialist companies.
6 **Magazines and supplements** usually have advertisements for specialist companies dealing in kitchens, bathrooms, loft conversions and conservatories.
7 **Leaflets** through the letterbox may be of use, but only in conjunction with thorough research on your part. Always get at least two other quotes and read the small print very carefully before signing.

Structural engineer

Members of the Institute of Structural Engineers are the people to call when work has to comply with building regulations, but doesn't justify the services of an architect. Structural engineers will also undertake consultation work. For example, when you knock two rooms into one, a structural engineer will specify the type and size of beam that has to go over the new opening. An architect will consult a structural engineer as necessary.

What does it cost? Charges are negotiated according to the work involved and vary from one part of the country to another.

Architectural consultant

Architectural consultants may also trade as design consultants or architectural advisers, but never as architects. They don't have to register with any professional body and therefore do not have to abide by a code of conduct. They may not be insured in the event of faulty work. However, many firms work to an excellent standard; if you find a well-established local firm with good references, they're worth talking to.

What does it cost? An architectural consultant will almost certainly cost less than a registered architect.

Specialist firms

These firms deal exclusively with one aspect of home improvement – such as loft conversions, conservatories, kitchens, bathrooms and replacement windows. They handle everything from design to the construction, usually in a temptingly short period – 'a new kitchen in four days'.

Avoiding possible pitfalls

- Get at least three specialist firms to submit plans and quotations. Make sure you clarify precisely what they will and won't do. Jobs such as levelling a floor or painting and decorating, for example, may be excluded – in which case their schedule must give you time to have the work done.
- A common ploy of specialist firms is to visit your home, spend several hours coming up with a design and a price, and then offer a substantial discount if you sign up there and then. Don't, unless you have already done enough research to know that the deal represents good value. Explain that you are considering all options and that you will get back to them. If they can give you 25% off one week, they can offer it a fortnight later!
- It's true that practice makes perfect and specialist firms are likely to have encountered most problems in their field. Be aware that they might work to a fixed formula rather than giving individual consideration to your requirements.

Managing the work yourself

Managing a building project involving a number of different contractors is almost a full-time job in its own right. It is true that you can save money by being your own manager, rather than hiring an architect or builder to oversee the work, but you must have:

Time

- To research the materials and quantities you need.
- To source the right materials at the best price.
- To find contractors to do the work.
- To be available to answer queries and make decisions.
- To inspect the quality of the work.

Organisational skills

- To prepare a schedule of the work.
- To ensure that labour and materials are on site at the same time and at the right stage of the work. Materials delivered too early are likely to be lost or damaged – late delivery wastes expensive labour time.
- To have contingency plans in the event of unexpected problems.
- To manage permissions, approvals, contracts and payments.

Experience

- To be realistic about timeframes and costs.
- To anticipate problems.
- To know if work isn't up to standard.
- To understand problems and discuss possible solutions – otherwise you are at the mercy of the contractor, who may want to do whatever is easiest.
- To stand firm in order to achieve the result you want.

Finding a contractor

Everyone has heard sensational stories about people who have been ripped off by bad contractors, but the majority of tradespeople are honest, reliable and capable. Some background research will help you find them, and some commonsense guidelines will ensure that you enjoy a good relationship with them. But give yourself plenty of time: good builders, for instance, are often booked up for months in advance and you don't want to be pressured into choosing someone just because they are available.

Ten questions to ask

1. Do you do the type of work I require?
2. Have you done a similar job recently and if so, is it possible to see it or talk to your clients?
3. Can you supply references for similar work?
4. How long have you been in business for?
5. Do you belong to the Federation of Master Builders or any other trade organisation?
6. Do you have a full-time team of people – if so, how many?
7. Are there any areas you don't cover, such as central heating or decorating?
8. If you sub-contract, do you regularly use the same people?
9. When would you be available to start?
10. Would you work exclusively on my job or do you work on two or more sites simultaneously?

Where to look for a reliable contractor

Nothing beats personal recommendation when it comes to finding professional help, but even that is not foolproof. One person's idea of a job well done is not necessarily the same as another's. So, before you make any decisions about which contractor to hire, check out the options outlined below.

Observation Walk round your local streets and note any work being done on houses in the area. Try to speak to the owner. At worst, you can knock on the door, though you might be met with initial scepticism. Explain your interest and ask about what they're having done and whether or not they're happy with the builders. Most people love to talk about their renovations and, once they've realised you are genuine, they may be delighted to help.

Small ads Tradespeople often place advertisements in the local newspaper as one job is coming to an end, so you may have an opportunity to visit their current workplace and assess the quality of the work. Before you phone, prepare a brief outline of the work you want done (see p158) and a list of questions (see left). Ignore any ads that only give a mobile phone number – they could be cowboys.

Yellow Pages You may have to make quite a few calls, most of which will be a matter of elimination. But if, after going through your preliminary questions, it is obvious that a company is not suitable for you, ask if they know of anyone who does handle your sort of work. Information of any sort helps narrow the field.

Professional bodies, such as the Institute of Plumbing, will supply a list of members in your area. Members of the Federation of Master Builders also have to have a good reputation and be able to supply bank references and proof of insurance. Bear in mind that not all bodies may be so stringent in their vetting procedures as these two.

Check out **websites**, such as www.improveline.com – but be sure you're happy with the terms of business indicated on the site.

Never, ever employ someone who touts for work on the doorstep.

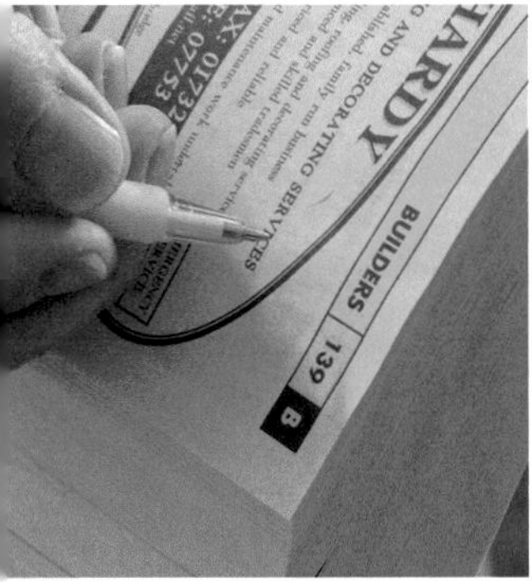

The Yellow Pages *is a useful source to find reliable builders*

Before work starts

- **Clear the area** – your contractor isn't paid to move furniture and take down curtains.
- Remove all **fragile and valuable items** from the premises or store them in a lockable room.
- **Protect your flooring**, removing carpets if possible, especially if they lie between the work site and, say, the bathroom. Builders don't stop to take their boots off.
- **Isolate the work area** as best you can, using masking tape to seal any doors that can be left closed. Building dust gets everywhere.
- **Dig up any precious plants** and store them away from the work. Any open space, however small, may be buried under building materials.

Asking for quotations

- Draw up an initial shortlist of between three and five contractors and make an appointment with each one in turn to meet you on site.
- Give them a copy of your initial specification and go through it with them. Take notes, especially if they suggest any changes. Inform all the other potential contractors of any changes you make at this stage.
- Never tell them what your budget is. Never say you want the job done as cheaply as possible. Never suggest that money is no object.
- Ask each contractor to submit a written quotation. Allow up to 28 days for a complicated job, but phone after a couple of weeks and ask how the

Comparing quotations

There are three main aspects to consider when comparing quotations from different contractors: how much the work is going to cost, what exactly gets done for the money and how long the job will take.

Price

- A high price can be an indication of top-quality work or it can mean that the contractor doesn't really want the job unless you pay a premium.
- A low price may come from someone who genuinely charges reasonable rates or it may come from a builder who will demand further funds half way through the job or use cheap materials.
- VAT, if applicable, makes a huge difference to the final price. Check it has been included.
- A contingency sum of between 5% and 10% should have been included as a matter of course to cover the cost of unforeseeable problems. Check whether this is listed separately or included in the total.
- If a contractor with whom you otherwise felt comfortable offers either a very high or very low price, ask them to go through the specification again to justify the quote. They may have made a mistake or have misunderstood the scope of the work required.

Who does what

- Will the contractor obtain planning permissions?
- Will the contractor supply materials? If you undertake any part of this, make sure you know exactly what is needed and when.
- Is the contractor insured for loss of or damage to materials and property, and for injuries to workers and to members of the public?
- Does the quotation cover clearance and removal of rubbish?

Timing

The quotation should indicate how long the work is likely to take and approximately when it could be done. If you have any specific timing requirements, you must tell the contractor at the outset.

quote is coming along. This sends a message that you're seriously interested in employing them and shows that you are not someone who lets things drift.

- Ask each contractor to itemise their costs. This will make it easier for you to see where your money is going and it will help you agree on payment stages, once you have decided which contractor to employ.

Making an agreement

As soon as you've made up your mind, phone the contractor and confirm the following:

- price and what it includes and excludes
- start date and estimated completion date
- any disruption that would require you to vacate the property, even for a night
- working hours
- number of workers on site
- procedures for changing the brief, the final price, or the completion date. Unless changes are very minor, they should be put in writing
- how payment will be staged, with an agreement to hold back between 5% and 10% until three months after the completion of the job in case of unfinished work or faulty workmanship that is not immediately apparent.

Put everything you agree into writing and send two copies of the letter to the contractor. Ask him or her to sign and return one copy. This is effectively a contract between the two of you. It will prove a valuable document should serious problems arise (*see* pp192–3 on getting redress).

Once the agreement has been signed, it's courteous to notify the other contractors who supplied quotes, especially if it was a difficult decision or was taken because of timing rather than price. It's worth staying on good terms, just in case your chosen contractor lets you down.

A set contract

If you would like to work with a **professionally drawn-up agreement**, you can use the Joint Contracts Tribunal (JCT) building contract for homeowners/occupiers. The JCT is an independent body and has produced an inexpensive, four-page, plain English contract to make life easier for you and your builder. It covers all the aspects dealt with on these pages. Some builders may be able to provide the contract, or you can order one direct from the JCT. Not for use in Scotland.

Rules and regulations

Whenever you make a structural improvement to your home, whether it's large or small, check first with your local authority. You may need to apply for planning permission and/or comply with building regulations.

An architect or consultant working on your behalf should do the planning or building regulation applications automatically. The rules and regulations can be complicated, but they have the force of law – they exist to provide a pleasant and safe environment for everyone. It's worth being on good terms with the staff of planning and building control offices, who are there to help.

Planning permission

The purpose of the Town and Country Planning Acts is to protect the character and amenity of an area. In England and Wales, this responsibility

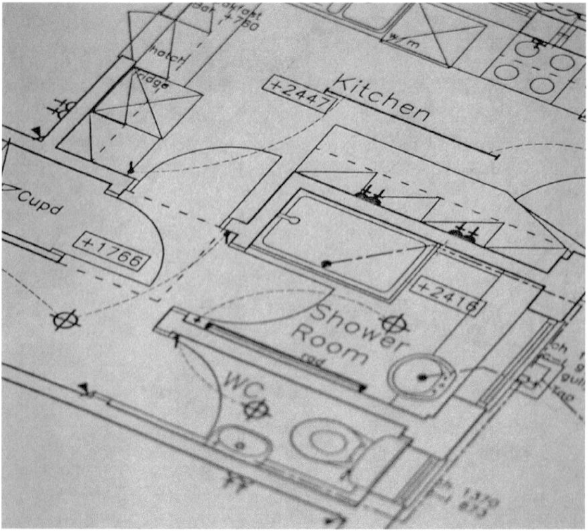

Architect's plans will need to be seen by the local authority to grant permission

lies mainly with local authorities. Scotland and Northern Ireland have similar regulations. In Scotland, these are enforced by the councils. In Northern Ireland, applications should be made to the Planning Service Office of the Department of the Environment. The aim of the regulations is to look after the public interest, not the interest of one individual over another. You do have the right to make some alterations to your property, but the onus is always on you to check whether planning permission is needed.

Operate on the principle that you should take nothing for granted, as interpretations of regulations may vary from area to area. You may discover, for instance, that alterations made by a previous owner mean your home has reached its maximum allowable size (*see* Volume and area, p156). In a Conservation Area, even repainting the exterior of your house may be controlled. If you don't find out where you stand, you can be forced to undo unauthorised work and restore it to the way it was before you started.

Watch out

- Work that is **exempt from building regulations** may still need planning permission.
- Work that does not need planning permission may still be **subject to building regulations**.

Points about plans

- **Site plans** should be drawn to a scale of not less than 1:1,250.
- **Detailed drawings** should be to a scale of not less than 1:100.
- If you cannot give **scaled drawings**, you should mark all relevant dimensions on your plan. New work or alterations should be crosshatched or coloured on the plan to make the proposed changes instantly obvious.

Six steps in applying for planning permission

1 Write to your local planning department to explain what you are hoping to do. Ask if they foresee any difficulties and, if so, what modifications might help get your plans through.

2 If planning permission is necessary, ask for the appropriate application form (some local authorities have them on their website, for downloading) and check the following:

- how many copies of the form do you need to return?
- what plans do you need to submit?

- how long will it be before you are given a decision?

3 Check what fee is payable, and what it covers. If the application is turned down, you can usually modify your plans and reapply free of charge within a set time. Equally, if you want to make minor adjustments once work is underway, you may not have to pay a further fee, but you will need to seek permission.

4 Send your completed application forms, necessary plans and the fee to the planning department. Keep copies of everything.

5 The council should acknowledge your application within a few days. It will also notify your neighbours, put up a notice near the site or advertise the application in the local paper. Members of the public can study your application at the council offices.

6 If permission is refused, you are entitled to know why. Planning staff may be prepared to advise you about changes that might make your scheme acceptable. If permission is granted, work must usually begin within a certain time.

Building regulations and control

The Building Control Service of each local authority has a wide range of responsibility for building regulations, from ensuring safety in public buildings, through naming streets and numbering houses, to making sure that dwellings are structurally sound. You need to comply with building regulations and get approval from your local Building Control Officer when you:

- erect or extend a building – here size is important (*see* Volume and area, p176)
- carry out structural alterations
- extend or alter a controlled service – for example, water and waste, by putting in a downstairs cloakroom
- change the use of a building – for example, sectioning off rooms for a self-contained flat or converting a warehouse or barn into a dwelling.

Additionally, building regulations cover some less obvious work, such as having cavity walls insulated. Seek advice as early as possible – unless the work is exempt, you have a legal requirement to tell the council about your intended work. You are entitled to start work two days after giving

Building rules can be strict if you live in a listed house or conservation area

notice, but for major work it is better to wait until approval has been granted.

How to apply for building control approval

There are two types of application. The Building Control Service will advise you on the best one for your circumstances.

Building Notice This is suitable for relatively simple work, such as putting in a new cloakroom or removing an internal wall. You need to submit:

- a completed Building Notice application
- a site plan showing the site boundaries and the position of the public sewers if the application is for a new building or a simple single-storey extension. This is available from the council
- the relevant fee. This is calculated according to the type and cost of the work involved.

Full Plans submission Required for more complicated work such as a double-storey extension or where the site presents problems with foundations or drainage. You may have to enlist professional help to draw up the plans (*see* p162). You will then receive a formal notification, if the plans have been passed. You need to submit:

- two completed Full Plans applications

Listed buildings and conservation areas

In England, listed buildings are those deemed by the Department of Environment, on the advice of English Heritage, to be of significant **historic or architectural importance**. Although most are old, a rolling 30-year rule allows buildings to be taken off or added to the list at any time, and some relatively modern buildings are listed. In order to preserve their character, **planning and building controls on such buildings are generally strict**, although they vary with individual councils and conservation officers. Listed building consent is required for many internal alterations, even though they do not affect the outward appearance of the building. Consult the planning office before you start work. Failure to obtain listed building consent can land you with a hefty unlimited fine, or even a jail sentence.

Conservation Areas, National Parks and Areas of Outstanding Natural Beauty are also carefully protected, and many alterations that normally do not require planning permission – from building a small extension to installing a satellite dish – must be approved by the council in these areas.

- two copies of the detailed drawings of the proposed work. The degree of specification required (such as foundations, roof construction and covering, and thermal insulation) depends on the extent of the work you are proposing
- two copies of a site plan showing site boundaries and the position of public sewers, available from the council
- the fee. This is calculated according to the type and cost of the work involved.

Proof of legitimacy

Planning permission Keep all correspondence regarding planning permission in case you ever need to prove that it was granted and whether or not there were conditions attached. A phone call will often establish that planning permission is not required. If you want a record of this, you can obtain, for a fee, a lawful development certificate.

Other people's building plans

You have a right to examine any **planning application** at the council's planning department. Contact the planning department if you think the proposed work would affect your privacy, block your light or overshadow your garden, increase the amount of traffic to an unacceptable level, cause problems with parking, create noise or other pollution (in the case of an industrial development), alter the character of your street or have any other environmental impact.

Put your **objections in writing**. There is no guarantee that the development will be stopped, but you may at least win some modifications that minimise its impact.

Building regulations If you write to your local Building Control Service it will give written confirmation if work is exempt – keep hold of this. No fee will be charged. If building regulations apply, you will receive written confirmation of compliance when the work has been finished and inspected. Again, keep documentation safe.

Financial assistance

Grants are few and far between.

- For home maintenance and improvement, they tend to be awarded to those most in need: the elderly, disabled and those receiving state benefits.
- If you live in a listed building or Conservation Area, you may be eligible for a percentage of the cost of repairs directly associated with the historic fabric of the building. But, as with all planning issues, the concern is with public rather than individual benefit. You are more likely to receive help with restoring a significant building you don't use, than you are for your own home.

Reduced or zero-rated VAT
Usually, VAT makes up a hefty proportion of the cost of any building work. The standard rate of VAT is applied to most construction work, but there are

Tell the neighbours

If your proposed work will affect your neighbours in any way, it is only fair to warn them. This may prevent problems arising.

Planning permission

- Tell your neighbours what you want to do, show them the plans and listen to any concerns they may have.
- They have the right to object to your application and, whether or not their objections are upheld, it may help your case in the long term to think through any possible modifications in advance.

Building regulations

Neighbours do not have the right to object unless the 1996 Party Wall Act applies. This covers:

- work on an existing wall or structure, such as the floor in a block of apartments, that is shared with another property, and which could affect its structural strength and support functions. This excludes minor work such as installing shelves or power points
- building on the boundary with a neighbour's property
- excavating near a neighbouring building.

The regulations require that you notify them in writing at least two months before starting work, and obtain their written consent.

While work is in progress

- Be considerate (or apologetic) about taking up kerb space with vehicles, building materials and skips.
- Keep the pavement and road clear of rubbish.
- Let the neighbours know when noisy work is due to start.
- Ask their permission on the day if your contractors need to enter their property in order to access, say, your side wall or roof.

some instances when a reduced or zero rate applies to material and labour costs, provided the work is carried out by a builder. If you are doing the work, you will have to pay the standard rate on all materials.

- New building work is zero-rated for VAT. Renovations, improvements and even new extensions don't count as new building work, but if you are demolishing and rebuilding on old foundations, you may have a case.
- Alterations to make a property suitable for a disabled person are zero-rated.
- Some alterations to listed buildings are zero-rated.

At the time of writing, a reduced rate of 5% applies to the installation of energy-saving materials. This covers:

- insulation for walls, floors, ceilings, roofs and lofts
- insulation for water tanks, pipes and other plumbing fittings
- draughtproofing for windows and doors
- central-heating controls, including thermostatic radiator valves
- hot-water system controls
- solar panels.

The importance of volume and area

Volume is a significant factor as regards planning permission. It is calculated from the external measurements.

- As a general rule, a building can be extended by whichever is the smaller: up to 70cu m (2,472cu ft) or up to 15% of its volume on 1 July 1948 (when the legislation came in) or of its original volume if it was built after that date. The allowances are different in Scotland and Northern Ireland.
- Terraced houses and houses in Conservation Areas, Areas of Outstanding Natural Beauty, and National Parks can be extended by up to 50cu m (1,766cu ft) or 10%, whichever is the smaller.
- If you are thinking of buying a property that you would consider extending, check with the local authority that it has not already been extended to its maximum size.

Area affects whether or not building regulations apply. This is calculated using internal measurements. Small building works, such as the construction of a porch, carport, garage, greenhouse or garden shed, will be exempt if:

- the building is more than 1m (3ft 3in) from the boundary and the new floor area does not exceed 30sq m (323sq ft).

As an approximate guide, a **flat-roofed extension** with a floor area of 4m (13ft) x 4m (13ft) and a height of 3m (10ft) would give a volume of 48cu m (1,695cu ft).

The floor area of a **double garage** is usually roughly 30sq m (323sq ft).

Which work requires permission or approval?

Type of work	Building regulations	Planning permission*	Other approval as appropriate
Repairs and decoration	✗	✗	✔ Listed building consent
Replacing an existing kitchen or bathroom	✗	✗	
Creating a new kitchen or bathroom, or altering existing drainage	✔	✗	✔ Must comply with water regulations; contact your supplier
Installing central heating	✔	✗	
Installing unvented hot-water system	✔	✗	
Adding insulation	✔ For cavity-wall insulation	✗	? Listed building consent, for external wall insulation
Adding damp-proofing	✗	✗	
Internal structural alterations	✔	✗	✔ Listed building consent
Replacing windows	✔	✗ Unless they face a highway and project beyond the foremost wall of the house	✔ Listed building consent
Converting loft	✔	✔ For dormer windows and windows over a certain size; check with local authority ✗ As long as house volume is unchanged and highest part of roof is not raised	
Adding extension	✔	✗ Unless it exceeds the permitted increase in volume ✔ If you live in a flat or maisonette	✔ Listed building consent ✔ Consent of freeholder/management company
Adding conservatory	✗ Unless floor area is more than 30sq m/ 323sq ft in area	? As for extension ✔ Listed building consent	
Adding porch	✗	? As for extension	✔ Listed building consent
Adding garden shed or garage	✗ Unless floor area is more than 30sq m/ 323sq ft, or it is 1m/ 3ft 3in of boundary	? Depends on size and position on the site – consult local authority	✔ Listed building consent
Adding carport	✗	? Consult local authority	✔ Listed building consent
Hardstanding for private vehicle	✗	✗ Unless you live in a flat or maisonette	✔ Consent of freeholder/ management company
Erecting greenhouse	✗	? As for extension	? Possibly listed building consent
Demolition	✗ For total demolition of a freestanding building ✔ For partial demolition	✔	✔ Listed building consent
Change of use (self-contained flat/office)	✔	✔	
Removing trees	✗	✗ Unless they are protected or you live in a Conservation Area	

Key: ✔ = requires permission/approval; ✗ = does not require permission/approval; ? = may require permission/approval.

* *This column does not reflect planning requirements in protected areas, such as Conservation Areas, National Parks and Areas of Outstanding Natural Beauty, where regulations may be stringent.*

Disruptive work

Taking up the floor coverings, lifting floorboards, cutting away plaster and knocking holes through walls are on the list of projects to do as infrequently as possible.

However, such disruptive tasks are unavoidable when you are dealing with urgent problems such as woodworm, damp, rot or carrying out improvements that involve plumbing or electrical work. Check the table (right) to find out what your proposed work will entail.

If some jobs will have to be done later, leave access to underfloor spaces – screw, rather than nail, floorboards in place and don't put down fitted floorcoverings until all the work is behind you.

Access to important areas may be disrupted...

Living with the work

It's home to you, but to the builder it's a work site. If you will be living in your property while renovations take place, specify the following in writing:

- Access to the property. Builders will take the shortest route, even if it crosses a new cream carpet, unless you state that they must always use, say, the back door
- Access to water and electricity for tea making
- Use of a lavatory
- Use of the phone – most tradesmen have mobile phones but, if not, they may need to use your phone for business purposes
- Arrangements for delivery and storage of materials, ensuring that access your property is not blocked
- Disruption of services – you should never be left without water or electricity at the end of the day.

How much disruption does the work involve?

Likely disruption – see key below

Type of work	1	2	3	4	5	6	7	8	9	10	Other
Woodworm Can affect timber in any part of the property	●						●		●		Wait six weeks before laying impervious floor covering such as vinyl
Wet rot Affects floors at ground level and exterior woodwork	●						●				Apply paint or other protective finish to exposed wood
Dry rot Most likely to start at ground level but spreads rapidly	●				●	●	●	● *	●	●	* May need to install airbricks or vents
Penetrating damp Damp patches often indicate source of problem					●	●				●	Gutters may need attention Brickwork may need repointing Check roof for missing slates or tiles
Rising damp	●				●	●	●		● *	●	* For chemical damp-proof course (DPC). Installing/ repairing dpc involves drilling into or cutting exterior brick walls
Electrical work	●	●	●	●		●				●	
Plumbing	●	●	●	●		●					Water system may need to be drained
Repairing/ upgrading central heating	●	●	●	●		●				●	Water system may need to be drained

Key:
1 Fitted floor coverings must be removed; floorboards must be lifted
2 Joists and rafters may be notched or drilled to accommodate pipes or cables
3 Solid walls and floors may need to have channels cut into them to house pipes or cables
4 Plasterboard may need to be cut away so that pipes or cables can run behind
5 Damaged plaster needs to be cut out
6 Plaster must be made good/replastering necessary
7 Rotten and weakened timber must be replaced
8 Holes need to be knocked through walls
9 Chemical solutions used
10 Redecoration required

Improvements to consider

Installing new, or improving existing, systems are expensive projects, but the outlay is justified in terms of comfort, efficiency and the value added to your home.

Much of the cost of using professional plumbers and electricians is accounted for by the hours they have to spend preparing underfloor areas and chipping away at the walls. By having the work done in one go you can at least save the cost of repeatedly lifting the floorboards – and any preparation work that you can do yourself will also save you money.

Replacing windows

Ill-chosen replacement windows can seriously devalue a property. Since 2002, new windows must comply with building regulations – and if you live in a Conservation Area, you will need to get planning permission to replace them. Generally, however, a house with double glazing is attractive when it comes to selling, as double glazing reduces draughts and cuts out some noise.

- If your windows are of architectural interest, consider secondary glazing instead of double glazing.
- If your windows are beyond repair and must be replaced, try to replace like with like. A local joiner will be able to make exact replicas – or even

A simple insulating improvement is to fix draughtproofing foam or rubber strips around doors and windows

sympathetically designed double-glazed windows.
- Even if the new windows are the same size as the old, internal plaster will need to be made good round the frames.

Fitting insulation

Insulation is one of the most cost-effective home improvements and, with planning, can be installed as you carry out other work.
- Draughtproof gaps round doors and windows with foam or rubber strip, but don't seal the room completely – ventilation is essential.
- Lag hot water pipes and tank to prevent heat loss.
- Lag cold water pipes and insulate cold water tank to prevent condensation and freezing.
- Loft insulation can be bought as rigid sheets, fibre rolls, or loose granules (which are useful for awkward spaces). Install it after all other work requiring access to the attic – plumbing, wiring, roof repairs – has been completed. Make sure the insulation material does not impede ventilation round the eaves.
- Underfloor insulation is now a requirement for new buildings. In an existing property it is easiest to install it while the floorboards are up. Tack plastic netting between the joists to support the insulation material.
- Double glazing is most effective at preventing heat loss if the gap between the panes is between 8mm (⅓in) and 20mm (¾in).

Regulations that affect improvements

Water bye-laws are principally concerned with preventing any risk of contaminated household waste water being siphoned back into the mains supply. Tell the local water supply company about the new installation of a bidet, flushing WC, tap with hose connection or any other fitting which might allow back siphonage. If in doubt, ask.

Building controls apply mainly to the disposal of waste water and sewage. They control the size and type of pipes used, and the angles at which they must fall towards the stack pipe. They specify ventilation requirements for any room with a WC, and also apply to the installation of unvented water heaters. Building controls also apply to the installation of boilers and unvented heating systems.

Gas connections must be carried out by an employee of British Gas or a member of the Council for Registered Gas Installers (CORGI).

Electrical wiring must comply with the wiring regulations of the Institution of Electrical Engineers (IEE).

Planning permission may be required if you want to install a fuel storage tank on your property, or if you need a chimney or flue that extends above roof level.

Unless you have the right skills, call in outside professional help for larger tasks

- Cavity wall insulation should be carried out by a professional. Consult your local Building Controls office before having the work done.

Increasing the number of power points

If you're having electrical work, think about how you may use different rooms in the years ahead and install extra power points now. Adding extra ones later will be far more expensive and disruptive. Eight or ten power points in a room is not excessive. Even a modest home office area is likely to need a computer, printer, scanner, fax machine, desk lamp and perhaps a music system.

Roof repairs

Unless the roof structure has been seriously weakened by rot or woodworm or the tiles and slates have started to disintegrate, most roofs can be repaired quite readily. If problems warrant a complete re-roofing job:

- re-use as much of the existing material as possible
- even if you are not in a Conservation Area, choose materials that are sympathetic to the style of the house – as well as to the neighbouring properties
- try to do the work during dry weather
- don't undertake any interior work until the roof is sound.

Combining/dividing rooms

Changing the shapes and sizes of your rooms by taking down or putting up walls often gives scope for dramatic improvements to your home.

To look at the possibilities, start with a scale drawing of your existing floor plan, a sheet of tracing paper, and a pencil and rubber. It's also helpful to have scale cut-outs of furniture so you can check it fits comfortably into your new scheme.

Advantages/disadvantages of removing walls

Reasons for

- Taking down a wall between two small rooms to make one room of a decent size can make the whole house seem more spacious.
- You may let in more light: knock down the wall that divides a north- and a south-facing room and you have a large south-facing room.
- A separate dining room may be rarely used, which makes it an obvious contender for combining to create a large living/dining room or spacious eat-in kitchen.
- Hall space can be incorporated into the living room.
- Combining two bedrooms may provide room to create a generous main bedroom suite with walk-in wardrobe and en-suite bathroom.

Reasons against

- Can you afford to lose a room that may be used infrequently, but which offers space for working or reading?
- You may be knocking down just one wall, but in terms of accommodating furniture, shelves and pictures, you are removing two – one from each room. Can you relocate (or do without) the things that used the wall space?
- Will losing a room affect the value of your property? A house that boasts one luxury bedroom suite plus a second bedroom may not be as saleable as a three-bedroom home. Check with an estate agent in your area.

Practicalities

- The first step is to consult a building surveyor to find out if the wall is load-bearing. If it supports the weight of the floors or roof above, it may not be possible to remove it. If it can be removed, the surveyor will recommend the correct size and type of beam to span the opening, and the correct way to install and support it.

- The floor in one room is not always level with the floor in the next. If the difference is minimal, you may not discover it until you have created the new opening. A shallow step is likely to cause accidents – the solution may be to raise the level of the lower floor by laying a new layer of flooring.
- Extra work will be involved if there are radiators or wall lights to remove.
- Closing off one door will give extra wall space. The neatest method is to remove the door, frame, and the architrave, and infill the opening with stud partitioning.
- Light switches may have to be relocated so that they can be operated from the new, principal doorway.
- There may be times when you would like, temporarily, to re-divide the room. Consider installing French doors in the new opening. If they are glazed, you still benefit from the increased light. Sliding or bi-fold doors use up less floor space but are more expensive.

Advantages/disadvantages of dividing a room

Reasons for

- Stud partition walls are quick and relatively easy to build. It is also easy to hide pipes and cables behind the plasterboard. The basic work can be carried out in as little as a day, with extra time for electrical and plumbing work, and for finishing off.
- Dividing a large bedroom to create an en suite bathroom or an additional bedroom can add value to your home.
- A kitchen can be improved if space permits you to section off part of it for a separate utility room.
- It may be possible to create a downstairs cloakroom by, for example, partitioning off part of the hall and using the space under the stairs.

Reasons against

- If you are dividing one bedroom into two, each new room must have its own window for light and ventilation. You may, therefore, have to install a new window.
- A high-ceilinged room may look terrible when divided in two if the floor space is not adequate. Don't divide a room if the proportions look wrong.

Dividing glass doors can still give you the option of two rooms

- Extra walls can make a home darker. Wherever practical, incorporate fanlights over new doorways and fit glazed doors.
- Make sure each room has its own access from a passage or lobby – you may have to sacrifice some floor space to create one.

Practicalities

- Solid walls offer greater soundproofing qualities than stud partition walls, but are less quick and easy to construct. They also need foundations for support.
- A new stud partition wall will need to be secured at floor and ceiling level. You may have to install extra supports between the joists of the floor below and the joists or rafters of the space above. This would mean lifting floor coverings and floorboards, and taking out a section of the ceiling.
- Make sure the new wall does not block future access to the space underneath the floors.
- Plan where to hang radiators, shelves and mirrors; make sure horizontal or vertical timber supports are in those places.
- Gas fires and other fuel-burning appliances need a minimum amount of air circulation to function safely. Consult your supplier to ensure that you will still have adequate ventilation to meet regulations.
- Run wiring and pipework through the wall before you put the plasterboard into place.
- The new wall should look as if it has always been there. Install skirting boards and cornice to match on both sides.
- Take soundproofing into account. Acoustic insulation can be installed between the timber supports. A double layer of plasterboard with staggered joints reduces noise.

Extensions and conservatories

Having an extension built is a far greater undertaking than adding on a conservatory, but they involve similar planning. When you're designing the layout of the new space, consider how you will use the space when it's finished and how that might change in the future.

Making an extension suit the house

The reason you need the extra space will dictate whether you choose a single- or double-storey extension and its position on the site. If you can afford only one storey now but would like to build up later, make allowances at this stage with foundations and walls that can support the extra storey.

Check the flow

Unless you are adding a separate 'wing' as a self-contained flat or office, it's important that human traffic flows smoothly between the old and new parts of your home.

- **Avoid conflicting interests**, such as having to cross the main work area of the kitchen to move from the new room to the back door or downstairs cloakroom.
- If a conservatory is to lead directly off a living room, you may have to **rearrange the seating** so that you can get to it easily.
- **New staircases and passages** (even those that are not partitioned off) can eat up floor space.

If the extension will include a kitchen, laundry, or bathroom, how easy will it be to connect into existing waste services, plumbing and electrical supplies? In a large extension it may be more practical to install independent heating and hot water systems, rather than place an extra strain on the existing system. Design the layout of your extension so that costs of providing new services are kept to a minimum.

Looking good

An extension must function well, and it should look as if it has always been there.

Windows and doors If the existing style is not available ready-made, have matching window frames and doors (both external and internal) made by a local joinery.

Bricks Although you should be able to match the colour of bricks fairly closely, modern bricks may not be the same

A conservatory is a popular choice for adding an extra living area to a home

size as old bricks. You may be able to find suitable secondhand bricks, but cost could rule this out. If you are working with different sized bricks, avoid butting directly up to the existing brickwork – even a slight recess will minimise the difference.

Roofing material Slates and tiles can look conspicuously new for years. To achieve an instant weathered look, buy secondhand. If this is not feasible, take old tiles from the least visible part of your roof and use those on the new extension. Put the new tiles in the less noticeable position.

Roof pitch The pitch should match or be sympathetic to the existing slopes and angles of the roofline. A flat-roofed extension on a pitched roof house always looks like an afterthought. If the location or your finances don't allow for a proper pitched roof, raising the roof at an angle for four or five rows of tiles will soften the effect. Alternatively, consider creating a roof terrace (take that decision early as it will affect construction).

Adding a conservatory

A conservatory can be an effective way to bring more warmth and light into your home without having to change the basic structure of the house. It also provides a way for you to enjoy your garden without having to brave bad weather.

A conservatory requires different materials to most extensions.

- If you want to use the conservatory all year round as an extension of your living space, central heating, lighting and the type of glass you use are important for its comfort.

- Conservatories can get extremely hot, especially during the summer, so allow for ventilation and heat-reflective blinds – which will also give privacy after dark. Automatic venting and blinds systems are effective but expensive.
- Before deciding on a glass roof for a conservatory, think about cleaning. A solid roof with skylights might be more practical, especially if you are building under a tree. It would also make the conservatory cheaper to heat in winter.

The components

Framework is usually made of timber, uPVC or metal.

- Timber requires the most maintenance and uPVC frames the least.
- Timber is sympathetic to older architectural styles.
- Most conservatories are made up of prefabricated panels, and their dimensions determine the final size of the room.

Windows should be double-glazed or the room will be too cold in the depths of winter, when you most want the sun.

- Full height glazing gives the maximum light and sense of space.
- Sill-height glazing gives some privacy and accommodation for radiators. You can also put plants on the sills. The pleasure of a conservatory comes from being able to sit in it and look out to the garden – the internal height of

Make the best of natural light

Planning considerations and the layout of your home will narrow down the possible positions for an extension or conservatory. Before you finally decide where to put it, consider how you can best utilise natural light.

- **A sunny aspect and good light** are vital for a conservatory and desirable for the rooms in which you spend most of your time – probably the living rooms and kitchen. If these rooms currently face north or northeast, it may be possible to switch your floorplan so utility areas and less used rooms are on the darker side of the house.
- If the new extension is to house a garage, laundry or spare bedroom, locate it so it has **minimal impact** on the light entering your home. South-facing living rooms sell, but no one will be impressed by a south-facing garage.

the sill should be less than 60cm (24in) or it will obstruct your view.

- All glass that you can fall on to or walk through must be toughened – check with building regulations.

Glass roofing is vulnerable to impact and a major escape route for rising heat.

- Glass must be toughened or laminated – which certainly puts the price up.
- Polycarbonate sheeting is a less expensive option. Choose twin- or triple-wall sheets to reduce heat loss. Be prepared for clicks and creaks as the plastic expands and contracts with changing temperatures.
- Fit guards along the gutters to protect the roof from falling tiles and, in harsh winters, compacted snow falling off the roof or trees.

Flooring depends on how you wish to use the room.

- In Victorian times (when conservatories first became fashionable), tiles were used. If you like the look but not the cold underfoot, consider installing underfloor heating before the tiles are laid.
- Warmer alternatives are timber flooring or concrete, covered with cork, vinyl or even a fitted carpet.

Ten things to consider

1. How will you **access** the new room/s from inside? Can you use an existing doorway, modify a window or will you need a new opening? Will you have to create a passage or can you walk through another room with an outside door?
2. Are there **obstacles** on the exterior wall – such as down pipes, soil pipes, boiler flues – that will have to be repositioned?
3. Can you **link the new gutters** to your current system or will you have to make alternative arrangements for dispersing rainwater, such as digging a new soakaway?
4. Are there **services or inspection chambers** that will have to be repositioned?
5. Is the ground outside at the **same level** as the existing floors? Will you step down (or up) into the extension or will you build up (or excavate) the land outside?
6. Do you want **access to the new room/s from the outside**? Will you need to construct new paths? What are the implications for security?
7. How easy will it be to bring **services** (electricity, plumbing, drainage, heating) to the site?
8. Will the conservatory **affect how you use the garden**? Consider adding exterior lighting over new garden doors.
9. Will you still be **able to reach the windows, walls and gutters above the extension or conservatory** to maintain them? If the exterior above a new conservatory needs work, do this first, as scaffolding is expensive.
10. Will the new building make upstairs windows **accessible to intruders**? You may have to fit window locks or modify your security system to monitor the new roof.

Loft conversions

There is a big difference between boarding over the floor of your loft to make full use of the space for storage and converting it into a proper room. A loft conversion is a good way to increase your living space without altering the volume or footprint of your property.

Although it involves meeting building regulations and possibly acquiring planning permission (*see* Rules and regulations, pp170–7), loft conversion is quicker and less disruptive than adding an extension.

Is conversion feasible?

There are three key factors to consider when contemplating a loft conversion: roof construction, access to the conversion and headroom.

> **Fire safety**
>
> **Building regulations** require:
> - **smoke detectors** to be fitted in loft conversions
> - recommended fire-rated materials and **fitting self-closing fireproof doors** to prevent the spread of fire
> - in a building with two or more storeys, a certain **maximum height of windows** above floor level and maximum distance from the eaves, to allow escape by ladder.
>
> **For details, check with your local authority's Building Office.**

Roof construction Traditionally, pitched (sloping) roofs were built on site, using rafters supported by high-level horizontal beams called purlins. The resulting framework leaves the central space unobstructed and fairly easy to incorporate window openings in the roof. Many modern roofs are built with prefabricated trusses, with lower, horizontal timber braces to give them strength. Yet these braces make it difficult to move around the loft space.

Access Decide where to locate the stairs leading up to the new room. In a single-storey house, space will have to be taken from the hall or one of the rooms. In a two-storey property, the usual location is directly above the existing stairs.

Headroom There must be adequate headroom above the stairs as you enter the new room. You may either have to position the stairs to enter the room under the highest point of the roof – which would use up

Natural light from a dormer window can give the conversion a light, airy feel

valuable floor space – or build up the wall and raise the roof over the stairs.

To move about the loft easily, you need a minimum height of about 2m (7ft). Consider whether you need one or more dormer windows. Lower-ceilinged areas around the edge of the room can be used for storage.

Conversion step by step

1 The first thing to do is to create safe access to the loft space. Do this where the stairs will eventually be positioned.
2 Will you be able to carry all the materials through the house and through this access? If not, make an opening in the roof – in a place where you will be installing a window. Builders should cover the gaps with plastic sheeting if the window is not fitted immediately.
3 Install services (electricity, central heating, other plumbing) before you put down the new floor.
4 Insulate the roof and the gap between the roof and sloping walls. Don't block ventilation around roof timbers.
5 If you remove insulation from under the new floor, heat rising from the rest of the house will keep the chill from the loft room.
6 If installing skylights, black frames look less obviously new than light timber ones, especially on older roofs. If you build a dormer window, make sure that the pitch, scale and style are sympathetic to the existing roofline.

Avoiding problems

The more thorough you are when preparing your specification for any contractor, the less likely you are to end up in dispute. Follow this advice, however, and you will hopefully avoid any dispute starting.

You should ideally agree in advance what procedures you'll follow if a dispute does arise. Play your part in maintaining a good working relationship by giving the contractor as much notice as possible, in writing, if you change the specification, or if there is good reason why payments will be late or withheld, and by paying promptly if there are no problems. Here are the six most common complaints about getting work done – and how to avoid them.

Keep a diary

If there is **any dispute**, a full record will help you present your case.

- Every week, compare **actual progress** with anticipated progress.
- Keep a record of **materials** as they are delivered.
- Make a note of all **payments**.
- Keep a record of all **conversations with the builder**, especially those in which either of you expresses concern about possible problems.
- Take **photographs** regularly, ideally with a camera that dates each shot.

1 **Undue pressure to have unnecessary work done** You should never agree to have work done that you don't want – but that is sometimes easier said than done. If you're up against someone particularly pushy, buy yourself time by saying that you have a friend or relative with whom you'd like to discuss the proposals, or say you need to obtain a loan to pay for the work and you'll have to submit three detailed quotations. Unscrupulous builders and cold-call salespeople will not risk being put under such scrutiny.

2 **Over-charging** Confirm every verbal quotation in writing, even if you are only having minor work done and are paying on an hourly basis. Your letter should confirm the hourly rate; whether it includes VAT; how materials will be costed; roughly how long the job should take.

To keep track of progress, take photos with a date and time facility

3 Lost deposits Some firms won't undertake work unless they receive a deposit. If they insist on this, ask for bank and insurance references – and follow them up before work starts.

4 Unnecessary delays In the absence of unforeseeable problems, you have a legal right to have the work completed within a 'reasonable' time frame. Before you accept any quotation, ask how long the work should take, when it will start and when it will finish. Include a penalty clause in your agreement, to reduce the bill by a stated amount if the job overruns beyond a set number of days.

5 Unfinished work Before accepting a quotation, especially for a major contract, check the company's insurance: it should protect you from financial loss, although it can't compensate you for the inconvenience of having to find another contractor. For smaller jobs, make sure that at all times, the money you owe the contractor more than covers the cost of finishing the job – otherwise unscrupulous traders may feel they have nothing to lose by abandoning you.

6 Poor workmanship Following up references and checking on membership of trade associations is your best safeguard. While the job is on, inspect the work at the end of every day. If you suspect the work is not up to standard, talk to the contractor immediately as it could jeopardise the quality of subsequent work. Hold back the final payment for three months in case problems arise once the contractor has left the scene.

Contact details

Useful websites and addresses about the information given in this chapter.

British Wood Preserving & Damp Proofing Association,
1 Gleneagles House, Vernon Gate, Derby DE1 1UP
Tel: 01332 225 100
Fax: 01332 225 101
e-mail: info@bwpda.co.uk
www.bwpda.co.uk

Chartered Institute of Arbitrators, International Arbitration Centre,
12 Bloomsbury Square,
London WC1A 2LP
Tel: 0207 421 7444
Fax: 0207 404 4023
e-mail: info@arbitrators.org
www.arbitrators.org

CORGI, 1 Elmwood, Chineham Business Park, Crockford Lane, Basingstoke, Hants RG24 8WG
Tel: 01256 372 200
e-mail: enquiries@corgi-gas.com
www.corgi-gas.com

ebuild
e-mail: info@ebuild.co.uk
www.ebuild.co.uk
A directory of building products and services for self-build, DIY and house renovation.

Federation of Master Builders,
Gordon Fisher House,
14-15 Great James Street,
London WC1N 3DP
Tel: 020 7242 7583
Fax: 020 7404 0296
e-mail: central@fmb.org.uk
www.fmb.org.uk

HM Customs and Excise
Tel: 0845 010 9000
www.hmce.gov.uk

HomePro.com, Quadrant House, The Quadrant, Hoylake, Wirral CH47 2EE
Tel: 08707 344 344
www.homepro.com
Find reputable tradespeople.

Improveline, Bond House,
347–353 Chiswick High Road,
London W4 4HS
Tel: 0845 359 3000
Fax: 0845 359 3001
e-mail: info@improveline.com
www.improveline.com
Directory of tradespeople; search by postcode.

Institute of Electrical Engineers,
Savoy Place, London WC2R 0BL

Tel: 0207 240 1871
Fax: 0207 240 7735
e-mail: postmaster@iee.org
www.iee.org.uk

Institution of Structural Engineers, 11 Upper Belgrave Street, London SW1X 8BH
Tel: 020 7235 4535
Fax: 020 7235 4294
e-mail: mail@istructe.org.uk
www.istructe.org.uk

Joint Contracts Tribunal, 9 Cavendish Place, London W1G 0QD
www.jctltd.co.uk
If you require a contract with your builder, the JCT have a standard contract you can use.

Office of the Deputy Prime Minister (ODPM), Enquiry Service, 26 Whitehall, London SW1A 2WH
Tel: 020 7944 4400
Fax: 0207 944 6589
www.planning.odpm.gov.uk
Planning procedures in England and Wales.

Planning Service, Clarence Court, 10–18 Adelaide Street, Belfast BT2 8GB
Tel: 028 9054 0540
Fax: 028 9054 0665
e-mail:
planning.service.hq@nics.gov.uk
www.doeni.gov.uk/planning
Planning process in N. Ireland.

Royal Incorporation of Architects in Scotland, 15 Rutland Square, Edinburgh EH1 2BE
Tel: 0131 229 7545
Fax: 0131 228 2188
e-mail: info@rias.org.uk
www.rias.org.uk

Royal Institute of British Architects (RIBA), 66 Portland Place, London W1B 1AD
Tel: 0207 580 5533
Fax 0207 255 1541
e-mail: info@inst.riba.org
www.architecture.com

Royal Institute of Chartered Surveyors, RICS Contact Centre, Surveyor Court, Westwood Way, Coventry CV4 8JE
Tel: 0870 333 1600
Fax: 0207 222 9430
e-mail: contactrics@rics.org.uk
www.rics.org/public

Scottish Executive, 2H Victoria Quay, Edinburgh EH6 6QQ
Tel: 0131 556 8400; Helpline: 08457 741 741
Fax: 0131 244 8240
e-mail: ceu@scotland.gov.uk
www.scotland.gov.uk/planning
For information on planning procedures in Scotland.

NatWest

Home Working

Working from home, either for yourself in a home-based business or salaried to a company, is fast becoming the chosen way of working that many of us are opting for.

Deciding whether home working suits the way you operate is a primary consideration, as organisational skills and discipline to get the job done are strong requirements. Then there is the matter of work space. Will you need a small office or just a desk in a corner of a room? Maybe the most important factor is money. If you are starting off on your own, make sure you have financial backing not only to pay for essential equipment, but also to cover you if business turns out to be slow at certain times.

First steps

It's estimated that by 2005 over 6 million people will be working at home in the UK. Some will be employed by large companies, but the majority are expected to be self-employed sole traders.

If you decide to use your home for work, whether it's the kind of work you already do for someone else or a new business idea that may involve others, you need to prepare thoroughly.

Making the decision

Be honest with yourself

Working at home can be lonely. It can also become addictive. Have you got what it takes to survive? Try to answer the following questions honestly.

- Could you cope with not having anyone to bounce ideas off if something goes wrong?
- Would you miss the social life of colleagues?
- Could you motivate yourself to meet targets and deadlines?
- Do you have the self-discipline to make yourself work, even if the sun is shining? Equally, would you be able to cut off mentally at the end of the day?
- Can you be organised and keep your work separate from your living space?
- How well would you cope with financial insecurity?
- Could you say 'no' to a client or customer, because the work would overstretch you?
- Will you be able to earn enough to live on?

You should feel confident in all these areas before you start on the practical preparations for working at home.

Will you be a nuisance or break any rules?

If you plan to work at home, you have to be careful that you won't fall foul of the law or upset your neighbours. In

Try and keep your work area totally separate from your living area

Weighing it up

For:
- It's comfortable and pleasant. Your surroundings are your own.
- It's cheap. No more travel costs and no need to rent an office.
- Instead of travelling to work, you can be earning money or doing something else.
- You can tailor the hours you work to your needs and those of your customers. You can generally work at your own pace.
- As your own manager, you are in control.
- No one ever got rich working for someone else!

Against:
- The lease or deeds of your home may prevent you from using it for business.
- You might need extra insurance and home security.
- If you work alone, you could feel isolated.
- You might find it hard to resist distractions.
- Your income may be irregular and you may have to chase late payments.

general, if you're engaged in a quiet, desk-based activity, no one is going to mind. But you may find that the terms of your mortgage or lease specifically exclude you conducting any business that creates noise, makes a mess, or involves clients' cars or large delivery vehicles parking in your street. And if you do cause disruption, your neighbours may complain to the local authority, which can take steps to limit what you do (*see* Make sure it's legal, p200).

Deciding where to work

If you are going to function well, you need a proper space in which to operate. It may seem at first that all you need is a desktop for your computer or whatever major equipment you require for your business, but in reality you need much more.

Whatever your business, try to establish a reasonable-sized area to work in, with enough storage space so that the things you need are close to hand. It also helps, psychologically, to keep everything associated with work separate from the rest of your home: this can make it quicker to settle into a work frame of mind and allows you to get away from it all at the end of the day. If you can't shut a door on your workspace, consider putting up a curtain to hide desk and shelves, so you don't feel work is hanging over you.

In deciding where to work, and depending on what you do, you may need to consider some of the following.

Make sure it's legal

When setting up a business, unless it's small-scale and entirely desk-based, it's best to make thorough enquiries with your local council's Trading Standards department to make sure that you are complying with **current laws and regulations**.

- Check your mortgage or lease and your house insurance to make sure that there are no clauses prohibiting the **business use of your home**. Change your insurer if necessary. Many house contents policies now include cover for basic office equipment but there's usually a fairly low limit. If you will be using other types of business equipment such as specialist tools, your normal contents insurance is unlikely to cover it. Also, you should inform all your insurers as a matter of course that you have become self-employed because it may affect premium and/or payment of future claims. This is particularly important if you use your car for business.
- You may need **planning permission** for change of use if using more than half your home as an office or an outbuilding as a workplace.
- You may need a **local authority or government licence** to run your business, particularly if you want to run an agency, look after children or animals, or offer physical therapies or treatments.
- You will have to be inspected by the **Environmental Health** department or other relevant authority if you work with food, look after children or animals or offer physical therapies or treatments.
- If clients or customers visit you, you should have **public liability insurance** and, if you handle money on behalf of clients, you should have professional indemnity and/or fidelity bonding.

- Changing the function of rooms to create a dedicated workplace. If you can clear away your things completely when your work is done, a room that isn't used much – a dining room or spare room – could double as a workspace.
- Ensuring there is enough natural light and ventilation – especially if you're thinking of putting a desk on a landing or in an area under the stairs.
- Installing extra shelving and other storage.
- Fitting up a basement, attic or outbuilding. Get estimates for how much this will cost and make sure there would be sufficient heating. If your business is noisy – for instance if you are a composer or a machinist – you might consider soundproofing.
- Providing safe storage facilities if your work involves hazardous materials.
- Providing parking facilities if customers will be visiting.
- Extra plumbing – sinks or a toilet – if you are offering treatments or therapy. You may need a special power supply for machines or you may have to make structural alterations to accommodate heavy equipment.
- Access for deliveries, if you are

Make sure you have the discipline required to work efficiently from home...

likely to need regular supplies for your work.

- Extra insurance – *see* p241. If you are investing in expensive equipment, your insurer could insist on extra locks, security lights or an alarm.

Basic forward planning

It would be rash to contemplate starting a business at home without the finances to tide you over in the early stages as you get yourself established. These could be savings, a loan or an overdraft facility (*see* Money and insurance, pp238–41). When working out your financial needs for the first year, take into account not just your usual bills but also items that you may not have had to purchase before, such as special insurance, licences, maintenance and repair of equipment, and so on.

Once you've worked out your various commitments, you'll be able to work out how much you need to earn. You also need to take into account periods when you have no work, cannot work or want to go on holiday.

Market research is a key part of your preparation. You need to be confident that there will be enough demand for whatever product, service or skills you hope to sell. It's also advisable to have some customers or potential customers in your sights when starting out.

Last but not least, inform your local tax office (*see* Dealing with tax, pp242–5). Both tax and National Insurance are now dealt with by the Inland Revenue, so you only need to register your self-employment once.

Planning the workspace

It's worth investing in quality furniture and equipment to make working at home comfortable and convenient. If your work area is on view to visitors to your home, you might want to choose furniture to blend in with your surroundings, concealing the fact that it's a work area.

Making yourself comfortable

Working from home is a great idea, as long as it doesn't eventually damage your physical or mental health because you are working in unsuitable conditions. You should make sure you have good lighting and ventilation at your workstation, adequate heating, freedom of movement, room to lay out your work, and suitable storage of papers, files and work tools close at hand. You should also be able to conduct your work in safety and to guarantee the safety of the public who may visit your workplace.

If you have a room or area dedicated to your work, you need to think about the following:

General conditions

Light Working under constant electric light without any natural light has been found to promote headaches and depression. If you don't have natural light, invest in some natural light spectrum bulbs that simulate daylight.

Ventilation If you're working in a room without a window that opens, you should consider installing a small air conditioner or – if it is, say, an attic – investigate the possibility of installing a new window.

Heating If a room is cold and damp, it will not only affect you but it will also certainly affect computers, photocopiers and fax machines, as well as any papers you store. Your computer printer will not feed paper through unless it is completely dry. If you are working in an outbuilding, you will need to insulate it and install some form of heating.

Work area

- Make sure you have a large enough work surface. Computers and computer equipment, for example, take

Make sure you have sufficient desk space to work on or lay out paperwork

up a lot of room. Do you have desk space to lay papers down and to read or write?

- Do you have enough shelving, filing cabinets or storage – preferably actually in your work area – so that you can access everything easily? If you work with tools, make sure you have hooks or racks so that you can put the tools away when you have finished with them.
- Make sure your work area is big enough. Can you move around it easily? Can you work without tripping over boxes of files on the floor, and can you open the door properly without it banging into your desk?
- If your work surfaces are too high or too low, you may develop neck, shoulder or back problems.
- Similarly, you will need a well-designed, adjustable chair to work from.

Equipment

- Do you have adequate power points for all your equipment? Plugging everything into extension leads is a potential

A well set-up office should have room for a computer, as well as storage

Taking steps to protect your work

Your working area at home should be well safeguarded.

- Make sure you have **sufficient security**. If it's known that you work from home, thieves may think you keep money there. You may need better locks, a security light, or perhaps an alarm system.
- **Protect any machinery** from tampering or theft by fitting safety guards and keeping them locked away. Protect computers and peripherals with dust covers.
- Make sure you're not overloading **power points** (*see* Your electricity supply, pp122–5).
- Keep relevant **fire safety equipment** close at hand (*see* Safety at home, pp406–9).
- Keep **back-up copies** of all work in a lockable fireproof filing cabinet in another area of the house.

fire risk and lots of trailing cables around a room can cause accidents. Can cables be hidden away?

- You will probably need a telephone point and extension in your work area. You might want a dedicated land phone number and perhaps a separate, dedicated modem line.
- It's vital to have fire safety equipment handy. You'll need to know what type of small fire extinguisher or fire blanket you need for any special pieces of equipment you have.

- If your work involves preparing food or providing therapeutic treatment, do you know what you need to do in order to meet hygiene standards?

It is a good idea to separate your work from your home life as much as possible. Make it a rule not to take work out of your work area. If your work is going through a difficult patch, you'll be able to lift your spirits simply by closing the door on your workspace and going to another part of your home to relax and get away from it all.

Wash hands regularly if working with foodstuffs

Useful equipment

Technology has made working from home very much easier, but think carefully about what you need each piece of equipment to do – equipment you already have for leisure use may not be sufficiently fast or reliable for your new work requirements.

If you're buying new, check the small print for technical and maintenance support (and what happens to these if the company goes bust), and what any warranties cover. Look for good deals but don't skimp on quality.

If specialist equipment is expensive and likely to need frequent upgrading, consider leasing some or all of it.

Computers Be sure your computer system has enough memory for the needs of your business and that you can upgrade easily. For e-mail, which is used extensively in business, you'll need a computer that can connect to the Internet and an account with a service provider.

Fax machine or a scanner linked to the computer Both enable you to send illustrations as well as text.

Answerphone/voicemail To take messages while you're out.

Mobile phone or WAP phone So that when you're on the move people can contact you and you can contact them, either verbally or with text messages or e-mail.

Laptop computer If you travel a lot, a laptop computer may be a better choice than a desktop, so that you can call up and amend files while you're in meetings or work on a train journey.

Photocopier A fax machine or scanner can double as a photocopier, but if you need to do lots of copying it's worth getting a photocopier. Small copiers can be leased quite cheaply and are easily upgraded.

Health and computers

If you're working from home, you'll probably have a computer. The following points will help you use your computer safely.

- Fit a glare filter to protect your eyes from glare and flickering.
- Make sure that your office space has sufficient overhead lighting and, especially, that it does not flicker. Lack of light or flickering lights can cause eye strain and bring on headaches. Using a desk lamp may also help, as long as the light does not reflect off the screen into your eyes and end up dazzling you.
- Take a break from working at the computer every hour – otherwise you risk getting headaches, eye strain and posture problems.
- Regulate the air in the room with an electric fan in the summer or portable heater during the winter to maintain a comfortable temperature.
- Look up from your computer every 10–15 minutes and focus on the middle distance, to relieve eye strain.
- Have regular eye tests.
- Guard against repetitive strain injury (RSI), a condition in which prolonged performance or repetitive actions cause pain in tendons and muscles. Stop working if your hands and wrists start aching.
- Ensure that your desk is at the right height so that you can work at your keyboard with relaxed shoulders, with your forearms straight at the wrist, parallel to the floor and not resting on the keyboard or desk.
- Sit at an adjustable chair when you're working – see above. Your feet should be flat on the floor, your thighs parallel to the floor or with

TOP TIPS

Staring at a **dirty screen** will simply bring on eye strain and headaches, so it is important to clean your equipment regularly. Computers can become dirty and dusty because of the effects of static. Reduce static by wiping the outside of your monitor and the surrounding wires with a cloth dampened with vinegar. Vinegar will reduce the static and so prevent dust from clinging to surfaces.

Using a mix of **half ammonia (or vinegar) and half water**, you can clean the dirtiest portions of your keyboard. This will get the grease out that has been accumulating from your skin. For a more thorough clean, use methylated spirits with a cotton bud to clean the most detailed pieces of your computer keyboard.

your knees slightly below your hips.

- Make sure that the screen is at the correct height, so that you're not bending your neck backwards to look up at it or bending to look down at it.
- Don't use the computer at night or have it in the bedroom. Computers throw out powerful electromagnetic fields and can disrupt sleep patterns.
- Plants can improve an office environment by releasing oxygen and freshening the air quality. A few, well-chosen indoor plants (*see* pp102–3) can restore moisture to the dry environment caused by printers, computers and other work equipment.
- Keep your work area clean and tidy. (If you deal in foodstuffs or any product that demands hygiene safety standards, this should already be a daily part of your work routine.) Put aside time every few weeks to properly clean office equipment. Switch off computers or other electrical equipment before dusting. Use a soft brush (eg. a make-up brush) to get between the keys on a keyboard to remove any dust or an old toothbrush for really stubborn stains.

TOP TIP

If you work with a laptop, the finger touch **control pad** quickly becomes unresponsive. Switch off, dampen a kitchen towel with a little vinegar and wipe all around the control pad. The pad is now responsive and smooth once again.

Typing on a keyboard day in, day out can bring on repetitive strain injury

Organising yourself

The most important element to consider when working from home is the effective use of your time. Discipline is essential as time can easily be wasted and you may find yourself becoming increasingly stressed by the lack of progress you have made at the end of a day.

Here are a few, simple guidelines to help you manage your work time more effectively – and therefore, hopefully, increase your earning potential.

Allocate tasks

Planning is the key to managing work time, whether you work from home or not. We are all different in our approach to work. Some of us are more alert first thing in the morning; other take time to get going and become more energetic after lunch. Decide when the best time is for you and schedule in the most demanding tasks to do during those hours. Other more routine jobs (such as filing, correspondence, sorting out data for backing up and storing) can be performed when you are not firing on all cylinders!

Use the spare minutes between big tasks to make phone calls or tidy your working space.

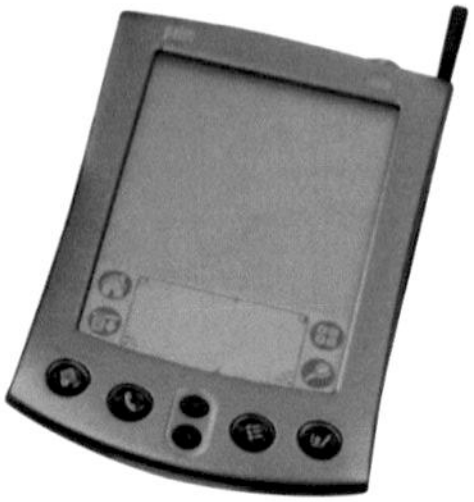

A palm pilot could help you to structure your working day

Plan ahead

Write down a work plan for the week, scheduling in the urgent or more difficult tasks during your peak working hours. Highlight any appointments or meetings, writing the time and place clearly so there will be no chance of any mistakes. Keep this work plan where you can see it at all times – maybe on the wall or a noticeboard – and cross off jobs once they have been carried out. This

Diaries, palm pilots or personal organisers are invaluable tools to keep you up with the day-to-day work plan

simple act of striking through an achieved goal can really boost your self-achievement and encourage you to fulfil the remaining tasks still left.

Appointments

Keep a diary or personal organiser with you at all times, as well as a larger diary that remains in your home office. As soon as you make an appointment, put it in your personal diary, as well as the home office one. If you mislay or lose one, you always have a backup record of any arrangements. Make a note the day before any meeting to confirm that you have the correct time and it is still going ahead. Enter all appointments on your weekly planner. Electronic palm pilots are extremely useful for carrying appointments, addresses, reminder notes or anything else you find useful around with you in one small, compact gadget.

Set financial goals

Make sure you keep track of your finances. Do not let relevant paperwork build up as you will soon lose track of your situation. Set targets that you can achieve, rather than over ambitious ones that will lead to disappointment.

Reward yourself

When you have completed all the tasks you have set yourself, give yourself a reward. This might be as simple as a mid-morning coffee break or a pamper massage at the end of a hard week. After all, working for yourself should be an enjoyable experience.

Computer needs

Buying a personal computer has become simpler, with high-street chains now offering after-sales support. Some larger stores even offer fully guaranteed upgrades.

Although many computer experts still say that having a PC built to your specification or building your own offers the best value, high-street chains can often undercut specialist shops through sheer purchasing power. Before buying a PC, it's a good idea to check what the various components do and which PCs are best suited to different types of tasks.

What do you get in a PC?

Operating system

This is the software that controls the basic operation of a computer. A typical operating system controls the peripheral devices such as printers, organises the filing system and runs other programs.

Central processing unit

The central processing unit (CPU), often called a processor, is the heart of any PC. Essentially it controls how fast applications run. Processors are classified in three ways:

- By manufacturer, of which Intel is the most common. Intel is the market leader, but rival AMD offers processors that are fully compatible with Intel chips and are often cheaper.
- With a description of the processor's class. The class is either a name or a number describing the level of advancement. For example, an Intel Pentium 4 is the fourth version of the Pentium-class chips and will have more

Think about whether you are going to need a laptop PC

features than a Pentium 3. However, some of the features of the Pentium 4 may not be relevant for home users or may work only with very specific applications.
- With a speed rating measured in megahertz (MHz) or gigahertz (GHz). This is similar to the litre rating on a car engine: a 1.1 litre car has less horsepower than a 2.4 litre estate. In the same way, an Intel Pentium 3 650MHz processor has less power than an Intel Pentium 3 running at 850MHz. The GHz rating means the unit is measured in thousands, so an Intel Pentium 4 runs at 1.8GHz (1800MHz).

The speed of the processor is not the same as the speed of the PC because, like a car, the PC is the sum of all its parts. A fast CPU will be hampered if the rest of the PC is unable to keep up with the speed and performance of the processor.

Upgrading tip Processors are upgradable, but consult the manual for details of the PC motherboard before upgrading. This will have crucial information about the types of processor your PC can use and which settings you need to change. Without this information you may destroy your CPU.

Upgradability

When buying a PC, upgradability is a key factor in ensuring that your PC doesn't slip into obsolescence too quickly. Check that what you are buying:

- has at least two free **PCI (peripheral component interconnect) slots** that will allow you to add internal upgrades such as a graphics accelerator card, a secondary sound card or the next big thing – whatever that may be
- has at least one free **RAM (random access memory) slot**. Adding more memory will generally give a flagging PC improved performance
- has not already been **upgraded to its maximum level**. Often, 'bargain' PCs will have a respectable basic specification, but further enquiry may reveal that you will not be able to upgrade or add more memory.

Hard disk

The hard disk drive is used to store all your software and files. There are two main criteria for hard disks.

- Type – normally either SCSI or IDE. SCSI is only used where speed is of the essence and is not normally found in home PCs. IDE is found in over 90% of home PCs.
- Storage capacity – this is measured in gigabytes (GB). Typically even the largest games or applications will not use more than 1GB of hard disk storage. Most hard disks start at 40GB but if you're on a

A typical PC specification	
Operating system	Windows 2000/XP
Processor	Intel Pentium 4 – 2000MHz (2GHx)
RAM	256MB
Hard disk size	40GB
Graphics card type	ATI 8500 LE
Graphics card memory	32MB
Devices	Samsung CD-2412 CD-ROM drive 1.44MB floppy drive Sound Blaster 16 sound card
Interfaces	2 serial; 1 parallel 2 USB

tight budget, even an 8GB hard disk will allow for plenty of applications to be installed on your PC. If you are running out of hard disk space, provided you have the original CD-ROM that installed your software, you can always remove software from your hard disk and reinstall it as required.

Upgrading tip Adding a second hard drive, although time-consuming, is a relatively simple upgrade. Nearly every PC will have at least one free connection for another disk.

RAM memory

Random access memory (RAM) is used by the PC to execute applications. A simple rule of thumb is the more the merrier. RAM is measured in megabytes (MB) and most applications will need at least 32MB of memory, but with memory prices dropping constantly, software developers are making their programs more memory-hungry. One word of caution – when buying a secondhand PC, it's wise to make sure that the PC uses the more modern type of DIMM memory, which is easily available, and not older SIMM memory modules, which are increasingly scarce and offer slower performance than DIMM.

Upgrading tip If you use any memory-intensive applications such as action video games or graphics, you may need more memory. Larger memory manufacturers offer a service where you specify the make and model of your PC and they send you the correct memory.

Graphics card

Computer games are the fastest-growing entertainment form. Consequently, the variety of graphics cards for the PC is huge. Manufacturers are constantly trying to outdo each other and the top of the pack changes weekly. A general rule of thumb is that graphics cards with a lot of memory will often provide good performance.

Upgrading tip Whether you are upgrading your PC, building your own or buying secondhand, you need to make sure that the interface on the graphics card matches the port on the computer's motherboard. The most modern type of interface is called AGP and provided your PC has an AGP port then any AGP card will work. The older format is called PCI. PCI cards are often found in older PCs and don't accept AGP-based graphics cards.

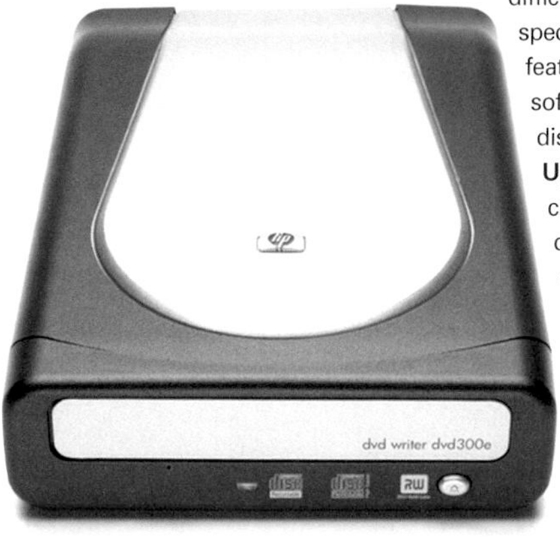

You can add a DVD-writer to your computer to create your own DVDs

CD-ROM and DVD drives

Most new PCs are supplied with a DVD-ROM drive which allows you to access conventional software and music CDs, as well as DVD films. A more common feature is the ability to write your own CDs or create your own DVDs. You can use the CD/DVD-writer to create your own video disks, music collections or digital pictures, or to back up your important files.

Both the software and music industries are concerned about piracy and, consequently, using a CD/DVD-writer to make duplicates of copyrighted material is illegal and often difficult to do because of special anticopying features on video, software and music disks.

Upgrading tip You can add a CD or DVD drive to an older PC using an external interface such as a Firewire or USB port. Although this is slightly more expensive than an internal drive, it doesn't require any special training and can be done in about five minutes.

Choosing the right computer

PCs are very adaptable but picking one that fits your needs is a matter of choosing the right combination of components to suit the type of software you intend to run. Identify what you will use your PC for, then find out what combination will match your requirements.

What do you want to do?

I just want to play games and maybe surf the Internet

When looking for a PC for games, a modern processor running at over 1.8GHz combined with a powerful graphics card such as a Geforce mark 3 is a good start. Memory is key for games, so look for lots of system RAM – 512MB is recommended. Games are often very memory hungry, so a graphics card with at least 32MB of video RAM is highly recommended. Any PC that can play the latest games will be able to surf the Internet comfortably using a modem. A basic operating system, such as Windows 2000 or Windows XP, should be sufficient for gaming. Games are generally quite large so a 80GB hard disk should be a minimum requirement.

Upgrading tip Using an Accelerated Graphics Port (AGP)-based graphics card as a separate component, rather than a built-in one, makes it easier to keep up with new versions.

TOP TIP

If you want to limit your spend, you may well be able to do without some of the more **expensive options** on offer, for now, and upgrade later. If the jargon is new to you, check terms in the glossary on pp220–5.

I just want to write letters and send e-mail

Word processing and e-mail are very low intensity applications and consequently don't require the fastest PCs. Simple tasks like writing letters and e-mail are the perfect reasons for finding a secondhand bargain. A PC such as an Intel Pentium 2 or an AMD K class processor with only 32MB RAM and less than 8GB hard disk space will be able to offer a comfortable level of performance. If you're doing a lot of writing, a larger screen could be a better investment as well as a printer.

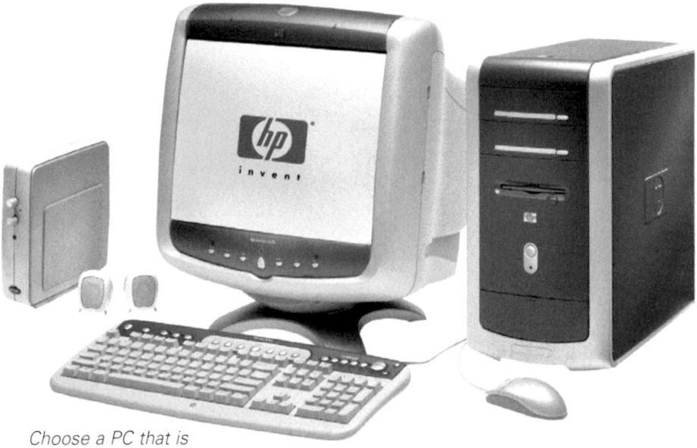

Choose a PC that is right for the sort of jobs you are going to use it for

I'm a creative sort of person and want lots of flexibility from my PC

The PC is fast becoming the tool of choice for musicians, artists, animators, and video producers. Most creative tasks are quite resource hungry but provided you have a good base to start from, the PC can grow over time to suit the task. Custom-built PCs are most suited to creative tasks. For example, you can specify a PC that can support two CPUs although you needn't have the second processor installed at the time of purchase.

Another example of forward planning is to have your hard disk bays fitted in a removable cage, so you can quickly add or switch between hard disk drives for large video files, pictures or music tracks. If you have a specialist application in mind, it's often worth talking to a local shop about building a machine dedicated to the task, instead of the high street chains that tend to treat PCs as a consumer commodity. For graphics and video, as much memory as possible will help speed things up.

Upgrading tip Upgradability is the key to flexibility. Buying a PC with a highly upgradable motherboard, and a big empty case where all your components will sit, is a good start for a person keen to create their own PC-based music studio or video editing suite.

I want to set up a computer at home similar to my work PC

If you want or need to work at home sometimes, it's probably best to pick a PC based on your office specification. This should also include software applications similar to your work PC. Many companies have a person or department responsible for information technology (IT) and, depending on your employer and work role, you may even be able to buy directly through your company (often at a discount). They might also configure your PC to access parts of the company network. The type of PC you need will depend on the type of applications you use at work but most workplace PCs will be devoid of multimedia features such as fast graphics or sound facilities.

I'm on a tight budget and just want a basic computer

The magic number touted by high street chains for a basic new PC is around £1,000, but considering that most of the basic computer applications such as word processing,

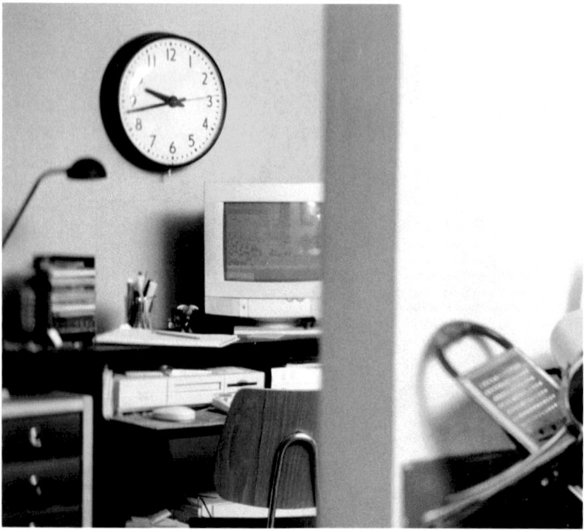

Set your computer up similar to your work PC if you occasionally work from home

spreadsheets, databases, e-mail, Internet surfing and simple games have been around for over a decade, a second-hand PC that is two or three years old is more than capable of performing these tasks.

The main difference is that the applications will need to match the older hardware. The most current version of the popular Microsoft Office application is MS Office XP. However, Office 95 still has 90% of the functions of its more advanced sibling and requires only a Pentium 133MHz processor, 24MB of RAM, and less than 1GB of hard disk space. A PC with this kind of specification can be bought fairly inexpensively. Buy the software first, since it's easier to match the PC to the software than the other way round. Software manufacturers are reluctant to sell older and cheaper software ahead of new expensive packages, but mail-order or second-hand PC suppliers generally also provide older software. Even bigger chains often offer old software at reduced prices. Whatever your source, check the specification sheet for compatibility with the PC you plan to buy.

Antivirus software

A **computer virus** is a small program that passes onto your computer without your knowledge or consent, with the intention to cause damage or to allow an outsider to break into your files. The virus will usually try to pass itself onto another computer by attaching a copy of itself to e-mails and files. Not all viruses have malicious intent but they can cause the computer to behave oddly and crash.

Antivirus software is available for nearly all types of computers. However, most manufacturers will require you to pay a yearly subscription to provide you with protection against the latest viruses. Without these regular updates, you will be vulnerable to new types of viruses and, in the event of a virus attack, you will not be eligible for technical support from the antivirus company.

Even with antivirus software you are vulnerable to attack, so take these precautions.

- If you receive **unsolicited e-mail** that has an attached program or document you should, before opening it, check with the sender that it was sent intentionally and not generated by a virus.
- **Illegally copied software**, often found at car boot sales and markets, is a notable source of viruses and should be avoided.
- If you often use **floppy disks**, remember to remove them from the disk drive before turning on your PC – floppy disks can carry viruses that can be transmitted as the computer is switched on.
- If you have **vital files** such as financial accounts, if possible try and copy them to floppy disk as a precaution against a virus attack or hard disk failure.

Apple computers

Apple fans extol the virtues of Apple's easy-to-use operating system, reliability, and sleek design ethic. However, there are far fewer business and leisure applications for Apple computers and accessories tend to be slightly more expensive. To be fair, the more recent Apple computers have tended towards using the more common components found in PCs but the selection is still reduced because, even though an item may have hardware compatibility, not all manufacturers will have the necessary software to make the hardware function.

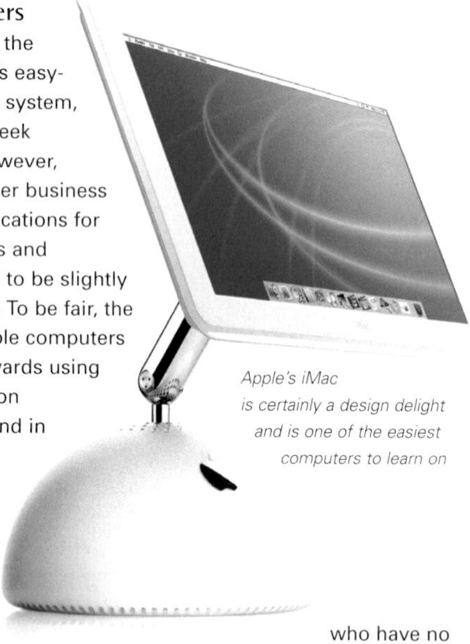

Apple's iMac is certainly a design delight and is one of the easiest computers to learn on

Apple computers are favoured by many people working in creative fields, and the reliability of the operating system and applications make it a good tool for music, video, and graphic design.

iMac

The iMac has won awards for its design chic and has been popular with first-time buyers who have no preference towards the PC. The design was primarily chosen because of the low build cost and consumer-friendly styling. The iMac comes with built-in Internet connectivity and is one of the easiest computers for the beginner to use.

Apple G4/G5 desktop computers

Apple has chosen to base its computers on chips developed by Motorola and IBM. These Power PC class processors use a completely different architecture from Intel and AMD Pentium class chips. Consequently, the associated speed rating for Apple computers, measured in megahertz, is, on paper, often considerably less than Intel or AMD chips. However, in practice, the fastest Apple desktops are normally equivalent to PCs due to the elegance of their design.

In contrast, though, to very high-specification PCs, which can also double as workgroup servers or powerful workstations, Apple computers tend to be aimed at individual users.

Apple iBook and Powerbook laptops

Like its desktop counterparts, the Apple notebook range has a striking look, offering light chassis designs and good performance. However, with an effective monopoly on pricing, Apple notebooks tend to be much more expensive than PC laptops that offer equivalent performance. Like its desktop range, Apple has included the high-speed Firewire port in its laptops to provide more external connections, but the range of optional bays is very limited.

PDAs

Personal Digital Assistant (PDA) is an umbrella term that is applied to personal organisers, handheld PCs or even, to use Microsoft's term, PocketPCs. All these devices:

- typically weigh less than 1 kilo (2lb)
- have a small LCD screen
- have a small internal memory to store a handful of built-in applications and a few optional ones.

Nearly all PDAs can connect to a **desktop PC or Mac** to allow files such as address books and diaries to be synchronised, and more advanced models have built-in mobile phones or the ability to connect to a mobile or land-based telephone line. When buying a PDA, you should think through how you may want to use it now and over the next couple of years.

Matching software to systems
Unlike the desktop PC market, which is dominated by Microsoft Windows, there are many operating systems for PDAs and software will only work on the corresponding operating system. The main rivals are Microsoft PocketPC, Palm OS and Symbian Epoc – these make up over 90% of the market. Few manufacturers develop software for all three operating systems, so if you have a particular application in mind, it's best to find out about the application's requirements before you decide which hardware to buy.

Each **operating system** will have basic diary, contact book, word processing and communication facilities. It's worth noting that PDA versions of popular applications will almost certainly be cut down and will not offer all the functions of their desktop equivalent.

Understanding technospeak

Technology comes with words and abbreviations that are confusing. In this glossary, what an acronym stands for and what the thing is used for may come before a technical definition.

AGP Accelerated graphics port. Improves the performance of 3D applications in a computer. AGP technology provides a high memory 'fast-lane' for graphics data by providing a dedicated high-speed port for the movement of data between a PC's graphics controller and system memory.

ADSL Stands for asymmetric digital subscriber line, loop or link. Used for transmitting data through existing copper telephone wires. A telephone line signal is effectively split into two, one for voice and the other for data. ADSL technology can transmit data 10 to 40 times faster than a normal telephone modem (depending on the service available).

Application Computer program or software designed for a particular purpose. such programs include word processors, desktop publishing programs, databases, spreadsheet packages, graphics programs, e-mail programs and Internet browsers.

Bandwidth In computing and communications, the rate of data transmission, measured in bits per second (bps).

Bits and bytes Bit stands for binary digit (0 or 1); the smallest unit of data in a computer. The speed at which information is transmitted is measured in bits per second (bps). Eight bits make a byte – enough computer memory to store a single character. For example, the capital letter A would be stored in a single byte of memory as the bit pattern 01000001.

Broadband Technology that provides fast data transmission for communications – it has a high bandwith, so can transmit lots of bits per second (bps). With broadband connection, you can have a computer, television and phone all working simultaneously on one line.

Browser Computer program which is used to navigate (browse) the Internet and to read html files, for example Microsoft Internet Explorer and Netscape Navigator.

Bus A set of parallel tracks – an electrical pathway – that carries digital signals within a computer's CPU (*see* below) and to peripherals (components outside the computer such as printers and scanners).

Cable modem Box supplied by cable companies as part of a cable connection to television, telephone and network services, including the Internet.

CD-ROM Stands for compact-disc read-only memory. A medium that can store programs, pictures, sound, films and other data. A computer needs a CD-ROM drive to be able to read a CD-ROM. The disk is read optically by passing a laser beam over the disk. CD-ROMs typically hold over 600 megabytes (MB) of data.

CD writer A computer component that allows you to write to, or copy to, CD-ROMs.

Central processing unit (CPU) The 'brain' of your computer – it executes individual program instructions and controls the operation of other parts (also called the central processor or a microprocessor). The speed of a CPU is measured in megahertz (MHz) – the greater the MHz, the faster the computer will work. A modern home computer might have 800 MHz or more.

Chip A complete electronic circuit on a slice of silicon (or other semiconductor) crystal only a few millimetres square.

Configuration The way in which a system, be it hardware and/or software, is set up.

Digital Information coded as numbers and transmitted as electronic pulses.

DIMM Dual in-line memory module. A DIMM is a double SIMM (single in-line memory module – *see* below).

Download To transfer data – programs, pictures, movie clips – from the Internet to a computer or from, say, a digital camera to a computer.

DVD Stands for digital versatile disk or digital video disk. Medium for storing digital information. DVDs can hold 14 times more data than CDs, but work in much the same way.

Ethernet Networking standard used for connecting several computers to make a local area network.

Firewall A security system built to block access to a particular computer or network while still allowing some types of data to flow in from and out onto the Internet.

FireWire A high-speed connection between as many as 63 electronic devices –

computers, camcorders, digital television sets, DVD players, scanners and colour printers – in one system.

Flash A popular browser-independent vector-graphic animation technology, which allows complex multimedia animations to be displayed on web pages with the necessary plug-ins.

Gigabyte (GB) A measure of memory capacity, equal to 1,024 megabytes (MB).

Hard disk The main storage media in a computer – data are read from and written to the hard disk by means of a disk drive. The hard disk may be permanently fixed into the computer or removable.

Hardware The mechanical, electrical and electronic components of any computer system.

HTML Stands for hypertext markup language. The standard for structuring and describing a document on the Internet.

IDE Intelligent drive electronics or integrated drive electronics standard. It is the most popular interface used for mass-storage devices where the controller is integrated into the disk drive.

Interface The point of contact between two computer programs or pieces of equipment. A printer interface, for example, is the cabling and circuitry used to transfer data from a computer to a printer.

Internet Global computer network connecting governments, companies, universities and many other networks and users. The world wide web (www) allows seamless browsing across the Internet via hypertext links.

ISDN Integrated services digital network. Internationally developed telecommunications system for sending signals in digital format, greatly increasing the amount of information that can be carried.

ISP Stands for Internet service provider. To access the Internet, you connect your computer via your phone line or broadband connection to an ISP, which is connected to the Internet. ISPs provide this access for a regular monthly fee or for free.

JPEG Joint Photographic Experts Group. A graphics file type used to display images on the Internet.

Kilobyte (KB) A unit of data equal to 1,024 bytes – stores about 1,000 characters of text.

LCD Stands for liquid-crystal display. Used in calculators, laptop computer screens, digital cameras and so on.

Link Short for hyperlink. Allows you to click with the mouse on underlined text or graphics and connect to another site in a web or computer document.

Mac Short for Macintosh, a range of computers manufactured by Apple, a US computer company.

Megabyte (MB) A unit of memory equal to 1,024 kilobytes (KB). Often called 'meg'.

Modem Short for modulator/ demodulator. Used for linking one computer to another anywhere in the world using an analogue telephone network.

Motherboard Also called a mainboard. Printed circuit board (pcb) that contains the main components of a microcomputer.

MP3 MPEG (Moving Pictures Expert Group)-1 Audio Layer 3. A way of compressing digital sound and audio files while retaining quality, allowing fast transmission via the Internet.

Network Method of connecting computers so that they can share data and peripheral devices, such as printers. One of the most common networking systems is Ethernet.

Operating system (OS) A program that controls the basic operation of a computer. A typical OS controls the peripheral devices such as printers, organises the filing system, communicates with the computer operator and runs other programs.

Parallel device A device that communicates binary data by sending the bits that represent each character simultaneously along a set of separate data lines, unlike a serial device.

PC Stands for personal computer, another name for microcomputer.

PDA Stands for personal digital assistant. Handheld computer designed to store names, addresses, diary information, and to send and receive e-mail.

Peripheral A device that connects to the computer and performs a role in its functions, such as modems, printers and monitors (screens).

Pixel Stands for picture element – a single dot on a computer screen. The number of pixels available determines the screen's resolution. Typical resolutions of microcomputer screens vary from 640 x 480 pixels to 800 x 600 pixels to 1,024 x 768 pixels.

Plug-in A small additional file that enhances a computer program's operations. Plug-ins can be downloaded easily from the Internet.

Port A socket in a computer that enables the processor to communicate with an external device. Computers may have ports for monitors, printers, modems, digital cameras and less commonly for hard disks and musical instruments (MIDI, the musical-instrument digital interface). Ports may be serial, parallel or USB.

Program A set of instructions that controls the operation of a computer.

Public-domain software Any computer program that is not under copyright and can therefore be used freely.

RAM Random Access Memory. Used by the computer to temporarily store information to and from the processor. Contents are lost when the computer is switched off.

RealPlayer Software for broadcasting live or pre-recorded sound and video over the Internet.

ROM Stands for read only memory. Loaded with permanent data and programs during manufacture.

Scart socket A 21-pin audio/video connector used in electronics equipment such as TV sets and video recorders.

SCSI Small computer system interface, pronounced 'scuzzy'. A method for connecting peripherals to a computer. A group of peripherals linked in series to a single SCSI port is called a daisy chain.

Search engine Computer program used for indexing, and finding, information on the Internet, such as AltaVista, Google, Lycos and Yahoo.

Serial device A device that communicates binary data by sending the bits that represent each character one by one along a single data line.

Shareware Software distributed free via the Internet or on disks given away with magazines. Users have the opportunity to test it before paying a small registration fee directly to the author. Shareware is not copyright-free, unlike public-domain software.

SIMM Single in-line memory module. Printed circuit board carrying multiple memory chips. A double SIMM is a DIMM.

Software A collection of programs and procedures for making a computer perform a specific task. Computers need two types of software: application software and systems software.

SVGA Super video graphics array. A graphic display standard for computer screens providing resolutions of either 800 x 600 pixels or 1,024 x 768 pixels.

USB Universal serial bus. Transmits data more quickly than serial or parallel devices, and allows devices to be connected and disconnected without switching off the computer. Allows up to 127 peripherals – including joysticks, scanners, printers and keyboards – to be daisy-chained from a single socket, offering higher speeds and improved plug-and-play facilities.

URL Stands for uniform resource locator – a website address. A series of letters and/or numbers specifying the location of a document on the Internet. Every URL consists of a domain name, a description of the document's location within the host computer and the name of the document itself.

Vector-graphic Graphic stored in computer memory using geometric formulae, allowing the images to be transformed without losing picture quality.

VGA Stands for video graphics array. A graphic display standard for computer screens providing 16 colours and a resolution of 640 x 480 pixels, or 256 colours and a resolution of 320 x 200 pixels.

Virus Software that can replicate and transfer itself from one computer to another, without the user being aware of it. Some viruses are relatively harmless, but others are dangerous and can damage or destroy data. Anti-virus software should be installed on all computers and kept up to date. This is especially important for home computer users connected to the Internet via broadband or those who share files by e-mail or floppy disk.

Windows In computing, originally Microsoft's graphical user interface (GUI) for IBM PCs and computers running MS-DOS. Windows has developed into a family of operating systems that run on a variety of computers from pen-operated palmtop organisers to large, multi-processor computers in corporate data centres.

WAP Stands for wireless application protocol. Used for transmitting data between websites and mobile phones.

WWW Stands for world wide web. Hypertext (linking) system for publishing information on the Internet. WWW documents (web pages) are text files coded using html to include text and graphics, and are stored on a server connected to the Internet.

Making use of the Internet

The Internet originated in the 1970s with a handful of universities and government organisations passing information around in a private network. Nowadays, the Internet comprises millions of pages and is an invaluable tool for those working from home, as well as the office.

Choosing a service provider

Whichever way you choose to get on to the Internet, you will need to decide on an Internet Service Provider (ISP).

Free ISPs

Following the phenomenal success of Freeserve, launched as a free ISP in 1998, other providers started to offer access to the Internet without a monthly charge. These services have relied on users reading the numerous adverts on the ISP's main website, and buying things through the services available there.

Few of these sites offer unique content, but collect content found elsewhere on the Internet into one convenient place. Typically, free ISPs will use fixed national rate numbers and, because of the large number of users, connection speeds are often not as fast as those of ISPs that charge.

Fee-paying ISPs

There are still many people who pay for Internet connectivity.

E-mails can also contain attachments – files such as a large text documents or images – which can take time to download to your inbox (e-mail post box)

The average cost lies between £5 and £15 per month for a no-frills service. One advantage of fee-paying ISPs is that they tend not to bombard customers with advertisements. Also, these services generally have more incoming telephone lines available, so you can connect even during busy times.

Content-providing ISPs

Content providers, also called portals, require a monthly charge, provide services such as interactive games, blocking junk e-mails, restricting access of inappropriate material to children and a host of other features available to members. However, some users complain about the 'big brother' mentality of some of these ISPs.

E-mail services

Basic e-mail software is free and is included as standard with Windows or Apple computers. Like sending a letter, you just need to type in the e-mail address of the person you wish to correspond with and click on the 'send' button. A typical e-mail address will look like this: 'John.Smith@freeserve.co.uk'. The e-mail will not be delivered if you fail to place any of the full stops or the @ sign correctly.

Search engines

To find something on the web, you need to use a search engine. These free services **index web pages** and search them using your query. For example, typing in the words *used car dealers in London* will find web pages – possibly hundreds of thousands of them – that feature any of these words. However, if you surround the words with quote marks, the search engine will look for the exact phrase. This produces more precise results but requires a website to use that exact phrase on its main page. A compromise is to use the plus sign between the words – +used +car +dealers +London. The plus sign means the search engine will find web pages that contain all of the words, but not necessarily in that order.

Search engines often offer different results and features. Have a look at:
www.google.co.uk
www.yahoo.co.uk
www.excite.co.uk
www.altavista.co.uk
www.yell.co.uk

Type in the query 'search engine' to get a list of others.

E-mails can also contain attached files, although some ISPs place a limit on the size of the attachments you may send. Most ISPs have a web mail service that allows you to access your e-mail from any Internet browser, which is great if you move around a lot. Have a look at www.hotmail.com, which is currently the most popular web mail service.

Equipment for accessing the Internet		
Type	**Approximate hardware cost**	**Approximate running cost**
PC with modem and standard telephone line	Nearly all PCs come with a built-in modem, but if you need to add a modem, it should cost about £30	Using a modem costs the price of a local-rate telephone call, and phone companies are under increasing pressure to reduce the cost for Internet users
PC with DSL adapter and DSL-equipped telephone line	Digital Subscriber Line, often called broadband, will have an initial set-up fee of about £100, and may require an additional telephone line	DSL is an 'always-on' Internet connection, and is not charged by the minute, although there will be a monthly charge of between £25 and £40
PC with ISDN adapter and dedicated ISDN telephone line	ISDN is an established technology favoured by small businesses; set-up cost, including hardware and installation, can run to several hundred pounds	ISDN is, like DSL, an 'always-on' technology, but phone companies also charge fees for sending and receiving data – however, this is less than a phone call
Cable modem connected either to a PC or a set-top box with a keyboard	Normally sold as part of a cable television system, set-up costs are generally less than £100	Cable modems are an 'always-on' connection, and have no running cost besides a fixed monthly fee, which is comparable to DSL but often slightly more owing to the faster connection speeds
Satellite modem connected to a PC	Although still rare in the UK, satellite transmission of requested Internet pages is catching on in the USA and Europe, but initial costs of equipment and sign-up fees are high	Satellite systems have monthly charges similar to DSL, but many companies also charge for the amount of data you download, with current prices of about £1 per 100 MB
Digital set-top boxes such as Sky digital, with a keyboard	Although the equipment is often free, setting up may require an installation fee and a one-year payment in advance	Cost of a phone call, but often at a fixed rate, irrespective of the time of day

Equipment for accessing the Internet

Performance	Notes	Availability
Using a modem is the slowest method of Internet connection with a maximum speed of about 5KB per second, or 56 kilobaud per second (Kbps)	Modems have a built-in facsimile ability and are great for people who just want to send the occasional e-mail or fax	Huge number of service providers, with many offering free connection
DSL offers better performance than a modem, but is subject to a drop in performance when many users within the same local geographical area all use their DSL at the same time	DSL is not available in all areas due to the slow and expensive process of upgrading phone exchanges, and inferior copper wiring, to DSL-compatible alternatives	Only a handful of service providers offer DSL, mostly in larger cities
ISDN performance ranges from 12 KB (128 Kpbs) to 96 KB (768 Kpbs) and, unlike DSL, there is no drop in performance with a high density of local users	ISDN is expensive just for Internet usage, and always has a one-year minimum sign up, but ISDN lines are very reliable	Most large telephone companies can offer ISDN across the whole of the country
Cable modems perform at speeds up to 2,048 Kbps (2 MB), which is faster than DSL, and, although performance can suffer from a high number of local users, this loss of performance is negligible	Cable modems are becoming increasingly common with the two largest providers NTL and Telewest providing services in most cities. Due to their residential nature, cable modems are often not designed for small-business use	Limited to areas that can receive cable
Satellite modems have a receiving speed starting at 2,048 Kbps (2 MB), but can run as high as 41,448 Kbps (40 MB)	Satellite modems offer the fastest download speed for people who download shareware, movie trailers, or music, but are not suitable for Internet browsing	No UK suppliers; available through mail order to connect to several European services, (www.europeonline.com/www.star speeder.co.uk)
Performance varies between services, ranging from speeds equivalent to a traditional PC modem in a box, to performance similar to DSL	Useful for those who just want limited access to e-mail and the Internet but the set-top box is not upgradable and picture quality is poor	Available across the UK

Internet business

If you will be using the Internet for business, bear in mind that your requirements are more demanding than those of the casual user. It is doubly important that all your e-mails arrive and that your dial-up service always runs efficiently.

Avoid the temptation of free Internet Service Providers (ISPs) – they are fine for leisure use but tend to have a very large number of accounts, which can cause problems of service supply. In fact many free services specifically exclude business use.

Your telephone bill

If you are working from home you'll depend on the telephone quite heavily for business, so it's essential to have a **separate phone line** for your computer.

To keep your phone bills as low as possible, investigate **cheap-rate or un-metered access dial-up ISPs**. Some of these offer a free telephone number for connecting your computer to the Internet for a monthly fee. Even having free access at night and weekends can produce a significant cut in costs if you are building your own website.

Broadband connectivity, supplied across normal telephone lines or by cable companies, provides an always on, high-speed Internet connection, plus telephone connection, for a monthly subscription fee. You can use the telephone and remain online at the same time. Find out whether BT supplies broadband where you live by visiting www.bt.com. For cable broadband information, contact your local cable company.

Your own domain name

Consider having your own domain name. This is a memorable name for your Internet presence. In business, it's much better to have an e-mail address based on your business name – me@mybusiness.com – than a complicated rigmarole that incorporates your name and your ISP. As with customised telephone numbers, the aim of the domain name is to make it simple for your customers to memorise.

Once you have registered your business domain name, it remains yours wherever you take your Internet account. So if you aren't happy with the service you're receiving from your current ISP, you can move to another one but still keep your own e-mail and website addresses.

You can access your website remotely from a laptop or PDA

A few years ago registering your domain name was an expensive and complex process, but nowadays it is a lot easier and need cost only a few pounds. You can start by discovering if your chosen name is available – surf to www.nic.uk for UK domain names and for global ones (such as .com and .net) to www.internic.net. You'll find useful information on these sites about choosing and registering your domain name.

There are plenty of companies with whom you can register. Some even offer 'free' domain name registrations, but look carefully into what's on offer as there may be restrictions on transferring your name to another server. Once again, the advice is to be cautious of free services. Companies that specialise in Internet services for business, on the other hand, often offer good value package deals.

Does your business need a website?

Many people assume that a website is essential for any 21st-century business. But some activities just don't lend themselves to this type of marketing – or it may be that creating the right website would not prove **cost-effective**.

For example, if you were running a local employment agency for casual labour, your website could enable employers to advertise and potential workers to register online. However, updating an interactive site is expensive and it's unlikely in a small business that it would generate enough additional revenue to be worth the investment. A more realistic option would be a simple website advertising the business and the range of jobs catered for, and giving contact details. This type of site is often referred to as **brochureware** because it is essentially a company brochure published on the web.

Before investing in a website – whether designed yourself or by a professional – ask yourself a few **critical questions**.

- What **extra value** will a website add to your business for you and your customers?
- How many **visitors** would your site need to earn an acceptable return on investment? If a website is designed to generate cash this is easy to establish.
- Do your clients or potential customers have **access** to the Internet?
- Can your products or services easily be **delivered** nationally or even worldwide?
- Can you accept **payment** by credit card?
- Could a website open up a **market** that you currently can't reach?

Keep browsers up to date

A website is viewed using a piece of software called a browser. This accesses the files on the website and translates them into a visually coherent page on your computer screen. A browser also enables hyperlink navigation (*see* How a website works, below) and functions such as downloading files, filling in forms and watching live video.

The two main web browsers are Microsoft Internet Explorer and Netscape. Some ISPs – AOL, for example – provide a specially customised browser that enables you to access additional services available only to subscribers. But the two major browsers are available free on the web or on CD-ROMs given away with computer magazines. If you plan to take browser software from the Internet, bear in mind that the programs can be very large and take a long time to download. Rather than running up a large phone bill downloading a file, it may be cheaper to buy a magazine offering browser software on a free CD-ROM.

To get the best from the web it's important to keep your browser up to date. Increasing numbers of websites today use advanced features to bring you rich multimedia content and if your browser is an old version you may not be able to access this material. Updates are available on the web or on CD-ROM and it's a good idea to check for the latest version every few months.

If you're designing your own website you should bear in mind that different browsers

How a website works

A website is made up of a number of separate items of data called files. These can be text files (the copy on the page), formatting information files, picture files, sound files, video files, animation files and document files that the visitor can download to his or her computer and view separately.

Any number of files can make up a web page and any number of pages can make up a website. Visitors to the site use a browser that combines all the files into a recognisable form. What makes a web page special is the hyperlink. This is a section of text or a picture that replaces one page on your computer screen with another when you click on it.

Once you have designed a web page on your own computer (*see* pp234–7 for more on what you need to do this), you publish it by **uploading the files to a web server**. This is a computer provided by your ISP and permanently connected to the Internet.

(and versions of browsers from the same manufacturer) are likely to display your web pages differently. This 'cross-platform compatibility' is the biggest bugbear for the web designer and if it isn't dealt with correctly it can result in your carefully designed pages looking messy or at worst being unreadable on some computers.

Is web design for you?

If you're not a natural technophile, you may prefer to find a good designer and brief them thoroughly. It's worth thinking through some of the following considerations first.

- Building a website can be time-consuming and can divert you from more important aspects of your business.
- You may need to acquire and learn how to use several pieces of software and install additional hardware as well.
- Like any other marketing activity, a website works best if it is carefully planned and executed to maximise its effectiveness – it may be hard to gather enough expertise to do a professional job.
- A poorly designed website can reflect badly on your business and discourage potential customers.

A recent technological development has made it possible to create web pages as easily as creating a Word document. As yet this technology is not widespread and there are various requirements, but using the system means you can create and update your website using any suitable computer with an Internet connection, anywhere in the world.

Types of website

Websites range from simple two- or three-page sites with little interactivity to huge multimedia affairs costing tens if not hundreds of thousands of pounds. But most fall into one of the following categories:

- e-commerce sites – where you can buy goods or services directly over the Internet
- brochureware – informing the visitor about a company's products or services
- news sites – widespread distribution of useful or interesting information
- download sites – sites that supply software such as games or music either free or at a charge
- special-interest sites – such as clubs, trade bodies or hobby sites.

Build your own website

Building a simple website, whether for business or for leisure, can be straightforward, but there are certain hardware and software requirements, as well as hosting considerations, which you should allow for in your budget.

You will first of all need to decide what to put on your site and how it should look. When it's live on the web, you need to make sure it works for your business.

Hosting requirements

You will need a computer and an Internet connection to enable you to build and upload your site. You should also have enough hard disk space to store your site off-line and to install software you need. To include pictures, you will need either a scanner to digitise printed and photographic material or a digital camera.

When choosing a web space provider, the main options are:

- your existing ISP
- a free hosting service; *see* www.freewebspace.net for availability (and *see* comments on free services, pp230–1)
- an independent commercial hosting service; www.webhostmagazine.com provides a useful guide.

Being part of the World Wide Web is not as daunting as it sounds

Tips for designing a website

- **If you are designing a business site**, your job is to promote your company's core products, services and values. Try to adopt a style that reflects your market image and ties in with any other material you use to market your business, such as brochures, advertising and letterheads.

- **In general, keep each page as uncluttered as possible.** Split the information into bite-sized chunks and link several pages together to produce a 'chapter'. Use lots of white space – it is easy on the eye, improves legibility and looks classy. Smaller pages will also give the user faster loading – try to restrict the number and size of images on your pages for the same reason. Some of the more sophisticated web design packages give an indication of the loading time of a page. If a page takes more than 30 seconds to load using a 56K modem – the most common and fastest modem in general use – the visitor may go to another site.

- **Use a commonly available typeface.** There are really only two choices – serif, which has decorative bits at the end of stems of letters (the most common serif typeface being Times Roman) and non-serif (like this text), where a letter upright is just a single vertical stroke (as in the typeface Arial). Of other fonts, Tahoma and Verdana are particularly popular, but the less common the font you use, the greater likelihood that the visitor will not have it on their computer and therefore that your site will not appear as you intended.

- **Make sure your site is visually consistent.** A jumble of different typefaces and layouts, inconsistent navigation, lots of meaningless flashing and flying images won't impress the visitor, who can go to a more restful and better-designed site at the click of a mouse button.

- **Good design is almost always simple.** That doesn't mean it's easy to achieve, but visual simplicity on a web page is a really attractive feature that will set your site apart. If you need to put in more information, consider creating a new page rather than expanding an existing one.

Check that commercial use of the service is acceptable and take into account:

- any set-up fee, and the monthly cost. This may vary depending on which services you opt for
- how much space will you be given on the server. A basic website shouldn't need more than 5MB, but a large product catalogue may need more
- any limit on bandwidth, affecting how many people will be able to look at your site at a time. Limits are unlikely, but it's worth checking, as there could be additional costs if your site is very successful
- whether the host offers all the features you'll need.

Software

You can get software from a variety of sources. Your local computer shop or superstore may be able to help you and may offer useful advice. Look out for the following, too.

Shareware Software you can try out for a limited period and only pay for if you decide it suits you. The most common way to get hold of shareware is on the Internet or from covermount CDs (*see* below).

Freeware Smaller pieces of software that cost nothing to obtain and use, often designed to perform a highly specific function, such as creating animations from existing graphics files. These can also be found on the Internet or on covermount CDs.

Covermount CDs CD-ROMs given away with computer magazines are a valuable source of freeware and shareware, as well as demonstration versions of full commercial products. Often you will find articles describing and reviewing the products in the accompanying magazine.

What software will you need?

Web design software

A web page is designed using a coding language called HTML (Hypertext Mark-up Language, *see* Understanding technospeak p222), but you don't need to learn HTML to design a web page. Your chosen host may offer a template service to help you create your site. Otherwise there is plenty of web design software available, ranging in price from free to hundreds of pounds.

Macromedia Dreamweaver
This professional-level package is one of the leaders in the field, and is the preferred package of many professional Web designers. For the amateur, it can take some time to learn.

Adobe GoLive Another professional-level package from a well-known design software company. May be rather oversophisticated for the amateur.

Microsoft FrontPage Easy to learn and has a WYSIWYG (What You See Is What You Get) editor. It is included in some versions of Microsoft Office. FrontPage Express – a cut-down version with fewer features – is available free when you install Microsoft Internet Explorer. They are user-friendly, good value for money and come with ready-made templates and design styles. But there are some drawbacks: to use some of the features you can only host your website on a server with FrontPage Extensions installed. Also, FrontPage uses some features that are only supported by the Microsoft browser – Internet Explorer.

Image-manipulation software
You need to have some software to get the pictures and graphics the way you want them and suitable for your website. As well as drawing and painting, your image software should allow you to scan in images; import pictures from your digital camera (if you have one); resize and crop; adjust brightness, colour, and so on; and save your work in a variety of formats (including GIF and JPG – the ones used in web design).

It will take time to learn how to use this software successfully, but it is an essential investment if you are serious about having a good-looking website. At the time of writing the most popular packages are Adobe Photoshop, which is very comprehensive but quite expensive, and JASC Paint Shop Pro, which is comparable but costs considerably less.

Software for loading the site
Having created your website, you have to load it on to your web space so the world can see the result of your efforts. To do this you use a type of software called an FTP (File Transfer Protocol) program, unless you are using a web design package that uploads your files for you. There are several shareware versions available, and some free of charge, on the Internet. Names to look out for include WS_FTP, CuteFTP and CoffeeCup.

Design pitfalls

The main challenge you have in designing your site is ensuring that it looks right on the many variations of hardware and software that will be used to view it. Key differences are browsers and screen resolution.

Browsers When designing your site, it is best to view it using at least Microsoft Internet Explorer and Netscape Navigator. Together, these two products account for over 90% of web browsers. Use an up-to-date version, as old versions will not necessarily show the site in the same way. Some web designers keep older versions of web browser programs so they can check how their sites will look under different conditions. PCs and Apple Macs can show sites completely differently.

Screen resolution Use a common screen resolution – for PCs, it's best to use 800 x 600 pixels, but also view it at the lower resolution of 640 x 480 pixels and the higher one of 1024 x 768 pixels, from time to time. To do this on a PC with Windows, open the control panel on your computer, select 'Display' and then the 'Settings' option. Some software includes a resolution selection feature to help you do this more simply.

Money and insurance

When you're running your own business, it's vital to spend time keeping track of your finances – the money side is where many new businesses come unstuck.

The key task in keeping track of your finances is to monitor cash flow, but you also need to plan for contingencies, so that you aren't totally floored if you hit a bad patch. The Internet has opened up new possibilities not just for handling money, but for making money too.

Bank accounts

If you are operating as a self-employed sole trader, you may not need a business account, but you will almost certainly need one if you are going to borrow money. Shop around for the business account that will give you the most flexibility and the lowest charges.

Internet banking may be attractive for the various added-value services it offers, such as allowing you to conduct credit enquiries online, receive regular updates of statements, and find new suppliers on the bank's database, as well as make all the usual banking transactions. Online banking can save time, but if you will be banking cash regularly you need to choose a bank that has a branch nearby.

As with personal banking, it's vital to keep good records with your business banking. On bank statements, check that bank charges haven't been changed without warning; that all transactions are included and correct; that all payments into your account have been cleared; and that the balance is correct.

Always keep on top of your finances when running your own business

Sources of money

While you may be able to get an overdraft facility from a bank, which is useful for tiding you over when cashflow is tight, you may find you're unable to get a straightforward loan if you don't have enough security – in other words, you don't have anything that can be redeemed against the loan if you default on your payments. It's inadvisable to offer your home as security against a loan: if you fail, you risk losing the roof over your head. And if you have a mortgage, you may not own enough of your home to borrow against it anyway. Contact Business Link (*see* pp246–7) if you're looking for funding.

Government loan scheme

Your bank may be able to offer you a loan under the government's Small Firms Loan Guarantee Scheme, if it feels that your business is eligible and relatively risk-free. The government guarantee covers 75% of new loans. Loans start at £5,000 and can reach £250,000.

Grants from public bodies

There are nearly 4,000 grants on offer in the UK each year. These are provided by all kinds of public bodies, ranging from local authorities and local and regional arts councils to central government and the European Union. Several publications give details of grants. These can be found in any good business reference library or bought from the Stationery Office, which has an online sales service, or try looking on the Internet for information – www.j4b.co.uk is a good place to start.

The amount of a grant is dependent upon a variety of

The business plan

A **business plan** is not just a document to present to a bank when you want to borrow money. It's also to show you how your business is going to succeed financially. It should contain some or all of the following:

- what your business **produces/provides**
- **details of the market** for the business, with figures, projected market growth and so on
- whether there's any **competition** and why you'll succeed against it
- how you'll **market** your products/services and how much that will cost; allow enough to be able to try different media – national newspapers, magazines, radio, a website, for example
- what **equipment and supplies** you need to start up with
- how you'll **price** your product/service
- **overheads**, including rent, mortgage, council tax, insurance and other regular payments
- **projected income** and whether you expect to have difficult periods.

Professional help

You should consider using the following: an **accountant**, to help with your tax affairs, running the business and raising money if you need it; a **solicitor** to help with terms and conditions of trade, litigation, contract law and so on; an insurance broker; an **independent financial adviser (IFA)** to advise on, among other things, pensions, especially if you plan to be self-employed for some time.

factors and you will certainly have to find a sum of money yourself, as a grant never pays the whole cost of a project. Although there appear to be many grants on offer, getting a grant may take considerable work. Companies called grant consultancies have sprung up to help applicants. There are various types of grant.

- A direct grant is a sum of money that is given to a business – usually no more than 50% of a proposed project – and needn't be paid back.
- A soft loan is made available to businesses not eligible for commercial loans. It may be interest-free, long term or offer other benefits. It has to be paid back eventually.
- A repayable grant is usually offered, interest-free, for special projects on the understanding that it will be repaid when the project succeeds, but not if it fails.
- Support in kind may take the form of free training, advice, professional services such as research and development, trips abroad for export planning or something else useful for your business.

Venture capital

The government encourages individuals and businesses to invest in small-to medium-sized companies needing an injection of cash in order to grow. The Inland Revenue gives tax relief to investors who provide venture capital. Nearly £23 billion has been invested in UK companies over the past 15 years. The British Venture Capital Association provides information, as does venturesearch.co.uk.

Business angels

Business angels are private individuals who invest small amounts in companies in the early stages of development. The National Business Angels Network comes under the aegis of the British Venture Capital Association, which publishes a directory listing all current sources of business angel capital.

What insurance do you need?

It's best to consult an independent business insurance broker or go direct to one or more insurance companies – some offer small-business packages that can be tailored to your requirements. These are the main types of insurance.

Home contents insurance
All your working equipment must be covered and you must inform the insurer if you add any new equipment, otherwise a potential claim could become invalid.

Professional indemnity
Desirable if you advise or perform a service for clients and the quality of your work could substantially affect their business.

Product liability
Important if you manufacture a product, no matter how modest, in case any member of the public is injured because your product is faulty.

Public liability and third party public liability
The first policy covers you against any injury to the public through your work or in your home. The second type of cover may be relevant if you subcontract any of your work to others who are deemed to be acting on your behalf.

Employer's liability
Required by law if you employ even just one person, to cover you if an employee should be injured in the course of employment.

Business category car insurance
Check whether your car insurance covers self-employed business use. You will certainly have to pay higher premiums if the business use of your car involves using the car as a taxi, transporting high-priced goods – for instance samples or stock – or you carry valuable or hazardous equipment.

Private medical insurance
Usually offers the option of private medical treatment or, if you opt for NHS treatment, a cash sum to compensate for lost income.

Accident cover
This policy will pay you money if you are out of work owing to an accident. Premiums can be quite high if you are in a high-risk occupation, such as the building trade.

Critical illness cover
Protection if you are ill and not able to earn money.

Keyman cover
A popular policy for very small companies where the loss of one particular individual through illness or injury can greatly damage the effectiveness of the company. The policy covers the cost of a temporary replacement employee.

Taxing matters

People tend to dislike the notion of tax and tax inspectors: the very words Inland Revenue or Customs and Excise can make even honest people freeze. But this is unnecessary, because tax inspectors can be extremely helpful to the self-employed.

Starting out as self-employed

The Inland Revenue (IR) classes you as self-employed and charges tax on your business profits if you're a sole trader – that is, in business on your own – or in a partnership. The alternative to being self-employed is to set up your business as a limited company that pays corporation tax. This requires the services of an accountant and is beyond the scope of this book.

If you are self-employed and don't register with the IR within the first full three months of self-employment, you can be fined £100. There are exceptions and rules for certain occupations and industries, like the construction industry. To be certain of where you stand, get the leaflet IR56 *Employed or Self-Employed?* from your local IR office, by phoning the Inland Revenue Orderline on 0845 9000 404.

After you have registered, the IR will send you a *Starting Up in Business* guide and arrange for you to start paying self-employed flat rate (Class 2) National Insurance (NI) contributions. You'll be sent a quarterly invoice for your NI contributions or you can arrange to pay them monthly by direct debit.

Completing a tax return

You can complete a **self-assessment form** and return it by post. Alternatively, the IR has an online tax filing service. You can register your intent to file electronically and then download the necessary self-assessment forms and the software program needed to complete and return the information.

If you miss the deadline for submission of tax returns of 31 January each year, you'll automatically incur a fine – currently £100. Further fines and surcharges can be levied if your tax return is delayed any further than that. If it is still outstanding by the following 31 July, you'll be fined a further £100 fine. A 5% surcharge is imposed on any tax bill that remains unpaid 28 days after the due date and an additional 5% if it remains unpaid after six months.

Shortly after the end of the tax year (currently 5 April) in which you started working for yourself, the IR will send you a self-assessment tax return. This is made up of a 'core' tax return and supplementary pages relevant to your situation. If you have registered as self-employed, the self-employment supplementary pages – where you should give details of your earnings – will be attached to the back of the core tax return. The information enables the IR to work out how much tax and Class 4 profit-related NI you owe, if any. This figure will also set the amount of advance payments of tax, 'payments on account', that you have to make for the following tax year.

Self-assessment: the principles

Different incomes and profits require different supplementary pages to be filled in, but the main points apply to everyone:

- one set of payment dates for tax – 31 January each year. Self-employed people, though, pay tax in two instalments – the first on 31 January made up of tax owed plus first payment on account and the second – the second payment on account – on 31 July
- fixed, automatic penalties for late returns and interest and surcharges for late payments
- clear obligations for keeping records. You must keep records of all financial dealings in support of information given on each tax return for five years and ten months from the tax year to which they relate.

Under self-assessment, you can ask the IR to work out how much tax you need to pay, in which case you have to send your completed tax form in by 30 September each year. If you want to calculate your own tax – or choose to pay an accountant to do this for you – forms are due back by 31 January each year, with the first payment.

Finding a good accountant

An accountant can advise you on **tax matters** and take on the responsibility of dealing with the IR on your behalf, as well as help you with other **financial matters**. Conventional wisdom is that hiring an accountant is worthwhile if they can save you the cost of their fee – and preferably more. You can find a good accountant through:

- **recommendation** from other business people
- your **bank**
- a **professional body** of which you're a member
- a business advice source, such as **Business Link**
- your **trade association**, if you have one
- a business club, such as the local **Chamber of Commerce**.

You can get tax relief on the price of a new car if you are self-employed

Tax relief

Employees and the self-employed get the same personal allowances. But the self-employed can usually claim tax relief on more of their work-related expenditure. Buy something for £100 and the real cost after tax relief will be £78 if you're a basic-rate (22%) taxpayer, £60 if you're a higher-rate (40%) taxpayer.

You can claim relief for expenditure that's exclusively to do with your work. And if you spend money on something that's partly to do with work and partly with your private life, you can claim tax relief on the proportion related to your work. For instance, tax relief on part of your gas and electricity bills if you work from your home.

As self-employed, you will be dealt with by a local tax office, which can advise on allowances. You might also consider using an accountant, at least when you first start in business. They can give advice on expenses you can claim and, where relevant, on the proportion you can claim.

Tax relief comes in two forms:

- you can deduct from your income in one tax year the full cost of allowable expenses for most work-related expenditure – including gas, electricity, phone, cleaning, insurance, mortgage interest or rent – or the appropriate proportion
- you can deduct from your income capital allowances for capital expenditure – including machines, computers, vehicles and buildings. But tax relief on most capital expenditure must be claimed over several tax

years. If you're a small business you can claim 40% of capital expenditure as a first-year allowance and 25% of the outstanding balance in subsequent years, such as on machinery. On other capital expenditure, for example vehicles, the maximum first-year allowance is 25%.

Registering for VAT

You have to register for Value Added Tax (VAT) with Customs and Excise if you supply goods and/or services that are not exempt from VAT and your total sales exceed £55,000 (the figure at the time of writing; it may change). You don't have to register if your total sales are less than this threshold, but you can choose to do so.

The advantage of being VAT registered is that you can claim back any VAT charged on things you buy for your business, which brings down your costs. This can seem quite attractive if you plan to buy a lot of expensive equipment. For example, if you buy a computer costing £1,175 (including VAT at 17.5%), being registered for VAT means that you can claim back the £175 in tax, so the computer ends up costing you only £1,000. However, you have to balance this advantage against the fact that you will have to:

- add VAT at 17.5% to all your invoices, which – unless your customers are VAT registered and so able to claim back the VAT they pay – pushes up the price of whatever you are selling
- keep accurate and detailed records and fill in a VAT return, usually every three months
- make sure that you have sufficient cash available to pay the VAT you have collected – less the VAT you can claim back – to Customs and Excise.

Employing others

At some point you may need to have someone to help you with your work. If so, until you have a reasonably large turnover, you should avoid taking on employees. Employment law is complex and **the real cost of hiring an employee may be almost double the salary** you offer. Also, it may be difficult for you to offer an employee continued employment, especially if you are in the start-up period.

It's better to **subcontract** – in other words, get another self-employed person to do some of your work – or to contract someone from an agency. An agency will take care of PAYE, National Insurance and all the other employer's responsibilities. There are plenty of agencies that can provide temporary staff in all employment sectors.

Contact details

Useful websites and addresses about the information given in this chapter.

Better Business, Active Information Ltd, Cribau Mill, Chepstow NP16 6LN
Tel: 0845 458 9485
Fax: 01291 641 777
e-mail: info@better-business.co.uk
www.better-business.co.uk
Free information and guidance for small businesses.

British Venture Capital Association, 3 Clements Inn, London WC2A 2AZ
Tel: 020 7025 2950
Fax: 020 7025 2951
e-mail: bvca@bvca.co.uk
www.bvca.co.uk

Business Connect Wales
Tel: 08457 969 798
e-mail: executive@businessconnect.org.uk
www.businessconnect.org.uk
Information for small to medium businesses in Wales.

Business Link
Tel: 0845 600 9006
www.businesslink.org
A national business advice service.

DTI Enquiry Unit, 1 Victoria St, London SW1H 0ET
Tel: 020 7215 5000
e-mail: enquiries@dti.gsi.gov.uk
www.dti.gov.uk
Area on the site dedicated to business and small businesses.

Federation of Small Businesses, Sir Frank Whittle Way, Blackpool Business Park, Blackpool, Lancashire FY4 2FE
Tel: 01253 336 000
Fax: 01253 348 046
e-mail: ho@fsb.org.uk
www.fsb.org.uk
Statistics, details of events and help for small businesses.

Inland Revenue
Tel: 020 7667 4001; helpline for newly self-employed: 08459 154 515; orderline for leaflets: 0845 900 0404
www.inlandrevenue.gov.uk
Detailed information about individual and business tax, including a separate section on self assessment.

InterNIC
www.internic.net

Internet domain name registration services.

Invest Northern Ireland, 64 Chichester St, Belfast BT1 4JX
Tel: 028 9023 9090
Fax: 028 9049 0490
e-mail: info@investni.com
www.investni.com
Small business scheme in Northern Ireland.

j4b, 51 Water Lane, Wilmslow, Cheshire SK9 5BQ
e-mail: enquiries@j4b.co.uk
www.j4b.co.uk
Explore the range of funding that might be available to you.

McAfee Security, Network Associates, 227 Bath Road, Slough, Berkshire SL1 5PP
Tel: 01753 217 500
Fax: 01753 217 520
e-mail: customer_service@nai.com
www.mcafee.com
Internet security company.

Nominet UK, Sandford Gate, Sandy Lane West, Oxford OX4 6LB
Tel: 01865 332 211
Fax: 01865 332 299
e-mail: nominet@nominet.org.uk
www.nic.uk
Registry of domain names.

SBS Loan Guarantee Unit, St Mary's House, c/o Moorfoot, Sheffield S1 4PQ
Tel: 0114 259 7308
Fax: 0114 259 7316
e-mail: sflgs@sbs.gsi.gov.uk
www.sbs.gov.uk
Details of the Small Firms Loan Guarantee Scheme.

Scottish Executive Enterprise and Lifelong Learning Dept, The Scottish Executive, 6th Floor, Meridian Court, Cadogan Street, Glasgow G2 6AT
Tel: 0141 248 4774
Fax: 0141 242 5665
e-mail: ceu@scotland.gov.uk
www.scotland.gov.uk/who/elld
Small business scheme in Scotland.

SearchEngineWatch.com
www.searchenginewatch.com
Information on how to promote your site in search engines.

The Stationery Office, PO Box 29, St Crispins, Duke St, Norwich NR3 1GN
Tel: 0870 600 5522
Fax: 0870 600 5533
e-mail: customer.services@tso.co.uk
www.tso.co.uk
Includes an online bookshop with a section dedicated to business publications.

Electricity bill
PAY YOUR
1454.38DR
alance
1454.38DR

Money Matters

Like it or not, money affects all of us in one way or another. For the householder, budgeting to pay for bills so that we can maintain our home is a priority and one that we cannot shy away from.

Planning for the future is important as well, so in this chapter we also take a look at savings, investments and pensions. Keeping our spending under control can help us avoid falling into serious debt. The prolific rise of the credit card can tempt all of us into buying beyond our means and this can obviously have a detrimental effect on the running of our homes. There are ways to save on household utilities, for example, as well as getting the best deal for where we keep our money.

Budgeting

One of the least attractive aspects of being a householder is coping with all the bills. The consequences of not paying them can be severe – ignoring utility bills can mean having essential services cut off, while failure to pay your rent or mortgage could lose you the roof over your head.

Ensuring that you have your regular bills covered should be a top priority. Once you have taken control of your day-to-day finances, you should also consider how you can plan for future financial commitments and meet unexpected demands on your resources.

Budgeting

Bills have a nasty habit of arriving all at once, which can wreak havoc with your bank balance. One way to avoid sharp dips in your finances is to pay bills monthly by direct debit. But not all bills can be paid in this way and sometimes paying monthly costs more. Insurance companies, for instance, often charge extra if you pay premiums in instalments rather than as a lump sum. Always check this before you fill in the direct debit mandate.

Another way to deal with bills is to open a second current account into which you pay a monthly amount to cover all your regular bills. To work out how much to pay – or just to get a view of your outgoings – draw up a table as shown opposite on the next page.

- Put the months of the year across the top and the bills you want to be covered down the side.
- Estimate how much you spend each month (or quarter or year) on each bill or use old bills for approximate figures.
- Enter the figures against each item on the list under the column for the month(s) in which you make payment.
- Total each column to get the total for each month. Add the totals and divide by 12 to give the monthly amount you need to pay into your bills' account.

If you can use spreadsheet software you will find it quicker than using pen, paper and a calculator. Once it's set up, you can also use your spreadsheet to find out the impact of any additional commitment on your finances.

How much to set aside for bills?

	Jan	Feb	Mar	Apr	May	Jun	Jul	Aug	Sep	Oct	Nov	Dec
Mortgage	250	250	250	250	250	250	250	250	250	250	250	250
Council tax			65	65	65	65	65	65	65	65	65	65
Buildings insurance	23	23	23	23	23	23	23	23	23	23	23	23
Contents insurance	18	18	18	18	18	18	18	18	18	18	18	18
Electricity	66			60			55			55		
Gas	80			80			65			70		
Water					110						110	
Car insurance	25	25	25	25	25	25	25	25	25	25	25	25
Car tax								155				
Parking permit										35		
Phone	75			75			75			75		
Mobile	20	20	20	20	20	20	20	20	20	20	20	20
TV licence			112									
Pension	100	100	100	100	100	100	100	100	100	100	100	100
TOTALS	**657**	**436**	**613**	**716**	**611**	**501**	**696**	**656**	**501**	**736**	**611**	**501**

Average monthly amount to set aside: **£602.92**

Warning signs

A key reason for keeping your finances under control is to avoid the risk of drifting into **serious debt**. If you answer 'yes' to any of the following questions, you should draw up a budget (*see* above) and include in your calculations a monthly amount to put towards clearing your debts, starting with the biggest.

- Do you regularly **spend** more than you earn?
- Are you always **overdrawn**?
- Do you repay only the **minimum** amount due on your credit card bill every month?
- Does your overdraft and/or the amount you owe on your credit card **go up** every month?
- Do you put off paying bills until the **final reminder** arrives?
- Have you ever missed a loan **repayment**?

If you answered yes to **all** of the above, your debts are already out of control (*see* Debt action points, p253).

Budget for the unexpected

It's not just today's bills you need to budget for – you need a strategy to help you deal with unexpected bills and continue to meet your living expenses if your income falls due to sickness or unemployment.

1 Aim to **clear your debts** – especially if you are at risk of getting into serious debt (*see* p251). Paying off expensive overdrafts and money you owe on credit cards makes a lot of sense, as the interest you pay on borrowing is higher than interest you earn on savings. Being in debt makes you more vulnerable to a sharp drop in income than if you were financially solvent.
2 Take out **buildings and contents insurance**. Such policies will protect you against the cost of dealing with damage or loss caused by things beyond your control, such as storms, theft or fire.
3 Build up your **savings**. Once you have cleared debts, build up a cash fund to fall back on. How big the fund needs to be depends on what you want it to do for you. It could be enough to meet the cost of household repairs or six months' worth of rent or mortgage payments.

Build up a cash fund to fall back on once you have cleared all your debts

4 Check what **financial protection** you have. Many people believe that the state will provide in times of trouble. It may offer some financial help, but state benefits for unemployment and inability to work due to illness or injury are unlikely to cover all your expenses. One way of coping is income protection insurance, which pays a replacement income if you suffer a long-term illness or disabling injury. If you have a mortgage, you could take out mortgage payment protection insurance. If you are an employee, first check the terms of your employer's sick pay and redundancy schemes to see whether buying your own private insurance is strictly necessary.

Building up savings

- If you want to save for up to five years but may need to get to your savings within that time, the best place to put regular amounts of spare cash is in a **savings account** (*see* Short-term investment options, p279).
- If you can tie up your money for more than five years and/or you are prepared to see the value of your savings go up and down, you could consider an equity-based savings plan such as a stocks and shares **ISA**, *see* p298.
- If you can commit to saving for at least ten years, life-insurance-based savings plans – also known as **'endowments'** – could be an option. You will have to commit to regular payments for the duration and wait until it comes to an end before being able to touch your lump sum. If you can't, avoid these.
- For the options available if you have a **one-off sum to invest**, *see* pp296–9.

Future planning

If you have any money left over after paying your bills, clearing your debts, and meeting your day-to-day living expenses, you are in the fortunate position to take steps to plan for the future. Two main priorities should be:

- paying into a pension, because the sooner you start, the better (*see* p254)
- building up savings for major expenditure in the future (*see* above) – such as putting down a deposit on a house, buying a car, paying for a wedding or taking an unpaid career break.

Debt action points

If you answered yes to most, or all, the questions in Warning signs (p251), your borrowing is already **out of control** and you need to tackle the problem. Doing nothing in the hope that your debts will disappear could result in your being taken to court, losing the roof over your head and having essential services – such as gas and electricity – cut off. **If you fail to pay your council tax, you could even face prison.**

- **Don't be tempted** to use the services of a company that promises to reduce your debts by consolidating them all into one big loan – professional debt advisers say that this can lead to worse problems.

- **Cut back on inessential spending** – your priority should be to make sure that you can pay your mortgage or rent, utility bills, council tax and, if self-employed, National Insurance and tax.

- **Tell your creditors** (the people to whom you owe money) that you are in financial difficulty – the earlier you contact your various lenders, the more sympathetic and helpful they are likely to be.

- **Consider getting free advice from a debt adviser** – contact a Citizens' Advice Bureau, the Consumer Credit Counselling Service, or the National Debtline (avoid companies that charge you for help). A debt adviser will help prioritise your debts, draw up a repayment plan, and negotiate with creditors on your behalf.

- **If you are threatened with court action**, don't try to deal with it by yourself. Seek outside help, such as a debt adviser, who can help you to present your case.

How much pension will you get?

Your age now	The monthly pension you might get at 65 if you pay into a defined contribution scheme and make monthly contributions of:			
	£20	**£50**	**£100**	**£200**
20	£123	£309	£618	£1,236
25	£99	£249	£498	£997
30	£79	£198	£397	£794
35	£62	£155	£310	£621
40	£47	£118	£237	£474
45	£34	£87	£174	£348
50	£24	£60	£120	£241
55	£14	£37	£74	£148
60	£6	£17	£34	£69

Source: The Financial Services Authority

Five reasons to pay into a pension

1 Pension planning is all about saving now to buy an income in retirement. It is vital if you want to live on more than the basic state retirement pension. How much you get of any type of state pension to which you are entitled depends on your National Insurance record during your working life.

2 The pension you get from the state won't be paid until you are 65 (60 for women born before 6 April 1950). If you don't want to carry on working until you reach that age, you have to save for yourself, otherwise you won't have anything to live on.

3 Paying into a pension is the best way to save for retirement because for every £100 you pay in, the government adds a further £28 in the form of basic-rate tax relief (higher-rate taxpayers get a higher subsidy). And when you retire, you can take part of your pension as a tax-free cash lump sum.

4 The younger you are when you start your pension, the bigger the pension you can expect to get (*see* above).

5 Joining an employer-run pension scheme (if you can) is like getting a tax-free pay rise. This is because, by law, employers who run their own schemes must contribute to the scheme on your behalf. This is also true of employers who do not run their own scheme but offer staff access to a personal pension rather than a stakeholder pension (*see* p256).

How pension schemes work

Employers' schemes

If you have the opportunity to join an employer's pension scheme, take it. The best type of employer-run pension is a final-salary scheme – also referred to as a defined-benefit scheme. With this type of scheme, your pension contributions buy you a pension that is guaranteed to be a definite proportion – up to a maximum of two-thirds – of your salary at retirement or at the end of the scheme, whichever is earlier. What you pay in is not directly linked to what you get out, because the onus is on your employer to ensure you are paid the pension you have been promised.

This is not the case with an employer's money-purchase scheme, which an increasing number of employers are offering in preference to a salary-related scheme. With a money-purchase scheme, your pension contributions (and the contributions your employer puts in on your behalf) are invested, typically in stocks and shares, to build up a fund. This fund of investments carries on growing until you decide to take your pension. At that point, the fund is converted into cash, the bulk of which is used to buy an annuity – a type of investment which pays a fixed sum to you at regular intervals for the rest of your life.

Some employers offer hybrid schemes – mixed-benefit schemes – which combine the two. The pension you get at retirement is guaranteed to be the greater of whichever method of calculating your pension gives the better result.

Whichever scheme your employer offers – and you are unlikely to be given a choice – joining it makes sound financial sense. Because your employer meets the costs of running the scheme and contributes on your

Personal pensions

Personal pensions work in the same way as stakeholder pensions except that they do not have to meet the minimum standards for charges, contributions levels and flexibility. The stakeholder option, however, invariably offers the better deal.

If you already have a personal pension you have **three options**:
- keep it going
- transfer the fund into a stakeholder
- stop paying into it and take out a stakeholder.

Which is the **best course of action** hinges on the projected financial outcome, taking into account penalty charges you face for transferring your fund or stopping your contributions. Check with your pension company or consult an independent financial adviser.

State pension: in or out?

If you are an **employee**, you can choose to opt (or 'contract') out of the state second pension.

Contracting out may happen automatically if you join a contracted-out employer's scheme. If you do this, your employer undertakes to replace the pension you would have got from the state and, in exchange for giving up your rights to this, you pay a lower rate of National Insurance.

If you're not already contracted out through an employer's scheme, you can **opt to replace your state pension** with a stakeholder (or personal) pension. You still pay full rate National Insurance but part of what you pay is repaid to your chosen pension plan.

There is **no guarantee** that the pension you get from contracting out in this way will be as good as the state pension you give up.

behalf, an employer's scheme will provide a bigger pension for the same money than either your own stakeholder or personal pension. The main cause of the pensions' mis-selling scandal of the late 1980s was people being wrongly advised to give up the benefits of an employer's scheme to take out a personal pension.

Stakeholder pensions

A stakeholder pension is a type of personal pension and it works on a money purchase basis.

Stakeholders have been available since April 2001. They are aimed at people who do not have an employer's scheme to join. This includes the self-employed and people who do not have a job.

The most important difference between stakeholder pensions and the earlier type of personal pension is that the government has laid down minimum standards that stakeholders must meet. Old-style personal pensions don't have to meet these minimum standards.

When you invest in a stakeholder pension, you can be sure that the company you buy it from will:

- charge no more than 1% of the value of your fund each year in fund management charges
- let you pay in as little as £20 at a time
- allow you to make both one-off and regular contributions
- not make you pay extra charges if you stop paying in or decide to transfer your fund to a different company.

If you don't currently pay into a pension, consider a stakeholder. It is also an option to consider if you are already paying into either an employer's scheme or a pre-April 2001 personal pension and want to increase your pension savings.

Flexing the plastic

Why bother with a credit card when you can just as easily use the debit card that you got with your current account? One good reason is that a credit card gives you access to free and flexible credit.

Another reason for using credit cards is that with the Consumer Credit Act, buying with a credit card gives you a valuable line of defence if something goes wrong with your purchases. The downside is that it can be a passport to unmanageable and expensive debt.

Benefits of credit cards

1 One of the main benefits of using a credit card rather than a debit card is the protection provided by the Consumer Credit Act. This says that if you have problems with goods or services – such as a supplier going out of business or failing to deliver – you can get your money back from the card issuer if you can't get it back from the supplier (provided that whatever you bought cost between £100 and £30,000).

2 Some cards provide purchase protection insurance, which pays out if something you have bought with the card is lost, damaged or stolen within 90 or 100 days

of the date of purchase. However, this type of insurance doesn't cover all purchases – secondhand or perishable goods, for example – and there's usually a limit on how much you can claim. This kind of insurance is not worth having if it duplicates cover you already have under your home contents insurance, which it probably will if you have 'all-risks' cover.

3 A credit card can cost nothing – if you pick a card that doesn't charge an annual fee and you always pay the bill in full every month. Most cards charge interest only if you leave part of your balance unpaid.

4 A credit card can save you money if you choose one that earns you cash every time you buy something. How much cash you get back is calculated as a small percentage of the amount you have spent on the card. Some cards offer incentives other than cash – Air Miles or shopping vouchers, for instance.

5 Even if you do not pay your monthly bill in full, a credit card can be cheaper than running an overdraft on your current account, especially if your bank charges a monthly fee as well as interest when you overdraw.

6 Using a credit card can work out cheaper than using traveller's cheques or foreign currency to pay for things abroad. This is because the exchange rate used by card companies to convert foreign spending into sterling is better than normal tourist rates. However, because of credit card charges for cash withdrawals (*see* Credit card traps to avoid, pp260–1), a

Charge cards

They look like credit cards, but **charge cards** – of which Amex and Diners Club are the most well known – are quite different. Unlike a credit card, a charge card:

- provides **unlimited credit**, but expects you to pay your bill in full every month – with hefty charges if you don't
- **does not provide the protection** of the Consumer Credit Act (*see* Seven benefits of credit cards, pp257–9)
- always has an **annual fee**, which can range from £40 to £150 a year
- can provide access to an **automatic overdraft facility** of up to £15,000 (for a charge card issued by a high-street bank)
- generally comes with various forms of **free insurance** – travel or medical insurance, for example
- is unlikely to be offered to you unless you earn **at least £25,000** a year.

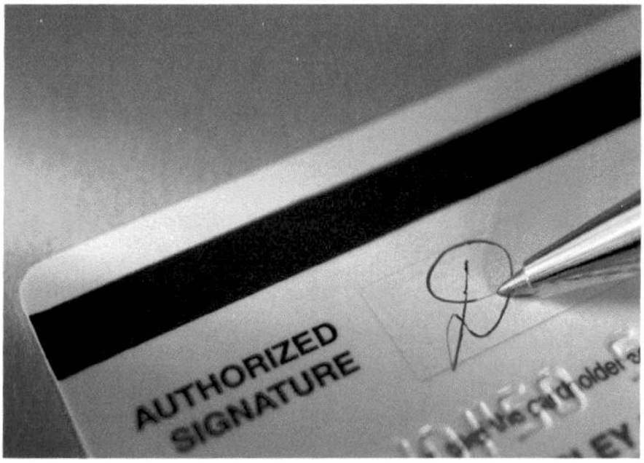

The credit card can be an extremely beneficial way of handling finances, but can equally become an easy way to build up soaring debts

debit card is better if you want to use plastic to buy currency, whether over the counter or from a foreign cash machine.

7 You can give to charity for free if you sign up for a charity credit card. When you first use the card, the card company makes a one-off donation of between £5 and £10. How much the charity gets after that depends on how much you spend, but it's typically 25p per £100 spent.

Get the best from your card

- Always check your statement. Credit card fraud is on the increase and if you don't spot a rogue transaction you will end up paying for someone else's purchase. This won't happen if you report it to the card company, because the disputed transaction must be removed from your account while it is investigated – and the onus is on the card company to prove it was your transaction, rather than you to prove it wasn't. A rogue transaction is as likely to be an unauthorised payment to an organisation you have already paid, as a payment to an unknown destination.
- Hold on to your credit card receipts at least until the transactions have appeared on your monthly statement. This makes it possible to check any payments you don't recognise. Bear in mind that if you query what appears to be a rogue transaction and it turns out that it was yours after all, you may face a charge of up to £10 for the inconvenience to your card issuer. If you use the card

to make major purchases, it's a good idea to keep the slips indefinitely.

- Always stay within your credit limit. If you go over it, your card may be refused. You could face a charge of between £10 and £20 each time you exceed your limit. If you are getting dangerously close to your limit, ask the card issuer to increase it. Or cut back on your spending.
- Pay your bill on time to avoid a late-payment charge of up to £25. This type of charge may also be levied if you pay your bill on time but the payment subsequently bounces. To make sure that you pay by the due date, consider paying by direct debit. All card issuers let you pay the required minimum amount each month, and all but a handful let you pay the full amount, by direct debit.
- If you run a debt on your card, keep an eye on the interest rate. If you have had the card for a year or more, it's likely that you could save on your interest bill by transferring the debt to a different card to take advantage of attractive rates for new customers. Many credit card companies are offering 0% interest rate to new customers on balance transfers for a specified term, generally between six and nine months. There are even cards that promise to keep this rate for a year. Some will additionally offer 0% on purchases over a specified period as well. Look for these rates in the personal finance pages of the weekend press or on the Internet.

Watch out – interest rates can vary enormously from card to card

- Keep copies of any letters cancelling arrangements made via your credit card (subscriptions, for instance), so that you can prove to the credit card company that you cancelled, should they continue make payment.

Traps to avoid

- Don't use your credit card to get cash. There is usually a minimum charge of £1.50 or £2 for making the withdrawal. Interest may also be charged – at a higher rate than on purchases – from the date of the withdrawal. The best way to avoid temptation is to destroy your credit card personal identification number (PIN) without looking at it.

- Don't use the cheques that several card companies issue alongside their cards. Writing a credit card cheque is like making a cash withdrawal and attracts the same sort of charges and interest. Using a credit card cheque rather than the card itself also means that you lose the protection of the Consumer Credit Act.
- Be wary of credit cards offered by shops and large retail groups to be used exclusively in those stores – the interest rates are usually very high.
- Don't be taken in by what looks like a low monthly interest rate. A monthly rate of 2.2% translates into a yearly rate of nearly 30%. On a debt of £500, this would mean paying approximately £150 in interest.
- If you are currently with a 0% interest free card, make a note of the date when the special rate expires. After this date, the balance of what you owe returns to the normal rate, typically anything from around 10% up to 30%. If you still owe a large amount, consider opening a new account offering 0% and transfer the balance when your 0% term expires on your present card.

Protecting your cards

It makes sense to be prudent with your card. Be wary, for instance, of traders who want to keep your credit card (as 'security', maybe) for even a short time. Beyond commonsense measures like this, there are two types of insurance that you are likely to be offered the chance to buy.

Card protection insurance allows you to register all your plastic cards so that if you lose your wallet or purse you only have to phone one number to report all of them missing. You may feel this convenience is worth the typical £10 charge, but the other 'benefits' are of limited value. Most policies, for example, offer up to £1,500 of cover against fraudulent use of the credit card, but the law already protects you against this: your liability is limited to £50 per card until you have notified the card company of the loss or theft. After you have notified them, it's zero. It is also zero if the card never left your possession but someone managed to get hold of and use your card details.

Payment protection insurance promises to pay your credit card bills if you are not earning as a result of illness, injury, or redundancy. However, such policies generally pay only a small proportion – typically 10% – of your outstanding balance and then only for a year.

Changing banks

Most current accounts offer the same package of cheque book, cash/debit card, direct debits, standing orders, overdraft facility and the option of accessing your account by phone or over the Internet, so you may assume that there's not much to choose between them.

Thinking that all current accounts must be similar is what the traditional high-street banks would like you to think. However, some accounts – particularly those from stand-alone Internet banks – offer a much better deal than others.

If your bank doesn't have a branch or cash machine nearby, change banks!

Six reasons to switch

1 You have moved or changed jobs and your bank no longer has branches and/or cash machines near to where you need them. Convenience is the most important factor when choosing a current account.

2 You can't remember the last time you set foot in a branch and you would be quite happy running your account by phone or over the Internet. Accounts from branchless banks tend to pay much better rates of interest than those offered on the high street.

3 You have a 'packaged' current account that gives you a range of extras – such as free travel insurance – in exchange for a monthly fee (that you have to pay even when you're in credit). The extras are rarely worth the £60 to £150 a year that these accounts can cost.

4 You tend to stay in credit and your bank pays only a paltry interest rate. On a balance of £500, for example, switching from the worst rate to the best could mean £25 a year in interest rather than 50p.

5 You run an overdraft and your bank charges a high rate of interest. Many banks charge around 18%, but you could easily halve this. On an overdraft of £500, this would bring the interest charged down from £90 a year to £45.

6 You regularly overdraw and your bank charges a monthly fee as well as interest. Although rare these days, this kind of charge can cost up to £100 a year, assuming you overdraw every month.

Comparing accounts

Here is a list of the main questions to ask:

- Does the bank provide access to cash machines and have branches where you are likely to need them?
- Are there any charges for using the cash machines of other banks and building societies?
- Can you access your account details in a way that suits you – for example, over the phone, via the Internet or WAP phone, or through digital TV?
- Is there a minimum amount that has to be paid into the account each month?
- Can you pay in cheques and cash in a way that you find convenient?
- Does the bank pay interest on credit balances? If so, how much?
- How much interest does the bank charge when you are overdrawn?
- What fees will you have to pay if you overdraw?
- Does the bank charge a monthly fee even when you are in credit?
- Will the bank help you switch your account to them, or will you have to do this yourself?

Extra questions to ask stand-alone Internet banks:

- Does the bank provide prepaid envelopes for paying in cheques through the post or will you have to pay postage?
- Is there a charge if you contact the bank by phone rather than by e-mail?

Switching made simple

In the past, **switching bank accounts** could be a time-consuming and tedious process. However, a recent scheme means that you don't have to endure the hassle of changing your standing orders and contacting all the organisations you pay by direct debit (or who pay you by direct credit) to advise them of the change in your bank details. Your new bank is likely to be able to do all this for you. They will:

- **produce a letter** for you to send to your old bank authorising them to pass to your new bank details of all your regular transactions
- **set up** all your standing orders, direct debits and direct credits on your behalf
- **close your old account** (if this is what you want to do) and transfer the balance to your new one.

Get the best from your bank

- Many people assume that banks don't make mistakes – they do. Always keep your own record of all your transactions and check this against your bank statements. Keep cash-machine receipts until your withdrawals appear on your statement.
- Even if you plan never to use it, it is worth arranging an overdraft limit on your account in case you overdraw accidentally. Some money may take longer than expected to reach your account, for example. Some banks automatically give you a limit when you open an account, but most expect you to ask for one. If you go over a pre-arranged limit, you will be charged a penalty rate of interest as well as a variety of fees. You will also have cheques bounced and cash withdrawals and debit card payments refused.
- If you lose your cash card and/or debit card, or you suspect that someone knows your personal identification number (PIN), contact your bank as soon as you possibly can. If someone uses your card without your permission, you are liable for the first £50 unless you managed to tell your bank before the fraudulent transaction occurred. Once you have told your bank, your liability is zero ... unless you wrote your PIN on your card. To avoid writing down your PIN anywhere, choose a number you will remember easily and make use of the option of changing your PIN – an option that the

The Banking Code

Nearly all banks follow the Banking Code – a **voluntary code of practice** that, among other things, commits a bank to making sure you have clear information on:

- how you can expect your bank to deal with you
- how your account will be run
- the charges, interest rates, and the terms and conditions governing your account
- the Direct Debit Guarantee (which offers certain assurances regarding your direct debits)
- the steps you must take to protect security information
- how to make a complaint.

If you are not given a copy of the Code automatically, you can ask for one. If you think your bank has failed to follow the Code, contact the **Banking Code Standards Board**, who can also tell you if your chosen bank subscribes to the Code. If you have a complaint about your bank that you are unable to resolve using the bank's own complaints procedure, contact the Financial Ombudsman Service.

Banking Code (*see* left) says all banks must offer.

- If you use Internet banking, all the banks say that you will not lose any money if you are an innocent victim of fraud. However, you do need to make sure that you keep secret the security details you use to access your account. Sensible precautions include not writing them down without disguising them, not saving your password on your hard disk, and always logging off properly from the bank's web site after you have finished. This is particularly important if you share your computer, use Internet cafés, or if you access your account from a computer at work.

Internet banking

Most banks offer Internet banking services with a current account. You can't use Internet banking to pay in cheques or withdraw cash, but you can:

- view your balance(s) and recent transactions on screen
- print statements
- transfer money between accounts
- pay bills
- make payments to any other UK bank or building society account
- set up, view, amend or cancel standing orders
- view direct debits
- order cheque books and other stationery
- send instructions to your bank via a secure e-mail system (which you should use instead of your normal e-mail).

At the time of writing, stand-alone Internet banks – such as cahoot (www.cahoot.com), Egg (www.egg.com), Intelligent Finance (www.if.com), smile (www.smile.co.uk), or the Internet account from First Direct (www.firstdirect.com) – offer all these services but differ from the traditional banks' add-on Internet services in two important respects. They don't have branches, and they pass on – in the form of competitive rates of interest – the cost-savings gained from operating over the Internet. Up-to-date rates are given on the banks' websites, which also feature online demonstrations.

All stand-alone Internet banks allow you to pay in cheques by post and withdraw cash through cash machines; some also use the Post Office. Check each for the particular services they offer.

Saving on utilities

We've all seen adverts urging us to switch suppliers of electricity, gas and telecoms. They promise big savings, especially those trying to get us to switch to a single supplier for electricity and gas.

So are there real savings to be made? The answer is yes, for the moment, and it may be less difficult to switch than you think. Even if you don't want to switch, you may still be able to reduce your bills. Phone companies may also provide Internet and cable television access. Before buying or changing, decide what you need and what you're prepared to pay for it.

Telecoms

Despite the fact that everyone has had a choice of company for their landline telephone for several years now, research by the Department of Trade and Industry showed that, up until June 2000, only 11% of people had taken steps to save on their land phone bills by moving away from British Telecom (BT). Choosing a cable company is one option. If you don't want to have a new line installed, or your street doesn't have cable, you can still save on your bills – up to 20%, for example, by keeping your BT line but changing the company that bills you for your calls.

Saving on the phone and the internet

There are several ways to save money on your phone bills, none of which involves changing your phone number.

- Stick with BT but switch from its standard line-rental package. Paying a little more each month for the BT Together package gives you a limited number of free calls, halves the cost of national calls and reduces the cost of your local and international calls. Another alternative is the BT Talk Together package. This has a higher monthly fee, but the first hour of every local call made at the weekend or on a weekday evening is free.
- If you make a lot of national and international calls, you can save a substantial amount by routing them through an 'indirect access' company. You still pay line rental to BT, but another company bills you for

calls. The company will give you a four-digit access code to dial before the number you want to call and/or you will get a special autodialler which re-routes calls.

- You can use different indirect access companies for different types of call, which is worth doing because some are cheaper for daytime national calls, while others specialise in cheap international calls. If you don't want to remember several access codes or have a number of autodiallers, sign up for 'carrier pre-selection' (CPS), offered by some indirect access companies. This allows calls to be switched through to the relevant company at the telephone exchange, doing away with the need for extra digits or kit.
- If you surf the Internet on a pay-as-you-go basis, it can add a big chunk to your phone bill, especially if you are a heavy user or you access the Internet at peak times. Unmetered access – where you pay a fixed fee per month to an Internet Service Provider (ISP) to cover all your surfing time – can be a much better deal. You can get up-to-date details of ISPs (offering both dial-up and broadband access), together with user comments on the quality of service, by going to www.net4nowt.co.uk. Some cable and other phone companies offer similar fixed-fee deals and some offer package deals.

Websites that enable you to compare phone costs – including mobile deals – include:
www.buy.co.uk
www.callforless.co.uk
www.saveonyourbills.co.uk
www.uswitch.com.

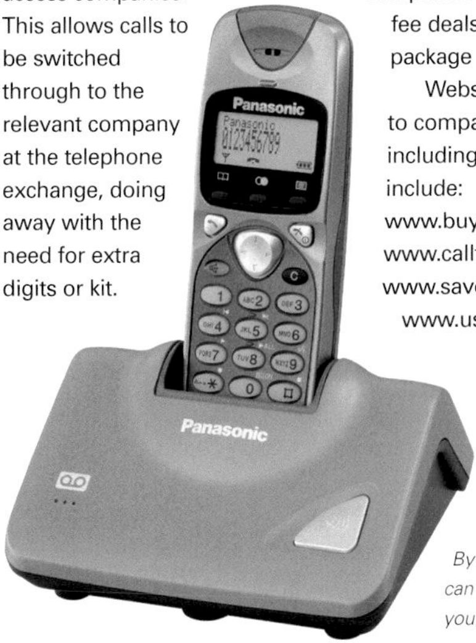

By shopping around you can really save money on your monthly phone bills

Gas and electricity

How to reduce your bills

Using less energy will reduce your bills (*see* pp131, 132, 138 and 144), but another way of saving money is to change from paying your bills by cash or cheque to paying by direct debit in order to take advantage of a price reduction of between about 5% and 10% (depending on usage and the company).

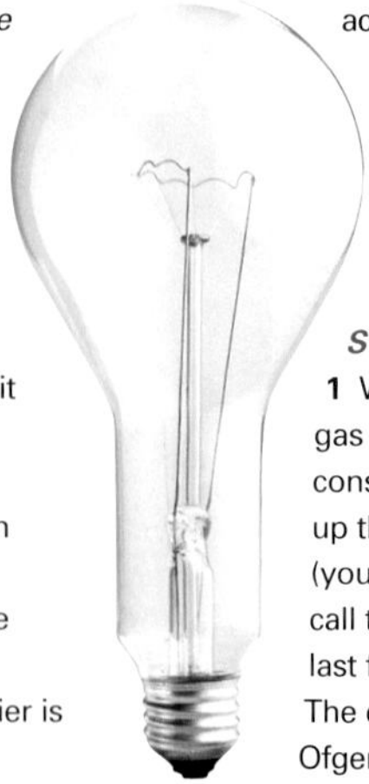

If your gas supplier is British Gas, paying promptly – which means paying a bill within ten days of the date it was issued – saves about £30 a year. Paying by direct debit is usually still cheaper, but how much cheaper depends on the size of your bill.

You can also save money by changing suppliers. According to figures published by the National Audit Office, people who have switched suppliers have saved, on average, £78 a year on gas and £45 on their annual electricity bills.

And since switching doesn't require any kind of physical upheaval (your gas pipes, electricity cables, and meters stay the same), the only hassle involved – if you want an accurate idea of how much you could save – is working out your annual consumption. See Switching suppliers.

Switching suppliers

1 Work out your annual gas and electricity consumption by adding up the kilowatt-hours (your electricity bill may call these 'units') on your last four quarterly bills. The energy regulator Ofgem estimates that average annual gas consumption is 10,000kWh in a flat or small house, 19,050kWh in a medium-sized house and 28,000kWh in a large house. The figures for electricity consumption are 1,650kWh, 3,300kWh and 4,950kWh.

2 Identify which suppliers will save you money. The easiest way to do this is to enter your annual consumption into the interactive calculators at www.buy.co.uk, www.unravelit.com or www.uswitch.com (which usefully gives each company a service rating). Alternatively, use the price information published in the free fact sheets published by Ofgem. The fact sheets also give suppliers' contact details.

3. Phone your chosen companies for quotes and to check what kind of contract is offered. With rolling contracts, the supplier is free to change the tariff after giving you 10 days' notice, but you are usually free to change to another supplier without penalty. With fixed contracts, the price can't go up during a set period but you could be charged a fee if you decide to switch again before the end of this period.
4. Sign the contract with your new supplier and tell the old supplier you want to switch. They may not let you do so until all bills have been paid.
5. Expect the whole process to take about 28 days, during which time either you will be asked to supply a meter reading or your new supplier will take one. Keep a note of this so you can check the old supplier uses the correct figure when calculating the final bill.
6. You should receive a letter from your new supplier telling you the date that the switch will take place.

Getting connected

When you move into a new home, you usually inherit the gas and electricity suppliers chosen by the previous occupant. If you are happy to stick with those suppliers, you should ask the relevant companies for **a contract** before you move in, as well as arranging to **have the meter read** when you move in. They will also be able to tell you whether the supply will need to be reconnected and whether there is a charge for this.

Changing suppliers If you want to change suppliers, ask the previous occupants for the gas **Meter Point Reference Number and Electricity Supply Number**. This helps to speed the change to a new supplier. If you can't get the information from the previous occupants and you want to find out who supplies your new property, contact the **Meter Number Helpline** for gas on 0870 608 1524. To find out which company supplies electricity and/or the Electricity Supply Number, contact the local electricity distribution company – under 'Electricity' in the phone book – and ask for the **Meter Point Administration Service**.

If you're renting If you rent a property and pay utilities directly, you may need your **landlord's permission** to change suppliers. If the landlord charges you for your gas and electricity, you will not be able to change supplier unless you can persuade him or her to do so. Note that there is a **maximum resale price** for gas and electricity, which is the most your landlord can charge you. This cannot be more than the price he or she has paid per kWh, although the landlord is also entitled to recover any standing charge.

Home insurance

There's an array of different types of insurance policies that between them offer a financial safety net to prevent you losing out on most of life's uncertainties.

In practice, there are limits on how many insurance premiums individuals can afford. However, when it comes to an insurance priority list, household insurance should be near the top for most people.

New-for-old cover

Most household policies will pay out on a **new-for-old basis**, which is especially important with contents cover. New-for-old means that if, say, your ten-year-old television is stolen, you should get the nearest current equivalent model or enough cash to buy one (though increasingly insurers prefer to replace goods from a named supplier).

No deduction is made for **wear and tear**. Be wary of policies that pay out on an indemnity basis – they do deduct for wear and tear when you claim.

Traditionally, even new-for-old policies have given only **indemnity cover** for some items, such as clothes. So if your entire wardrobe were ruined following a burst pipe in the attic, you wouldn't get enough cash to replace everything as new.

But some policies now do give **new-for-old cover on clothes** – something to watch out for if you like buying designer items.

What is household insurance?

Household insurance falls into two distinct types of policy: contents and buildings. You can choose to have just one type or both.

Buildings insurance protects the structure and fabric of a home you own, including the walls, windows, doors, floors, ceilings, roof, pipes, gutters, decorations, outbuildings, and fixtures and fittings such as baths, basins, radiators, boiler, fitted kitchen cupboards and the garage. In short, it protects things you couldn't take with you if you moved home.

Contents insurance protects things that you normally keep in your home, whether you own or rent the property. These are items that aren't an integral part of the building, such as furniture and furnishings, carpets and curtains, electrical appliances, kitchen and bathroom equipment, sports equipment, clothes, books, CDs and jewellery. In short, it protects movable possessions.

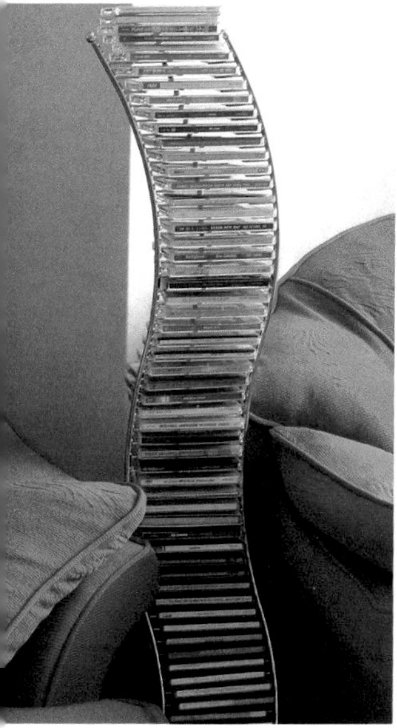

Contents insurance covers possessions such as CDs and music equipment

In certain cases, a policy may cover these possessions elsewhere, for instance while you are away from home (called all-risks, *see* Policy extensions, p273) or the place where a student member of the family lives in term-time. Cover can only extend to people who have what the insurers call an identifiable interest in your property, so members of the same family and common-law spouses can be covered by the same policy, but a group of friends sharing a flat, for instance, could not.

When do policies pay out?

Buildings and contents insurance policies typically pay out for damage and loss caused by fire, flood, storms, theft and attempted theft, vandalism, riots, leaks of oil and water, explosions, subsidence, (though there's usually a substantial excess for subsidence), heave, landslip, earthquakes and impact – for example by vehicles, animals (but not pets), trees, lamp posts, telegraph poles, aerials and aeroplanes.

Excess is an initial figure that the insurance company will not pay on a claim – you have to meet this and the insurer pays the balance on the sum you are claiming. The insurer will not meet claims below the excess.

Basic cover also usually includes your legal liability as owner or occupier, for example if a visitor or tradesperson sues you after an injury resulting from disrepair in your home.

It also usually pays for the cost of alternative temporary accommodation, for instance if you were flooded and had to leave your home.

How much buildings cover?

- Insure for the total rebuilding cost – what it would cost to rebuild your home from scratch if, for example, it were destroyed in a gas explosion or burnt to rubble.
- It's rare for anyone to have to claim the total amount. But if you don't insure for total rebuilding costs you'll be under-insured and any claim you submit is likely to be scaled down in proportion to the level of under-insurance.
- Rebuilding costs are based on the size of the property and are not the same as the market value of your property. This is partly because even if your property were to be demolished, you would still own the land. Don't insure for market value.
- If you have a mortgage, the lender's valuer will usually provide a sum to insure. If you need to work out rebuilding costs yourself, you can get a leaflet from the Association of British Insurers. Alternatively, you could pay for a quotation from a qualified surveyor, such as a member of the Royal Institution of Chartered Surveyors (RICS).

After some years your original sum insured could be out of date. For example, it may not have been correctly updated each year to match rebuilding cost inflation in your part of the country or you may have carried out major building works such as an extension or loft conversion. Reassess the sum insured from time to time.

How much contents cover?

- Work out the cost of replacing as new all your possessions, with the possible exception of clothes and household linen, for which you should make a deduction for wear and tear. Which items are to be costed as new and which are to be costed with a wear-and-tear deduction will depend on the policy you are buying (*see* New-for-old, p270).
- The cost of replacing everything (either as new or with a wear-and-tear deduction) is the sum you must insure for. If you under-insure, any claims, including small claims, could be scaled

down in proportion to the level of your under-insurance.

- Putting a replacement cost on every item in the home could be huge task and it may involve a lot of guessing, making the final figure an approximation only. Inevitably, many people make an intelligent estimate. If that's your approach, don't underestimate. You might be surprised at how much you would have to pay out if you needed to replace every item.
- You could err on the side of caution by overstating the replacement cost of all your possessions. Bear in mind that your premium would then be higher than it need be. And while there's a serious disadvantage in under-insuring, when it comes to claiming there's no advantage in being over-insured.
- Many policies automatically index-link your cover each year – that is, they increase the sum insured by the rate of inflation as measured by the retail prices index. Do review the level of cover from time to time. Index-linking may not be sufficient if you are steadily getting more prosperous and acquiring more valuable possessions.

Policy extensions

- Most policies will offer **limited cover for accidental damage**. A contents policy will usually pay out if you damage your television, a hand basin, or the glass in doors, for example. But extensive cover for damage caused by accidents is usually an optional extra, for which you have to pay an extra premium. Check what's covered in the basic policy and decide whether you or your household are sufficiently clumsy enough to make paying an extra premium worthwhile.
- Other things may be covered by the basic premium or **may be covered only if you pay an extra premium** – for example, your bike, the contents of a freezer (in case there is a power cut) or a computer you use for work. If these aspects of cover are important to you, check the small print or discuss with the insurer.
- Most policies offer an **all-risks extension**, also known as personal possessions cover, for an extra premium. This protects things you take outside your home and will usually pay out if you accidentally damage or lose them. It could be especially useful if you often have expensive items on you, such as jewellery, cameras, or sunglasses. But it could be an unnecessary expense. For example, you may want this protection only when you go on holiday and you could find similar cover is provided by the travel insurance you buy.
- Some policies cover you when you lose **stored oil or metered water**. Ask insurers about this cover if it sounds useful.
- Some policies include **cover for legal expenses** as a basic or an extra. Find out precisely what you would get in the event of a claim before you buy this cover as an extra or rely on it if it's included.

Benefits of using a broker

The cheapest insurance tends to come from **direct insurers** – those that sell direct to the public (usually over the phone and on the Internet) and that don't give commission to a broker or other intermediary. But direct insurers usually cater only for fairly standard risks and you will have to make all the price comparisons yourself – and check the small print.

What if you are in an area blighted by floods? Or have a holiday home to insure? Or have a home full of valuable antiques? Or have **other special needs** – perhaps a member of the household has a criminal conviction. Consider visiting a competent broker, even if you end up paying a higher premium.

A good broker should have a **thorough knowledge** of the market and be able to match the best policy to your needs. Another advantage is that the broker should be able to help if you ever need to make a claim.

Buying and claiming

Household insurance pays out only on items that are covered and for certain perils – such as fire and theft. Be aware of exclusions and limits on claims. Getting to know how policies work will improve your chances of buying the right one for you and of claiming successfully.

Tips for buying

Household insurance premiums are set by various factors beyond your control, including your postcode. Your area may suffer high crime, for instance, pushing up your premium even if your home has Fort Knox-style security. Despite this there are a few of ways to keep costs down.

- Household insurance offered through a mortgage lender can be expensive. Lenders get a big commission. Get alternative quotes.
- Mortgage lenders require borrowers to have buildings insurance but often let you choose your own insurer if you ask. They may charge £25 or so if you don't use their insurance, but it's often worth paying to get a lower premium. Some insurers will pay this fee for you if you switch to them.
- Buying buildings and contents from the same insurer should ensure there are no gaps in your cover and you will have to deal with only one insurer if you claim. But an insurer that's competitive on buildings premiums may not be so competitive on contents – or the other way round.
- An excess is the amount of any claim (loss) you must pay yourself. Most policies have compulsory excesses – and it's worth comparing these – but also let you choose voluntary

excesses. You get a reduced premium in exchange for a higher voluntary excess.

- Get several quotes before renewing your policies. In the financial services world, loyalty is rarely rewarded and is often penalised. If you do find a cheaper deal than your existing insurer, tell your existing insurer what you've been quoted, if you would rather stay with the company. It may be able to come up with an improved premium.
- Treat discounts cautiously, for example those marketed at people in particular trades and professions, of a certain age or in a neighbourhood watch scheme. Compare a discounted premium with non-discounted premiums.
- A cheaper policy could have unwelcome gaps in cover. Check the proposed cover carefully. And what's an insurer like when disaster strikes? Listen to friends who have claimed. Are some companies worth considering, others to be avoided?
- Check restrictions and exclusions carefully for any that would affect you particularly. For instance, many insurers reserve the right to replace lost items from specified suppliers (*see* below), and in some cases this extends to jewellery. If you own valuable antique jewellery, or prefer an unusual style, you may not want to replace it from a high-street chain.

Tips for claiming

- Keep receipts of things you buy, especially of expensive items. These could be useful if you ever need to claim. Take photos of the inside of your home and particularly of high-value items, such as antiques, including jewellery.
- Many insurers offer a no-claims discount. If you have one, find out what it would

Flood alert

If you live in a UK area at high risk from flooding and are worried about insurance, check with your local **Environment Agency** office whether there are plans to improve flood defences in your area by 2007. The Association of British Insurers intends that, if there *are* plans:

- you should be able to renew insurance with your current insurer, but the premium and excess may increase
- anyone buying your house should in principle be able to get cover from your existing insurer, but this may depend on their claims record.

However, if there are no plans:

- insurers may not guarantee to maintain cover. Properties could be considered individually.

cost you to lose it and also the amount of any excess you may have to pay, before you decide whether it's worth claiming.

- People often put in claims for things they are not covered for. But the reverse is also true. You may be unaware that your policy covers you for a particular loss or damage.
- You should put in a claim as soon as possible after you are aware that you have suffered damage or loss. Delayed claims may be refused.
- Report all crimes, such as break-ins or vandalism, to the police. The same applies to losses, even if you are sure something has been lost rather than stolen. A claim may be refused if you haven't reported it to the police and been given an incident number to quote.
- Don't buy a replacement item without checking with your insurer. Some insurers may want you to replace an item from a named supplier (from whom they will get a discount for the volume of their business) rather than offer cash. Most policies give the insurer the right to repair rather than replace items.
- Ask whether your insurer would agree to an upgrade. Even where insurers give replacement goods rather than cash, some allow you to pay the difference to upgrade your replacement. So if your video player were stolen, you could bring forward plans to buy a DVD player.
- After certain types of disaster – such as a flood, fire or break-in – contact your insurer as soon as possible to find out what you can do in terms of instant repairs. After a burglary, for example, you may need to secure the property with new locks or replacement glass.
- Don't embark on longer term or less urgent repairs until you have agreement for the work from the insurance company.
- Get the insurance company's permission before throwing anything out, for example a carpet ruined by flooding.
- If you have access to a camera, take pictures of your home showing the results of the damage and loss. Photos could provide useful evidence to support your claim.
- If you can't agree the value of your claim with the insurance company, consider paying a loss assessor to present your case (not to be confused with loss adjusters, whose job is to value your loss on behalf of the insurance company).

Borrowing to buy

The best way of financing a major purchase is to save up for it. If you can't wait that long, your only other option is to borrow. But taking out a loan can push up the price of your purchase quite considerably.

The repayment figures on a loan can work out quite expensive. The interest on a personal loan of £5,000 from a high street bank, for example, could add between £1,400 and £2,600 to what you pay. So if you want to borrow to finance a major piece of furniture or a home improvement, it pays to check the different types of loan available, and the charges involved, before you commit yourself to a lender.

Six thing to consider

1 Don't borrow if you don't have to. Buying on credit can add substantially to the cost of your purchase. You should also think twice before borrowing if you would still be repaying the loan long after your prospective purchase has stopped being of any use to you – if you want to finance a holiday, for example, or buy something that will quickly go out of fashion.

2 Don't overstretch your budget. Although it is best to pay off a loan as quickly as possible to keep interest charges to a minimum, the most important thing is to estimate how much

Look at the different loans available if you want to buy a brand new sofa

Comparing the cost of credit

All advertisements and marketing material for credit cards, mortgages and other loans (with the exception of overdrafts on bank accounts) have to show the cost of credit as **APR – Annual Percentage Rate**. This provides a standardised way of comparing the cost of one loan with another. The APR is not an interest rate – it is an annual rate, and takes into account how much you pay, how often you make payments, and the term or duration of the loan.

As well as the interest you will have to pay on the loan, the APR also covers fees and other charges for arranging the loan and may include the cost of **compulsory insurance** on repayments. When comparing credit offers, check whether insurance is included or not (*see* box, p279).

you can realistically afford to repay each month.

3 Check your credit card limit. Provided you have sufficient availability – or you can persuade your card issuer to increase your limit – using a credit card to borrow may be cheaper and more flexible than taking out a personal loan. Of course, this is true only if you have a card with a low rate of interest and you are disciplined enough to make regular monthly repayments to clear the debt.

4 Avoid borrowing on impulse. Some retailers use credit promotions to encourage impulse buying. This usually takes the form of some kind of discount if you use their store card (which works like a credit card) or apply for the store's fixed-rate loan (which works like a personal loan). Either way, the interest on the credit can be staggeringly expensive.

5 Beware interest-free credit deals. Although some genuinely are free, others offer interest-free credit for a limited time only – six months, say – and charge a high rate of interest after that. Buy-now-pay-later deals can also end up being expensive. With these, you pay nothing for a few months and then either settle the debt in full or start to make monthly repayments that tend to carry a high rate of interest.

5 Do your homework. It's easy to think that the best place to get a loan is from your bank but this is rarely true, especially of high street banks. Keep your borrowing costs to a minimum by checking the 'best-buy' tables published in the personal finance pages of the weekend press or by using one of several web sites that provide information on the various loan deals available.

What sort of loan?

A bank overdraft – which is repayable on demand by the bank – is unlikely to be the best way to finance a major purchase, especially if you want to spread the repayments over a number of years. Other options are described below.

Personal loans

If you want to borrow between £500 and £15,000 and you are prepared to pay it back over six months or within up to seven years, a personal loan can be a good choice.

For The monthly repayments are fixed for the duration of the loan, which makes budgeting easier and means that you don't have to worry about facing increased interest rates.

Against If you want to repay the loan early, a lot of lenders charge an early repayment penalty, which is typically the equivalent of two months' interest.

Flexible personal loans

A handful of lenders offer flexible personal loans, which work a bit like a credit card. You are given a borrowing limit when you take out the loan, there is no fixed repayment period and you are not required to make a fixed monthly repayment (although there is usually a minimum regular amount that you have to pay).

Payment protection insurance

When looking at the cost of monthly repayments on a personal loan, check whether they include **payment protection insurance**. This kind of cover aims to meet some or all of your loan repayments if you become ill, lose your job or, with some policies, if you die before the loan is paid off. However, payment protection insurance doesn't always pay out. Definitions of illness may be very restrictive, often excluding existing medical conditions and stress. Redundancy may be hard to prove if you are self-employed or work part time. So check the details in the small print before committing yourself. Insurance can also add a substantial amount to the overall costs of the loan.

Lenders rarely make buying this kind of insurance compulsory, because if they did it would have to be included in the APR and would make the loan look very expensive, but they do **use various ploys** to encourage you to take it out. These include:

- making monthly repayments that include insurance look more eye-catching in marketing literature than those without insurance
- using much smaller type for the figures for repayments without insurance so that they are harder to read
- printing payments without insurance over the page where you might not even notice them.

Refused credit?

No one has the right to credit. Lenders are likely to refuse you if they think that you are a bad risk and will not be able to repay the loan. This could happen if:

- you scored less than the pass mark in **credit scoring** – a kind of financial marking system that allocates a score to answers you give when applying for a loan
- the lender consulted a **credit reference agency** – the main two are Equifax and Experian – and information on your file suggested you have had borrowing problems.

If you can't think of a good reason why your application has been rejected, **ask the lender**. Lenders don't have to reveal why they turned you down but they must tell you whether they checked with a credit reference agency and if so, which one. You can then check with the agency that the information held about you is correct (you can also do this if you simply want to find out what is on your file).

A free leaflet, *No credit?*, from the Office of the Information Commissioner, tells you how to go about doing this and explains how to get your file corrected.

TOP TIPS

- **Don't borrow as a couple** – or guarantee someone else's loan – unless you're prepared to pay up if the other person can't (or won't).

- If you buy on **hire purchase (HP)**, you won't legally own the goods until you've paid the last instalment. If you default on payments the goods can be repossessed and you won't be entitled to any refund.

For A flexible loan can be useful if you want to be able to vary your monthly payments and you don't have a sufficiently large credit limit with your credit card.

Against Interest rates tend to be higher than with a normal personal loan, so it can be an expensive way of borrowing. If you want this kind of flexibility, and have sufficient credit limit, a credit card can be cheaper.

Secured loans

If you want to borrow to finance home improvements, a relatively cheap option is to extend your mortgage with your current lender. Alternatively, you could take out a loan secured on your home with another lender. However, the interest charged is usually higher than it would be if you simply increased your mortgage.

Against The disadvantage of taking out a secured loan is that you will have to pay a fee to set up the loan. You should also be aware that with any kind of loan secured on your home, if you do not keep up repayments, you risk having your home repossessed. This is not the case if you take out a personal loan, for which no security is required.

Purchasing matters

We all want a good deal when we buy goods and services and we need to know that we will be treated fairly if there is a problem.

While home shopping and Internet sites have made browsing and buying much more convenient in some respects, it isn't always easy to know who is actually supplying your purchases. The information and advice on the following pages comes from the Office of Fair Trading (OFT). The OFT runs a comprehensive web site with consumer rights advice and also runs a telephone service giving information about where to go for help if you have a problem (*see* pp300–301).

Your rights

Safety

It is an offence for a supplier to sell you goods – whether new or secondhand – unless they are safe. But this does not apply to antiques or to goods needing repair or reconditioning, provided you were clearly informed of this fact. If you believe you have bought unsafe goods, you should contact the Trading Standards department of your local authority. If new goods turn out to be unsafe you may have a legal claim against the manufacturer.

If things go wrong

If you decide to complain, bear in mind how the item was described. A new item must look new and unspoiled as well as work properly, but if the goods are secondhand or seconds then you cannot expect perfect quality. Many shops have goodwill policies that go beyond your statutory rights. For example, some stores allow you to exchange goods that aren't faulty, such as clothes that are the wrong size. If there is something wrong, tell the seller as soon as possible. If you can't return to the shop

Your legal rights

The law says that **goods** must be:

- of satisfactory quality
- fit for their purposes
- as described.

If you're buying a **service**, it should be carried out:

- with reasonable care and skill
- within a reasonable time – particularly if you have not agreed a completion date.

within a few days, it's a good idea to phone the trader with your complaint.

Rejecting faulty goods

You have a right to 'reject' faulty goods. If you tell the seller promptly that the goods are faulty and you don't want them, you should be able to get your money back. As long as you have not legally 'accepted' the goods you can still 'reject' them – that is, refuse to accept them.

One of the ways you accept goods is by keeping them without clearly saying that you want to return them after you've had a reasonable time to examine them. What is 'reasonable' however is not fixed: it depends on all the circumstances. Normally you can at least take your purchase home and try it out. But if you delay in examining what you've bought or in telling the seller that you wish to reject the goods, then you might lose your right to reject.

Sale goods

You have the **same rights** when you buy goods in a sale as at any other time. The seller can't get away with notices saying there are no refunds on sale goods.

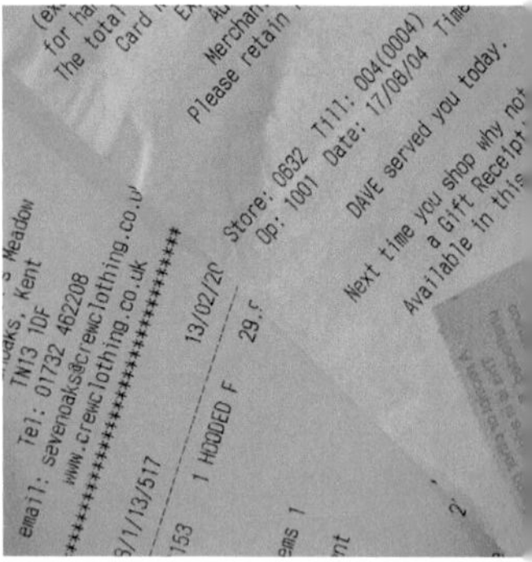

A receipt is evidence of when and where you bought the goods

Even if you signed an acceptance note, this does not mean you have signed away your right to reject the goods. If you agree to let the seller try to put faulty goods right, this also does not affect your rights. Make it clear that if the repair fails, you will be rejecting the goods and seeking a refund. You can insist on a full refund. You do not have to accept a replacement, free repair or credit note. But if you do accept a credit note you probably won't be able to exchange it for cash later on. Some credit notes are only valid for a limited period.

Once you have, in the legal sense, 'accepted' goods you lose your right to a full refund.

You can only claim reasonable compensation. Normally you have to accept an offer to put the goods right or the cost of a repair. But if the faults can't be put right you are entitled to appropriate compensation which, in many cases, may be the cost of buying an alternative.

Receipts

If you lose your receipt your rights still apply. A receipt, however, is important evidence of when and where you bought the goods and, if you don't have a receipt, some alternative proof of purchase is likely to be necessary – a credit card bill or bank statement might do. If you received faulty goods as a present, ask the person who bought them for the receipt or proof or purchase, or to complain for you.

Sending goods back

You're not legally obliged to return faulty goods to the seller at your own expense, unless you agreed this in advance. If a bulky item is difficult or expensive to return, ask the seller to collect it. This does not apply when you complain about faults after having 'accepted' the goods – or if the goods were a present.

Ways to complain

If you complain on the telephone:

- make a note of what you want to say
- have receipts and any other documents handy
- get the name of the person you speak to
- note the date and time and what is said
- follow up your call with a letter, particularly if your complaint is serious.

If you complain in writing:

- describe the item or service you bought
- say where and when you bought the item or when the service was done and how much it cost
- explain what is wrong, any action you've already taken, to whom you spoke and what happened
- say what you want done to remedy the situation, for example a refund or repair, or the job done again without charge
- consider using recorded/special delivery so you can check your letter has been received
- keep copies of any letters you send – send photocopies, of original documents.

Further tips:

- Consider getting an expert's opinion in writing to back up your complaint. Motoring organisations offer reports on cars, but any reputable trader with relevant experience can count as an expert. You might have to pay for this.
- If you did not fix a price but you think you've been overcharged, get quotes from other traders for comparison when you complain. Some may charge to do this.
- Take photographs if appropriate.
- If you bought the goods or services on a credit card, you might have additional protection.

Complaining

The law says it's up to the seller to deal with complaints about defective goods or other failures to comply with your statutory rights. Don't accept the excuse 'it's the manufacturer's fault', although you might also have rights against the manufacturer under a guarantee.

If you have to make a complaint about goods to a trader, most will try hard to deal with it properly. Go back to the shop as soon as possible. It's useful to have a receipt or other proof of purchase to take with you. Explain what the problem is, say what you want done about it and set a deadline. If you're still not satisfied put your complaint in writing. If the shop is part of a chain, write to the customer services manager at its head office. If none of this works, get further advice from your local Trading Standards department, a trade association that may be able to offer arbitration or consider whether you want to go to court (*see* Making a small claim, p289–91).

Equally, if you have a complaint about a service, give the supplier a chance to put the matter right. If you're not satisfied put your complaint in writing, saying what you want done and set a deadline. If you're dealing with a large business, address your letter to the customer services manager or company chairman/woman. Consider withholding further payments until the problem has been sorted out, but check the small print of any contract.

Be careful about withholding payments if you have a credit agreement. If you stop paying, it could affect your credit rating in the future. Continuing to pay will not undermine any claim you have against the lender for any unsatisfactory service by a supplier. You might want to take advice on this.

Home shopping outside the UK

Shopping in the EU Always check the details before you shop. Your additional home shopping rights in the UK stem from a European Directive and they therefore should also apply in other European countries. However, it may take longer for some European countries to amend their laws to provide you with equal protection. Also, they may not be exactly the same as in the UK.

Shopping beyond the EU In countries outside the European Union, your rights and responsibilities are likely to vary even more – so check these out too. Always try to check out the small print. If anything does go wrong, it might be more difficult to pursue a complaint against a trader who's based outside the UK – and particularly outside the EU.

If your goods arrive in a faulty state, you are entitled to your money back

Shopping from home: your rights

Under The Consumer Protection (Distance Selling) Regulations you have special rights as a consumer when you shop from home. You still have your normal statutory rights if something goes wrong.

With home shopping you have the right to:

- clear information before ordering
- written information about a purchase
- a 'cooling off' period during which an order can be cancelled without any reason and a full refund made
- a full refund if goods or services are not provided by an agreed date or within 30 days of placing an order if no date was agreed
- protection against credit card fraud.

Faulty goods

You are entitled to reject the goods and get your money back if the goods:

- are faulty
- are not of satisfactory quality
- do not match how they were described
- are different to the ones that you ordered.

If it takes a while before you notice the goods are faulty, you might only be entitled to claim compensation. This could be the cost of repair or the cost of returning the goods for a free repair. Check whether you are covered by a guarantee.

Returning goods

If your contract says that you should return the goods, you will probably have to pay the cost of returning them. If you choose not to return the goods yourself, the supplier can arrange to collect them – but still charge you for this. Before the seller can collect the goods, you must be given a written notice in a letter, e-mail or fax at the time the goods are collected, at the latest. Your rights may vary when you have a contract with sellers outside the UK.

Search engines will provide many examples of online shopping sites

Buying online

Once you have decided to buy something over the Internet, be sure you know what is being sold, the total price, the delivery date, the return and cancellation policy, and the terms of any guarantee.

Other points to remember:

- Save all information possible relating to your order. This might be pages from the supplier's web site (for example the advertisement), the completed order form, and any e-mails. Suppliers in EU countries should provide you with key pieces of information before your order is finalised. For example, they have to give you the identity of the supplier, the main features of the goods or services, the price, the arrangements for payment and any rights you have to back out. All of this must be given in a clear and understandable way.
- The supplier also has to send you confirmation of the order.
- Be wary of giving out your bank account numbers, credit card numbers or other personal information to a company you don't know or haven't checked out. And don't provide information that isn't necessary to make a purchase.
- Good companies are likely to have privacy statements on their web sites. In these they will explain what they do with the information they have about you and how secure the information is. Such companies will also allow you to say whether or not you want your information passed on to

other companies. Any company that sells or passes on details about you without your consent could be breaking UK and European law. Outside the EU there may be little action you can take against, say, a US-based company that has information about you.

- You may have some extra protection if you pay by credit card. If you have a claim against the seller for breach of contract or misrepresentation – for example, if goods were not supplied or were faulty – you may also have a claim against your credit card issuer. This could also be useful if the seller goes out of business. This applies to goods or services costing more than £100 for one item (but less than £30,000), even if you have only used your card to pay a deposit. You do not have the same protection if you pay by a debit or charge card.
- Many companies allow you to send your credit card details via a secure (encrypted) page and you should aim to buy from companies that give you this choice. You will be able to see on the screen whether the page you are on is secure. Often it will flash up a warning as you enter a secure page and you might see a closed-padlock symbol in the status bar at the bottom of your screen. If a padlock is not there and there are no other guarantees, you should think twice about buying.

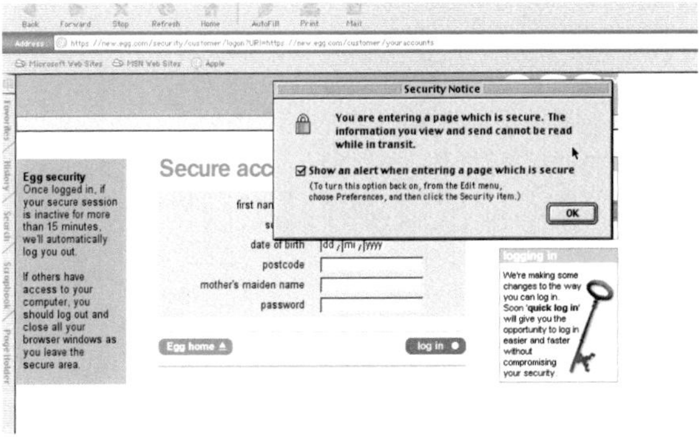

This website guarantees that any dealings – financial or otherwise – are secure

Online buying tips

Many tips for buying on the Internet are the same as for buying from a shop, such as:

- shop around. That great deal might well be on offer somewhere else
- use retailers and services you know about – or ones that have been personally recommended to you.

But there are also other aspects of shopping online:

- a company might have a great web site but that doesn't mean it is law-abiding
- make sure you know the trader's full address – especially if the company is based outside the UK
- don't assume an Internet company is based in the UK just because its web address has 'uk' in it – check out the address and phone number
- look for web sites that have a secure way of paying (known as an encryption facility) – these show a padlock at the bottom of the screen for payment details
- check whether the company has a privacy statement that tells you what it will do with your personal information.

Look for firms that are part of an independent approval scheme such as TrustUK. These have signed up to particular standards, including measures to:

- protect your privacy
- ensure your payments are secure
- let you know what you've agreed to
- tell you how to cancel orders
- deliver goods or services within agreed timescales
- protect children
- sort out complaints – regardless of where you live.

There are many trader approval schemes worldwide, so check out what their particular approval means.

Buying online from abroad

The general advice on buying online should always be followed when buying from abroad. But there are additional issues.

- Standards vary between countries. Ask the supplier to confirm compatibility of, for example, electrical goods.
- Check that any guarantee is valid in the UK and whether you will have to return the product to the supplier's country if there is a problem.
- Check for hidden costs such as VAT, customs duties, delivery charges, postage and packaging. The Customs and Excise website gives information on when VAT and duty has to be paid. However, if your supplier is based in the EU, prices should include tax.
- If problems arise, you might have to take legal action in the country of the seller.

Buying privately and at auction

In a private sale, the **goods must be as described**, but a seller who is not acting as a business is not covered by the rules on satisfactory quality and fitness for purpose. An auction house is, in principle, covered by the rules on quality of goods, but it may be able to get out of this by putting an exclusion clause in its contract. Always read the terms and conditions before you bid.

Making a small claim

Faced with a genuine complaint, most firms are prepared to exchange goods or give a refund or appropriate compensation without the threat of court action, but some dig in their heels.

If you find yourself in a dispute claiming up to £5,000 from a manufacturer, retailer or service provider, you can take your claim to the county court. The defendant may settle on delivery of the summons, but if not, your case will be considered for the small claims track. Going to court needn't be daunting or expensive as long as you're well prepared and have worked out your costs.

How to sue

You'll need patience if you sue, as your claim may take six months or so to get to court. But before contemplating going to court, give the third party a chance to settle. If nothing happens, write threatening action. State that if they have not settled to your satisfaction by a certain date – seven or 14 days – you will issue a claim in the county court.

In England and Wales, you can go to any county court to start the action. Ask for the claim form N1 and its notes for guidance. Fill in the form and return it to the court. The fee for issuing a claim will be between £27 and £115, depending on the amount you are claiming for, or £120 if you are claiming for something other than money.

It is possible to take a claim of more than £5,000 down the small claims track, but only if the defendant agrees with your suggestion and the judge thinks your claim is sufficiently straightforward. The fee for issuing a claim under these circumstances is up to £500.

The court will send the defendant the necessary papers. The defendant must reply within 14 days and can apply to have up to 28 days to send in a defence. If there is a hearing, it may be in the court for the area where the defendant is based.

TOP TIP

www.courtservice.gov.uk gives a full account of the small claims track and other aspects of using the courts in England and Wales.

The small claims track

The small claims track is a relatively informal court procedure designed with the do-it-yourself litigant in mind. **You don't need a solicitor or any legal knowledge.** You won't normally risk big legal costs if you lose.

Claims must be simple and not involve large numbers of expert witnesses or grey areas of the law. There's usually an **upper limit of £5,000** for each claim, although see How to sue (p289) for claiming over £5,000. The limit on claims for personal injury or housing disrepair is £1,000.

Typical small claims concern faulty goods, services inadequately delivered, bad workmanship, damage to property, road traffic accidents, personal injury, debts and disputed ownership. You can also use the procedure to **force action** – for example, to compel a landlord to carry out repairs.

The defendant's response

- The papers may be returned to the court undelivered, in which case the court will send you a notice of non-service. You will then have to serve the claim form yourself. Court staff can tell you how to do this. You must serve the claim within four months of the date it was issued or apply for an extension if four months is not long enough – for instance, if you cannot track down the defendant's current address.
- The defendant may admit your claim and offer to settle with you immediately.
- The defendant may challenge your claim at first, but then admit it and offer to settle as the date for a court hearing approaches.
- The defendant may admit your claim and offer a sum of money where you have not specified an amount. If you accept the offer, ask the court for a judgement to be registered. This will allow you to take further steps to enforce the judgement should the defendant fail to honour the promise. If not, a judge will decide the amount of money, possibly at a court hearing.
- The defendant may agree to pay the amount you want but under terms you don't like, perhaps in instalments. Court officials can impose a solution.
- The defendant may ignore your claim. You can then ask for judgement in your favour. If you haven't specified an amount of money in your claim, a judge will decide the amount.
- The defendant may dispute your claim, saying that you are asking for too much or rejecting the claim outright. It's only when this happens that you discover whether your case will be channelled to the small claims track.

When a claim is disputed

It is only when a claim is disputed that you discover whether your case will be allocated to the small claims track. A judge will decide whether it fits the criteria – see left. If it doesn't fit the criteria, a judge will allocate the case to a different track (fast track or multi-track) of the county court. You'll have to decide whether to proceed or withdraw, taking account of the more formal procedures and the risk of incurring the defendant's costs should you lose the case.

You will be sent a copy of the defendant's case and asked to fill in allocation questionnaire form N150 to put your case on the small claims track. On the form you can apply to put forward evidence from an expert witness. There is an allocation fee of £80 for claims of more than £1,000.

Assuming your case is accepted for the small claims track, you'll be told when and where the hearing will take place and what you need to do. Sometimes a judge requires a preliminary hearing. If not, there's only one hearing and typically it will last for no longer than an hour. A judge may not even require a hearing if a decision can be taken on the paperwork alone.

If you win but the defendant ignores the judgement, it will be up to you to enforce the judgement, which might require you taking further legal action. County court staff can advise on the procedure.

Eight tips for making a small claim

1 **Gather your evidence** – brochures, letters, contracts and other documents, records of phone conversations or visits to a shop, photos, witness statements – and work out how strong your case is.
2 A **Citizens Advice Bureau** may be able to advise on how your case might fare under the small claims track.
3 Find out when your local county court has **small claims hearings** and whether you can observe as a member of the public. This will give you a feel for how proceedings work.
4 County court staff can advise on **procedures** and have a range of leaflets on going to court.
5 **If you don't wish to speak in court**, you can ask someone to do it on your behalf – a relative, friend, advice worker or even a solicitor if you're prepared to foot the bill.
6 Keep **copies of all documents** that arise as your case goes forward.
7 **Read all court documents carefully**. Watch for deadlines, pay fees on time and don't get to court late – otherwise your claim could be struck out.
8 You may be able to object to or **appeal against decisions** taken by officials or the judge as your case proceeds, but watch out for time limits at each stage.

Taxing matters

According to an investigation carried out in 2002 by Tax Action (a company set up to promote independent financial advice), as a nation we paid out nearly £4 billion in unnecessary tax in the year 2001–2002. Apart from fines and interest, most came from people paying more tax than they legally had to.

Tax-saving tips

1 Check your PAYE tax code, which appears on your payslip. If it is wrong, you could be paying too much – or too little – tax. If you have not received a coding notice, ask for leaflet *P3(T) PAYE: Understanding your tax code,* which explains how your code is worked out and what the letter in your code means, from your tax office.

2 Avoid incurring a penalty. If you fail to file your tax return (and pay any tax due) by 31 January following the end of the tax year to which the tax return relates, you face an automatic fine of £100. This is also the case if you become self-employed and you fail to register with the Revenue within three months from the end of the month in which you started working for yourself. Ask your tax office for a copy of leaflet *CWL1: Starting Your Own Business?*

3 Make the most of your ISA allowances (*see* p298). Keeping cash in an ISA rather than in a bank or building society account increases the interest you get by 20%. If you prefer to invest in equities,

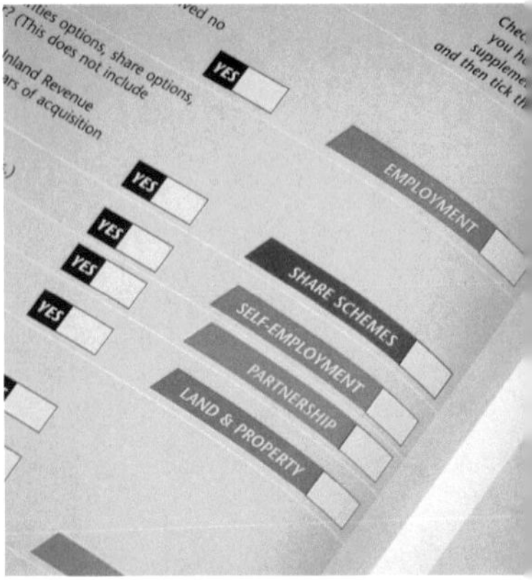

Tax returns need to be returned to the Inland Revenue by 31 January or you face an automatic £100 fine

you get back the 10% tax that is deducted from the income from equities – and there's no capital gains tax to pay when you finally cash in your investments.

4 If you are asked to make tax payments on account – advance payments against tax to be paid at the end of January and July – check that you are not paying more than you need to. The amount you have to pay is based on last year's tax bill, so if your income has gone down, the amount of tax due will also fall. You can request that the Inland Revenue reduce the amount of payment required.

Your tax obligations

Your obligations as a taxpayer are to be honest, to give accurate information, to keep records and – if you receive one – to file your self-assessment tax return and pay your tax on time. **Even if you don't receive a tax return, you are still legally obliged to tell the Inland Revenue about income and capital gains that have not been taxed.** You should also tell the Revenue about taxable work perks (or 'fringe benefits'), such as a company car. However, if all your perks are listed on the P11D provided by your employer, you can safely assume that the Revenue has been informed. The deadline for notifying the Revenue is six months after the end of the tax year in which you made the income or gain or received the work perk.

Capital gains tax

As well as having to pay tax on the income you get from savings and investments, you may also have to pay capital gains tax (CGT).

CGT becomes liable when you sell assets that have increased in value, such as antiques and investments like shares, unit trusts, and open-ended investment company shares held outside the tax-free wrapper of an ISA. There's no CGT to pay when you sell your main home (broadly, one you've been living in), but you may face a CGT bill if you sell a property you inherited or bought to let.

The tax bill is based on the capital gain, which is the difference between what the asset was worth when you got it and the price at which you sold it (or gave it away), less any costs – such as share-dealing commission – involved in buying and selling.

For example, in the 2002–2003 tax year, you would have to pay CGT at a rate of 10%, 20% or 40%, depending on your income on any gains over £7,700. Gains lower than this were tax free for that year.

Why make a will?

A will sets out what you want to happen to what you leave behind after your death. If you don't make one, the law decides who gets what (unless your heirs draw up a deed of arrangement – *see* **Avoiding inheritance tax**). What the law decides varies according to whether you are single, married, have children and/or other close relatives. If you are all alone in the world and fail to leave a will, everything goes to the Crown.

Making a will (or revising an existing will) is essential if:
- you want to **stipulate** who gets what
- you start acquiring **substantial assets** such as a home
- you are **co-habiting** and want your partner to inherit your worldly goods
- you are **divorced** and your ex-partner is still alive and/or you have children from a former marriage
- you have **young children** and you want your wishes about who looks after them taken into account
- you marry – **marriage** automatically revokes any will you made as a single person, unless you specified it was 'in consideration of marriage'
- you run your **own business** or farm.

You don't have to use a solicitor to draw up a will – costs start at around £50, as opposed to £5 for a do-it-yourself pack – but unless your circumstances are absolutely straightforward it is advisable to get legal advice.

Inheritance tax

You won't have to pay inheritance tax on your own estate (broadly, what you leave behind when you die) for the simple reason that you'll be dead. But you may face an inheritance tax bill if you inherit money, property or other items of value from someone else. At the time of writing, there would be no tax if you inherited from a husband or wife, or if the total value of the estate of the person you inherited from was worth £250,000 or less and the death occurred in the 2002–2003 tax year.

If the total value were more than £250,000, whether or not you would have to pay tax would depend on two factors. First, it would depend on how the will was worded. If the will said that:

- your gift was 'free of tax' (or didn't mention tax at all), you should get the amount specified in the will and any tax due would be paid for out of what was left of the estate after all other gifts had been paid from it
- your gift was 'subject to tax' or 'bears its own tax' – there could be a tax bill.

Second, whether or not there would be a tax bill would depend on the taxable value of the estate. This is worked out by taking the total value of the estate and then subtracting debts, funeral expenses and tax-free gifts, including those to a spouse, charity and/or political party.

To this figure would then be added the total amount of gifts that the person whose will it is made in the seven years before death less tax-free lifetime gifts, which would include:

- wedding gifts worth up to £5,000 from a parent, £2,500 from a grandparent and £1,000 from anyone else
- small gifts of up to £250
- the first £3,000 of any other gifts made in each of the seven years before death.

If the resulting total were less than the nil-rate band of £250,000, there would be no inheritance tax to pay. If it were more than the nil-rate band, tax at 40% would be charged on the taxable value of the estate less £250,000. So if the taxable value of the estate came to £275,000, tax would be due on £25,000 – £275,000 minus £250,000.

These are the rules and limits that apply for the 2002–2003 tax year. Changes to inheritance tax rules, if any, are announced in the budget and are generally featured in press budget reports.

Avoiding inheritance tax

A lot of people worry unduly about inheritance tax, which is paid on **fewer than 6% of estates**. If you stand to inherit under a will and you think you could face an inheritance tax bill, your options for avoiding the tax are limited to encouraging the person whose will it is to take steps to reduce the possible inheritance tax liability. But since most of the ways of reducing a potential tax bill involve either giving money and possessions away before death and/or paying for professional advice on inheritance tax planning, you may feel that, as a potential recipient, you could come across as a little grasping. Another barrier is that a lot of people don't like talking about money and death – even to their nearest and dearest.

However, even if someone takes no steps to reduce a possible tax bill, it may not matter, because it is possible to alter someone's will after death by getting a solicitor to draw up a **'deed of rearrangement'**. Provided you act within two years of a death and all the beneficiaries agree, rearranging a will – which can mean adding beneficiaries who weren't originally included – can reduce the tax bill. You can also use a deed of rearrangement to create a will for someone who died 'intestate' – without making a will.

Acting as an executor

If you are an executor for someone's will and their estate is not owned jointly with a surviving partner, you will need to apply in person to a **probate office** to get probate – an official form allowing the executors to take charge of the dead person's assets. If the probate office advises you that inheritance tax is likely to be due, take legal advice, paid for out of the estate.

Lump sums

If you've built up a solid chunk of savings, you've just had a handsome bonus or perhaps have been lucky enough to inherit some money or win a few thousand on the lottery, you can be left wondering what to do with the extra cash. Here are a few pointers.

A lot depends on your personal circumstances, what you want the lump sum to do for you and how big it is. But on no account should you make a hasty decision or assume you must rush to invest the money. Take time to explore all the options and consider getting financial advice.

Before blowing your windfall, consider all your options carefully

Six priorities

1 Clear short-term debts such as bank overdrafts, credit-card debts and personal loans. A debt is an unnecessary drain on your finances and the interest you save by paying them off will be higher than the interest you can earn from putting money on deposit.

2 Put some cash aside to cope with the unexpected. You should also consider setting aside enough cash to cover major expenditure in the future, so that you avoid the expense of borrowing.

3 Boost your retirement savings either by starting a pension or by paying extra contributions into an existing scheme. If you already belong to an employer's scheme (and, in the 2002–2003 tax year, you earned less than £30,000) you can choose between taking out a stakeholder pension and paying into an additional voluntary contribution (AVC) scheme, which employers have to run alongside their main pension scheme.

4 Buy a home if you know that you will be staying in the same place for at least three

years. Buying your home is often cheaper than renting and by the time you finish paying off the mortgage, you will have acquired a substantial financial asset.

5 Pay off some of your mortgage. This can either help to boost your monthly income or reduce the mortgage term. The downside of paying off your mortgage debt is that you may not be able to get at your cash again without selling or re-mortgaging. However, this is not the case with flexible mortgages that link your mortgage to your savings. Instead of paying you interest on your savings, the lender offsets your savings against the amount you owe, which in turn reduces the amount of interest you pay – while still giving you ready access to your cash. Swapping to a flexible mortgage is no different from switching any other kind of mortgage, although you will have to take penalty clauses into account.

6 Put any money left over after you have covered the basics in an easy-access savings account paying the highest rate of interest you can find, while you consider your investment options.

Short-term options

Unless you can leave your money untouched for more than five years, you will find that your options are pretty much limited to putting your cash into savings accounts and other products where the value of your money does not rise and fall, but grows by having interest added to it. Short-term, low-risk options include:

- savings accounts that pay a variable rate of interest (the rate varies in line with interest rates generally)
- cash mini ISAs
- term accounts, where you lock your money away for anything from six months to five years
- fixed-rate deposit accounts
- local authority bonds, where you lend money to a local authority in exchange for a fixed amount of interest
- products from National Savings and Investments (NS&I).

Long-term options

The first decision to make is whether you want your savings to provide you with income or growth, or a mixture of the two. Although many investments suit both these aims, some are particularly

Different types of ISA

Taking out an **Individual Savings Account (ISA)** is a way of sheltering investment returns from tax. Pick one or more of the three types of account to suit your needs: a cash ISA; one that invests in the stock market (i.e. shares, unit trusts and investment trusts); or one that's life-insurance-based. Bear in mind, however, that unless you are a higher-rate taxpayer, the charges you will pay on stock and shares ISAs and insurance-based ISAs may outweigh the tax savings.

Mini or maxi?

Each tax year you can choose between having one maxi ISA or up to three different mini ISAs – but you cannot have both. If you opt for a maxi ISA, you must use a single provider to invest in stocks and shares. With mini ISAs, you can choose a different provider for each type of investment.

Annual ISA limits

Up to 2006, the most you can save in cash is £3,000 per year, and the most you can spend on life-insurance-based investments is £1,000 per year. If you take out a mini stocks and shares ISA, the most you can invest is £3,000. With a maxi ISA, you can invest a maximum of £7,000 in stocks and shares, but if you do this, you cannot invest in cash and insurance.

CAT-marked ISAs

CAT-marked ISAs – the acronym stands for Cost, Access and Terms – meet certain minimum standards laid down by government. For cash ISAs the CAT mark means that, among other things, the interest paid is guaranteed to be no less than 2% below bank base rate. For stocks and shares ISAs, it guarantees that you pay no more than 1% in charges – for insurance ISAs the maximum charge is 3%.

geared to producing an income while others will be better for producing a larger lump sum at a future date. You must also decide how much risk you are prepared to take on your investment – generally, the higher the risk, the greater the return over the long term.

Medium to high risk

If you are happy to see the value of your lump sum go up and down, consider investments that provide capital growth – where the lump sum itself changes in value (as with shares) rather than growing by having interest added (as with money in a savings account). It's generally considered unwise to choose fluctuating investments if you can't lock your money away for at least five years. This is because in the short term there is a very real risk that you will get back less than what you put in. Options include:

- corporate bond funds (investment funds that invest in corporate bonds)
- unit trusts or open-ended investment company shares (OEICS, an investment fund that works like a unit trust)
- investment trusts

- unit-linked insurance (like unit trusts with a bit of life insurance thrown in)
- shares.

Low to medium risk

With some investments you can be sure of what you get back, provided you hold the investment for a minimum period of time, although the value of your lump sum can fluctuate in the meantime. Long-term, medium-risk investments include:

- gilts (these are British Government Stocks)
- corporate bonds
- guaranteed growth bonds (offered by life insurance companies, these guarantee to return your lump sum plus a fixed amount of growth at the end of a fixed period)
- guaranteed income bonds (as above, except that they guarantee to pay a fixed amount of monthly income for a fixed period of time)
- with-profits bonds (a unit-linked life insurance that offers a degree of certainty but not a guarantee. Your money grows by having bonuses added. Bonuses can vary from year to year, which is why the return on your money is not guaranteed).

Variable, fixed or index-linked?

The majority of investments pay a return that is variable, which means that the amount of money your investment pays you goes up and down in line with market conditions. However, if you want a degree of predictability, you can choose investments such as Savings Certificates from NS&I, where the return is fixed. This can work in your favour if, after investing, interest rates generally fall – but the reverse is true if they rise.

If you choose an index-linked return, the return is guaranteed to keep pace with inflation – usually with a bit on top. You won't normally get the highest return possible but you can be certain that your money isn't losing its spending power.

Premium Bonds

One way to gamble, without the risk of losing your stake, is to buy Premium Bonds from **National Savings and Investments (NS&I)**. The money you 'invest' buys you numbers that are entered into a monthly draw. This gives you the chance of winning as much as £1 million or as little as £50 – or of not winning at all. Financial experts are divided over whether premium bonds are a serious form of investing as the actual value of your bonds will decrease (they will not keep up with inflation), so redeeming them will give you less spending power than you put in.

Contact details

Useful websites and addresses about the information given in this chapter.

Association of British Insurers, 51 Gresham Street, London EC2V 7HQ
Tel: 020 7600 3333
Fax: 020 7696 8999
e-mail: info@abi.org.uk
www.abi.org.uk

Banking Code Standards Board, 33 St James's Square, London SW1Y 4JS
Tel: 020 7661 9694
Fax: 020 7661 9784
e-mail: helpline@bcsb.org.uk
www.bankingcode.org.uk

Consumer Credit Counselling Service, Wade House, Merrion Centre, Leeds LS2 8NG
Tel: 0800 138 1111
e-mail: duty.counselling@cccs.co.uk
www.cccs.co.uk

Equifax Credit File Advice Centre, PO Box 1140, Bradford BD1 5US
Tel: 0870 010 0583
www.equifax.co.uk
Area of the site devoted to your credit file and how to obtain a copy.

Experian, Consumer Help Service, PO Box 8000, Nottingham NG1 5GX
Tel: 0870 241 6212
www.experian.co.uk
Your credit file and how to obtain a copy.

Financial Ombudsman Service, South Quay Plaza, 183 Marsh Wall, London E14 9SR
Tel: 0845 080 1800
e-mail: enquiries@financial-ombudsman.org.uk
www.financial-ombudsman.org.uk

Financial Services Authority, Public Enquiries Office, 25 The North Colonnade, Canary Wharf, London E14 5HS
Tel: 0845 606 1234
e-mail: consumerhelp@fsa.gov.uk
www.fsa.gov.uk/consumerzz

HM Customs and Excise
Tel: 0845 010 9000
www.hmce.gov.uk

Inland Revenue
Tel: 020 7667 4001
www.inlandrevenue.gov.uk

Insolvency Service
Tel: 020 7291 6895
www.insolvency.gov.uk

Law Centres Federation, Duchess House, 18–19 Warren Street, London W1T 5LR
Tel: 020 7387 8570
Fax: 020 7387 8368
e-mail: info@lawcentres.org.uk
www.lawcentres.org.uk
Information about Law Centres which provide free legal advice.

moneysavingexpert.com
www.moneysavingexpert.com
Independent guide to saving money on virtually everything.

Money Supermarket, 1 Chantry Court, Sovereign Way, Chester, Cheshire CH1 4QA
Tel: 0845 345 5708
e-mail: moneysupermarket@mortgage2000.co.uk
www.moneysupermarket.com
Offers comparison tables for personal finance products.

MX Moneyextra, Customer Services, 66 Queen Square, Bristol BS1 4JP
Tel: 0845 077 7085
Fax: 0117 943 7693
e-mail: customer.services@moneyextra.com
www.moneyextra.com
Guidance on financial products.

National Association of Citizens Advice Bureaux, Myddelton House, 115–123 Pentonville Road, London N1 9LZ
e-mail: adviceguide@nacab.org.uk
www.adviceguide.org.uk

National Debtline, The Arch, 48–52 Floodgate Street, Birmingham B5 5SL
Tel: 0808 808 4000
Fax: 0121 703 6940
www.nationaldebtline.co.uk

Northern Ireland Court Service
Tel: 028 9032 8594
Fax: 028 9023 6361
e-mail: informationcentre@courtsni.gov.uk
www.courtsni.gov.uk

OPAS, 11 Belgrave Road, London SW1V 1RB
Tel: 0845 601 2923
Fax: 020 7233 8016
e-mail: enquiries@opus.org.uk
www.opas.org.uk
Independent organisation providing advice on the full range of pensions.

Scottish Court Service
Tel: 0131 229 9200
Fax: 0131 221 6890
e-mail: enquiries@scotcourts.gov.uk
www.scotcourts.gov.uk

LET
COURT SECURITY
SOHO W1

Letting and Renting

Advantageous mortgage rates have led more people than ever to buy property to let as an investment for the future. However, whether you let a property or rent it as a tenant, there are certain rules to follow.

Renting a property can be the best option, especially if you do not have sufficient funds for a mortgage deposit, do not want to be tied to a particular area or are relocating and want to get a feel of the place before you look into buying a property. In this chapter, whether you are a tenant or the landlord, we cover key letting issues, rights and obligations of the tenant, tenancy agreements, as well as the tax implications on letting property for the landlord.

Deciding to let

Letting out a property has become an attractive option for long-term investment and a useful short-term solution if you have to move but are reluctant to sell.

In the last decade or so, the number of people renting in Britain – and the number of properties available to rent – has increased enormously. This was first triggered by the recession of the early 1990s. More recently, the rise in property prices increased the pool of people unable to afford a mortgage and therefore increased demand for rental accommodation.

Buy to let

The logic behind buy-to-let is simple. Over the years, the value of property has gone up by more than the rate of inflation. If you can buy a property and then let it at a rent that is more than the cost of repaying the loan financing the purchase, then you have the perfect investment – an income-producing asset that will also increase in value. But there are pitfalls you need to avoid.

- Don't get carried away by dreams of wealth. In many parts of the country there is already a surplus of accommodation to let and thus no guarantee that you will get a tenant or have a steady succession of tenants.
- Buy a property that will be easy to let – size, location and the rent you will need to charge to make a decent return on your investment will be paramount.
- Ask letting agents which types of property, and in which areas, are easiest to let and how much rent these properties will command. Don't just ask the agent who is trying to sell you the buy-to-let loan – go for someone who has no self-interest.
- Like any other business, a letting business has to be run. Be prepared for things to go wrong – such as burst pipes and other problems that need fixing quickly. You will have to organise these and you will be liable to compensate the tenant if you are not able to act quickly enough. Or you can delegate the responsibility to an agent, as part of a full management service.

The demand for rented property is still on the increase

Buy-to-let mortgages

Unless you can buy a property outright, you will need to raise the cash by taking out a mortgage with one of the increasing number of lenders who offer buy-to-let loans. These work just like the mortgage you take out to buy your own home (*see* p366–75), except that:

- you may have to pay a slightly higher interest rate than you would if the loan was for a home for you to live in, although at the time of writing increased competition in the buy-to-let loan sector is bringing interest rates down
- you will usually need to put down a deposit of between 20% and 25% of the value of the property
- the size of mortgage the lender will allow you is based not on your personal earnings but on the expected rental income for the year

TOP TIP

If you are going to use a **letting agent** to manage your property, invite two or three local agents round to appraise the property. This way, there will be a consensus on pricing and you can compare their various services and charges.

- the mortgage payments, together with other expenses involved in letting the property, can be deducted from the rental income, which reduces the amount of the income on which you have to pay tax.

Use an interactive calculator such as that on the website of Paragon Mortgages (www.paragon-mortgages.co.uk) to work out how much money you may make both in terms of rental income and in likely profit from the eventual sale of the property.

Risk assessment

Letting property can be risky. You only need one bad tenant who stays for six months without paying any rent and then disappears, leaving the house in need of hundreds of pounds' worth of redecoration to bring it back into a decent condition, and your profit for that year – and probably the next – could be gone.

You should take out property insurance, which would cover damage, but the rent is not insurable. If you employ an agent and they failed to check references properly, you could claim negligence. You can also get legal-costs insurance to cover your costs if you have to sue a tenant.

No matter what happens with your tenant, you will still have to go on paying the mortgage and the other outgoings on the property. If you cannot keep up the mortgage payments, then your lender will have the right to take

Reasons for letting

- If you're **moving jobs** within a company and need to move to another area, perhaps for a short time, there is a good case for keeping your present property and letting it out in case you need to return. Often the rent you receive will more than cover the mortgage payments you will have to continue making on the property.
- It has become **easier to get a mortgage on a property with the specific intent of letting it** (*see* Buy-to-let mortgages, p305). This is because in 1989 the security of tenure that previously applied to tenants was relaxed, making a let property less risky for mortgage lenders, who always want to know they can realise their investment if they need to.

possession of the property and sell it in order to recover their loan and interest.

Tax implications

- You will have to pay income tax on any profit you make over and above your outgoings on the property, and will therefore have to inform the Inland Revenue and fill in a tax return every year. These outgoings will include decorating costs, maintenance charges for servicing gas and electricity appliances, buildings insurance, and, in addition for a leasehold property, annual ground rent and any annual service charges made by the management company.
- When you come to sell a property you have let out, you will also be liable for capital gains tax (CGT) on any profit you make on the sale. CGT doesn't apply to your own home as long as you have resided there throughout your ownership.

The Inland Revenue publishes the following useful leaflets: *IR87: Letting and your home*; *IR150: Taxation of rents – A guide to property income*; *IR250: Capital allowances and balancing charges in a rental business.*

Using a letting agent

Having decided that you are going to let, **how do you go about finding the perfect tenant**? You could simply place an advertisement in your local shop or newspaper and take complete responsibility on yourself for finding a tenant. Alternatively, you can use a letting agent. Before deciding which agent to go with, do your homework.

- **Most agents offer two options – full management or just collection of rent.** Check their fees and what these fees include. In addition to a percentage of the rent, there will typically be one-off fees for finding a tenant, preparing a tenancy agreement (necessary for each new tenant), preparing and agreeing an inventory, and so on.
- **Ask friends or colleagues** whether they have any experience of renting property through the local agencies – they may be able to tell you which are the most efficient in dealing with queries.
- **Agents vary in how carefully they vet prospective tenants.** If you feel up to it, go round the agencies as a prospective tenant to see how efficient they seem at 'selling' the properties they have to let and what they want to know about you.
- There have been several instances of letting agents holding on to rents received and then either going bankrupt or disappearing, leaving landlords out of pocket. It's, therefore, wise to go for an agent who is a **member of one of the recognised professional bodies** – the Royal Institution of Chartered Surveyors or the Association of Residential Letting Agents. These bodies have codes of conduct and compulsory insurance schemes to protect clients from problems such as money disappearing due to insolvency or fraud.

Key letting issues

Preparing to let a property takes considerable planning and effort and, even once a tenancy is under way through an agency, you need to be ready to devote time at short notice to talk through any problems.

Where you will be living in the meantime may affect your choice of agent – if you'll be a long way away, you may want to choose the most reliable agent you can find, which may also be the most expensive. If you will be living nearby, a smaller or newer agency may be quite adequate.

Factors to consider

Before you sign up with an agent, or start looking for a tenant, there are some important factors you will have to bear in mind.

Consent of insurer Whether you are letting the house furnished or unfurnished, you will need to contact your house insurer (and your contents insurer if letting furnished) to discuss with them your plans to let. It is likely that the insurer would see this as an increased risk and would wish to vary the terms of the policy, often by increasing the amount of the excess and/or charging a higher premium. Failure to get the insurer's consent could result in them refusing to meet any claim you make on the policy.

Consent of mortgage lender Consent to let will be required as a term of your mortgage. The lender will be concerned that the existence of a tenant could reduce the value of the house should they need to sell it to recover their loan. It is possible that the lender may charge a higher rate of interest as a condition of giving their consent. In any event, there is likely to be a fee to cover the lender's administrative costs in deciding whether or not to give consent.

Planning permission This is not normally required to let property, but if you are going to let the house to more than one family group, or divide it into flats, then permission may well be required. You should contact the planning department at your district or unitary council to discuss your plans with them.

Length of tenancy You will need to decide for how long you

Before signing up with an agency, check that your house insurer is agreeable

want to let the property. Is the let intended to be a semi-permanent arrangement (a buy-to-let arrangement probably will be), or is there a chance you may want the house back in a few months' time, either to live in yourself or to sell with vacant possession? If you let the house on a five-year tenancy, you will not be able to get possession back until the end of that time, unless the tenant agrees, and why should they unless you make it worth their while? Many lets are for six or 12 months, which gives you as the landlord some degree of flexibility should circumstances change. However, it may well be that you'll attract a better tenant if you opt for a longer let.

References Every landlord wants a tenant who will look after the property well, pay the rent on time every month, and at the end of the letting will voluntarily vacate the premises without the need for a court order. Insist on references being provided – and be sure, if you use an agent, that they obtain references on your behalf. Ideally, you should obtain an employer's reference, to show that the prospective tenant is in employment and therefore has the means to pay the rent (this

The tenancy agreement

- Don't rely on word-of-mouth agreements, even if letting to friends. You need the protection of a **properly drafted tenancy agreement** that covers all eventualities.
- **Most letting agents have their own form of agreement.** Check that the proposed agreement includes: what the deposit can be used for and whether the tenant is entitled to interest on it; obligations on the tenant not to cause a nuisance or damage the property/contents; that the tenancy can be terminated prematurely if terms are breached.
- **If the agreement is too onerous on the tenant**, you may well find that no one will want to rent the house. Also, under the Unfair Terms in Consumer Contracts Regulations, any term that is deemed unfair to a tenant will be void and so unenforceable.
- The Consumers' Association publishes an agreement that tries to maintain a **fair balance between the rights of both landlord and tenant**.

will not, of course, guarantee that they will actually pay it). Many people also recommend getting a reference from a previous landlord to say that your prospective tenant was a good tenant. However, landlords are generally not amenable to giving such references and insisting on one would rule out someone who has never rented property before. A personal reference as to the person's character is a good alternative.

Be vigilant, however, with all references – it's not unknown for people to write their own. Check the names and addresses of all those giving the references, whether employers or individuals. You can search the British Telecom website for phone numbers and addresses (except for individuals who are ex-directory). Bear in mind that even impeccable references are no guarantee that you'll have a trouble-free time as landlord – there is always an element of luck involved.

Guarantors If there's a doubt over the prospective tenant's ability to pay the rent regularly, it is not unusual for a landlord to insist on the tenant providing a guarantor. A guarantor signs an agreement to the effect that if the tenant does not honour the terms of the agreement (for example, by not paying the rent regularly), then the guarantor is liable. Such an arrangement is often used in the case of a student renting property – a parent will be required to guarantee the obligations under the lease. Again, such a guarantee is only as good as the financial standing of the person giving it, so references should be obtained for the guarantor, too.

Rights and duties

Repairs

Under the Landlord and Tenant Act 1985, the landlord is liable for repairing the structure and exterior of the house, and the installations for supplying gas, water, electricity, and for sanitation. As the landlord you cannot avoid this responsibility by trying to put the burden on the tenant in the tenancy agreement. If you do not carry out the necessary work speedily, the tenant may have a claim against you for substantial damages to compensate them for living in an unrepaired house.

Gas, fire and electrical safety

There are stringent safety regulations to be complied with in relation to all of these – *see* p322 for details.

Outgoings

The tenancy agreement should make it clear who is responsible for paying the council tax, phone, water, gas and electricity bills. Although the law implies that the tenant will normally be responsible, it is best for this to be set out clearly in the tenancy agreement to avoid any disputes later on.

What happens at the end of a tenancy

In the case of a **fixed-term letting**, even when the fixed term has expired, the tenant does not have to vacate the house – they are allowed to remain in possession, on the same terms as previously, unless and until the landlord follows the correct procedure to obtain possession.

What the correct procedure is will depend on which of the two following **types of tenancy** has been granted. It will be obvious that landlords are going to prefer shorthold tenancies.

Shorthold

Unless the landlord has served a notice on the tenant stating that the tenancy is to be an 'assured' tenancy, the letting will be a 'shorthold' (sometimes referred to as an 'assured shorthold') tenancy, no matter how long it is.

The landlord will have an **absolute right to obtain possession** if he or she follows the correct procedure. They must serve a notice on the tenant, under section 21 of the Housing Act 1988, requiring possession in two months' time.

If the tenant does not vacate at the end of the two months, the landlord will still have to go to court to force the tenant to leave, but **the court must order possession** – there is no discretion.

Assured

If the letting is an 'assured' tenancy, then the landlord must follow a different procedure and **must establish a 'ground' for possession** – a reason recognised by statute as being sufficient to entitle the landlord to possession. Rent arrears or breaches of some other term of the tenancy agreement may be sufficient.

TIPS OF THE TRADE

1 Decide which market you are selling to and choose finishes accordingly. For students, for example, an inexpensive laminate worktop is fine and you won't get any extra rent for anything fancier. Granite would be more suitable for a top-end corporate let – and the potential rent will be decreased if finishes lack the luxury touch or costs have been cut.

2 At every rental market level, **everything must be simple to use and strong**. Tenants do not take extra care or make allowances for weaknesses. For example, a shower rail must be robust – tenants won't take the extra few seconds to pull the curtain back carefully. Likewise, if no chopping board is supplied in a 'fully-equipped' kitchen, they will use, and therefore damage, the worktop.

3 Cater for basic needs, like **laundry and rubbish removal**, with adequate and efficient equipment. With no other option for drying clothes, tenants will have damp washing hanging round, to the detriment of the decoration.

4 Minimise wear and tear on expensive items. A large, good-quality doormat will prolong the life of the hall carpet. A chair rail in the eating area will stop the wall from getting scuffed – and save redecorating the whole room.

5 Tackle problems and have them **professionally repaired** so that tenants do not take matters into their own hands. Their solution to, say, draughty windows, is likely to be newspaper stuffed into the gaps or sticky tape.

6 Choose light, bright, non-patterned colours for walls, curtains and so on (pastels are ideal) to give all types of accommodation a cheerful, positive atmosphere.

7 Tenants like character. Never remove original design features such as fireplaces, cornices or skirting boards.

Bob MacKinnon, landlord

Increasing the rent

Long lets Once a tenancy agreement has been signed, it is a binding contract between the parties. Just as the tenant is bound to pay the rent throughout the length of the tenancy, so the landlord has also agreed to accept that stipulated amount for the length of the letting.

The landlord cannot increase the rent without the tenant's agreement – and why should they agree? In a short-term tenancy (for example, six or 12 months) this will probably not be a problem, but in a longer let the effects of inflation will soon adversely affect the value of the rent agreed. Therefore, it's essential for the tenancy agreement for a long let to include a provision allowing the landlord to increase the rent.

Periodic tenancies In the case of a periodic tenancy – one that runs from week to week or from month to month – the 1988 Housing Act includes a provision that allows a landlord to increase the rent, even if there is nothing in the tenancy agreement allowing this. However, the procedure for this is slow and complicated and gives the tenant the right to refer the matter to the Rent Assessment Committee (a public body run by the Lord Chancellor's Department on a regional basis), who will have the final say as to what the rent is to be. So even in the case of a periodic tenancy, it is best not to have to rely on this procedure, and to include a provision in the tenancy agreement allowing the landlord to increase the rent.

Fairness Any provision in the agreement allowing for an increase must be fair, within the meaning of the Unfair Terms in Consumer Contracts Regulations. A provision that allows the landlord to increase the rent at any time, for any reason, and to any amount he or she thinks fit, will probably be held to be unfair and thus void.

Why it is important to take a deposit

As well as requiring a tenant to pay rent in advance (usually a month's rent), it is also usual for a landlord to insist on the tenant **paying a deposit at the start of the letting**. This deposit is usually the equivalent of one or two months' rent.

Reasons

- The idea behind the deposit is that if the tenant misses a month's rent, the landlord has the money in hand and does not need to resort to court action to recover it. Similarly, if at the end of the letting there is damage to the house or contents, the landlord can take the **cost of the damage from the deposit** and only return the balance.

Disputes

- There are probably more disputes between landlords and tenants over the return of deposits than any other matter. **The tenancy agreement should make it quite clear what the deposit is to be used for** (whether it is just for rent or for breakages as well).

  Also, at the start of the letting, a **detailed inventory** of the property's contents and their condition should be agreed between the landlord and the tenant. Otherwise, when the landlord holds on to part of the deposit to pay for damage, there is nothing to stop the tenant claiming that the damaged item was in that condition at the start of the tenancy.

Renting a property for holiday let still needs written agreements and managing

Evicting a tenant

Even if the tenant is not paying the rent regularly or is in breach of other terms of the tenancy agreement, the only way you can evict them is by obtaining a court order for possession. This, of course, will take time and will cost money.

You are not allowed to use or threaten force, or in any other way harass or try to persuade a tenant to leave. Harassment and unlawful eviction are criminal offences and the tenant would also be able to obtain substantial damages from you.

Expenses

Keep **records of all your costs** when you set up a property for letting, both for insurance purposes and for setting the costs of running the let against tax on rental income. In the first year you may want to consult an accountant about what you to claim.

Right of entry

Many landlords do not realise that although they may regard the house as 'their property', once they have granted a tenancy they have no more right to enter that property than anyone else who doesn't live there. If you want to keep a key to the property, to look round and check that everything is in order, then this must be provided for in the tenancy agreement. Any provision in the agreement allowing for access by the landlord must still be fair, however, within the meaning of the Unfair Terms in Consumer Contracts Regulations. A provision that allows the landlord access at any time, for any reason, and without giving reasonable notice, is likely to be held to be unfair and thus void.

Tenants on housing benefit

Housing benefit is a means-tested benefit, administered by the local housing authority, that can meet some or all of an applicant's rent. Many landlords ask for the benefit to be paid directly to themselves rather than to the tenants, which gives them a form of extra security. Direct payment requires the tenant's consent, which can be included as a term of the tenancy agreement.

The downside of direct payment is that if benefit is overpaid – as a result of a claimant failing to disclose their full financial circumstances, for instance – the local authority can reclaim the overpayment. If the benefit has been paid directly to the landlord, the overpayment can be reclaimed from the landlord, who would in turn have a right to recover this amount from the tenant – that is if the tenant is still around and there is a chance of successfully suing for the money.

Property for holiday lets

Running holiday lets is similar to any other kind of letting. You will:

- need to **obtain consent from your insurers** (buildings and contents) and mortgage lender
- **be liable for all the repairs**, for maintaining gas appliances, and other safety issues
- have to **meet all the outgoings**.

Many holiday lets are granted fairly informally, but there is still a need for a **written agreement** to make it clear that the letting is for holiday purposes only. This is often included on the booking form, if the let is offered through an agency, and will prevent a tenant claiming the right to live in the property and thus the right to continue in possession after the end of the let.

When you're choosing **furnishings**, you might choose stylish, practical tableware and bedding, that can be replaced fairly cheaply, but pay extra for a good-quality sofa and beds (*see* Buying beds and sofas, p104–7). You need to budget for:

- **dining chairs and easy seating** to match the number accommodated for
- plenty of **crockery and glassware**, with spares, plus a full set of cutlery, pans, cooking utensils and serving dishes
- at least **two sets of bedding for each bed** – polycotton dries quicker than pure cotton and anything with pleats or frills will add to the ironing time – plus mattress covers, ample pillows and perhaps new duvets.

Most guests will also expect:

- **a washing machine and tumble dryer** or space for drying clothes
- **a microwave**
- **a dishwasher**
- **a colour television** and ideally a video recorder, which will require a TV licence.

Somewhere to rent

There's been an increasing trend towards renting accommodation. It's the obvious option if you're going to be in an area for only a short period.

If you're planning to settle in a particular area, renting gives you time to consider the type of property that would suit you and to save up to buy. Before you rent, make sure you can't get caught out by the small print in the tenancy agreement, so that your time renting goes as smoothly as possible. If you're sharing with friends, there are some special issues about being joint tenants that are worth thinking about at the outset – *see* p323.

Take the right steps to a happy tenancy by reading the agreement

Things to consider

Deposit It's usual for a landlord to require a prospective tenant to pay a deposit as well as a month's rent in advance. Normally the deposit will be equivalent to one or two months' rent. You should not agree to pay more than the equivalent of two months' rent as a deposit – this would almost certainly be unfair. The idea behind a deposit is that if you fail to pay the rent, or cause any damage to the house or contents, the landlord can use this money as compensation without the need for expensive court proceedings.

Many tenancy disputes arise out of the repayment of deposits at the end of the tenancy. Landlords sometimes claim that there is damage, which is then disputed by the tenant. Equally, there may be a disagreement as to the amount that should be deducted as compensation for the damage caused. Here, the landlord has the advantage – as the tenant you have already handed over your money and it is unlikely to be returned unless you go to court.

The tenancy agreement should make clear the following:

• what the landlord (or the letting agency) can use the deposit for – either just for arrears of rent, or for breakages as well
• whether, if the landlord makes use of the deposit during the tenancy, for the agreed purposes he or she can require you to top it up to the original amount
• whether the tenant is entitled to receive interest on the deposit for the time it is held by the landlord
• that the deposit is held on trust for the tenant. Otherwise there is a risk that the money will not be recoverable by the tenant if the landlord should become insolvent.

The government has introduced a Tenancy Deposit Scheme, which aims to provide security for tenants' deposits and independent resolution of disputes. Ideally, you should ensure that your landlord is willing to participate in this scheme. More details are available on the Department of Transport, Local Government and the Regions' website www.housing.dtlr.gov.uk.

Tenancy length What length of tenancy are you looking for? Be wary of signing up for too long, because if you decide to leave early, you will be liable for rent for the rest of the time you agreed. However, most landlords will take a favourable view if you can find an acceptable replacement tenant for them.

Tenancy agreements and the law

The tenancy agreement you will be asked to sign is a **binding legal document**. Unlike many legal documents it will not carry a 'health warning' cautioning you against signing it unless you wish to be bound by its terms – but you must not sign it without understanding exactly what you are letting yourself in for.

Under the **Unfair Terms in Consumer Contracts Regulations 1999**, any term in a tenancy agreement that is deemed unfair by the tenant is void. But the regulations are very vague as to what may or may not be 'fair' and the only way that this can be decided upon is by going to court, which could be expensive and time-consuming. Best not to sign an agreement that strikes you as unreasonable in the first place.

Finding a property

Through an agent:
If possible, ask friends in the area who have rented property before to recommend an agent.

- Use an agent who is a member of a **professional body**, such as the Royal Institution of Chartered Surveyors (RICS) or the Association of Residential Letting Agents (ARLA). These bodies have professional standards to uphold and membership shows a commitment to behaving professionally.
- Remember that the agent is the **landlord's agent** and although the existence of a buffer between landlord and tenant can help in settling disputes, the agent is in the pay of the landlord.
- When you sign up with an agency they will want to see **evidence of your identity**, such as a passport and at least two months' pay slips. They may check with a credit reference agency to see if you have a satisfactory credit rating. They may also ask for an administration fee for signing the tenancy and a further fee at each renewal.

Direct from the landlord:

- Many landlords advertise privately in the **small ads** of local papers.
- Beware of landlords who insist on **rent payments in cash** – their disregard of the tax laws might mean they would disregard your rights too.
- If the property is in **poor condition** when you look round, think twice before signing up for it. The landlord may promise to carry out the repairs when you have signed the agreement, but a good landlord would have done the repairs before advertising it. Once you have signed up, the landlord will have little incentive to carry out repairs.

Inventory If the property is being let furnished, ensure that there is a detailed inventory of the contents. This should not only include everything in the house, but also describe its condition, detailing any damage. Go through it carefully and don't sign it unless you are sure it is accurate. This can save all sorts of arguments at the end of the tenancy when it comes to the repayment of the deposit. The landlord will often make a deduction because of a damaged item, despite a tenant's claim that it was in that condition to start with. A detailed inventory can prevent this.

Rules and regulations It is usual for a landlord to include in a tenancy agreement various rules and regulations that state what you can or cannot do in the property. These will often aim to avoid causing a nuisance to neighbours. Whatever it is you have agreed to, your signature on the tenancy agreement binds you to it. If you do not comply with these provisions, the landlord may well be able to bring the tenancy to a premature end. However, what a landlord cannot do is to impose new rules after you have signed the agreement – unless, that is, the agreement allows it.

Right of entry Landlords frequently keep keys to the properties they let, but the law does not allow them right of entry unless this is specifically stated in the agreement. A landlord may arrange to come round to see what repairs need doing, but otherwise, they have no more right to enter the property than a stranger has. The whole essence of a tenancy is that the tenant has the right to exclude anyone and everyone from the property – including the landlord.

Shorthold or assured?

Most lettings these days are what are called shorthold tenancies (sometimes called assured shortholds, but they are the same thing). Unless your tenancy agreement states expressly that it is an assured tenancy with no mention of the word 'shorthold', then it will be a shorthold. In the case of a shorthold, the landlord will have an absolute right to possession of the property at the end of the tenancy, as long as he or she gives you two months' notice. Although the landlord cannot evict you without obtaining a court order, he or she will have an absolute right to such an order.

If your tenancy is an assured tenancy, then the landlord can only obtain possession if he or she can prove the existence of one or more 'grounds for possession', that is, circumstances which justify him or her requiring possession. These are many and various and outside the scope of this book, but include non-payment of rent and breaches of other terms of the tenancy agreement. Some grounds are 'mandatory', which means that on proof of the ground, the court must make an order for possession against the tenant. Other grounds, however, are discretionary, so that even if the ground is established, the court has discretion whether or not to order possession.

If you have an assured tenancy and you receive a notice claiming possession, you should immediately seek legal advice as to your rights.

Responsibility for outgoings

All outgoings on the property – council tax, gas, water, electricity and telephone bills – will normally be **your responsibility as the tenant**, whether or not this is stated in the tenancy agreement.

Think before you sign

It cannot be stressed enough that you must **read the tenancy agreement carefully and thoroughly before signing it**. If in doubt, seek advice from a Citizens Advice Bureau (CAB) or free housing aid centre if there is one in your area. Be wary of pressure to sign immediately because of a queue of eager applicants behind you. There may well be others waiting to snap up the property, but any reasonable landlord will give you time to make sure you understand what you are signing – after all, this is in the interest of both parties.

Rights and obligations

Your rights and obligations as a tenant are, to a large extent, governed by the terms of the tenancy agreement, but the general law may also sometimes be relevant.

Responsibility for damage and repairs

The Landlord & Tenant Act 1985 places the obligation for repairing the structure and exterior of residential properties on the landlord. This is so in cases where the tenancy is for a term of less than seven years – which will cover most tenancies – and applies even if there is a provision in the tenancy agreement saying that the tenant must carry out the repairs. The same Act also provides that the landlord must keep in repair and proper working order the installations in the property for the supply of gas, water, electricity, and sanitation. This includes sinks, baths, toilets, and drains, though if drains are blocked because of the tenant's unreasonable behaviour, then the tenant is responsible for unblocking them.

The words 'structure' and 'exterior' are not defined by the Act, but will include the main fabric of the house, such as walls, roof, window frames, gutters, drainpipes, and paths and steps that form the main access to the house. Interior decorations and fittings are not included in the Act.

The landlord will not be liable for damage that was the tenant's fault – say the tenant cracked a washbasin by dropping something into it. The landlord will equally not be liable to repair items other than those within the Act or to redecorate, unless stated in the tenancy agreement. You, as a tenant, are liable for matters not covered by the Act if you have agreed to such repairs in the tenancy agreement – another reason for reading it through carefully.

If the agreement does not deal with the repair of an item that does not feature within the Act, then neither landlord nor tenant is under an obligation to repair. However, if the damage was the tenant's fault, the tenant is responsible.

Getting repairs done

Landlords can be expected to do repairs only if you tell them what needs doing – until you have done this, they are not liable. Many landlords are very conscientious about maintaining their property. It is, after all, in their interests to keep it in good condition. But some landlords are not helpful and repairs can remain outstanding for a long time, often at great inconvenience to the tenant.

Going to court to force your landlord to carry out repairs is an option (*see* p290), but can be lengthy and expensive. What you cannot do is simply stop paying the rent – the fact that the landlord has failed to do the repairs is not grounds for defence if he or she sues you or tries to evict you for non-payment.

If persuasion or persistence, does not work, you can warn the landlord that unless he or she carries out the repairs, you will have them done and then deduct the cost from future payments of rent. In such a case get at least two estimates first and send these to the landlord, so there can be no argument that the cost is excessive.

Tenants are entitled to compensation in reduced rent

Taking in a lodger or subletting

If you are yourself a tenant and want to sublet all or part of your accommodation, then you will **probably need your landlord's consent**. The law says that you can sublet or take in a lodger unless your tenancy agreement says otherwise, however most tenancy agreements contain a **prohibition on subletting**. If you don't comply with the terms of the agreement, your landlord will probably have the right to go to court and seek your eviction from the property, even if the tenancy agreement has not yet expired.

Remember also, that if you grant a sublease, you will be taking on the role of landlord to that subtenant. So you will need to **check up on references** and make sure that you have a proper agreement, just like any other landlord.

As a landlord you will be **liable to that subtenant to carry out repairs** when they need doing and you will be liable if a gas fire is defective. Of course, your own landlord may be liable to you to carry out those repairs, but that is between the two of you. Your tenant will look to you and you alone for compensation (*see* p308–15 for more on letting).

for disruption while major repairs are carried out.

The garden

Neither landlord nor tenant is responsible for the garden – unless the agreement states otherwise. The tenant need not keep the garden tidy, and the landlord can't be forced to either.

Alterations

Often a tenancy agreement will forbid alterations, but if it does not and you as the tenant make improvements, you are allowed to remove them at the end of the tenancy. If they are left in place, the landlord does not have to pay you compensation.

Insurance

The landlord may well insure the structure of the building, but he or she will not insure your contents. If these are lost, stolen, or damaged, for instance by fire, you will have no comeback against the landlord. So consider taking out your own contents insurance.

Unlawful eviction and harassment

The landlord cannot evict you without first obtaining a court order – even if your tenancy has come to an end. If he or she tries to do so, or threatens or harasses you into leaving by unreasonable behaviour, such as excessive noise or cutting off services, he or she is liable to criminal proceedings. You can also bring legal action against a landlord to claim compensation and reinstatement to the property if you are evicted.

Gas, fire and electrical safety

There are various **government regulations** dealing with safety. The landlord is responsible for the safety of the electrical system, any oil or solid-fuel heating and any appliances included in the let. There are criminal penalties for supplying unsafe electrical equipment.

If the property is let furnished, upholstery, soft furnishings and mattresses must **comply with various flammability criteria**. Older furnishings that have no swing ticket or label showing compliance with the regulations are illegal, unless classified as antiques.

If the property contains a **gas appliance**, the landlord must ensure that it and any flue or pipe serving it is maintained in a safe condition. The appliance must be inspected at least **once every 12 months by a CORGI-registered plumber** and a record of these inspections kept.

The landlord must produce this record to the tenant on the grant of the tenancy and within 28 days of each annual inspection. If you are not shown this record when taking a tenancy, or it cannot be provided when you ask, do not take the tenancy.

Sharing with others

If you plan to share with others, you may be asked to sign the same agreement and become joint tenants. This means each tenant can be held responsible in full on all the terms of the agreement. If one tenant leaves, the rest will have to pay the monthly rent between them.

A joint arrangement also means that if one tenant breaks the terms of the agreement by causing damage, the landlord can again claim against any one tenant for that loss or retain some of the deposit at the end of the letting.

If one joint tenant leaves, the rest will almost certainly need the landlord's consent to bring in another person to share. If you do this without consent, the landlord might be able to obtain possession of the property.

Alternatively, you may be asked to sign a separate agreement, promising to pay a specified amount of rent. If one of the tenants leaves your liability doesn't change – but it is up to the landlord to find a replacement tenant.

In the case of breakages or damage, the agreement usually allows the landlord to hold any tenant liable for any damage, no matter who caused it.

When can the landlord increase the rent?

The **amount of rent**, and your ability to pay it, is a crucial factor to consider before entering into a tenancy. But once you have signed the agreement, can the landlord increase the rent?

- In the case of a **letting for a fixed term** (usually six months) there can be no rent increase, unless it is built into the tenancy agreement. So again, read the agreement carefully – you will be bound by any provisions contained in it that allow an increase.
- In the case of a **periodic tenancy** (one that lasts from week to week or from month to month), the law does allow a landlord to increase the rent, even if there is nothing in the tenancy agreement permitting this. But in order to increase the rent, the landlord must follow the correct procedure. This involves him/her serving a **two-months' notice** on you in the form laid down by the Housing Act 1988, stating the proposals for the new rent and detailing your right to refer the increase to the Rent Assessment Committee (a government body) to see if it is fair. You need not agree to any increase where the correct procedure has not been followed.
- Landlords are **not entitled to increase rent after carrying out repairs**, such as replacing an old gas boiler with a new one. However, an improvement, such as installing central heating when it wasn't there before, could be a reason for reviewing the rent. The landlord would then need to follow the procedure of notice, as above, again giving you the right to refer the increase to the Rent Assessment Committee.

Contact details

Useful websites and addresses about the information given in this chapter.

Association of Residential Letting Agents, Maple House, 53–55 Woodside Road, Amersham, Bucks HP6 6AA
Tel: 0845 345 5752
Fax: 01494 431 530
e-mail: info@arla.co.uk
www.arla.co.uk
Site has a Buy to Let area with detailed information on what 'buy to let' is and which lenders will offer the finance. Detailed information for both tenants and landlords.

Government housing information
www.housing.odpm.gov.uk
General housing information, including government housing policy and the housing choices available to homeowners, tenants and landlords.

Inland Revenue
Tel: 020 7667 4001
www.inlandrevenue.gov.uk
Information about individual and business tax, including a separate section on self assessment. Details of the regional offices are also provided on the site. A range of leaflets covering letting issues are available from the Inland Revenue Orderline (0845 9000 404) or through the website.

Law Society, The Law Society's Hall, 113 Chancery Lane, London WC2A 1PL
Tel: 020 7242 1222
Fax: 020 7831 0344
e-mail: info-services@lawsociety.org.uk
www.lawsoc.org.uk
Enables you to search for a law firm or individual solicitor in England and Wales.

let-a-property
www.let-a-property.info/
A downloadable electronic book (e-book) providing practical buy to let mortgage, UK rental property investment, landlord advice and guidance.

MarketPlace
www.marketplace.co.uk
Helps you to find the right property, mortgage, loan, pension, investment or insurance for you.

moneynet.co.uk, 4 Cobden Court, Wimpole Close, Stanley Road, Bromley BR2 9JF
Tel: 020 8313 9030
Fax: 020 8464 1971
e-mail: info@moneynet.co.uk
www.moneynet.co.uk
The site provides comprehensive, impartial and independent advice on the products available in the personal finance sector.

National Association of Citizens Advice Bureaux, Myddelton House, 115–123 Pentonville Road, London N1 9LZ
e-mail: adviceguide@nacab.org.uk
www.adviceguide.org.uk
Covers advice for England, Scotland, Wales and Northern Ireland, as well as a wide range of topics from money and employment to housing, education, consumer affairs and the legal system. Enables you to pinpoint your nearest Citizens Advice Bureau.

Paragon Mortgages Ltd, St Catherine's Court, Herbert Road, Solihull, West Midlands B91 3QE
Tel: 0800 375 777
Fax: 0121 712 2547
e-mail: mortgages@paragon-group.co.uk
www.paragon-mortgages.co.uk
Site includes an interactive calculator which allows you to work out how much money you are likely to make both in terms of rental income and the profit from the eventual sale of the property.

propertyfinder.co.uk, 182-194 Union Street, Union House, London SE1 0LH
Tel: 0870 075 8888
e-mail: info@propertyfinder.co.uk
www.propertyfinder.co.uk
A website that will search for areas by postcode whether you are looking to buy, sell, rent or let a property.

Up My Street
www.upmystreet.com
Enter your postcode to find information on services in your area. Useful to know if you are going to be renting and will be new to the area.

Which?, 2 Marylebone Road, London NW1 4DF
Tel: 020 7770 7000
Fax: 020 7770 7600
e-mail: which@which.net
www.which.net
Visit the bookstore area of the site where a number of publications on selling, letting and conveyancing are available.

GLASS
THE BIG YELLOW
SMALL BOX
THE BIG YELLOW SELF STORAGE

Selling a **Property**

When it comes to selling any property, the aim is to get the best possible price for it, particularly as most people will be buying another home from the proceeds.

Preparation is the most important aspect in selling the property. Not only does your home need to attract buyers by looking good, you have to decide whether to sell through an agent or privately, either over the Internet, in local papers or your own advertising. The legal process of the sale needs to be fully understood and adhered to, which finally leads to the moving day itself. Finding a removal firm, packing up and moving out can be the most stressful part of the sale.

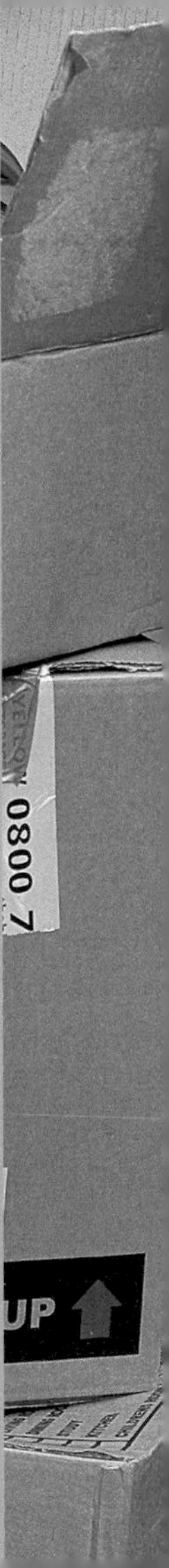

Preparing to sell

In today's fast-paced and highly mobile society, it's not unusual to own five or more homes in one lifetime. Home ownership is no longer just equated with shelter – the term has become synonymous with investment.

Buying and selling homes has become a national pastime in the UK, with many people amassing a considerable amount of capital by following the adage 'buy low, sell high'. Much of the advice here is relevant if you're also preparing to let your home.

Space, function and potential

Just as you the seller are looking to get your highest and best price for your house, the buyer is also looking to get the best possible deal. Your job is to make the buyer think that your house is just that deal. With the high prices of homes today, buyers have become more and more particular. They want to get the most they can for their money – the most space, function and potential. Also, today's buyers are usually extremely busy people, and prefer to use what little leisure time they have for recreation. Most of them are looking to pay as much as they can afford for a home that they can move straight into, without having to spend a lot of time or money on alterations. As a seller you need to present your home so that it meets the needs of the greatest buying audience in order to realise your best sale price.

Kerb appeal

Begin outdoors. Stand across the road from where you live and assess how your home measures up to the rest of the homes on your street. Does it grab your attention? Prospective buyers are likely to drive past your house first and will only bother to come inside if they like what they see from the street. This is kerb appeal – and it is critical. Your house should be appealing and welcoming, one of the nicest on the street, yet in keeping with the style of the neighbourhood. Fresh paintwork, a well-manicured garden and the overall first impression of a cared-for home are important factors in getting buyers inside.

Create an atmosphere of calm when potential buyers come round to view

A pleasing ambience

Buyers probably make the decision whether or not to buy within the first 60–90 seconds of entering a house. A buyer may not even be aware of this decision because it has been made subconsciously. Although most buyers have a list of requirements for their purchase, the decision whether or not to buy a particular house is usually based on intangibles. The place has to feel right. And if it doesn't, they are out of the door as fast they came in.

What can you do as a seller to make a house feel right? Pay close attention to those subliminal messages, a technique that is used often in advertising. Potential buyers will experience your house with their senses – sight, hearing, touch and smell. Ask a good friend to do an inspection before buyers come.

Inside the house, good lighting is essential, both natural and ambient, to create a cheerful atmosphere and colours should be soft, neutral

Bathrooms should be spotlessly clean and tidy, but also with a lived-in feel

Three key ingredients

Getting the highest and best price for your home usually requires more time and energy than money. However, before getting started, you need three key ingredients:

Commitment Unless you are truly committed to selling your home – and are mentally and emotionally prepared to move on – you will not take all the steps necessary to getting it sold. Be very clear of your motivation before embarking on the marketing process.

Detachment You need to be able to step back and view your home through a buyer's eyes, a vision not clouded by personality, memories or emotion. You are not selling your home – you are selling a house.

Co-operation Unless you have the co-operation and involvement of any other household members as well as your estate agent, the task at hand will be extremely difficult. It's all energies on board, working toward the same goal – the sale.

and easy on the eye. Cleanliness and order throughout evoke a looked-after feeling in the home. Clean windows, curtains and surfaces, especially in the kitchen, are reassuring.

Soft background music puts the buyer at ease. Subtle fresh scents, as well as plants and flowers, add life and vitality to a room. A fire in the fireplace on a chilly day creates the feeling of homeliness, as does the old trick of something yummy baking in the oven. If you have a garden, remove weeds and trim plants and lawn. Sweep paths. Pets, children and sellers themselves should remain unobtrusive in order to let the prospective buyers view the home in a relaxed and comfortable manner.

An image of spaciousness

Buyers have to be able to imagine living in the house that they are viewing, with their own possessions and furniture. It is your job to make it as easy as possible for them to visualise this. Since space is always at a premium, you need to make the most of what you have.

- Edit your belongings ruthlessly and arrange furniture to allow freedom of movement. Now, more than ever, 'less is more'

Ten steps to making a successful sale

1 **Clear away all clutter** – *see* p22–31. Pack up and store anything inessential. You'll be ahead of the game when moving day comes along.
2 Do an effective **spring clean**, whatever the time of year. Pay special attention to kitchens and bathrooms. Take care of any minor repairs.
3 **Fresh paint** can do wonders to brighten up a room. Use a light, warm, neutral colour.
4 **First impressions** are crucial. Be sure your home looks appealing from the front door through the entrance hall. A tidy garden, clean windows, polished door furniture and a welcome mat will invite buyers to step inside.
5 Indoors and out **replace or trim plants** that are overgrown or unsightly. Buy fresh flowers for the house.
6 Pay careful attention to **subliminal messages**: soft music, adequate lighting and pleasing scents elicit a positive emotional response.
7 Pick a **colour scheme**, preferably based on something you already own, like a painting or rug, and use these colours as accents throughout the house.
8 Now that you have cleared and cleaned, reinstall some of your favourite things. But remember, **'less is more'**.
9 If necessary, buy a few **accessories** to give your house that pulled-together feeling. Things like colourful rugs, fresh towels, decorative cushions, new curtains and prints can all be taken with you when you move.
10 Finally, the most artful preparation in the world will not sell a house if it is **overpriced**. Accept that you may need to hire a qualified estate agent and listen to their advice.

A modern, well-equipped kitchen is a key selling point for buyers

(money in your pocket, that is). If a buyer cannot see a room for clutter, there is no chance of them mentally moving in. Clear out all shelves and cupboards, and put everything back in a neat, organised manner. Buyers need to feel that there is adequate room for all their belongings, not get the impression that even you are struggling for space. Take advantage of unused storage areas in the house, in lofts, basements, garages, under the stairs, and so on, and present it neatly as an asset, not an eyesore. Never, ever, present one of your bedrooms, no matter how small, as a junk room. You will be doing yourself out of money.

- Pay special attention to the kitchen and bathroom. As these are two rooms that can be the most costly to redo, buyers tend to scrutinise them carefully. Few buyers have the money left over after purchasing their new home for any major renovations, so they need to feel that the kitchen and bathrooms are in good, useable condition. Sometimes it takes as little as a lick of paint on walls or cabinets, new flooring and/or tiling and some updated lighting to make a kitchen or bathroom look and feel good.

Selling your home

It's easy to feel you lack control when you sell a property, especially if you need a speedy sale and a good price to secure your next purchase.

With estate agency fees and legal costs adding up to a significant sum, you could save considerably by selling the property yourself or trying for a house swap. Whichever route you go down, do all you can to maximise your property's selling power and be aware of the issues involved in the legal contracts that selling or exchange entails. If you decide to sell through an agent, choose carefully.

Choosing an estate agent

Most property sales are conducted through an agent, whom the seller pays to represent them in the selling transaction. Ideally you should ask three agents to value your property and recommend a selling price. Personal recommendations are a good place to start, especially from someone who has sold a property similar to yours – perhaps a former neighbour.

- Look at the sort of details your chosen agents produce for properties like yours.
- Ask each agency what they see as your home's main selling points, and get detailed information on how they plan to advertise it. How often will it appear in the local paper? Do they have a website or do they supply details to a composite website, such as www.propertyfinder.co.uk?
- Look for an agent who demonstrates a good knowledge of the area and shows a genuine interest in handling your sale.
- Choose someone you get on with. A good relationship with

Your responsibility as a seller

You and your solicitor or conveyancer should together fill in two legally binding documents: the **Fixtures and Fittings** form and the **Property Information** form. These should cover all the basic information about the state of the property and exactly what you're selling.

As the seller, it's best to be honest if a potential buyer asks about something you know is dodgy – for instance, if you know of some dry rot or have very difficult neighbours. **Sellers can be sued for not revealing the truth.**

Consider the pros and cons with sole agency or multiple agencies

> **Swapping homes**
>
> Swapping your home is an **alternative to selling the traditional way**. Several websites allow you to advertise the property you have and outline what you're looking for. If you want to stay in the same vicinity, you might even find a neighbour with whom to swap. If the two properties to swap are valued differently, there will be a balance to pay. A significant financial advantage is that in a property swap, **stamp duty is payable only on the higher priced property** – and you could agree to share that cost with the other owner.

the agent is important and will make it easier to sort out any problems that may arise.

- Consider using a smaller agency – they may depend more on your sale and make more effort than a large agency, which may have so many properties that they can't give yours their full attention.

Comparing agents

- Look at the charges carefully – most agents charge a

percentage of the final sale price, which means you only pay if and when the property is sold, but some may offer a lower percentage and charge fees for advertising, putting up the sale board and arranging viewings, all of which you may be liable to pay for immediately.

- Check the small print and ask what happens if you sell to a neighbour, friend or colleague – some agencies claim 'sole selling rights' (not the same thing as 'sole agency' rights, *see* below), which means you have to pay their fee even if you sell the property without their help. This may apply for a set time after your contract with the agent has expired.
- Don't automatically opt for the agent quoting the highest sale price – they may just be desperate for your business. A difference of 5% is acceptable, but if the estimates are adrift by more than this, ask the agent quoting the highest rate to justify their figure with actual examples of recent sales of similar property in the same area.

Sole or multiple agency?

- A sole agency agreement, where you let just one agent try to sell your property for a set number of weeks, is the cheapest option. Multiple agency, where you place the property with several agents at the same time, can increase the cost by as much as one per cent of the sale price or even more, and as most buyers will visit or contact all the estate agents in an area, you may not gain much by signing up with more than one.
- If your start with a sole agency agreement and the

The seller's pack

New legislation, likely to take effect from 2004 or 2005, will oblige anyone selling a property to pay to provide prospective buyers with a seller's pack, consisting of:

- a completed **local authority search** on their property (indicating, for example, whether there are any development plans for the area)
- a **full survey of the property** – though this will not be a valuation.

While the pack is **expected to make the selling and buying process quicker** in England and Wales, it may increase property prices a little to start off with, to offset the money sellers have to spend on preparing the pack. Banks and building societies will probably still want to conduct their own valuations before lending on the property and this cost will probably be passed on to the buyer one way or another.

Cost of selling a home in England and Wales

Property price (£)	Legal fees (£)	Estate agent's fee (£)	Total funds you will need (£)
25,000	347	629	976
50,000	354	826	1,180
60,000	361	915	1,276
80,000	379	1,115	1,494
100,000	401	1,335	1,736
150,000	438	1,933	2,371
200,000	483	2,553	3,036
300,000	574	3,777	4,351
500,000	719	6,114	6,833

Source: The Woolwich Cost of Moving Survey 2004. Figures compiled by the University of Greenwich, School of Architecture and Construction. *Note*: This table gives the average cost of selling in England and Wales. Actual costs vary by region and tend to be highest in the Southeast and Southwest of England.

agent doesn't manage to sell your property within the agreed sole agency time, you can try multiple agency as the next step. Multiple agency may be worth considering from the start, however, if you want to sell very quickly, or if your property falls between two areas of potential buyers (whether districts of a city, or nearby towns) and your first choice of agent doesn't have a branch in both areas.

- An estate agent may well agree to a shorter sole agency period than their terms and conditions state. Try to get this amended when you sign up, rather than challenge it later if they haven't found a buyer.

Selling without an agent

Selling your property privately, without involving an estate agent, may entail more work on your behalf, and you might find it hard to reach as many prospective buyers as an estate agent would. On the other hand, if you're successful, you'll save the commission you would have to pay an estate agent. If you have already signed with an estate agent, however, don't agree a private sale unless you are absolutely certain that you aren't breaching the terms of your contract or you could still be charged a fee – *see* Comparing agents, p334–5.

First steps

- Find out how much estate agents are asking for similar properties in your area.
- Pay for an independent valuation from a surveyor.
- Decide the asking price.
- Draw up a short description of the property, using the conventional abbreviations used in the local property paper. Ask a friend to check it, in case you've forgotten anything vital.

Advertising your home locally

- Pay for a small ad in the local paper, giving a telephone number but not your address.
- Drop details into local letterboxes. It's cheeky, but people do it – your home may be just what someone local is looking for, whether it has a special feature, bigger garden or is simply larger or smaller than their own.
- Ask to display an advertisement on staff noticeboards in large offices, universities or hospitals.

The legal transaction

The legal side of selling a house is more straightforward than buying, when you may need extensive legal help you be sure of what you're getting. Ask **three solicitors or licensed conveyancers** to quote an all-in price to handle the sale. Alternatively, it is possible to **undertake conveyancing yourself**, though you will need to be able to devote considerable time to the procedure and not be daunted by the paperwork. Consumers' Association publishes a book, *Which? Way to Do Your Own Conveyancing*.

Find a solicitor by:

- personal recommendation
- looking in *Yellow Pages* or on the Internet
- writing to the Law Society for a list of local registered legal practices. The Law Society also has a website with the directory of solicitors on it and a search facility for local firms – www.solicitors-online.com.

Find a licensed conveyancer by:

- looking in *Yellow Pages* or on the Internet

See Buying a property, p390–5, for the sequence of a property sale once an offer's been accepted.

Advertising further afield

- Sign up with a company on the Internet. One way Internet companies can afford to advertise your home without charging you or the eventual buyer is by passing your details to other companies who are interested in people

Selling property in Scotland

The process of selling and buying property in Scotland differs from transactions in England and Wales in several ways.

- Property is advertised either at a **fixed price or inviting offers** over a certain sum. With a fixed price, the first offer of that sum should secure the purchase, though a seller can accept a lower offer.
- **If more than one buyer is interested in a property**, the seller's estate agent may set a date and time for sealed bids to be submitted. The seller can then choose the highest price offered.
- The **seller's legal representative** accepts the chosen offer in writing. There still isn't a legally binding contract until negotiations on the terms of the contract have been settled – called Conclusion of missives. Once this has been reached, if either the seller or buyer wishes to withdraw, they must pay the other party compensation.

who are moving and might want their products/services. You aren't committed to buying any of these. Read the small print carefully.

- Set up your own website dedicated to selling the property (*see* Build your own website, pp234–7). This may be worth doing if the value or location of your property makes it of special interest. Don't give the exact address, but emphasise if it's in a tourist area or employment hot-spot, especially if employees come to the area from a long distance or from abroad.
- If you're in a popular area but don't want to go on the web, an advertisement in a national Sunday newspaper

If the offer is revised down

Sometimes, when a seller has accepted an offer, the buyer later reduces his or her offer. This may well be immoral, but **gazundering**, as this is called, is not illegal. So what can you do about it?

The first thing is to find out precisely **why the offer has been reduced**. There will usually be some good reason – the survey has revealed problems or repairs that need doing, which justify the reduction. In that case, carrying out the repairs yourself should mean that the offer can be restored to its original amount, but you will still have to find the cost of the repairs.

More often, the house has simply been **valued at a lower amount** by the buyer's mortgage lender, so reducing the amount of the loan the lender is prepared to make. It is then a case of bluff and counterbluff – how keen are you to sell (at a lower price) and how keen is the buyer to buy (by finding more money from their own funds)?

As a seller you may have little choice but to agree – or risk losing the house that you are buying because your sellers will not wait until you have found another buyer.

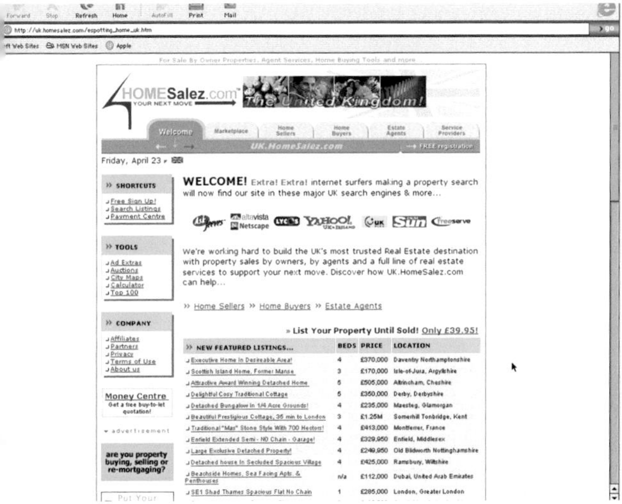

Advertising your home on the Internet is becoming a popular way of selling

or a magazine may produce a buyer.

Showing people round

- Create a demand for your property. Estate agents often arrange for potential buyers to view at more or less the same time, to make the property look popular. Hold an 'open house' viewing on a single afternoon so that prospective buyers find the place buzzing and realise that they need to make a good offer quickly.
- Always have another person there with you when you show potential buyers around your house.

Making a sale

- Ask for all offers to be put in writing to your solicitor or conveyancer, even if you're being offered the asking price. This gives you time to consider the implications of the offer, for instance, does the prospective buyer have funds already available?
- Insist that any subsequent negotiations on price or contents are done via your legal representative.

A few property transaction terms

Completion When title deeds are signed over to the buyer's solicitor/conveyancer and ownership of the property is transferred.
Scottish equivalent: Date of entry.

Covenant Usually a restriction in a lease or freehold that prevents tenant or owner from doing specific things in the property, for example running a business.

Deeds Usually Title deeds. A legal document, signed and witnessed, stating the official owner of a property.
Scottish equivalent: Disposition.

Exchange of contracts When seller's and buyer's legal representatives swap contracts; this should be the point of no return.
Scottish equivalent: Conclusion of missives.

Fixtures Fixed items usually left in a property, such as baths and toilets.

Freehold Property or land that is wholly owned by the freeholder, who can lease it (rent it) to someone else or sell it outright.

Ground rent An annual sum payable to a landlord who owns the lease on a property.

Land Registry fee Payable to the Land Registry to record ownership of property or land.

Lease A contract setting out the conditions under which the freeholder allows a leaseholder to live in a property or use a piece of land.

Service charge Usually an annual sum paid to a landlord or management company for services provided to tenants, such as cleaning, maintenance and repairs.

Sitting tenant A person who has a legal right to occupy a property, even though it has been sold by the owner to another person.

Subject to contract Applies to the period between an offer being made on a property and contracts being exchanged.

Subject to tender System whereby property (usually repossessions) are advertised and potential buyers submit sealed bids.

Title deeds The documents that state the name of the legal owner of a property.

Vacant possession Describes a property with no occupants, ready to be occupied by buyers.

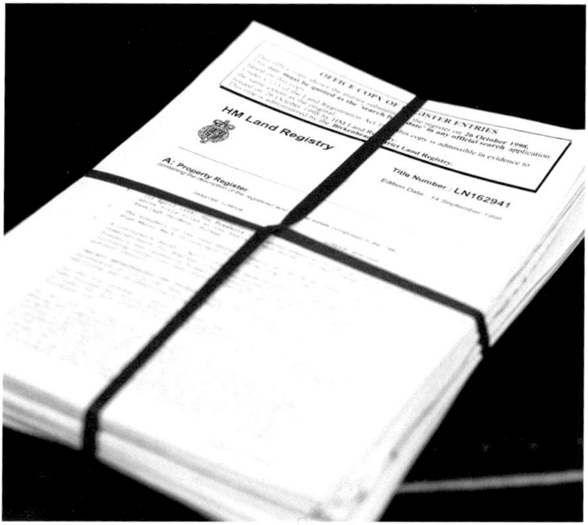

The Land Registry document records ownership of the property

Accepting an offer

Work out what you need to make on your sale, so that you know whether an offer is worth accepting. This will depend partly on your circumstances: if you are buying another property you will probably have a specific figure in mind that you need to reach in order to make your new purchase, allowing for all your legal costs of the sale and purchase. If you are downshifting to a smaller home or less expensive area, or moving into rented property, you may be able to be more flexible about what price you accept.

- If the property market in your area is strong, it might be worth making it clear that you won't negotiate: state on the property details that you won't drop the asking price even if a survey reveals minor defects.
- Don't stick to an unrealistically high figure for the sake of it, however – it will probably take longer to find a buyer and you may have to drop the price if the

Once you have accepted an offer

- Let your **agent** deal with the buyer, if you are employing one. If you're selling privately, it is best advised not to get too friendly with your buyer, however well you appear to get on. This is a business deal and there may be tough negotiations to handle.
- Don't encourage **gazumping** by accepting a higher offer after you have agreed a price with a committed buyer.

buyer's survey and valuation suggest that you're asking too much.

- Don't jump at the highest offer without carefully thinking it through – more money doesn't necessarily mean a more committed buyer. Opt for a buyer who you feel really wants your home and has the resources to pay for it.

Hang in there – a genuine buyer will finally come along with the right offer

Questions for the agent

If you use an estate agent they will advise whether or not to accept an offer, but you should specifically ask whether your potential buyer:

- needs to sell a property before they can buy. The more links there are in the chain, the more delays there are likely to be before completion.
- has finance arranged. A genuine buyer will be able to produce proof that a lender has provisionally offered them a mortgage. If they claim to have a large proportion of the purchase price available as cash, ask your agent to check out the details. Buyers desperate to have their offer accepted sometimes promise more than they can deliver.

On the move

Moving home is not only exhausting, it's also an intense experience. It calls for careful planning, plenty of decision-making and lots of hard physical work.

If you opt to get help with your move, go for the best service you can afford. The Internet has made it easy to get quick preliminary estimates for how much your move will cost.

Employing a removal firm

Invite several removals firms to provide free quotes. Ideally, get personal recommendations. Firms should be members of the Road Haulage Association (RHA) or the British Association of Removers (BAR) or both.

Company estimators visit you at your home to take stock of your belongings and requirements, and make a note of any potential problems, such as large pieces of furniture.

Each firm should then send you a clear list of what is to be moved, a step-by-step description of the process and a detailed price quotation,

Removal firms can take a lot of the hard work out of the moving process

Services offered by removals firms

Removals firms vary in the services they offer, though **all should provide a free quotation** – not an estimate, which by definition is not a final figure for the job. Expect to be **offered some or all of these services:**

- full or part packing service
- full or part loads
- supply of packing boxes, wrapping paper and travelling wardrobes
- specialist removal of pianos, antiques, clocks, fine art and Rayburn and Aga stoves
- containerised packing for shipping overseas
- full insurance cover
- seven-day-a-week service
- cleaning of the property you're leaving and/or cleaning your new home before you arrive
- transport of garden equipment, second car or boat
- organisation of temporary accommodation if required.

including clearly explained insurance terms.

Compare services and quotes, and get back to the firms with any questions. Consider whether staff are helpful – an important part of their service is to give you peace of mind.

Once you have made your decision, sign the acceptance form.

Questions to ask removals firms

- How many staff will work on the removal?
- What training have staff had?
- Are coverings used to protect banisters and carpets?
- Are special packing materials, such as acid-free tissue, used to protect valuables?
- Are padded jackets used to pack grand pianos and other awkward items?
- How often are lorries serviced?

Questions for van-hire firms

- What capacity van do I need, given the size of the property?
- Are vans cleaned between rentals? How regularly are they serviced?
- How much fuel will the van have? Must it be returned with the same amount?
- Does it have a hydraulic loading-lift?
- Are blankets provided?
- Are there side straps to secure upright items?
- What are the insurance terms?

Questions if you have to use storage

- What is the monthly rent and what are the available insurance terms?
- Is storage in bays or containers?
- Are large items of furniture packed individually?

Moving pets

Caged pets will settle quickly once the move is complete. Make sure that cages are secured during transport, and that animals inside are protected from bangs and bashes. Special boxes can be bought for transporting birds safely.

Dogs will usually settle easily too, but don't leave them alone in the new property until they seem confident.

Move aquariums with extreme care. The **fish** should travel separately in special water-bags stored in a polystyrene box, both available from an aquatic dealer. Empty the aquarium, but keep the filtration system wet and get it going again within eight to ten hours.

Few **cats** take kindly to moving. They travel best in secure wicker baskets with a familiar blanket, a good air supply, and a restricted view. Place the basket on a wad of newspaper on a plastic sheet, and make sure the basket is wedged or belted in place. Cats fight against the effects of tranquillisers, so they aren't worth using. Putting butter on their paws may distract them for a while, as they lick it off.

If there were previously cats in your new home, buy a **pheromone spray** that will override their scent and stop your pet from spraying to mark its territory. Sprinkle catnip (catmint, available from pet shops) around the house to make your cat feel at home. Give your cat the free run of your new home straight away, but don't let it out for two weeks. Then let it out ten minutes before feeding time and gradually increase the time outside.

- At what temperature is the storage area kept? Is access restricted?

For self-storage:

- Check what storage capacity you will need and what size is available.
- Is there a covered loading area?
- Easy parking, free trolleys?

Ideally visit the premises first to check them out and meet the staff.

Countdown to removal day

7 If using a removals firm, give them a provisional date for moving as early as is practical and confirm it as soon as you can.

6 Check in advance what time of day the property will be vacant, so that you won't arrive too early, then arrange times for the move and for keys to be handed over to you.

5 Contact suppliers of water, electricity and gas at both ends. Arrange for telephone and cable/satellite television accounts to be terminated/opened. Several companies offer services via the Internet, where they handle all the contacting of suppliers when someone moves. All you need

Tips for loading a van

- Load weight **evenly**.
- Put large, **heavy items** on first.
- Use the space **above the cab** – good for large lampshades.
- Stack **flat items** (like pictures) and tall items (like standard lamps) at the sides, held in with straps.
- Cover furniture with **blankets**.
- Put lighter things, like **bedding and open boxes of house plants**, on top.
- Stand garden pots on the **floor** of the truck.
- Put the **freezer** in last.
- Make sure everything is **securely wedged** or belted in place to withstand cornering and braking.

to do is register online and select, by tick-box, the suppliers you have arrangements with.

4 Send out change of address cards.

3 Make sure there is adequate parking and access for the removals van at both ends of the journey. Is a parking permit required? Do any overhanging branches need to be clipped?

2 Measure your new home and decide where furniture will go, so that furniture and boxes can be labelled in advance. Check that large pieces will be able to pass upstairs, round corners, through doorways. In some cottages and small terraced houses, there will be a 'coffin hatch', allowing larger pieces to be passed up through the ceiling. It may also be possible to remove a window to allow access. Some pieces of furniture may have to be dismantled and reassembled.

1 If possible, plan for any children and pets to stay with friends for at least the day of the move.

Packing up

Books

Dust the books as you take them down from the shelves. Stack books of similar sizes on their sides, no higher than to make a cube. Wrap each stack in bubble wrap, seal with masking tape and fit the books on their sides into a tough box. Don't force books in. Only part-fill large boxes, otherwise they will be too heavy to carry. Pack light things, such as pillows or duvets, on top. Pack odd spaces with crumpled paper or packing beans.

China and ceramics

- Wrap each piece individually, including the lids. Wrap first in tissue, then in bubble wrap

Packing materials

Most removals firms supply packing materials free or at a nominal charge, even if you opt to do the packing yourself. Some self-move van hire firms may also supply packing boxes. If not, look in *Yellow Pages* under 'Packaging Materials' and 'Boxes, Cardboard'. Be prepared with the following:

- **Custom-made packing cases.** These are preferable to supermarket boxes, which will be of different strengths and sizes, making it more difficult to load the van evenly and safely. Avoid old-fashioned tea chests, which have sharp corners and get very heavy when full.
- **Travelling wardrobes** or suitcases.
- **Bin bags** with ties (for duvets and clothes).
- **Acid-free tissue paper.**
- **Bubble wrap.**
- **Polythene sheeting** (for paintings).
- **Packing beans**, either polystyrene or biodegradable.
- **Masking tape.** Better than clear or parcel tape because it's easy to tear, see and remove. It sticks well on cardboard and, providing you don't overfill the box, is strong enough to hold it shut.
- **Felt-tip pen.**
- **Self-adhesive labels.**

and secure firmly with masking tape.

- Don't use newspaper, as the print will rub on to the china and you will be faced with a mountain of washing-up.
- Pay particular attention to protrusions, such as teapot spouts and handles. Pad them with wads of rolled or folded tissue.
- Fill hollow vessels with scrunched paper.
- Stack plates flat on top of one another.
- Pack bundles carefully into boxes, filling gaps with packing beans.

Clocks (long-case)

Grandfather and grandmother

Things to pack in the car

- Kettle, mugs and everything you need for making **hot drinks**, including milk.
- **Picnic food** and cold drinks.
- **First-aid kit.**
- **Nightwear** and clothes for the next day.
- **Toilet rolls.**
- **Light bulbs.**
- If you have room, **bedding**.
- **Mobile and plug-in phones**, plus useful telephone numbers, including that of your conveyancer and the office where you are to pick up keys. Let the removals firm know if you are delayed on your journey. Many removal vehicles have in-cab phones – ask for the number before you leave.
- If children are travelling with you, **toys and games** they can do on their own.
- **Champagne and glasses!**

When packing up, mark boxes clearly so either you or the removal firm know exactly which room they are to go in at the new place

clocks must be dismantled before moving. If you decide to do it yourself:

1 Wait until the clock has wound down.

2 Remove the hood. (There may be a swivelling catch inside the case.)

3 Lift the weights off their pulleys.

4 Stabilise the movement with one hand on the edge of the face.

5 Lift the pendulum up and back off the suspension block, taking care not to damage the suspension spring.

6 Lift the movement out. In some clocks you will need to unscrew the seat-board first.

7 Wrap the pulleys carefully round the seat-board.

8 Pack the movement in acid-free tissue paper in a padded box.

Clothes, bedding and curtains

Clothes on hangers are best transported in travelling wardrobes. Otherwise, use sports bags or suitcases. Other clothes, bedding, linen, and curtains can be rolled or folded and transported in bin bags. If bedding for the first night won't travel with you in a car, keep it separate and easily accessible.

Kitchen/utility

- If you are taking kitchen appliances with you, disconnect the cooker (get a professional to do this if necessary), washing machine, and fridge before the removal van arrives. Secure the washing machine drum with brackets from an authorised agent to prevent any damage during transit.
- Empty the fridge and discard or pack its contents.
- Tightly seal jars, bottles and packets, wrap and pack upright, wedged in boxes.

Packing tips

- **Seal boxes** with tape. Label with a brief description of contents and which room they're for.
- Mark which way is **up**.
- Overfilling a box prevents **level stacking**.
- If a box is getting **too heavy**, fill the remaining space with light things, like cushions.

Tips for moving furniture

- The best time for **discussions on manoeuvring** is before a piece of furniture is lifted, not after the operation has begun.
- A **tape** is a more efficient tool for measuring the width of a doorway than the piece of furniture that has to go through it.
- Protect banisters with **blankets**, making sure there are no long edges to trip over.
- **Protect your back** when lifting by squatting down, getting a firm grip on the object and lifting from the knees, taking the weight on your legs, not with your back. Put things down in the same way.
- Wear **gloves** to protect your hands against knocks and dirt, but choose a material that grips well, such as leather.
- Move hi-fis, televisions, video equipment and computers in their **original packing** if possible. If not, wrap in bubble wrap and fill gaps in boxes with packing beans.
- Removal firms may require the householder to dismantle and reassemble **self-assembly furniture**. Have it flat-packed, ready for the move.
- Loop **lamp flex** and secure with masking tape to the lamp to avoid accidents. Use this method for other electrical items.
- **Remove drawers** to make furniture lighter and use them as packing boxes.
- **Secure cupboard doors** to prevent them swinging open while being carried.

Areas of the house to pack up as early as possible

The attic
Sort and pack the contents and store in a bedroom where they will not be overlooked. The removals team will want to see the entire scale of your move when they arrive, so they can plan how to load up the van.

The shed
Sort and pack the contents of sheds and garages, discarding flammable substances (such as old tins of paint, creosote and gas bottles), which would invalidate your insurance if put on the van. Clean any tools before tying them together.

The garden
Don't forget about patio pots, garden seats, bird tables and the clothes line.

Priorities when you arrive at your new home

- Install **fridge and freezer**.
- Stick **labels** on doors of rooms to correspond with labels on boxes.
- Plug in **phone**.
- **Unload.**
- Chill **champagne**.
- Make up **beds**.
- Sort the **kitchen** out so that you can at least use the kettle!
- **Leave the rest until tomorrow.**
- **Open the champagne** and toast your new home!

- Put the contents of a chest freezer into the minimum number of large polythene bags so they can be quickly put back in the freezer once it's on the vehicle. Switch an upright freezer to fast-freeze first thing on moving day. Unplug freezers at the last minute. They should be the final things to be loaded on to the vehicle and the first to be unloaded at the other end. Freezer contents should stay frozen for up to 12 hours. If the freezer is going to be disconnected for any longer, empty out the contents and defrost beforehand.

Paintings and mirrors

Protect the corners of framed paintings and mirrors with pads of bubble wrap, then seal in a polythene parcel. Load paintings upright, supported on soft padding and strapped to the van's sides with flat webbing. Crated paintings should also travel upright and be secured.

Pianos

With a grand piano, the instrument is moved separately from its stand. Rods and linkages must be disconnected, and are sometimes difficult to re-engage. The pedals are loose once the rods have been disconnected – care needs to be taken to avoid catching them on the floor when the instrument is moved. Experts will put the piano in a padded jacket and move it on a trolley. It can take up to five people to negotiate stairs.

Rugs

Never crush a rug by folding it right side in. Roll fringe to fringe, right side outside, so that the pile is stretched, not squashed. For more valuable rugs, interleave with acid-free tissue paper.

Roll carpets round a core of PVC or a cardboard roller. It can take three people to roll a large carpet. Clear the carpet of furniture. Stand on the carpet, in a row, facing one end. Lift the edge and walk backwards until about 3m (10ft) of the carpet is lying face down. Put the roller in position and roll up this part of the carpet. Pick up the roller and walk backwards again, repeating the process until the whole carpet is on the roller.

Silver

Wrap all silver items in acid-free tissue paper. Newspaper is acidic and will cause tarnishing. If you use cling wrap or plastic bags, condensation will form inside.

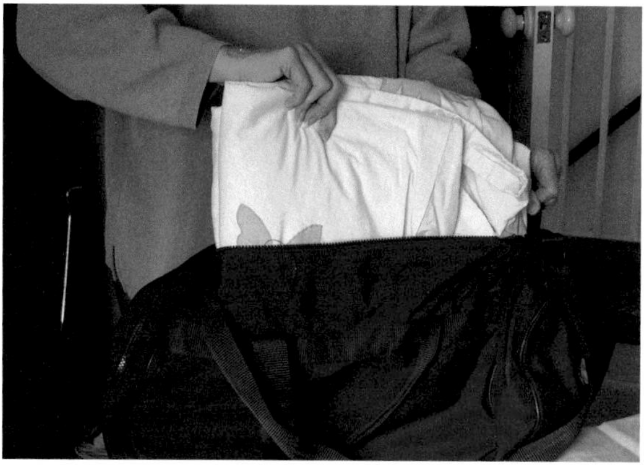

Pack bed linen for the first night in your new home

Contact details

Useful websites and addresses about the information given in this chapter.

British Association of Removers
e-mail: info@bar.co.uk
www.barmovers.com
Enables you to search and locate a removals company.

fish4
www.fish4.co.uk/homes/sguide/index.jsp
Provides a seller's guide to selling your property, including getting a better price, improving your chances of a quick sale, information on auction houses and advice on estate agents.

homesalez.com
www.homesalez.com
Advertise your home for sale on this site for a low, fixed fee, with nothing to pay until your house sells.

House Network Ltd, PO Box 6150, Basildon, Essex SS14 0WH
Tel: 0870 446 0406
Fax: 0871 733 4193
e-mail:
info@housenetwork.co.uk
www.housenetwork.co.uk
A website enabling you to sell your house online, with no time limit, for a low, fixed fee.

Inland Revenue
Tel: 020 7667 4001
www.inlandrevenue.gov.uk
Information about individual and business tax, including a separate section on self assessment. Details of the regional offices are also provided on the site. A range of leaflets covering letting issues are available from the Inland Revenue Orderline (0845 900 0404) or through the website.

Law Society, The Law Society's Hall, 113 Chancery Lane, London WC2A 1PL
Tel: 020 7242 1222
Fax: 020 7831 0344
e-mail: info-services@lawsociety.org.uk
www.lawsoc.org.uk
Enables you to search for a law firm or individual solicitor in England and Wales.

reallymoving.com
www.reallymoving.com
Provider of online home-

moving services. Gives information for house buyers on mortgages, surveyors, solicitors, removals, change of address services and home improvements.

Road Haulage Association, RHA Weybridge, Roadway House, 35 Monument Hill, Weybridge, Surrey KT13 8RN
Tel: 01932 841 515
Fax: 01932 852 516
e-mail: weybridge@rha.net
www.rha.net
Search for a haulier by place or postcode. One of the categories is removals.

the-big-move.com
Tel: 0700 510 2727
Fax: 024 7667 9251
e-mail: info@the-big-move.com
www.the-big-move.com
The website is an internet-based solution for all your removal needs within the UK mainland.

The Move Channel.com
www.themovechannel.com
A useful web resource to help with property related activities. Click on the How To Guides for advice on selling.

UK Property Web,
40 The Woodpeckers, Weymouth, Dorset DT3 5RS
Tel: 01305 814 721
e-mail: wendy.hyde@ukpropertyweb.co.uk
www.ukpropertyweb.co.uk
Dedicated to buying and selling property privately. No commission charge. Also offers a property matching service.

Which?, 2 Marylebone Road, London NW1 4DF
Tel: 020 7770 7000
Fax: 020 7770 7600
e-mail: which@which.net
www.which.net
Visit the bookstore area of the Which? website where a number of publications on selling, letting and conveyancing are available.

WhoToUse.co.uk
www.whotouse.co.uk/removals.html
Provides a customer recommendations guide to good local removal firms. The WhoToUse company (www.whotouse.co.uk) provides over 2,500 customer recommended tradesmen and professional people from all over England, Scotland and Wales. Those tradesmen or companies whose performance falls to an unacceptable level are removed from the list.

nking
Credit Card
Insurance
Investments
oans
Mortgages
Pensions
Savings
Mortgage
Help with buying, moving or improving your h

Buying a **Property**

Whether you are a first-time buyer or on the housing ladder already and wanting to move on to a bigger property, there are still valuable tips every buyer should be aware of before diving in.

Before even viewing property, you have to decide if you have sufficient funds. Although interest rates have been low in recent years, overstretching yourself financially at the beginning may lead to disaster in subsequent years if rates start gradually rising. The cost of the mortgage is not the only financial commitment. You need to take into account the many insurances that are part and parcel of owning a property today. Work out the nitty-gritty finances before even glancing in an estate agent's window.

Finding funds

Buying a home of your own could be the biggest financial commitment you ever make. So it's not something you should rush into – especially if you don't envisage staying in the same place for at least three years.

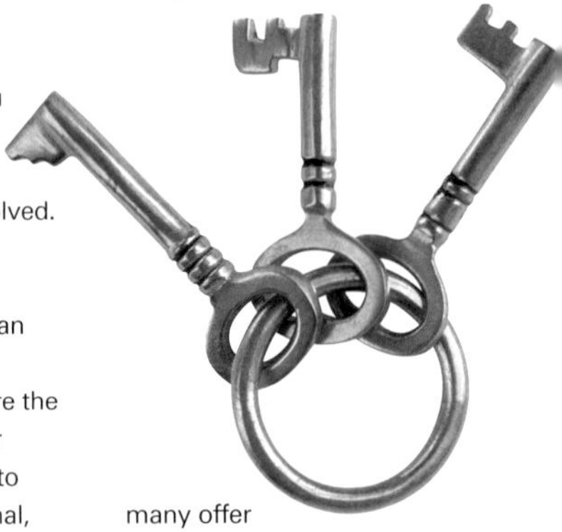

Buying will be a realistic option, however, only if you can amass the substantial amount of cash you'll need to meet the costs involved.

Reasons to buy

1 Buying can be cheaper than renting – largely because mortgage interest rates are the lowest they have been for over 25 years. According to research by Abbey National, even taking into account the costs involved in maintaining a property, on average it is 57% cheaper to buy than rent over 25 years.

2 Owning your home gives you security. Providing you keep up your mortgage payments, you know that you can stay in your home as long as you like.

3 When you have paid off the mortgage, you will have acquired a substantial financial asset and a home that costs very little to live in.

4 Because lenders are so keen to attract new customers, especially first-time buyers, many offer to help out with some of the upfront costs involved in buying a property, such as valuation and legal fees, either by refunding them if the mortgage goes ahead or by providing a cash lump sum. For more on finding a good mortgage deal, *see* pp366–75.

5 Providing your property goes up in value, buying your own home can mean that if, in the future, you want to finance home improvements – or any other large purchase, such as a car – you can extend your mortgage rather than using more costly types of loan.

Can you afford to buy?

The biggest single cost you face when buying a property is the cash deposit. The deposit needs to be at least the difference between the purchase price and the size of mortgage a lender is prepared to grant you. Most lenders will not lend more than 95% of the valuation of the property, so the minimum deposit you will need is 5%. If you plan to buy at auction (*see* pp398–9), you will need a deposit of at least 10% of your maximum bid price.

Your income also affects how big a mortgage you can get. If you are buying on your own, the most you can borrow is typically 3–3½ times your annual income, although some lenders will lend up to four times your income. So if you earn £20,000 a year, you could get a mortgage of between £60,000 and £80,000. Assuming you could borrow 95% of the value, this would buy you a property costing between £63,150 and £84,200, for which you would need a deposit of between £3,150 and £4,200. You also need to budget for:

- stamp duty, which you will have to pay if the property costs more than £60,000. The rates are: 1% on properties worth £60,001 to £250,000; 3% from £250,001 to £500,000; and 4% on £500,001 or more
- Land Registry fee, which is a flat fee of: £40 if the purchase price is up to £40,000; £60 from £40,001 to £70,000; £100 from £70,001 to £100,000; £200 from £100,001 to £200,000; £300 from £200,001 to £500,000; £500 from £500,001 to £1 million; and £800 on property costing more than £1 million
- search fees, which cost an average of £126 and pay for general checks – such as whether or not the property is in the path of a planned road development.

Shared ownership

If property prices in the area you like are out of your reach, it could be worth considering a **shared-ownership scheme**. These are usually run by housing associations. Instead of buying a property outright, you buy a share, with the help of a mortgage, and pay rent on the remaining share owned by the housing association. You then have the option of increasing your share as you can afford to.

Whether or not a shared-ownership scheme is an option depends on whether you meet a particular housing association's **eligibility criteria**. Preference is usually given to housing association and council tenants, and first-time buyers. Get more details by phoning the Shared Ownership Advice Line or contacting the Housing Corporation.

No stamp duty

You can buy property costing £150,000 or less in some 2,000 **'disadvantaged' areas** of the UK without having to pay stamp duty. Details from the Stamp Office.

Improve your chances

- If you plan to buy a home, saving up a **deposit** should be your top priority. Although the minimum you are likely to need is 5% of the property value, if you can save a deposit of at least 10% you will be in a much stronger position when it comes to finding a good mortgage deal.
- Before applying for a mortgage, pay off as much of any **existing debts** as you can. Although most lenders base what they are prepared to lend on your annual salary, they also look at your ability to repay the loan. The more debt you have in the form of overdrafts, outstanding credit card bills, and personal loans, the less income you will have available to make mortgage repayments.
- Work out whether you can afford the **regular monthly costs** of buying a home. This includes not just the mortgage repayments but the cost of insurance.
- If buying a place of your own doesn't seem affordable and you don't want to get involved in shared or joint ownership, **consider taking a lodger** to help pay the mortgage. Currently the first £4,250 of rent taken each year is tax-free. Some mortgage lenders will take the rent into account when they calculate your mortgage related to your earnings, but are more likely to do so when assessing your ability to repay, which looks at all income and outgoings.

- legal fees, of around £400 to £1,000, depending on the value of the property (*see* table). However, your lender may cover this expense.
- upfront mortgage costs, which can vary according to the size of the mortgage and the type of deal you choose.

Moving up the ladder

If you already have a foot on the property ladder but are considering a move, the costs you face are the same as those for a first-time buyer (*see* table), with one major difference. As long as your current home has risen in value since you bought it, the sale proceeds will provide you with the deposit for your next property. How big a deposit depends on how much you have left after:

- negotiations with your own buyer – you may end up reducing the asking price by as much as 10%
- paying off what you owe on your current mortgage – together with any charges for repaying early (if applicable, though these charges may be waived if you take out your next mortgage with the same lender)
- paying the estate agent –

Average cost of buying in England & Wales

Property price (£)	5% deposit (£)	Administration costs (£) *Solicitor/ Conveyancer*	*Land Registry fee*	*Searches*	*Stamp duty*	**Total admin costs (£)**	**Total funds you will need (£)**
25,000	1,250	369	40	167	nil	576	1,826
50,000	2,500	377	40	167	nil	584	3,084
60,000	3,000	383	60	167	nil	610	3,610
80,000	4,000	401	60	167	800	1,428	5,428
100,000	5,000	423	100	167	1,000	1,690	6,690
150,000	7,500	463	150	167	1,500	2,280	9,780
200,000	10,000	514	150	167	2,000	2,831	12,831
300,000	15,000	612	250	167	9,000	10,029	25,029
500,000	25,000	775	250	167	15,000	16,192	41,192

Source: The Woolwich Cost of Moving Survey 2004.
Figures compiled by the University of Greenwich, School of Architecture and Construction. This table gives the average costs of buying in England and Wales with a 5% deposit. Actual costs vary by region and tend to be highest in the South East and South West of England.

Moving up the property ladder can be expensive in the short term

unless you choose to sell privately (*see* pp336–9)

- meeting the legal fees involved in selling – unless you do the conveyancing yourself
- covering the costs involved in buying the next property, as well as removal expenses.

If all these costs reduce the potential sale proceeds to zero – and you have no other way of paying the costs – trading up is not an affordable option. You will need enough out of what's left to put down a deposit of at least 5% on the new property and, of course, you must also earn enough to get the size of mortgage you need.

Upfront mortgage costs

As well as budgeting for all the costs involved in buying a property, make allowance for the fees you may be charged for setting up your mortgage. These include:

- **Valuation fee**, which pays for a professional mortgage valuation – the figure on which the lender will base your final mortgage offer. You can avoid this fee by choosing one of the special deals where the lender bears the cost of the valuation or refunds the fee if the mortgage goes ahead.
- **Arrangement fee**, to cover the administrative costs of setting up the mortgage, although not all lenders charge a one-off fee for this.
- **Booking fee**, which you are likely to have to pay if you choose a mortgage deal where the rate of interest is fixed, capped, or discounted. For more details on interest rates, *see* box opposite.
- **Legal fees**, for the cost of creating the mortgage document, unless – as it usually is – this work is undertaken by your conveyancer and so already included in the other legal fees.

There is an awful lot of careful budgeting involved before putting out the welcome mat

What will the mortgage cost every month?

(£) Size of loan	3%	4%	Interest rate (£) 5%	6%	7%	8%
30,000	144	160	177	196	215	234
40,000	192	213	236	261	286	312
50,000	240	267	296	326	358	391
60,000	287	320	355	391	429	469
70,000	335	373	414	456	501	547
80,000	383	426	473	522	572	625
90,000	431	480	532	587	644	703
100,000	479	533	591	652	715	781
125,000	599	666	739	815	894	976
150,000	719	800	887	978	1,073	1,172
200,000	958	1,066	1,182	1,304	1,430	1,562
250,000	1,198	1,333	1,478	1,630	1,788	1,953

Source: MoneyFacts

Adding up the costs

Just as important as working out whether you can afford the one-off costs of buying (and selling, if you have to do that too) is checking that you will be able to meet the ongoing monthly cost of home ownership. To give you an idea of what your mortgage repayments will be, the table above gives the monthly cost, for different sizes of loan, of a repayment mortgage paid back over 25 years.

If you have overstretched yourself financially when interest rates are low, think about how much more a month an additional 1% will affect your ability to pay. Don't forget, your home is at risk.

Seven ways to save

1 Before you make your mortgage application, check whether you will be charged a **'high lending fee'**.
2 Don't assume that taking the **insurance** that a lender offers will improve your mortgage chances.
3 Get insurance quotes from **independent providers** to compare with your lender's quote.
4 **Don't assume** that because a mortgage offer gives quotes for insurance you have to buy it.
5 **Don't borrow from a high-street lender.** Lenders operating by phone or over the Internet are more likely to give you a free choice of insurer.
6 Don't be panicked into buying **MPPI** and/or critical-illness cover.
7 Find out what your **employer** offers in life insurance, sick pay and pension in the event of early retirement due to ill health. Check how much you would get if made redundant.

Buying with others

Sharing the cost of buying a property with another person can make the upfront costs more affordable and also **increases the size of mortgage** you can apply for. Most lenders will either consider lending the same income multiples as if you were buying on your own, plus one times the second person's income, or they will lend 2½ – 2¾ times your joint income.

If you share the purchase of a home with a friend, make sure that you own the property as **'tenants in common'**. This means that you each own a distinct share in the property (the sizes of the shares should reflect how much you each put into buying it). You should also ask a solicitor to draw up a trust deed to set out what happens if one of you wants to sell but the other doesn't. This costs about £75.

Being tenants in common also allows each of you to specify who will get your share if you die. This is not the case if you own the property as **'joint tenants'** – ownership of the whole property automatically passes to the other if one partner dies. However, a joint tenancy is worth considering if you are buying with a significant other and you would want him or her to be able to continue living in the property after your death.

Insurance

Although your lender may offer the types of insurance detailed below, you will not necessarily need all of them.

Buildings insurance

This is a must – without a suitable policy you won't get your mortgage. If you don't take the policy offered by your lender, you may have to pay an administration fee of around £25, although the insurer you decide to use may pay this fee for you.

Contents insurance

Covers the cost of replacing (or repairing) belongings if they are lost, stolen, damaged, or destroyed. If you are moving, you'll need a new policy for your new address.

Life insurance

Lenders like you to have life insurance because it pays off the mortgage if you die. Paying for life insurance is unavoidable if you choose an interest-only mortgage backed by an insurance-based savings plan (*see* p369). But with other sorts of mortgage (such as repayment mortgages) you usually have a choice. If you are unattached and dependent-free, you don't necessarily need life cover. If you have a joint mortgage and/or children, you probably do.

You need buildings insurance to get a mortgage on any property

Critical-illness insurance

Critical-illness policies pay out a lump sum if you are diagnosed as having one of a defined list of life-threatening or seriously debilitating conditions (such as cancer, multiple sclerosis, loss of limbs/eyesight/hearing/ speech). Whether you need critical-illness insurance or not depends on several factors: the likelihood of serious illness striking before your mortgage is paid off, how serious illness would affect your finances (and those dependent on you) and what other resources you have available.

Combined life and critical-illness insurance

A drawback of critical-illness insurance is that, typically,

The cost of 100% mortgages

One very good reason for making sure that you have as **big a deposit as possible** to put towards your property purchase is the fact that if you don't have a lump sum of at least 5% of the value of the property, you may face a 'high lending fee'. This is almost certain to be the case if you can scrape together only the difference between the purchase price and the mortgage valuation and so have to take out a 100% mortgage.

The high lending fee pays for an insurance policy called a **mortgage indemnity guarantee (MIG)**, which protects the lender from the risk of not being able to recover the full amount of the loan if you fall behind with your mortgage repayments and the property has to be repossessed.

A limited number of lenders do not charge a high lending fee and you are unlikely to face a fee if you borrow less than 75% of the lender's valuation of the property. But if you need to borrow more than 90–95%, you can generally expect to be charged 5–9% of the difference between 75% of the valuation and the amount of your loan. With a mortgage of £95,000 on a property valued at £100,000, paying for your lender's peace of mind could cost anything from £1,450 to £1,790. **If you borrow 100% of the valuation, the fee can be as much as 12% of the amount of the loan over 75% of the valuation.** If you can't pay this fee up front, it is added to the loan, which means that you end up paying interest on it too.

As an added precaution, as well as charging a high lending fee, some lenders will make buying **mortgage payment protection insurance** (*see* below) a compulsory part of the mortgage deal.

it will not pay out if you die within 28 days of the diagnosis of a serious illness. So, to plug this gap, many lenders sell policies that combine life insurance with critical-illness cover. If you decide you need both, combined cover tends to be cheaper.

Mortgage payment protection insurance (MPPI)

Also called 'accident, sickness and unemployment' (ASU) cover. It aims to meet your mortgage repayments for up to 12 months (sometimes 24) if you are not earning as a result of redundancy or illness. So this type of cover is not really necessary if your ability to meet your monthly mortgage repayments would be unaffected by illness or unemployment.

However, if you're self-employed, having a policy that pays out if you are too ill to earn could be useful, but you are unlikely to benefit from unemployment cover. The reverse may be true, however,

Mortgage protection insurance can cushion the effects of redundancy

if you are an employee with a decent sick-pay scheme. You are unlikely to benefit from MPPI if already out of work, work fewer than 16 hours a week, have not been in continuous employment for at least six months or are a contract worker.

Independent advice

With all these forms of insurance, if you are at all unsure, get yourself some independent financial advice from an adviser who will not receive commission from any of the policies.

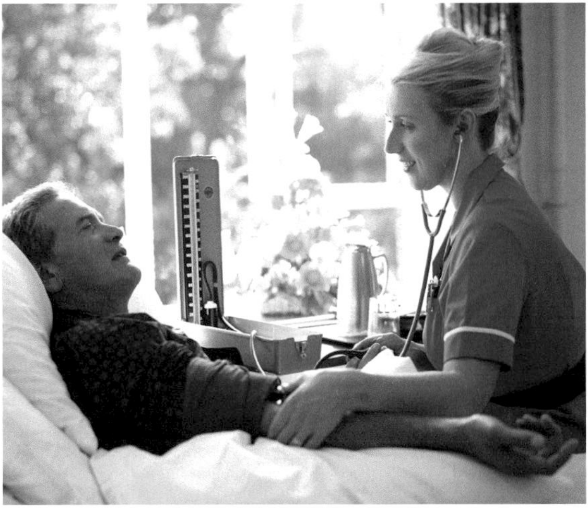

Sickness cover can help you through times when you are too ill to work

Choosing a mortgage

The days are long gone when everyone paid pretty much the same mortgage interest rate and you could get a mortgage only if you had dutifully saved with the same financial institution for a number of years.

Nowadays, lenders vie with each other to attract business with a constant stream of new deals for both first-time buyers and borrowers looking to switch mortgages, resulting in hundreds of mortgage deals to choose from. See How to get a good deal, p374, for where to look on the Internet for interactive advice on what type of mortgage might be appropriate for you.

Repayment options

The most important decision you have to make when choosing a mortgage is how you will repay it. There are two ways of doing this. Which of these you choose depends to a large extent on your attitude to risk. The stability of your income and whether or not it may rise or fall over the foreseeable future is also a consideration when deciding on a mortgage.

Repayment mortgages

A repayment mortgage – sometimes called a capital repayment mortgage – is the only risk-free way of making sure that you (rather than your lender) will own your home after the mortgage has come to an end. With this type of repayment method, part of your monthly mortgage payment is used to pay interest and part is used to pay back the capital you have borrowed, although in the first few years most of your monthly payment is interest (however, *see* Five mortgage myths, p368). This means that you gradually pay off the loan and – providing you keep up your repayments – you are guaranteed to have repaid it in full by the end of the mortgage term. If you don't want to take any chances with your mortgage, this is often the best repayment method to go for.

Interest-only mortgages

More risky than a repayment mortgage, as there is no

Most of us need to take out a mortgage to finance our home purchase

guarantee that you will pay off the loan and so own your home when the mortgage comes to an end. This is because, instead of paying back the loan little by little, the whole of your monthly mortgage payment is made up of interest. None of the capital you have borrowed is paid back until the end of the mortgage term, when you will be expected to pay off the entire loan in one go.

To make sure that you have a sufficiently large lump sum to be able to do this, as well as making mortgage payments you should make payments into some kind of savings plan (*see* below for the options). The risk you take is that the savings plan may not produce the lump sum you need to repay the mortgage, although if your investments do exceptionally well you could end up with more than you need to clear your mortgage debt.

Five mortgage myths

1 You have to pay back your mortgage over 25 years.
You can arrange a shorter or longer mortgage term than this. The shorter the term of the mortgage, the lower the overall cost of the loan.

2 In the first few years of a repayment mortgage, you pay off hardly any of the money you have borrowed.
Not true. After five years of a repayment loan of £70,000, for example, you would have paid off around £6,000 of the loan. By contrast, with an interest-only loan you would have paid off nothing after the same number of years.

3 Repayment mortgages cost more than interest-only mortgages.
Interest-only loans only seem cheaper. Once you add the amount you have to pay into the savings plan to the monthly mortgage interest, the total mortgage-related payments on an interest-only mortgage are higher.

4 Interest-only loans are better if you plan to move in the future, as they are more flexible than repayment mortgages.
There's no difference in flexibility between the two types of mortgage. And a repayment mortgage can be better because you will have a smaller capital sum to pay back when the property sells, releasing more funds to put towards the purchase of your next property.

5 Endowment-backed mortgages are still suitable for some people.
The only people who benefit from endowment mortgages are the advisers who get paid commission for selling them.

Backing up an interest-only mortgage

If you are attracted by the idea of combining the purchase of a property with the discipline of regular, long-term saving, you will need to decide on the kind of savings plan you are going to use to back the mortgage. Lenders make it very clear that it is

Before you buy, you have to choose the type of mortgage to best suit you

your responsibility to make sure that you are saving enough to build up the lump sum you will need to repay the loan. If you fail to keep up the payments into the savings plan, or you don't pay into a savings plan at all, when the mortgage comes to an end the lender can make you sell your property if that is the only way you have of raising the cash needed to repay the full amount of the loan.

With an endowment

In the past, the most popular form of savings plan to back an interest-only mortgage was an endowment policy. This is essentially a life-insurance policy linked to stock market investments. The main disadvantages of this kind of savings plan are that it includes life insurance that you may not need and you are tied to paying the monthly premiums for the full term of the mortgage. If you don't, you risk getting back less than you paid in.

Even if you do manage to keep up with the monthly premiums, there is no guarantee that your savings will grow sufficiently to produce the necessary lump sum. In recent years, thousands of people have been told that their policies are not on track to repay their mortgages because the underlying stock market investments have not performed as well as had been expected. This 'endowment scandal' has prompted most lenders to give up recommending interest-only mortgages backed by an endowment, in favour of ISA-backed mortgages.

Flexible mortgages and who they suit

Unlike traditional loans, where you pay a set amount each month over a fixed number of years (typically 25), flexible mortgages allow you to **vary your monthly payments** and make extra, lump-sum payments. This means that you can pay off your mortgage more quickly and so reduce the total amount of interest you pay.

This sort of mortgage may not suit first-time buyers on a tight budget, for whom choosing a low rate of interest is a top priority, but flexible mortgages can be very attractive for anyone with **unpredictable earnings**, for example people who are self-employed. This is because, as well as allowing you to make overpayments, most flexible mortgages also allow you to make underpayments or even stop making payments for a while.

Check on penalties for switching

If you choose a **special mortgage package**, such as a fixed, capped, discounted or cashback deal, there are usually strings attached in the form of (sometimes quite hefty) fees if you decide to pull out of the deal early. Most lenders charge a penalty only if you change your mortgage during the period of the special deal, but some will tie you in beyond that period.

This is not a worry if you plan to stay with the same lender. However, if there's any possibility you will want to change lender in the near future or else repay some or all of the mortgage early, look for a deal that has a **short penalty period**.

With an ISA

The attraction of a mortgage backed by an Individual Savings Account (ISA) is that an ISA is a more flexible and tax-efficient way of building up a lump sum than an endowment, and it doesn't have to include life insurance (*see* p298 for more on ISAs). The main disadvantage is that your investments are still linked to the stock market, so there is still no guarantee that you will build up the lump sum you need. You also need to be prepared to keep an eye on how well your investments are performing.

In addition, at the time of writing there is no guarantee that ISAs will continue after 2009, which means that you might have to look for another type of savings plan at some stage.

With a personal pension

Using a personal pension to back an interest-only mortgage is tax-efficient but also very risky. The idea is that you pay into a personal pension (which includes stakeholder pensions – *see* p256) with the aim of building up a fund that will be used both to pay you a pension and pay off your mortgage. However, only 25% of this money can be used to pay off the mortgage, so the fund built up in the pension plan has to be at least four times the size of your mortgage.

You should also be aware that if you have more than 25 years to go before retiring, you will have to pay mortgage interest for longer than you would with a mortgage linked to another sort of investment – in other words, you'll be paying until you decide to take your pension.

Also, if you join an employer's pension scheme,

The vast number of interest deals around can be daunting to a first-time buyer

you may have to find another way of saving to pay off your mortgage, because you cannot normally pay into an employer's pension and hold a personal pension at the same time.

Options for paying interest

Once you have decided how you are going to repay the mortgage, you need to choose the type of interest deal that will best suit you. The type of interest deal you choose can affect how long you are tied to the same lender and the kind of penalty fee you may have to pay if you move house or switch lenders in the future (*see* box, top p370).

Standard variable

All lenders offer mortgages where the interest is charged at their standard variable rate (SVR), which goes up and down in line with interest rates in general. In terms of monthly mortgage payments, this is unlikely to be the cheapest deal available, but there is usually no penalty to pay if you decide to switch your mortgage.

What if you are not a standard borrower

If there's a chance that you will be refused a mortgage because you don't fit the standard borrower profile of a full-time employee with a regular salary, you shouldn't give up on the idea of buying your own home. Using a **mortgage broker** can increase your chances of getting a mortgage, as can approaching one of the growing number of lenders who offer:

- **self-certification mortgages**, for people who can't supply evidence of two years' worth of earnings, such as the recently self-employed, new contract workers or divorcees living on maintenance from an ex-spouse
- **impaired-credit mortgages**, for people who have had problems with credit in the past, which may even have led to a county court judgement (CCJ) or bankruptcy.

Cashback deals

As well as offering different ways of paying the interest, several lenders have **special deals** that give back, as a cash payment shortly after the loan starts, a percentage of the amount you have borrowed. Providing the monthly payments are manageable, the attraction of this kind of deal is that you get a lump of money to spend as you wish.

The **disadvantage** is that the lender may want some of the money back if you decide to move or change lenders within five or so years of taking out the mortgage.

Discounted variable

As the name suggests, with this type of mortgage deal you pay a lower than normal variable rate for a fixed period of time, which can be as little as six months or as much as five years. Some deals keep the same discount for that period, while others gradually reduce the discount each year. A discounted rate is worth considering if you don't mind the fact that your repayments will still rise and fall in line with interest rates in general, and – more importantly – you like the idea of paying less for your loan to begin with.

Base-rate tracker

This type of deal is a variation on the standard variable theme. The difference is that the lender guarantees that the interest rate you pay will never be more than a fixed percentage above bank base rate (the interest rate set by the Bank of England on which lenders base the rates they charge) and that changes in base rate will be passed on immediately. This is an advantage when interest rates fall, but not so good when they rise.

Five steps to a successful application

1 Register to vote When assessing your application, as a way of confirming your current address, lenders will check that you are on the electoral register. Not being registered to vote can count against you.

2 Have your papers ready When applying for a mortgage, you will need to produce between three and six months' worth of payslips or bank statements that show how much you were paid. If you are self-employed, lenders usually want to see your accounts or tax statements for the past two or three years. If you currently rent your home, you may also be asked to provide evidence that you pay your rent on time and a reference from your landlord.

3 Clean up your credit record Most lenders consult a credit reference agency to find out what other debts you have, how good you are at keeping up repayments and whether you have ever been credit blacklisted. So, in the months leading up to applying for a mortgage, be scrupulous about paying all your bills on time and – if possible – reduce overdrafts and credit-card balances.

4 Apply early You don't have to have found a property to apply for a mortgage – many lenders will make an 'in principle' mortgage offer based on your earnings. This is worth having because it establishes the price of the property you can afford to buy, reassures prospective sellers that any offer you make is genuine and helps to speed up the buying process.

5 Be realistic If you apply to borrow more than you can afford, it's very likely that your mortgage application will be turned down. This will show up on your credit record and may deter other lenders from giving you a mortgage. *See* p14 for working out costs.

Fixed

With fixed-rate deals, the interest rate you are charged is fixed for a certain number of years – you are guaranteed to be able to pay that rate irrespective of changes in interest rates in general. At the end of the fixed-rate period, you revert to paying the lender's SVR. Fixed rates are ideal if you are on a tight budget and want the security of knowing that your mortgage payments won't go up and down for the first few years. However, you need to be aware that you are generally locked into a fixed-rate deal, so you won't benefit if there is a fall in interest rates in general.

Capped

With a capped-rate deal, the rate you pay is semi-fixed in that it is guaranteed not to go above a certain level – the 'cap' – during the period that the capped rate applies. With

How to get a good deal

- **Check the personal finance pages of the weekend press** for up-to-date information on the best mortgage deals available.
- **Look beyond the high street.** Some of the best deals available are from small building societies and the banks who operate only over the telephone or Internet.
- **Use the Internet.** One of the big advantages of going online to find a mortgage is that most mortgage websites provide interactive comparison tables – you enter your preferences and are presented with a list of possible mortgages. Useful sites include:
  www.charcolonline.co.uk
  www.marketplace.co.uk
  www.moneyextra.com
  www.moneynet.co.uk
  www.moneysupermarket.com.
- **Look out for CAT-standard mortgages.** CAT (charges, access, terms) marks are a government-backed initiative designed to make it easy to spot a mortgage that is low-cost and penalty-free. Although CAT-standard mortgages aren't guaranteed to be the cheapest, you can be confident that there are no nasty surprises lurking in the small print.
- If you don't have the time or inclination to search for a good deal, **consider using a mortgage broker**, who can search the market for you. Brokers usually charge you a fee, but may also be paid a fee by the lender. If so, the Mortgage Code says they must tell you that the lender is paying a fee and disclose the exact amount if it's more than £250.

some deals, there is also a lower limit – the 'collar' or 'floor' – which means that the interest rate you are charged cannot go below a certain level either. A capped-rate mortgage can be more attractive than a fixed-rate mortgage if you have some flexibility in your budget (allowing you to cope with limited rises and falls in interest rates) and you want the certainty of knowing that there is a limit on how much interest rates can go up and down.

The Mortgage Code

Until October 2004, when the sale of mortgages will be regulated by the Financial Services Authority, lenders and other mortgage advisers have to abide by the Mortgage Code. This is a voluntary code of practice that aims to improve the quality of mortgage advice and service levels from lenders, brokers and other mortgage advisers. Under the Code, every potential borrower must be given a copy of the leaflet *You and Your Mortgage* (which explains your rights under the Code) as early on in the buying process as possible.

Mortgage advisers have to abide by the Mortgage Code

Lenders and mortgage intermediaries must tell you what kind of service they offer, which can be:

- information on one type of mortgage deal, which may apply if you have made up your own mind about the mortgage you want
- information on different mortgages but no specific advice about which one is best – you use the information to make your own choice
- advice and a recommendation as to the most suitable deal for you, following in-depth questions about your current circumstances and future plans, with regards to your employment, for example.

In addition, mortgage intermediaries must tell you whether they:

- search the whole market looking for the best deal
- look only at mortgages offered by a limited number of lenders
- only make recommendations about mortgages offered by one lender.

An intermediary who searches the whole market is more likely to find a competitive deal than one who looks only at the mortgages of one particular lender.

Finding a property

In the property world location means everything – it is the cornerstone of the asking price. But your decision to buy will be based on what the location means to you and how long you plan to stay there.

Before you consider any properties in a particular area, ask yourself a few fundamental questions. Is this property going to be a stepping stone to a larger home or will you stay in it for the foreseeable future? Are you buying to let a property in an area that will appeal to a particular type of tenant, such as students or business people?

Think carefully about your needs and how they might change, how an area may change over time, and keep in mind possible resale values.

What you need from where you live

Make a list of the facilities you need or would like to have nearby and rate every property you view against it. The list might include good access to:

- public transport
- a motorway
- school
- college
- hospital
- workplace
- family and friends
- the countryside
- swimming pool or gym
- golf course
- shops
- cinemas and restaurants

Choosing the location

After finding an area that offers what you want, focus on specific locations within it. You might even compile a list of streets that you particularly like. Consider not just how a property will suit you while you live there, but how local features will affect its value when you come to sell. The website www.upmystreet.com gives extensive local information by postcode.

- **Near a public house** This may offer a handy extension to your social life, but pubs can generate traffic and noise, particularly at closing time.
- **Near a school** If places at the school are sought after, the property could have a

The setting looks idyllic, but does the river have a past history of flooding?

good resale value to a family with school-age children. In the meantime, how will you be affected by noise from the playground and school-run traffic?

- **Rivers and flood plains** Since the bad flooding in 2000, we're all more aware of the dangers of low-lying areas. Check the past history of the area with the Environment Agency at www. environment-agency.gov.uk/flood.
- **Local amenities** Unfortunately, many villages are losing their shops and post offices. Could a lack of local amenities be restricting for you – and the resale value?
- **Public transport** Does your chosen area provide good transport links?
- **On the sea front** Still a dream for some, but consider the possibilities of coastal erosion before you buy.
- **Proposed building projects** You or your solicitor needs to do a thorough local search to ensure that there are no major building projects planned. Future road creation or widening schemes would dramatically affect traffic levels. However, not all

projects are bad news financially. The creation of giant shopping malls and extensions to the London rail system have been known to push up property prices.

- **Electricity pylons or mobile phone masts** There is currently a debate about the health issues of living close to pylons and phone masts. Check out if the property you like has pylons or cables nearby by contacting www.home-envirosearch.com.
- **Crime rate** Click on www.upmystreet.com to check crime rates in your area.
- **Seasonal traffic** Be aware of how traffic in the area changes. It may come alive with tourists in the summer or host an arts festival in the winter.

Start your property hunt

There are many more options open to the house-hunter now than just the local estate agent. The Internet has opened up a whole new way of discovering and viewing properties. Other possibilities depend on the type of property that interests you.

The estate agent Still most people's first port of call. Be firm about your requirements and price range but be prepared to receive details of properties that don't quite fit all your specifications. Estate agents know that would-be buyers will often compromise or change their mind on what they're looking for. It's worth stressing that you are genuinely looking to buy and make it clear what you're hoping to find. Developing a good working

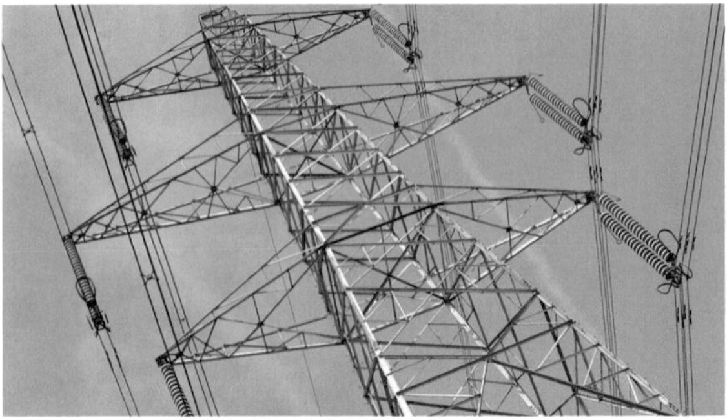

The close proximity of electricity pylons may be a cause for concern

relationship with an individual at each agency makes it more likely that they will think of you when a new property comes onto their books.

The Internet Useful if you are planning to move some distance and can't visit local estate agents. Download details of properties from sites and register at the same time. They will then e-mail or post you details of suitable properties that come on the market.

Private sales Some people prefer to sell their property without incurring an agent's fee. Check advertisements in the local paper. More unusual properties, or those in very popular locations, may be advertised in the national press – or on the Internet.

Property developers If you are interested in a newly built property it is worth contacting the National House Building Council for a list of members. Check whether any of them has building projects in your chosen area. Most of the larger companies advertise their new projects in local papers.

Buildings at risk You may be hoping to renovate a building that is in need of extensive repair or even reconstruction. Estate agents are usually

The environmental search

Several companies offer a **free environmental search** based on a property's postcode. Try www.home-envirosearch.com and www.homecheck.co.uk. The latter can e-mail their findings to your conveyancer.

A full search can be commissioned by a solicitor or conveyancing professional for a fee. A basic free report would offer information on the following.

- **Flood risk** More properties than ever are at risk of flooding.
- **Subsidence risk** Perhaps owing to a natural geological anomaly or the age of the building.
- **Radon risk** The naturally occurring radioactive gas, radon, is prevalent in certain parts of the country, especially the southwest of England.
- **Coal mining** Working or disused mines could present under- or above-ground problems.
- **Landslip risk** From naturally occurring or industrial sites.
- **Landfill sites** May contain household or industrial waste.
- **Waste sites** Could be tips or waste incinerators.
- **Contaminated sites** Adjacent former chemical works, radioactive sites, or other chemical hazards.
- **Air quality** A breakdown of air-quality readings.
- **Pollution risk** A breakdown of possible pollution sources.

Self-build websites can offer useful advice if you are thinking about this approach

reluctant to handle such properties. Contact your local authority or try English Heritage. The Society for the Protection of Ancient Buildings and the Scottish Civic Trust publish lists of such properties in Scotland.

Auctioneers Auction houses often have unusual properties on their books that may be in need of renovation or have a sitting tenant and would not easily sell on the open market. Look in *Yellow Pages* for details of local property auctioneers. You will be sent information about future auctions and can purchase the catalogues. See p398–9 for more on the process of buying property at auction.

Self-build Not quite as DIY as it sounds, though some people do choose to build their own. Basically, you buy a plot of land which has outline planning permission, then approach a company that designs and makes self-build houses. The manufacturer recommends a builder in your area who can construct the house to the required specifications. Self-build companies usually handle planning applications if the house you want doesn't fit your outline planning permission. Useful websites include www.ebuild.co.uk and www.selfbuildit.co.uk.

Shared ownership Some housing associations operate a rental scheme in which a proportion is taken from each monthly payment and put towards eventual ownership of the property.

Viewing properties

Try to visit a property for the first time in daylight. If the place appeals to you, arrange to view it again at another time of day, so you can see it in a different light.

Take a good look at the immediate neighbourhood and drive past at commuting times to check the traffic. Give the inside and outside a thorough check – any potential problems you see may affect your decision whether to make an offer, how much you are prepared to pay and what professional advice you will need.

Looking at the outside

This is something you will need to do extremely thoroughly if you're interested in buying. Check the structural soundness and security, and imagine what it would feel like to live there.

Structure checklist

- Are the walls in good repair? Does brickwork need repointing? Are there any dark patches on render that may indicate damp?
- Is the chimney stack straight? Ask the seller if it works.
- Does the guttering look sound? Can you see any damp patches that may be caused by leaky gutters?
- Is the roof in good shape? Ask the seller if there is a roof guarantee certificate.
- Do windows and sills look rotten or rusty? In a Conservation Area, there are

What to ask the seller

Be friendly **and ask questions**, whether you're with an agent or not. Many of your queries will relate to the specific property, but general questions may include the following.

- **Why** is the seller selling?
- Has he or she another **property** to move to?
- Is the seller's move dependent on another property purchase – in other words, **is there a chain**?
- Does the seller want a **quick sale**?
- How **long** has he or she lived there?
- Has the seller made any **improvements or changes** to the property?
- What are the **neighbours** like? Have there been any disagreements about boundaries, access and so on? (Be aware, though, with this question. The seller may be economical with the truth if there has been a history of bad feeling with the residents next door...)

restrictions on replacement windows – *see* p174.

- If there is a conservatory, is it generally in good repair? Do the foundations look sound and is the flashing – the metal strip where the conservatory roof abuts the house – intact?
- Are there any large trees nearby that might damage foundations with their roots or block the light? The trees could have a preservation order on them – check with the planning department of your local authority.
- Can you see any shared elements with the neighbours, like a drive, right of way or flying freehold (where part of one dwelling is built on top of a neighbour's property)?

Access and security

- If there is shared entry for a block of flats, is there an entry phone or electronic pass card system? Does the door shut automatically? Ask whether there is a resident or part-time caretaker.
- A public walkway or footpath through the garden or going round the boundary of the house might compromise your security.

Check that the shared entry is secure and that the door shuts automatically

Looking inside

Go prepared with a tape measure, pen and paper so that you can note fixtures that the seller wants to either leave or sell. It may be useful to have rough measurements of your current accommodation for comparison and sizes of any bulky furniture. Then really ask yourself some searching questions.

Is access to the property or garden awkward?

Might anyone need to get through a front or back door

with a bike, pushchair, or wheelchair? Is access to the property and up the stairs generally easy for removals? Is it straightforward to get to the garden?

Is there enough storage?
If there are no built-in cupboards or wardrobes, you may need to install some or buy freestanding storage. Either way, it will reduce the size of the rooms.

Is there space for your furniture?
Is there enough space in the kitchen/dining room for the size of table you need? You might need to move radiators to make your furniture fit.

Will the kitchen be suitable?
If you're not planning to replace units, check whether there are enough work surfaces and that the utility area is big enough for your appliances – and any you may want to install in the future.

Which way do the rooms face?
When do they get the sun?

Is there enough water pressure?
If you can, turn on a tap on each storey to check.

Is there room to expand?
Would it be possible to convert the loft or build an extension? Even if you don't need it yourself, the capacity to expand adds to the value of a property.

Possible changes

MAJOR EXPENSE:

- new roof
- new kitchen
- new bathroom
- building an extension
- adding a conservatory
- converting the loft
- rewiring the property
- installing central heating
- new boiler
- repointing external brickwork
- replacing a damp course
- replacing windows with double-glazed units.

LESSER EXPENSE:

- redecorating
- adding more units and worktops to the kitchen
- adding a downstairs toilet
- adding fitted wardrobes
- adding shelving or more storage
- insulating the loft
- knocking down walls
- adding a shower.

(*See* Getting work done, pp154–7)

Use your senses

By using your senses as you walk around the property, you can spot lots of small details that may indicate problems. You can then ask a surveyor to check these out, if you're still interested.

Use your eyes

- If the floorboards are covered up by carpet, ask to see a corner of them in each room, if possible. If you are planning on bare wood floors, rotten wood and boards with big gaps may need to be replaced. Boards in bad condition may also be a sign that there is dry or wet rot or beetle infestation.
- Look for signs of condensation and mould in the kitchen, bathroom, and toilet. This means that there is a ventilation problem. Windowless bathrooms and toilets should have an adequate extraction system to remove moisture.
- Have a good look around the loft. Check whether it offers good storage space, whether the roof timbers are sound, what sort of insulation it has and whether the water tank is insulated.

Check for safety

- A flat above ground level should have a **fire escape** or some means of exit over a balcony or roof.
- Look at the **fuse box**. Ideally the fuses should be modern with trip switches.
- Modern **electricity regulations** require cables to be housed in plastic trunking.
- **Stair banisters** should be good and firm. If you may be buying the stair carpet, check that it's not worn and that it's fixed firmly against the stair treads.

Use your ears

As you walk from room to room and out into the garden, what can you hear?

Neighbours Visit when the neighbours are likely to be home and check if you can hear them through any party walls. If you are viewing a flat, can you hear people upstairs? Noise carries more easily if a flat has bare wood floors. Although they are currently very popular, some flat leases do not allow bare floors.

Traffic Try to visit when the traffic in the street outside will be at its worst. Can you hear it from the back garden?

Noisy plumbing Run a tap or flush the loo, then listen in the bedrooms. Loud plumbing could mean that the pipes are

Visit the property during rush hour to see just what the traffic will be like

faulty. Check the location of the boiler. If it's on the other side of the bedroom wall it might wake you up when it comes on in the morning.

Use your sense of smell

Try to overlook smells that you will be able to get rid of – cats, dogs, cigarette smoke or old carpets. It's the smells that may point to problems that you have to watch out for.

Damp A musty odour, rather like potting compost. You would not expect a lived-in property to smell damp unless it had problems such as cracked walls, water penetration or bad ventilation.

Gas If you think there is a faint whiff around a boiler, then it may need to be replaced.

Toilet If a WC smells dodgy, it could mean there is a leak into the floorboards.

Making the purchase

Now you've found the property you want to buy, it's time to get the professionals on board. Your mortgage lender will send a surveyor to do a valuation and you should commission a more detailed surveyor's report.

One of the next steps to take is to appoint a solicitor or licensed conveyancer to deal with the conveyancing – the transfer of the property from the present owner to you. See p390–5 for more details. There are a number of documents your conveyancer needs to collect. For definitions of some property transaction terms, *see* p340.

How to find a surveyor

Surveyors can be found through your mortgage lender, in the *Yellow Pages*, on the Internet or through advertisements in local newspapers, through your estate agent.

Ask a **friend in the area** if you want a truly independent recommendation.

Surveyors should be members of **RICS (Royal Institute of Chartered Surveyors)**. The letters MRICS after a surveyor's name mean Member of RICS. After practising for 12 years a surveyor can apply for Fellowship (FRICS).

A specialist surveyor could be a member of the **Association of Building Engineers (ABE)** or the **Architects and Surveyors Institute (ASI)**.

Lender's valuation report

The purpose of the lender's valuation report is to reassure the bank or building society that the property is worth the money that you want to borrow. It is, in other words, to protect the money lent to you. It is not a detailed survey, but it will establish whether there are any major structural defects that affect the asking price. It assesses the market value of the property, taking into account:

- accommodation and land
- condition of the property
- location
- traffic density
- neighbourhood amenities
- market value of properties in the area
- resale potential.

If, in the surveyor's opinion, the property is overpriced, you have three options. You can find the extra money, taking the risk that you might not get your money back when you come to sell. You can back out and look for another property. Or you can enter into negotiations with a revised offer.

Equally, bear in mind that if you are putting in a sizeable proportion of the asking price yourself, you might want to have the valuation confirmed by a second opinion, as it will be your money that's at risk if the valuation is overgenerous.

Collecting information

Your conveyancer will need to **assess information about the property**. The sources of this information are the seller, the local council, the deeds and one or more surveyors' reports. The government has plans to make it a **legal requirement** for the seller to collect this information before putting the property on the market, which would speed up the process. However, the **seller will provide relevant paperwork**, such as guarantees covering work done on the property, including timber treatment, chimney repair, electrical work, damp-proofing, repointing of brickwork, roof repair or replacement, tanking (water-proofing) of the cellar, loft or cavity wall insulation and major plumbing jobs.

The seller should also provide any correspondence from the local authority about **pending or approved planning permissions** or restrictions on parking, removal of trees, change of use or extending the property.

Commissioning your own survey

If you are buying a new house it should have a National House Building Council certificate. This is a warranty that covers the house for ten years and precludes the need for commissioning your own survey – the lender's valuation report is sufficient. For older properties there are three types of survey:

- Homebuyer's Report and Valuation Survey
- Building Survey
- Specialist Report.

Homebuyer's Report and Valuation Survey

If you are buying a property built since 1900 that has no obvious problems (see Building Survey) it's wise at least to commission your own Homebuyer's Report and Valuation Survey. This will reveal whether there are any hidden defects that might affect your purchase. Most mortgage lenders encourage you to use the surveyor who carries out their valuation report. Most surveyors offer a discount if you book a more detailed survey that can be done at the same time as the valuation report. If, however, you use a different surveyor you will have to pay the full price for the

What is checked in a homebuyer's report

THE PROPERTY AND LOCATION
Summary of the type and age of the property, its internal and external construction, and its surroundings.

THE EXTERIOR
Movement Any signs of subsidence, structural movement or cracking.
Dampness and condensation Whether there is a damp course. Signs of condensation. Moisture readings to check for damp.
Roof, chimneys and gutters Ground-level inspection.
Walls Whether the walls are true, cracked or show structural movement.
Windows and doors Condition of frames and panes.
Decoration Paintwork, metal and timber finishes.

THE INTERIOR
Roof space The internal roof structure, insulation and ventilation. The surveyor may not go up into the loft if it's not easily accessible.
Ceilings Condition and structure.
Floors Signs of subsidence or settlement are noted.
Walls and partitions What they are made of and any structural problems.
Fireplaces Not tested.
Woodwork Condition of doors, kitchen fittings and skirting boards. Signs of infestation, damp and dry rot.
Decoration Plaster and paintwork.

SERVICES AND SITE
Electricity and gas A visual inspection of meters and outlets.
Water Visible plumbing, storage tanks, cylinders and immersion heaters, and boilers. None of these will be tested.
Heating Central or other heating will be visually inspected but not tested.
Drainage Visual inspection only.

survey, but you will have the benefit of a second opinion on the property.

The report is presented in a standard format of about ten pages in length. The surveyor groups observations under four headings:

1 Defects that are a threat to the fabric or structure of the building, such as subsidence, rotten roof timbers, or other major problems.
2 Defects that could have a significant effect on the purchase price – rotten window frames, central heating not working, for instance.
3 Health and safety aspects, including wiring requiring replacing or asbestos lagging around a water tank in a loft.
4 Legal matters, for instance whether access is over

another person's land, requiring a right of way.

Electricity, gas, plumbing and central heating are given a visual examination but not tested. Also, be aware that surveyors cannot usually lift fitted carpets for a floor inspection unless the house is uninhabited or there are obvious signs of dry rot or rising damp. However, they will lift a carpet covering a floor hatch that needs to be accessed. The Homebuyer's Report costs around £300 and takes no more than half a day to complete. For a list of what's checked, see box, p388.

Building Survey

For unusual properties and properties built before 1900, a full Building Survey is a good idea. This is not a standard format report and you can instruct the surveyor to address areas of special concern or, equally, to disregard, say, the condition of the decoration, if you know this needs attention. The survey should cover the condition of:

- the structure of the building (noting any unsoundness, such as subsidence)
- special features, such as beams, thatched roofs, balconies, tanked (waterproofed) cellars
- any extensions to the original building
- RSJs – reinforced supporting joists put in to carry a load where a supporting wall has been knocked down
- electrical wiring and plumbing – these will be inspected for health hazards such as lead pipes, but not actually tested.

The cost of a Building Survey is usually between £400 and £500 and it can take a day or more to complete, depending on how large the property is.

Specialist Report

Arising from a Building Survey, the surveyor may recommend that you commission a Specialist Report to examine any serious problem in detail. The specialist concerned could be a structural engineer, or an expert in timber preservation or damp treatment. You may well benefit from a specialist's opinion if the property:

- has been empty for a long time
- is very run down
- has had several extensions added

- is a conversion (say from an oast house or a barn)
- has suffered subsidence in the past or is in a terrace where subsidence has occurred to neighbouring dwellings.

A general surveyor will usually be able to recommend a specialist company that could undertake the survey. Agree the price beforehand, though timber and damp treatment firms should provide a free full report and quote at the same time for any action they recommend.

Conveyancing – what happens and why

Conveyancing – the process by which the house or flat changes hands – has developed somewhat haphazardly over the years. A government survey in 1999 found that the system used in England and Wales is the slowest in Europe. However, the good news is that it is also the cheapest. There are two landmarks in a typical conveyancing transaction – exchange of contracts and completion.

Procedure up to exchange of contracts

Have a proper survey carried out – otherwise your dream home could turn out to be your worst nightmare

Once you have agreed a price with the seller, the seller's conveyancer draws up a formal contract laying down the terms on which the seller is prepared to sell the house. As well as dealing with the price, it will prove that the seller does actually own the house and state whether there are any restrictions on the use to which the property can be put. The original oral agreement is not legally binding – the law requires that any contract for the sale of property be in writing.

Your conveyancer checks the contract to ensure that the terms are acceptable and that the seller really does own the land. He/she will also make several searches, asking public bodies questions such as:

- Has the local authority any development plans that may affect the house, such as for a new road?
- If the house is in a mining area, has it been affected by subsidence?
- Was planning permission obtained for any building work done on the property? Does this work comply with building regulations?
- Have any restrictions on the use of the house been complied with? Will they affect your use of the property?

You, as the buyer, should also commission a survey at this stage and your mortgage lender will organise a

Eight negotiation tips

1. **Do your research.** You need to assess how fair the asking price is and how fast houses in the area are selling. Scour the property papers and estate agents' windows, and view similar houses in the area. Ask the agent how long the house has been on the market, and whether there have been any other offers.
2. Only offer well below the asking price if you're prepared to irritate the seller and **risk losing the property**. But if the price is high and you aren't set on getting only that property, it can pay off.
3. **Offer slightly less than you think you'll end up paying**, hoping to meet the seller in the middle.
4. **Sellers normally want a quick sale**, so put yourself in as strong a position as possible and emphasise this to the agent or seller: you're at an advantage if you have nowhere to sell, you have a buyer for your current property, you already have a mortgage approved and if you're flexible on completion dates.
5. **Appear serious and committed** but not desperate – don't let the agent or seller know that this is your dream house.
6. Make it clear that your offer is **subject to contract and survey**.
7. Ask the agent (or, if it's a private sale, the vendor) for a commitment in writing to **take the property off the market once your offer is accepted**. The agent may not be prepared to do this, but it's always worth asking.
8. **Use carpets and curtains as a negotiation tool** by offering to pay a specified amount over the asking price of the house to include them. Second-hand furnishings aren't much use anywhere else, so don't pay over the odds.

E-conveyancing

Much of the conveyancing process is still paper-based. Although the actual exchange of contracts can be done over the telephone, **drafts of contracts and transfers are documents that must be sent through the post** and this can cause delay. The government plans that in the future contracts and transfers will exist only electronically. They will be transmitted and signed via computer, saving time and expense. Some conveyancers already allow you to track your purchase via their website, with a password.

A major initiative is the **National Land Information Service (NLIS)**, which enables local authority searches to be made online, providing the results in hours rather than weeks. Information held at the Land Registry on the ownership of property can be accessed online. These advances will speed up the conveyancing process dramatically. There may also be cost savings, although the new technology involves expensive investment, which conveyancers may want to pass on to their clients.

valuation report (*see* p386–7). The object of all these investigations is to discover as much as possible about the house before you legally commit to buy. If you discover something unfavourable (such as plans for the new M100 at the bottom of the garden), you can withdraw from the transaction without any comeback from the seller. The law does not require the seller to disclose this information to you – it is up to you to find it out. The government has produced plans for a Seller's Pack, in which sellers would be legally required to disclose much more information to a buyer at the start of a transaction, but these plans are at present on hold – *see* Selling your home, p333–6.

Exchange of contracts

- Once you and your legal representative are completely satisfied with the house, the contract is drawn up in two identical copies – you sign one and the seller the other.
- The contract becomes legally binding only when the copies are exchanged, so that each party has a copy of the contract signed by the other and both could sue on the contract, should the need arise.
- Contracts are normally 'exchanged' over the telephone – the hard copies are physically sent later.
- If the transaction is one of a chain, each dependent on the next (*see* box, p394), all the contracts in the chain

must be exchanged at the same time.

- You, as the buyer, will be asked to pay a deposit of up to 10% of the purchase price on exchange. This is held by the seller's legal representative until completion and is non-returnable if you decide not to proceed with the purchase.

After exchange, your conveyancer draws up a document known as a Transfer. This is the document that concludes the transfer of ownership from the seller to you, the buyer. Once you have signed it, the Transfer is sent to the seller's conveyancer to be signed by the seller. The seller's conveyancer will keep it until completion (*see* pp394–5). Your conveyancer must ensure that you have the rest of the purchase money ready for the day fixed for completion. Your conveyancer will deal direct with your lender, if you have arranged a mortgage, and will also draw up the mortgage document for you to sign. Some final

Only when the property has been transferred over to you does the seller leave the keys, care of the conveyancer or estate agent, for you to collect

Some problems you might encounter

The chain breaks

One of the major causes of problems in property sales is the chain. This is where a chain of people are all dependent on selling their existing home before they can proceed with the purchase of their new one – A is buying from B, who is buying from C, and so on. It only needs one sale to fall through for the whole chain to fail. So through no fault of your own, your sale and purchase may fall through, at great expense and inconvenience. This is why exchange of contracts should ideally take place only when everyone in the chain is ready, and why it helps if everyone in the chain can exchange at exactly the same time.

Gazumping

As there is no binding contract until exchange, and as exchange often occurs several weeks after you make an offer on a house, there is a time where the seller may back out. If the seller backs out right at the last minute before exchange with the object of forcing up the price, this is called gazumping. The seller may be playing you off against another prospective buyer. You may have incurred expenses in legal, search and surveyors' fees and feel that you are at the seller's mercy. The government's plans for a Seller's Pack (*see* p335) and for electronic conveyancing (*see* box, p392) are designed to shorten the delay between acceptance of offer and exchange, thus reducing the likelihood of gazumping.

searches by your conveyancer ensure that there have been no last-minute changes in the legal ownership of the property at this stage.

Completion

On completion, your conveyancer hands over the money and the seller's conveyancer hands over the Transfer deed, transferring the ownership to you. The seller leaves the keys to the property with the conveyancer or estate agent for you to collect. But the legal work is still not finished. Your ownership

Buying in Scotland

The legal process for buying property in Scotland is **significantly different** from that in England and Wales, and is often looked to as a model for a system where chains and gazumping are much less of a problem (*see* p338).

must be registered at the Land Registry (a government body that records the ownership of land) and you must pay stamp duty – your conveyancer will arrange both of these. Stamp duty is a government tax levied as a percentage of the purchase price on all purchases of houses and flats for more than £60,000.

Finding legal help

When you're looking to buy a property, it is worth asking three solicitors or licensed conveyancers to give you a rough estimate of their likely costs, based on the property price and whether there are issues that may require extra time to resolve. These might include leasehold queries on a newly built flat, for instance, concerning parking, management company responsibilities and so on, or queries on a repossessed property, where the other party might wish to complete the sale with minimal expenditure of effort. Both of these cases would increase the burden on the buyer's legal representative.

There are many ways to find a solicitor or licensed conveyancer, including:

- personal recommendation
- looking in *Yellow Pages* or the Internet
- contacting the Law Society. You can search on their website, www.solicitors-online.com.

A long chain is one of the major causes of problems in a property sale

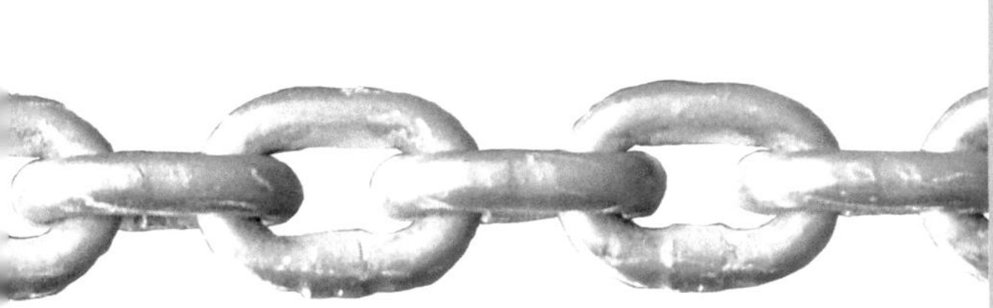

Other ways to buy

Perhaps you cannot afford to buy a standard property on your own, or perhaps you have seen a plot that is being developed and looks just right for you. Here is some help on what to do.

How to go about self-build

If you want a new property but don't want to buy from a developer, the answer could be to self-build. This doesn't mean that you have to lay the bricks yourself – unless you have the time and the right skills – but that you buy a plot of land, usually with planning permission, and **supervise the construction of your own home**.

A good place to start is the website **www.ebuild.co.uk**, which allows you to search for a suitable building plot on ebuild's UK building plots database, and buy step-by-step guides and home-plan books in their online bookshop. The site also has a directory of building companies manufacturing self-assembly houses, most of whom will help you obtain planning permission, should you need it, and recommend builders in your area who can erect the house for you.

Building your own home takes **time and commitment**. Over the period of construction you have to either live in a caravan on site or bear the cost of living in one home while building another, as well as devoting your life to being site foreman. You also have to organise a self-build mortgage, which is released in tranches to cover the cost of ongoing work.

Self-build is a **route to achieving an impressive property** that will cost very much less to build than it will be worth in the end.

Buying a home off-plan

Developers often sell properties before they have been built, sometimes with exchange of contracts taking place before building even begins – this is called buying off-plan. Sometimes all the purchaser has to go on are the architect's plans, specifications and drawings, though some developers may have a virtual reality computer programme that allows you to 'walk through' the proposed building or a show flat or house that you can inspect on site.

When you are ready, you can sign reservation papers to reserve a home in the complex. There will be a reservation fee of a few hundred pounds. Don't put your own house on the market or give notice on a rented home until you have been given an absolute date for completion of building works.

Before you commit

- To help you imagine the space offered in the new

Buying off-plan – before the property is even built – may be an option to consider

property, check the internal and external measurements on the plan against the measurements of your current home.

- Pay regular visits to the site. Check boundaries and measurements against the plan as soon as possible. If in doubt about the developer's intentions, contact the local planning department to check if specifications have changed.
- If looking round a show home, note whether artificial light is used during the day. Has the furniture been scaled down to make the rooms look big?
- Check the small print of the reservation agreement to make sure that the property you are reserving has the same specifications as the show home or the property in the plans.
- Ask the developer the following questions:
- Has final planning permission been granted or is it still pending for some aspects of the development?
- Has the heating system been tested in other developments?

- What fixtures, fittings, and finishes are included in the total price? Are any of these to be paid for as they are installed? Some developers include decorating, carpets, and even curtains.
- Make sure that there are penalty clauses if the developer misleads you or is late completing.

Investment opportunity

Sometimes people consider buying a house off-plan as an investment. There is an element of risk involved and you get a better price to reflect this. In times of high demand, it may be the only way to get your hands on a hot property in a sought after area.

Historically, investors have fared well from buying property off-plan. Good quality new homes can often get revalued shortly after completion with surprisingly high gains for the original buyers. In times of a rising property market, it is perfectly possible to turn in a significant profit even before a brick has been laid.

Of course, we have been in a rising market for some time, and it is also perfectly possible for a rising market to fall, meaning that you would lose money...

How to buy at auction

If you want an unusual property or one that needs renovation, the auction route can offer some good bargains. Repossessed homes are often sold by auction, too.

1. Contact property auctioneers in the relevant area and order catalogues for forthcoming auctions. Check when you need to register, should you want to bid.
2. Arrange to visit any properties that interest you.
3. Make a shortlist and go to the local authority with questions about your chosen properties. Find out if they have rights of way, boundary problems and so on.
4. Arrange to revisit properties you are still interested in. Organise a survey and ask a surveyor/builder to advise what, if any, work would need to be done and how much, roughly, it would cost.
5. Visit a mortgage provider to set up a mortgage offer on any property you would be prepared to buy. This has to be done before you go to auction. You can only bid if you have the money available or it could be accessed within three weeks of your bid being accepted.

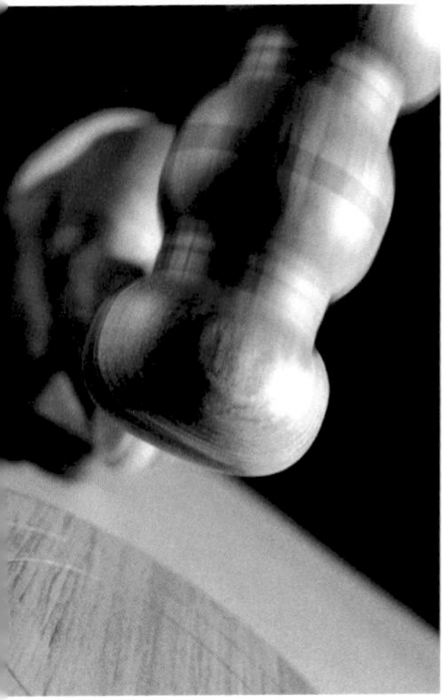

Do your homework before buying at an auction. Once the gavel falls...

6 The day before the auction, phone the auctioneers to check that the properties have not been withdrawn.
7 Attend the auction having decided the maximum amount of money you can afford to bid – and stick to it.
8 If your bid is successful, your contract to buy the property is binding as soon as the hammer goes down. You will usually be asked to sign a contract, though there is no actual legal need – you are bound anyway. You will be asked to pay a 10% deposit or £1,500, whichever is the greater. You will lose this if you back out later.
9 Insure the property immediately.
10 Pass details of your property to your mortgage lender for fast-track processing.
11 Instruct your solicitor or conveyancer.
12 Completion should take place within three weeks.

The auction

An auction, although it can be stressful, is actually quite a civilised place and many are now held in respectable hotels and conference halls. In recent years, auction houses have taken great strides towards modernising the way they do business and one of the benefits of this is a much better level of customer service. This means that you will be able to get useful guides, financial advice and even seminars that guide you through the bidding process and beyond.

Preparation is a vital component in a successful purchase at auction. You need to research the properties, sort out your finances and be ready to quickly progress with the sale.

Pooling resources with a friend is one way of getting into the property market

Shared ownership – buy and rent

Shared ownership was first introduced to help people who cannot afford to buy a home outright. Through shared ownership, you buy a share of the property and pay a rent on the remaining share you do not own. Gradually you may buy further shares and eventually own your home outright.

Registered social landlords are non-profit making organisations who provide and manage homes for rent and sale for people who cannot afford to rent privately or buy.

A social landlord can be a housing association, a housing society or a non-profit making housing company. Most of these landlords provide housing with the help of public money given by the Housing Corporation or a local authority; in some cases, the social landlord may provide housing using its own money.

Housing associations and charitable trusts sometimes offer first-time buyers – who may be single people, single

Buying a property with other people

Pooling resources with friends is one way of buying a home that's beyond your means. The problem comes when one party wants to sell their share.

- Up to **four people** can be named on a property deed as owners.
- Get a solicitor to **draw up a contract** between the co-owners so that if anyone wants to leave, the other co-owners get the first option on buying their share. If they can't afford it, then there should be a joint effort to find a mutually acceptable replacement.
- It's simpler if everyone owns and pays **equal shares** of everything – mortgage payments and other outgoings – even if one of the co-owners is away a lot. A solicitor can draw up a deed of trust to specify everyone's obligations.
- All co-owners should have **adequate insurance cover** that will pay their share of the outgoings in the event of redundancy or illness.

parents or students – the chance to part-buy/part-rent low-cost properties. Most local authority housing departments have lists of shared ownership schemes in their area. If you are eligible for a particular scheme you can fill in and submit an application form. If you are accepted, you will be offered a vacant property or put on a waiting list.

Conditions associated with shared ownership include:

- payment of a reservation fee, usually a couple of hundred pounds, which is non-returnable but does go towards the price
- getting a mortgage to buy your 50% or 75% share of the property
- your mortgage lender will carry out a valuation report (*see* p386–7), which will cost you around £150
- you will need to appoint a conveyancer to carry out the transaction (*see* p395). This may cost around £400
- when you move into the property you will be paying a mortgage to the lender and some rent to the association each month
- after you have lived in the property for a certain time, you can buy more shares in it (until you own it outright) or sell your shares back to the association (at a fair market rate)
- once you own the property outright, you can sell it on the open market.

For more information, visit the Housing Corporation at www.housingcorp.gov.uk.

Contact details

Useful websites and addresses about the information given in this chapter.

Association of Residential Letting Agents, Maple House, 53–55 Woodside Road, Amersham, Bucks HP6 6AA
Tel: 0845 345 5752
Fax: 01494 431 530
e-mail: info@arla.co.uk
www.arla.co.uk
Site has a Buy to Let area with detailed information on what 'buy to let' is and which lenders will offer the finance.

Charcol, Lintas House, 15–19 New Fetter Lane, London EC4A 1AP
Tel: 0800 718 191
e-mail: coe@charcolonline.co.uk
www.charcolonline.co.uk
Independent financial adviser.

ebuild
e-mail: info@ebuild.co.uk
www.ebuild.co.uk
For self build, DIY and house renovation. There is an extensive web directory of building products and services.

English Heritage, Customer Services Department, PO Box 569, Swindon SN2 2YP
Tel: 0870 333 1181
Fax: 01793 414 926
e-mail: customers@english-heritage.org.uk
www.english-heritage.org.uk

Government housing information
www.housing.odpm.gov.uk
General housing information, including government housing policy and the housing choices available to homeowners, tenants and landlords.

HM Land Registry, 32 Lincoln's Inn Fields, London WC2A 3PH
Tel: 020 7917 5996
Fax: 020 7917 5934
e-mail: marion.shelley@landreg.gsi.gov.uk
www.landreg.gov.uk
Reports on property prices, links to regional offices and details of how to obtain online access to registry documents.

Homecheck, Imperial House, 21–25 North Street, Bromley BR1 1SS
Tel: 0870 606 1700
Fax: 0870 606 1701

e-mail: info@homecheck.co.uk
www.homecheck.co.uk
A guide to flooding, subsidence, landfill sites etc in an area.

Housing Corporation, Maple House, 149 Tottenham Court Road, London W1T 7BN
Tel: 020 7393 2000
Fax: 020 7393 2111
e-mail: enquiries@housingcorp.gsx.gov.uk
www.housingcorp.gov.uk

MarketPlace
www.marketplace.co.uk
Helps you to find the right property, mortgage, loan, pension, investment or insurance for you.

Law Society, The Law Society's Hall, 113 Chancery Lane, London WC2A 1PL
Tel: 020 7242 1222
Fax: 020 7831 0344
email: info-services@lawsociety.org.uk
www.lawsoc.org.uk
Enables you to search for a law firm or individual solicitor in England and Wales.

National House Building Council, Buildmark House, Chiltern Avenue, Amersham, Buckinghamshire HP6 5AP
Tel: 01494 735 363
www.nhbc.co.uk
A warranty and insurance provider for new homes.

National Housing Federation, 175 Gray's Inn Road, London WC1X 8UP
Tel: 020 7278 6571
Fax: 020 7833 8323
e-mail: info@housing.org.uk
www.housing.org.uk
Website for the independent social housing sector.

Royal Institute of Chartered Surveyors, RICS Contact Centre, Surveyor Court, Westwood Way, Coventry CV4 8JE
Tel: 0870 333 160
Fax: 020 7222 9430
e-mail: contactrics@rics.org.uk
www.rics.org/public
Information on residential surveys, boundary disputes and advice on finding a surveyor.

SelfBuildit
www.selfbuildit.co.uk
Help and advice on building your own house.

Stamp Office
Tel: 0845 603 0135
www.inlandrevenue.gov.uk
Details of 2,000 'disadvantaged' areas where land and property sales of £150,000 or less are not subject to stamp duty.

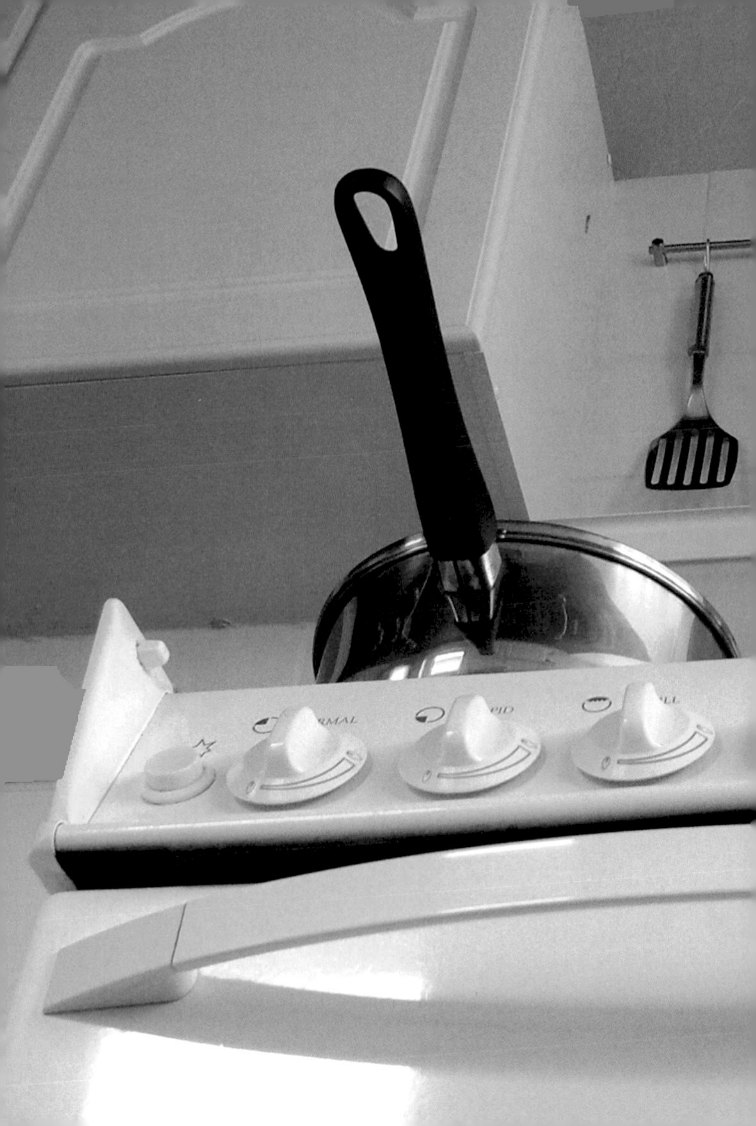

Safety in the home

Accidents in the home are all too commonplace, but if you take a look at your home with a view to safety – and not just for accidents involving children – you can easily reduce the risks.

More disabling injuries occur in our homes than at work or on the road combined. Simple steps such as installing railings on the top of stairs, putting up smoke alarms and childproofing your home can lower the risk of injuries significantly. Children are especially vulnerable as their sense of exploring the unknown can lead them into all sorts of dangers involving the most innocuous household objects. And with the increase in popularity of DIY, this is another major source of avoidable injury.

Room-by-room guide

Every year, more than 4,000 people die and 3 million are injured in the UK through accidents in the house or garden – these figures exceed those who are killed or injured in road accidents.

Falls, burns, choking and electric shocks are among the most common accidents, and many involve poorly maintained or badly placed everyday items. Others are caused by the careless use of electrical equipment. Give your home a thorough safety check.

Kitchen

- If you are planning a kitchen from scratch, keep safety in mind – more accidents happen in the kitchen than anywhere else in the home. There should be adequate workspace beside the cooker, so you have plenty of room both to work and to place hot dishes safely. Ideally, the hob should be close to the sink so that pans don't need to be carried far.
- Turn saucepan handles towards the back of the hob when cooking so they are not knocked off.
- Check that all burners are turned off when you finish. Don't test electric hotplates with your hands.
- Don't use wet cloths to pick up hot pots or lids – the water acts as a highly efficient conductor, making the cloth extremely hot very quickly.
- Don't hang tea towels or oven gloves on oven handles and keep them away from the hob.
- Be careful when pulling out oven racks with hot dishes on them. Some racks tilt as they slide out and can tip the dishes towards you or into the back of the oven. Take the dish right out and deal with it on top of the stove or counter.

Keep medicines or hazardous chemicals shut away

- Plates and other china can get extremely hot in a microwave – always use oven gloves to take them out.
- Children should always be supervised in the kitchen.
- It's easy to get distracted and leave pans to boil dry. Get into the habit of setting a kitchen timer if you are leaving the kitchen. Be particularly careful when using a chip pan and never leave frying food unattended.
- Keep kettles, coffee-makers, and toasters towards the back of worktops. Ensure flexes don't hang off worktops or trail across the hob. Choose coiled flexes when buying new.
- Switch off and unplug the kettle before filling it.
- If a slice of toast is stuck in the toaster, switch off the appliance at the wall before trying to prise the toast out.
- Wipe spills off the floor immediately, making sure the area is completely dry. Spills that contain oil or grease may have to be washed several times with soapy detergent before they lose their slipperiness.
- Keep knives sharp so that they are easy to use without undue force. Store them in a block, or use blade guards if kept in a drawer. Never leave knives or other sharp objects lying disguised in a sink of soapy water. If you use a dishwasher, store knives point down in the machine. Food-processor blades should be treated with the same caution.
- Wash the insides of glasses, jars and bottles with a brush or bottle-washer – don't put your hands inside in case the glass breaks.

Hazardous chemicals

- **Read labels** and follow instructions when dealing with hazardous substances, including wearing any recommended protective clothing.
- **Keep hazardous substances in their original containers** and make sure the label remains legible. Never put them in old food containers.
- **Don't mix chemical products** – some react dangerously with one another. A common mistake is to mix bleach with other cleaning products. Rather, choose a cleaning product that already contains bleach.
- **Never pour car fuel, engine oil, paint, paint-cleaning products or similar substances into the ground.** They can contaminate the earth and water supply. Likewise, hazardous chemical waste should not be put in the bin or poured down the drain. Check labels for recommended disposal methods, or contact the Environmental Health department of your local health authority.

Stairs

- Wooden stairs can be slippery, especially if polished or waxed. A non-slip matt paint finish would be safer. Fitted carpets are the safest option, though make sure that stair carpets are well fitted and secured, and check edges regularly.
- Don't put rugs near the top of stairs.
- Stairs should be well lit from top to bottom and there should be a light switch at both ends.
- Don't leave items lying on the stairs.

Living room, hall and bedrooms

- Ensure that carpet edges at doorways are well secured.
- Either avoid using rugs on polished floors or secure them with carpet tape.
- Arrange furniture so that you have a clear path through the room.
- Keep rooms well ventilated if you use gas, solid fuel or oil heaters.
- Always use a fireguard on an open fire.
- Don't place burning incense, candles or cigarettes near beds or curtains, and be careful about using these items late at night, in case you fall asleep with them still burning (*see* Fire precautions, pp412–5).
- Check electric blankets regularly for wear – some local authorities offer free checks. Turn off an electric blanket before you get into bed.

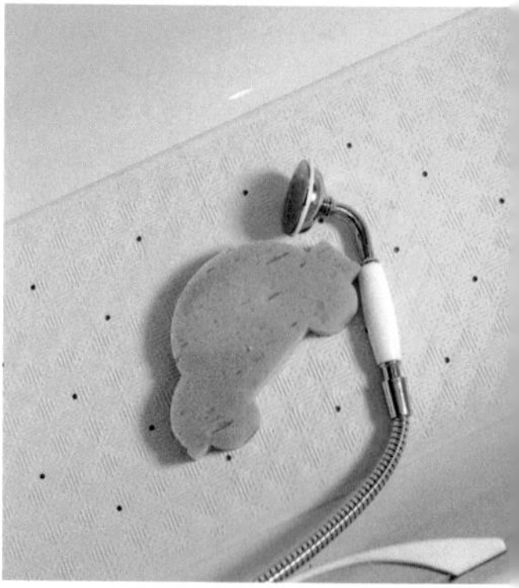

An anti-slip mat can help prevent falls when showering in the bath

Bathrooms

- Plug-in electrical appliances such as radios, hairdryers and portable heaters should never be used in the bathroom. Low-voltage electric shavers and toothbrushes that plug into two-pin sockets are fine. Standard battery-operated radios should be put where they won't get wet.
- Baths and showers can become very slippery,

particularly if you live in a soft-water area or have a water softener fitted. Use a rubber anti-slip mat to prevent falls.

The garden

- Put rakes and other tools away after use. Don't leave them where they could be trodden on.
- Uneven paving slabs, broken concrete and holes in lawns can cause falls.
- Fit plastic caps (available from garden centres) on the tips of bamboo canes to avoid eye injuries.
- Keep garden chemicals safely out of sight and reach of children.
- Use a plug-in residual current device (RCD) when using any electrical appliance (*see* Your electricity supply, p126–7). Keep cables well out of the way when cutting grass and don't use equipment in wet conditions. Always switch off and unplug garden appliances before checking, lifting or adjusting. Don't clean electrical items by immersing them in water – wipe with a cloth.
- Wear sturdy shoes to protect your feet when mowing or strimming grass.

Ten electricity safety tips

1. **Broken light switches and sockets are dangerous.** Cover with insulating tape as a reminder not to use until mended.
2. **Don't leave lamps without bulbs in them** – they could cause an electric shock if touched.
3. **Water and electricity are a lethal combination.** Always switch electricity off at the mains before washing down walls or using water anywhere near light switches or electric sockets.
4. **Always dry your hands before plugging in electrical equipment.** Don't turn appliances on if you're standing on a wet floor or if your other hand is in water.
5. **Keep small appliances where they can't get wet or fall into water.** If electrical equipment or plugs get wet accidentally, allow them to dry completely before using.
6. **Make sure extension leads are suitable for the intended task** – read the manufacturer's instructions. Add up the wattage of the appliances you're plugging in and check that figure against the wattage the extension lead can carry.
7. **Don't leave extension leads coiled while in use**, as they may overheat. The longer the lead, the greater the danger of overheating – use the shortest lead you can. Don't plug one extension lead into another.
8. **Check plugs to ensure that they have the correct fuse.**
9. **Don't overload sockets with adaptors** – have more sockets fitted instead.
10. **Have electrical equipment serviced regularly.**

DIY dangers

DIY can be a rewarding activity, but it can also be a dangerous one. Around 100,000 people need hospital treatment for DIY accidents in Britain every year.

The two main causes of injuries are failure to read instructions and use tools or materials properly, and carelessness when it comes to commonsense jobs, such as securing ladders.

Safety with tools

Bladed hand tools Use the right tool for the job and make sure the blade is sharp. You are more likely to have an accident using a blunt tool, because it needs more force to do its job. Keep your hands behind the cutting direction. Fit blade guards when not using the tool.

Power tools Power saws and routers (a tool for gouging) need handling with particular care. With all power tools, read instructions carefully. Never try to remove, bypass or deactivate a blade guard or other safety feature. Let the motor stop before setting the tool down and switch off tools whenever you are not using them, even if only for a short time. Keep clothes and hair away from moving parts. Wear safety equipment when appropriate.

While you work Tie back long hair, wear shoes that protect your feet and avoid loose-fitting clothes or dangling jewellery. If a job takes longer than you'd anticipated, don't rush or take

Power tools need handling with particular care – wear safety equipment if at all possible

short cuts. Take frequent breaks – tiredness is the underlying cause of many accidents.

Safety with electricity

Power tools Before using, look for damage to the flex sheath, for exposed cores where the flex enters the plug and cracks in the plug casing. Make sure the tool casing is securely closed and undamaged.

Outdoors Plug power tools into a special socket outlet or a plug-in adaptor with a residual current device (RCD). This cuts off the power supply if you touch any live parts on the tool, flex or plug.

Wiring work Don't take on wiring projects unless you know what you are doing. Badly executed wiring work can kill. Always turn the power supply off at the main fuse box or consumer unit before you start work. Isolate individual circuits by removing the fuseholder or turning off the miniature circuit breaker (MCB). Double-check all connections have been correctly and securely made.

Cable detector Use this inexpensive battery-powered tool to check the whereabouts of circuit cables (and water pipes) that may be concealed behind walls on which you are working.

Setting up ladders

Most falls are from **ladders and other access equipment**, and almost all are avoidable.

Ladders are designed for use at one **optimum angle**, with the foot of the ladder set 1m (3ft) away from what it's leaning against for every 4m (13ft) of ladder height. A steeper angle, and you risk overbalancing and falling off. Shallower angles strain the ladder and its foot may slip away.

1 Set the ladder down flat with its foot against the wall, and extend it to the required height.

2 Lift the top of the ladder and walk towards the wall, moving your hands from rung to rung until the ladder is upright. Rest the top against the wall, then lift or slide the ladder foot out to its final position.

3 Rest the top of the ladder against a firm surface, never against window glass or plastic guttering. If necessary, fit a standoff before erecting the ladder and rest this against the wall to hold the top of the ladder clear of such surfaces.

4 On uneven or soft ground, place the foot of the ladder on a flat board, securely packed underneath if necessary. Nail a batten along its length for the ladder feet to push against. Never put wedges or packing directly under one stile to get a ladder to stand upright.

5 Secure the ladder at the top and bottom whenever possible. Tie the stiles to stakes driven into the ground beside the foot and tie them higher up to an open window frame if possible. Don't trust downpipes to be strong enough.

Fire precautions

Fire is swift, often stealthy, sometimes deadly. In the UK alone, nearly 500 people die in house fires each year and there are around 60,000 accidental blazes.

Chip-pan fires are on the increase, as are fires started by candles and aromatherapy oil burners. Even a small fire can be highly destructive, as well as leaving a trail of smoke damage. As precautions against fire, equip your home with smoke alarms and fire extinguishers, make an action plan in case of fire and get into the habit of making some basic checks before you go to bed.

Fitting and using extinguishers

There are four main kinds of fire extinguisher. Fire extinguishers are colour coded usually, but not always, as follows.

Red

These are water extinguishers, the most commonly used type, but are suitable only for fires of ordinary solid materials such

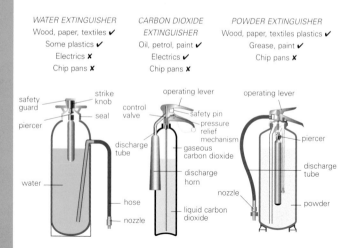

WATER EXTINGUISHER
Wood, paper, textiles ✔
Some plastics ✔
Electrics ✘
Chip pans ✘

CARBON DIOXIDE EXTINGUISHER
Oil, petrol, paint ✔
Electrics ✔
Chip pans ✘

POWDER EXTINGUISHER
Wood, paper, textiles plastics ✔
Grease, paint ✔
Chip pans ✘

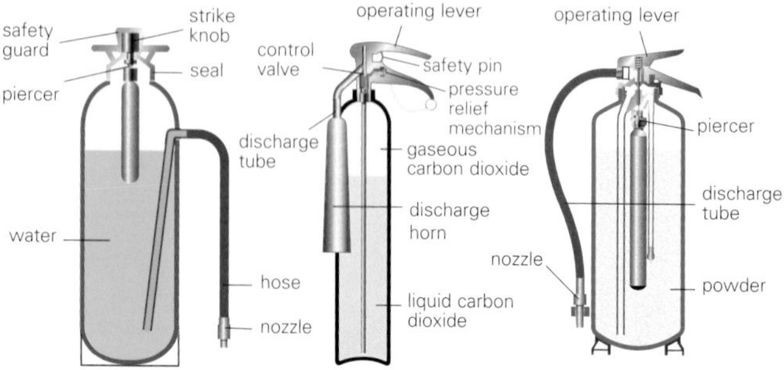

Check your furniture

All new furniture must by law be manufactured to meet **fire-resistance regulations**. This means that upholstered pieces must have fire-resistant fillings, the cover fabric must be match-resistant, and the combination of cover and filling cigarette-resistant. Some covers, mostly those made from natural fibres such as cotton or silk, are exempt from the match-resistance requirement. However, items with these covers must have a fire-resistant interliner. Check for details on an item's swing ticket and permanent labels. Second-hand furniture sold privately may not meet the fire-resistance requirements.

If you own upholstered furniture that was made before the regulations came into effect in the UK in 1988, you can improve its fire-resistance.

- **Fit secondary covers** – all covers sold nowadays must be match-resistant.
- **Use a fire-retardant spray.** Check that the spray is water-resistant and suitable for the furniture fabric.
- Have the furniture **reupholstered with fire-resistant fabric**. You could also replace the filling at the same time or have a fire-resistant interliner fitted between the old filling and the new outer cover.

as wood, paper, some plastics and textiles. Do not use around electrical equipment or on chip-pan fires.

Black

These carbon dioxide extinguishers will tackle fires of flammable liquids, such as oil, petrol and paint, but not chip-pan fires. They need to be used at close range and work by starving the fire of oxygen. They can be used for fires involving electrical equipment.

Blue

These dry powder extinguishers are effective on fires involving paper, wood and plastics, and for liquids containing grease and paint, but should never be used on pans containing fat, including chip pans.

Cream

These foam extinguishers are not recommended for home use.

In addition, fire blankets are useful for tackling a chip-pan fire in its early stages,

Smoking in bed

Every year people fall asleep either **in bed or in an armchair** smoking and start a fire. They are often killed. It is also dangerous to smoke when you're sitting down and feeling sleepy or if you've been drinking.

providing you can cover the pan entirely and without hurting yourself, and for wrapping round someone whose clothes are on fire.

- Keep at least one 0.45kg (1lb) dry powder extinguisher on each floor of your home. Place in the hallway, on landings, in the kitchen and in the garage.
- Mount extinguishers securely near likely sources of fire, though don't put them near radiators or cookers.
- Make sure extinguishers are clearly visible and easily accessible.
- Make sure everyone in the household knows how to operate extinguishers.
- Replace an extinguisher after use or when the five-year guarantee expires.

Chip-pan fires

- **Don't use water** or a fire extinguisher to tackle the fire.
- **Don't try and move the pan.**
- **Switch off the heat** under the pan only if you can do so without hurting yourself.
- **Use a fire blanket or damp tea towel** to smother the fire only if it is small.
- **If in any doubt** – get out and call the fire brigade.

Overfilling chip pans

It is dangerous to fill chip pans more than a third full. If the oil starts to smoke don't put food in – leave the pan to cool. Make sure the food you're cooking is dry.

Every week nearly **90 people** are injured by chip-pan fires.

Fitting smoke alarms

Smoke alarms are essential, since without them there is little chance of escaping a fire that starts when you are asleep.

Ionization alarms are the cheapest type and detect flaming fires before the smoke gets too thick.

Optical alarms cost more and are better at detecting slow-burning fires, such as those caused by smouldering upholstery.

Either type can be powered by battery or mains, and some models can be connected so that fire detected in one spot raises the alarm throughout the house.

Where to fit

- In a single-floor home, fit a minimum of one, preferably optical, alarm in the area between bedrooms and living rooms.
- To protect two or more floors, fit one alarm at the foot of the

The South Yorkshire Fire & Rescue Service demonstrates what happens when you throw water on to a chip-pan fire to try and put it out

stairs and another on each landing. For the best protection, use both ionisation and optical alarms, and if possible connect them. If you use just one alarm, site it where the noise will be heard throughout the house even when you are asleep, such as at the top of the stairs.
- Don't put smoke alarms in the kitchen, bathroom or garage.
- Mount as close to the centre of the ceiling as possible, a minimum of 30cm (10in) from walls and lights.

Maintenance

- Test batteries monthly. Fit new ones annually.
- Keep the casing clean.
- If cooking fumes trigger false alarms, don't remove the battery. Reposition the alarm where cooking fumes won't trigger it or fit a silencer attachment, which allows you to turn off nuisance alarms without disabling the alarm permanently.

Fire action plan

Does everyone in your home know what they should do if a smoke alarm goes off during the night? Make a **fire action plan** that caters for every member of the household.

- Choose a **back-up escape route** in case you can't get out by the door you usually use to leave the building. Always keep escape routes clear. In a block of flats, if the main stairs were blocked or smoke-filled, you would have to avoid the lifts and use the fire escape.
- Make sure everyone knows where **door and window keys** are kept, and that they are able to use them easily.
- Choose a **room with a window** (and, if possible, a telephone) that you would stay in if your way out was blocked.
- Once you've made your action plan, **walk through it** with everyone in the household. Remind yourselves of the plan at frequent intervals.

Have you fitted a smoke alarm?

Smoke alarms are relatively cheap nowadays. If your home is on more than one floor, you should **fit at least one smoke alarm on each floor**.

Emergency procedures

The advice here comes from the website run by the Office of the Deputy Prime Minister – www.firekills.gov.uk – which gives useful advice about preventing and dealing with fires, and provides links to other sites.

What to do in an emergency

ALERT EVERYONE
If you become aware of a fire in your home you need to act instantly, swiftly, and calmly. Make sure everyone in your home knows about the fire. Shout. Get everyone together.

DON'T DELAY
You cannot afford to waste any time. Don't:

- investigate the fire
- go looking for valuables – whether that's jewellery, photographs, documents or whatever
- go looking for pets.

SHUT DOORS
As you go out, open only the doors you need to. Before you open a door check it with the back of your hand. If it's warm, don't open it – the fire is the other side. Close any open doors.

GET EVERYONE OUT
Use a set escape route (*see* p415 for planning this). Stay together if you can.

CRAWL ON THE FLOOR
Smoke is poisonous and can kill you. If there's smoke, put your nose as low to the ground as possible; the air is cleaner near the floor.

DIAL 999
Once you've escaped, use a mobile, a neighbour's phone or a phone box – 999 calls are free. Don't call the local fire station's number – it will probably take longer to be answered. You should:

- speak slowly and clearly
- give the whole address of your home, including the town
- say what is on fire (eg. a two-storey house)
- explain if anyone is trapped and what room they are in.

The more information the fire brigade has, the quicker it can get to you and act when it gets there.

What to do in an emergency

DON'T GO BACK IN
Don't go back in for anything. If there's someone still inside, wait for the fire brigade to arrive. You can tell them about the person and they will be able to find them quicker than you. If you disappear inside the building, that will slow down the firefighters' efforts to rescue anyone else missing, apart from putting your life in great danger.

WAIT NEARBY
Find somewhere safe to wait. When the fire brigade arrives, give them as much information as possible about the fire and the building.

CAN'T GET OUT OF A DOOR?
- Go out of a window if you're on the ground or first floor.
- Throw bedding or anything soft down to cushion your fall and hang at arm's length before dropping to the ground.

CAN'T GET OUT AT ALL?
- Get everyone into one room.
- Shut the door and put clothes, bedding, etc. round the bottom of it.
- Open the window and call for help.

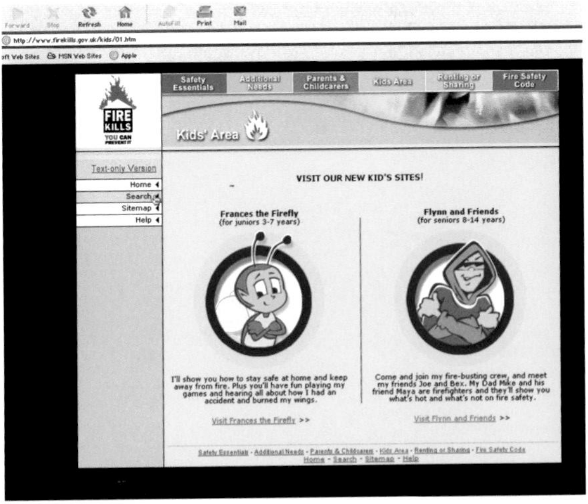

There is even an area for kids on www.firekills.gov.uk website

Six night-time checks

1. **Close all internal doors.** This slows down the spread of flame and smoke, giving you longer to escape.
2. Switch off, at the wall, as many **electrical appliances** as possible.
3. Make sure **cigarettes and candles** have been properly extinguished. Contents of ashtrays should be cold before you tip them into the bin. Never smoke in bed.
4. Make sure the **oven and burners** are turned off.
5. Turn off any other **gas appliances**, such as heaters.
6. Put **fireguards** in front of open fires.

Fire safety

Most of us, if we're honest, believe that a fire will never happen to us and don't really give much time thinking about fire safety in our own homes.

However, people who lose their homes to fire face a nightmare of insurance claims, temporary housing, endless form filling, insecurity, the threat of poverty and the pain of loss. And they're often just the lucky ones.

By following the precautions outlined on pp412–5, you should have enough information to prevent a fire in the first place.

However, if a fire does take place, the advice given on the previous pages (*see* pp416–7) provide the essentials in dealing with the emergency of a fire.

Above all, never think that a fire will happen to someone else and so put off considering an action plan.

House fires are easily prevented, but can cause devastation when they occur

Carbon monoxide dangers

At least 50 people die in the UK every year from carbon monoxide poisoning and many more have to have hospital treatment.

Even in small amounts, this invisible, odourless gas is harmful. Carbon monoxide is given off by gas-, oil-, coal- or wood-burning appliances if they are faulty, the room is badly ventilated or the chimney or flue is blocked.

Symptoms

If you feel drowsy or develop headaches, chest pains, giddiness, nausea or diarrhoea and stomach pains when there is no obvious cause, carbon monoxide could be affecting you. Turn off all appliances and see a doctor immediately.

Spotting the danger signs

Carbon monoxide causes:

- sooty stains to appear on or just above appliances
- gas flames, which usually burn blue, to burn yellow or orange
- coal or wood fires to burn slowly or go out.

Protecting yourself

- Get your boiler and gas appliances serviced annually by an engineer who is a member of the Council for Registered Gas Installers (CORGI).
- Keep your home properly ventilated.
- Never allow vents or outside flues to become blocked, for example, by climbing plants up the outside of the house.
- Have chimneys swept regularly.
- Consider fitting a carbon monoxide detector.

Carbon monoxide detectors

- Buy one that complies with the British Standard BS 7860.
- Fit the detector on the ceiling or wall in any room that contains a boiler, fire or water heater.
- Place it above door and window height and at least 15cm (5in) from corners.
- Test the alarm to judge whether it is loud enough to wake you. If you don't think it would wake you, fit a second alarm closer to your bedroom.

Children's safety

Every week three children die from accidents in the home in the UK, with under fives being at most risk. Annually, domestic accidents bring more than a million children under 15 to a hospital emergency department, while many more have less serious, but often painful, mishaps.

Whether you have children living in the house or as occasional visitors, there are effective precautions you can take to ensure that your home is safe for them.

Preventing accidents in the home

The most serious accidents happen in the kitchen and on the stairs. Young children, up to age four, are most at risk, with boys more accident-prone than girls. Younger children are at more risk of burns, scalds and poisoning accidents, while older children are more likely to suffer fractured bones. Accidents tend to happen in the late afternoon and early evening, and during holidays or weekends, when tiredness, hurrying, distraction or

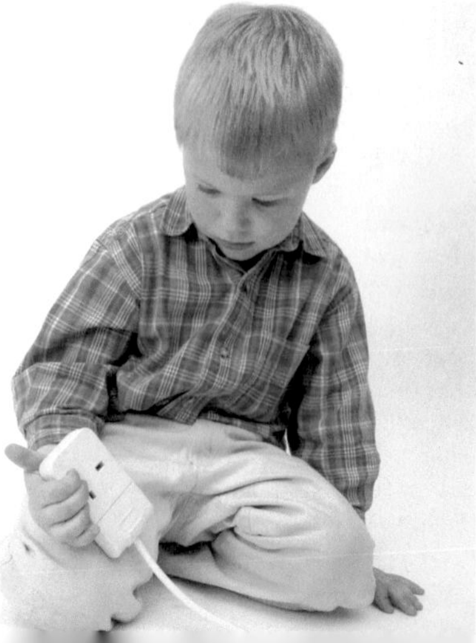

Young children are vulnerable to accidents in the home, especially as they get older and become more inquisitive

unfamiliar surroundings may play a part.

Burns and scalds

Fires cause almost half of all fatal accidents to children, while scalds can cause painful and disfiguring injuries.

- Keep matches and lighters where children can neither see nor reach them.
- Use a full-sized fireguard with fine mesh, secured to the wall.
- A hot drink spill can still scald a small child 15 minutes after being made. Never hold a hot drink while you have a child on your lap, pass a drink over a child's head or put a drink down on a low table.
- Turn down your boiler's thermostat a couple of degrees. Always run cold water into a bath first and test the temperature with your elbow before a small child gets in.
- Place pans on the cooker's back rings and keep handles turned in.

Choking and suffocation

- Keep tiny items, like marbles, watch batteries and coins, away from under-threes. Teach older children to keep small toys out of reach of younger ones.

Small children and their movements

0–6 months Not fully mobile, but can wriggle or roll into danger. Never leave on a raised surface, even a bed or sofa.

6–12 months Crawling and pulling themselves up. Keep small objects out of reach. Remove or secure free-standing furniture and other items that could topple onto child.

1–2 years Fully mobile, very inquisitive. Never leave unattended. Will probably taste or spill anything they encounter. Take care with hot drinks when near child. Use a fireguard and a stair gate.

2–3 years Can climb, pull, and twist. Will watch and copy. Will run around and knock things over. Keep valuables out of reach. Don't let child see you do anything dangerous.

3 years onwards Child's skills increase steadily. Continued safety training and frequent reminders of safety rules are important.

- Children under six should not be given peanuts to eat. If accidentally inhaled, these could lodge in the lung, causing severe illness.
- Flatten and knot plastic bags when using them for storage.
- Pull-cords on blinds and curtains should be short.
- Shut cats out of rooms where babies sleep and use a pram net or cot net.

Cuts

- Fit safety glass in low-level windows and doors or make non-toughened glass safer with shatter-resistant film. Buy greenhouses or cold frames that are safety-glazed or fence them off.
- Put stickers on large expanses of glass, such as patio doors, to draw attention to them.

Drowning

Small children can drown in less than 3cm (1in) of water. Always supervise children when in and near water, and be vigilant when visiting gardens and garden centres.

- Fit safety tops on water butts and drain ponds or fence them securely.
- Empty paddling pools between uses.
- Don't leave buckets or bowls of water unattended.

Immunisation

The NHS argues strongly in favour of immunisation and offers **nine vaccinations** against infectious diseases for children between two months and 14 years.

You can get information from your **GP and NHS-sponsored websites**. For arguments against immunisation, check out the website of The Informed Parent, www.informedparent.co.uk.

- Never leave babies or children younger than five alone in the bath. Stay in earshot at bathtime at least until they are six.

Falls

Over one third of all children's accidents are falls, most of which involve tripping. The worst consequences follow falls from a height, including toppling from high-chairs or prams. Always use, and check, safety harnesses.

- Put safety gates, made to BS 4125 specification, at the top and foot of staircases.
- Board up horizontal balustrades and vertical ones with wide gaps between struts. Discourage climbing.
- Secure carpet and rugs firmly.
- Fit safety locks on all upstairs windows, but make sure you can locate keys swiftly in an emergency. Don't put furniture – or a pram or buggy – under a window if a child could use it to reach the window.
- Never put baby bouncers on top of tables.

Poisoning

- Always keep household or garden chemicals in their original containers. Buy containers that have child-resistant caps.

- Keep chemicals and medicines out of children's sight and reach, preferably locked away. Even seemingly innocuous preparations, such as iron supplements, can be harmful to children.
- Don't leave alcoholic drinks in view where children could sample them.
- Check, before buying plants, that leaves and fruits are not poisonous.

Internet safety

The Internet can be a **great tool for children**, helping with study and research, as well as offering fun. Unfortunately, there are also dangers out on the World Wide Web.

1 **Set ground rules** and discuss them with children, so that they understand the reasons for them. Display the rules near the computer.

2 **Limit the amount of time** children spend on the computer. Set a kitchen timer near the computer.

3 Keep the computer in a **general living area**, not in a child's bedroom, so you can see what they are looking at.

4 Teach children **never to give their name, age, address or phone number** to anyone online.

5 Learn enough about computers and the Internet so that you are able to **understand** what children are doing.

6 **Encourage** children to tell you which websites they are visiting. This promotes trust and respect.

7 Don't let children enter **Internet chat rooms** unmonitored.

8 Get to know who the children's **online friends** are.

9 **Install software** that will block specific websites or filter out those site which contain suspect keywords.

Home treatments for common ailment

Colds In babies, the nose may become blocked, leaving them unable to suck properly. Nose drops help to clear the mucus. For babies over three months and young children, liquid paracetamol helps relieve aches and pains.

Coughs Your pharmacist can advise on the right type of cough medicine, depending on whether the cough is dry or not.

Fever Give liquid paracetamol. Make sure you use the correct dosage for the child's age – too small a quantity will not reduce the temperature. You can also give relief by sponging the top of the child's body with tepid water and allowing it to evaporate.

Diarrhoea and vomiting Give plenty of fluids. Babies under six months become dehydrated more easily than older children,

Although many childhood illnesses get better over a few days, keep a close eye on the symptoms and call a doctor if at all worried

so seek medical advice if they refuse liquid.

Tummy ache Children often complain of this when they have colds or other viral illnesses, because glands in their abdominal area swell and become tender. Give liquid paracetamol to ease the discomfort. Tummy ache can also be caused by constipation. Make sure children have sufficient fibre from fruit, vegetables and wholegrain cereals and bread. They should also have plenty to drink, every day.

Getting medical help

NHS Direct (*see* p443) offers healthcare advice over the telephone or Internet. You're asked a set of questions about symptoms, then advised on how to treat the condition at home or advised to see your doctor. Going online in the first instance may be quicker than using the telephone and you will still be put through to a qualified nurse.

Many common childhood conditions disappear by themselves over a few days, without needing medical intervention. Call a doctor if:

- a child has persistent abdominal pain with vomiting, which could indicate appendicitis
- you suspect meningitis – this disease is relatively uncommon, but symptoms include vomiting, headache, sensitivity to light, a rash that does not disappear when pressed and wanting to lie down undisturbed.

In the event of a burglary

If you find that you have been burgled there are certain things that you can do to increase the police's chance of catching the burglar. Preserving as much evidence as possible is the most important consideration.

If you have returned home and believe that the offender may still be inside or are at all unsure about checking the house, DO NOT ENTER THE PREMISES. Your safety is most important.

Contact the police

If your property has been burgled, contact your local police station, either in person or by phone, and give:

- your name, address and a contact telephone number
- details of where the burglary has taken place
- the name, age and address of the owner of the property and where they can be contacted
- if known, the time the crime happened and what type of property is involved
- details of witnesses or anybody you think may have been responsible for the burglary.

You should make a note of:

- anything you think has been stolen – especially any serial numbers
- any damage to your property caused by the burglars.

Let the police know if you later find:

- an item of property that you thought had been stolen
- that additional items have been stolen.

Other calls to make

You may need to contact:

- a locksmith or glazier if locks or windows are broken
- your bank if you notice any credit cards or chequebooks are missing
- your network provider if your mobile phone is missing
- your insurance company if you plan to make a claim
- the authority that issued official identification papers, such as a passport, if any of these are missing.

TOP TIP

If you have returned home to find that you have been burgled and the offenders are clearly long gone, **try not to touch anything that the offender has touched**. If there is something that you need to touch, put on a glove. This will limit the damage to any fingerprints that the offender may have left.

In the event of flooding

The information in this section comes from the Environment Agency. You can obtain a local Flood Directory, with a flood map and local contact numbers, from the Floodline, on 0845 988 1188.

Be prepared

In a flood you may find you're without lighting, heating or a telephone line. The following simple actions will help you to be prepared.

- Make sure you have adequate insurance if you believe your home may be at risk. Check your existing policy.
- Make up a flood kit – including key personal documents, torch, battery or wind-up radio, rubber gloves, wellingtons, waterproof clothing, First Aid kit and blankets.
- Keep details of your insurance policy and your insurer's emergency contact number somewhere safe, preferably as part of your flood kit.
- Get into the habit of storing valuable or sentimental items upstairs or in a high place.
- Buy sandbags or floorboards to try and block doorways and airbricks.

Flood warnings

- Listen for warnings on radio and TV; phone the Floodline for more information.
- Move pets, vehicles, valuables and other items to safety.
- Alert your neighbours, particularly the elderly.

If you live in a flood-prone area, preparations before flooding are essential

- Put sandbags or floorboards in place – but make sure your property is ventilated.
- Be ready to turn off gas and electricity (get help if needed).
- Co-operate with emergency services and local authorities – you may be evacuated.
- Do as much as you can in daylight. Doing anything in the dark will be a lot harder, especially if the electricity fails.

Stay safe in a flood

- Floods can kill. Don't try to walk or drive through floodwater – 15cm (6in) of fast-flowing water can knock you off your feet and 60cm (2ft) of water will float your car.
- Manhole covers may have come off and there may be other hazards you can't see.
- Never try to swim through fast-flowing water – you may get swept away or be struck by an object in the water.
- Don't walk on sea defences or riverbanks, or cross river-bridges – they may collapse in extreme situations or you may be swept off by large waves. Beware of stones and pebbles being thrown up by waves.
- Move your family and pets upstairs or to higher ground. If the flooding is severe the authorities may move you.

Switch off water, gas, and electricity at the first sign of flooding to your property.

If you have been flooded

- Call your insurance company's 24-hour emergency helpline as soon as possible. They will be able to provide information on dealing with your claim and assistance in getting things back to normal.
- Find out where you can get help to clear up. Check with your local authority or health authority firstly, or look under Flood damage in the *Yellow Pages* for suppliers of cleaning materials or equipment to dry out your property.
- Open doors and windows to ventilate your home but take care to ensure that house and valuables are secure. It takes a house brick about a month per inch to dry out.
- Contact your gas, electricity and water supply companies. Have power supplies checked before you turn them back on. Wash taps and run them for a few minutes before use.
- Throw away food that may have been in contact with floodwater – it could be contaminated. Contact your local authority's Environmental Health department for advice.

First aid advice

The first aid information on the following pages is based on advice from the British Red Cross. It is, of course, no substitute for a thorough training in first aid.

First aid is the term given to describe the care given to a casualty before professional help arrives. It can come from a member of the family, a friend or even a stranger who happens to be on the spot, but the help they give can sometimes mean the difference between life and death.

The aims of first aid are:

- to preserve life
- to prevent the worsening of any injuries
- to promote recovery.

To book a course in your area call your local British Red Cross branch. To order a first aid kit or other learning materials such as books and CD-ROMs, call 0845 601 7105. Visit www.redcross.org.uk/firstaid for more information.

Other organisations such as St John Ambulance, St Andrew's Ambulance Association and the Health and Safety Executive (mainly for work-related first aid

Recovery position

An unconscious casualty who is **breathing and lying on their back**, but has no other life-threatening conditions, should be placed in the **recovery position**.

- **Remove spectacles**, as well as any bulky objects, from the casualty's pockets.
- **Straighten** the casualty's legs.
- Place the arm, which is **nearest to you** at right angles to their body, palm up.
- Bring their other arm **across their chest** and hold their hand, palm facing outwards, against the cheek nearest to you.
- Using your other hand, hold the **knee furthest from you** and gently draw the leg up until their foot is flat on the floor.
- Keeping their hand pressed **close to their cheek** to support the head, pull the leg towards you and roll the casualty onto their side.
- Finally, pull the bent leg up at **right angles to the body** – both hip and knee are bent at a right angle.

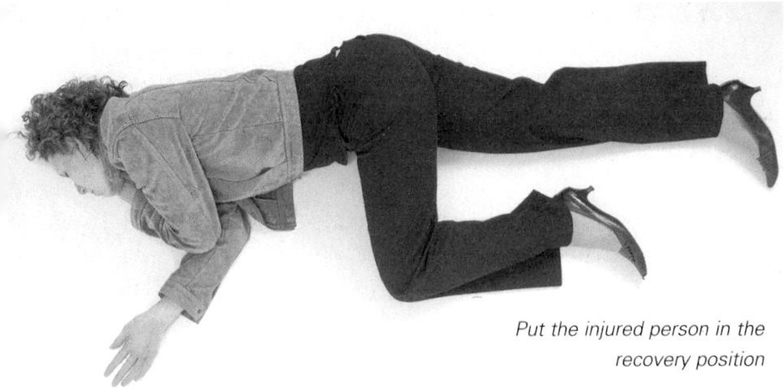
Put the injured person in the recovery position

training) can also offer courses in first aid.

So, what should you do if you are in a situation where someone has collapsed?

Danger

Firstly, make sure that neither you nor the casualty is in any further danger as you approach.

Response (adult)

You then need to check for any response from the casualty by gently shaking their shoulder and speaking loudly and clearly. Try asking what their name is (if you don't know them) or tell them to open their eyes.

- **If they respond**, then leave them in the position you found them and get help if necessary. Treat any injuries if you can.
- **If there is no response**, then the casualty is unconscious and you need to check the airway and their breathing.

Airway and breathing

When someone falls into unconsciousness there is the danger that, due to loss of muscle control, the tongue may fall back and block the airway, making breathing difficult or impossible.

- **To open the airway**, place one hand on the casualty's forehead and carefully tilt the head back. This will open the casualty's mouth. Check for any obstructions and remove objects such as broken teeth from the mouth.
- With the index and middle fingers of your other hand, lift the casualty's chin.
- **To check for breathing**, look

along the chest for signs of movement, listen for sounds of breathing and place your cheek close to their mouth for 10 seconds to try and feel for any breath.

- **If there are signs of breathing**, check for any life-threatening injuries and place them in the recovery position (*see* p428).
- **If the casualty is not breathing**, then send someone else (if available) to phone for an ambulance while you carry out rescue breathing (see below).

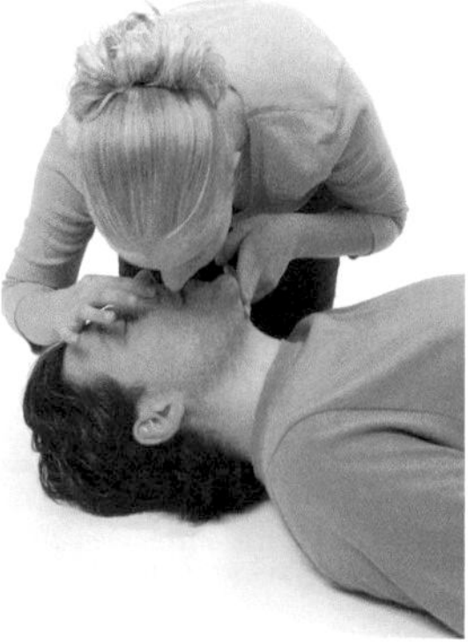

Pinching the nose, seal your lips around the casualty's mouth

Resuscitation techniques

If a casualty is unconscious, then their breathing may not function as it should, which in turn will affect the circulation and result in starving the body's cells of oxygen. However, by using reviving – resuscitation – techniques, oxygen can be supplied to the casualty until medical aid arrives at the scene.

British Red Cross

The British Red Cross Society
9 Grosvenor Crescent
London
SW1X 7EJ

Tel: 020 7235 5454
www.redcross.org.uk

These techniques can be easily remembered by thinking of them as the ABC of resuscitation: A is for keeping the airway open (*see* pp429–30); B is for breathing for a casualty; and C is for maintaining the circulation.

Rescue breaths

If an adult or a child over eight years' old has stopped breathing, then you will need to force air into the casualty's lungs by giving rescue breaths.

- Make sure the casualty's head remains tilted back to keep the airway open (*see* pp429–30). Next, pinch their nose, take a deep breath and seal your lips over the casualty's mouth. Breathe out firmly and steadily for roughly two seconds, watching for the chest to rise.

- If you are unable to blow into the mouth, close it and seal your lips around the nose and repeat the breathing out process. Open the mouth after each breath to let any air escape from the lungs.
- If their chest visibly inflates as you blow and falls when you take your mouth away you have performed an effective rescue breath. If this does not happen, make sure that the casualty's head is tilted back enough and that you have closed the nose completely by pinching it shut.

Keep trying up to five times to carry out two effective rescue breaths. If you are unable to carry this out, check their circulation.

Circulation

Check for signs of circulation, such as breathing, movement and coughing, but for no longer than 10 seconds.

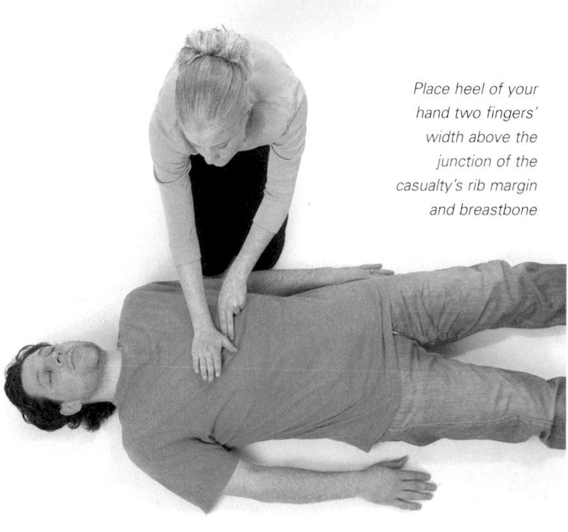

Place heel of your hand two fingers' width above the junction of the casualty's rib margin and breastbone

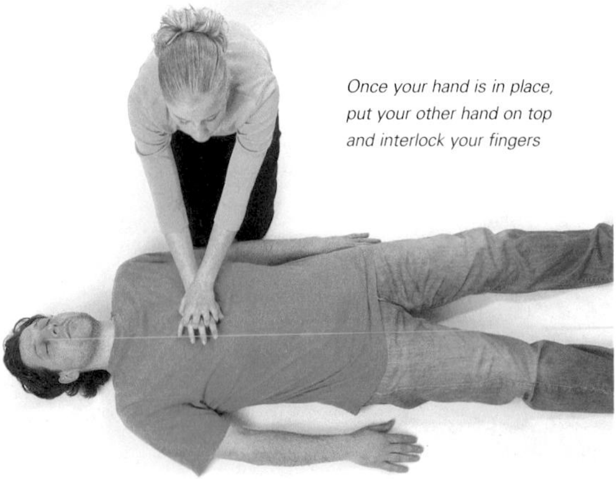

Once your hand is in place, put your other hand on top and interlock your fingers

- If there are signs, continue giving 10 rescue breaths every minute, checking circulation again after every minute. Once the casualty has started to breathe again, place them in the recovery position (*see* p428) and keep an eye on them until help arrives.

However, if you cannot give two effective rescue breaths and you know that the casualty has choked or there are no signs of circulation, then you should start a combination of chest compressions and rescue breaths, also known as CPR (cardiopulmonary resuscitation).

CPR (adult)

- Start by placing the middle finger of one hand on the point where the lowest rib meets the breastbone. Position your index finger next to your middle finger on this point. Place the heel of your other hand above and next to your two fingers on the breastbone.
- Next, cover the hand on the breastbone with your other hand, interlocking your fingers. Place the heel of the uppermost hand on top of the wrist of your underneath hand. The fingers of your underneath hand should be lifted clear of the casualty's chest (*see* image above).

- Kneeling with your shoulders over the breastbone and your arms straight, press down roughly 4–5cm (1½–2in). Release the pressure, but keep your hands on the casualty's chest. Give 15 compressions in total. Aim for a rate of around 100 per minute. To help in this, try counting out loud 'one and two and three and...' to get the correct rhythm.
- After performing 15 chest compressions, give two rescue breaths and continue this pattern – 15 compressions and two breaths – until medical help arrives or the casualty starts moving or breathing again.

Response (child)

This information is for a one to seven-year-old child. Check if the child is conscious by calling out their name (if known) or asking them to open their eyes. Gently tap them on their shoulder.

- **If there is a response**, then leave them in the position you found them and get help if necessary. Treat any injuries if you can.
- **If there is no response**, then the child is unconscious and you need to check the airway and their breathing.

Airway and breathing

- **To open the airway of a child under eight**, place one hand on their forehead while carefully tilting their head back.
- Check for any obstructions and remove objects such as broken teeth from the mouth.
- With the index and middle fingers of your other hand, lift the child's chin.
- **To check for breathing**, look along the chest for signs of movement, listen for sounds of breathing and place your cheek close to the child's mouth for 10 seconds to try and feel for any breath.
- **If there are signs of breathing**, check for any life-threatening injuries and place them in the recovery position (*see* p428).
- **If the casualty is not breathing**, then send someone else (if available) to phone for an ambulance while you carry out rescue breathing (*see* p434).

British Red Cross

The British Red Cross Society
9 Grosvenor Crescent
London
SW1X 7EJ

Tel: 020 7235 5454
www.redcross.org.uk

Blow firmly and steadily into the child's lungs until you see the chest rising

Rescue breaths

Make sure the child's head remains tilted back to keep the airway open (*see* p433).

- Next, pinch the child's nose, take a deep breath and seal your lips over the child's mouth. Breathe out firmly and steadily for roughly two seconds, watching for the chest to rise.
- If you are unable to blow into the mouth, close it and seal your lips around the nose and repeat the breathing out process. Open the mouth after each breath to let any air escape from the lungs.
- If their chest visibly inflates as you blow and falls when you take your mouth away you have performed an effective rescue breath. If this does not happen, make sure that the child's head is tilted back enough and that you have closed the nose completely by pinching it shut.

Keep trying up to five times to carry out two effective rescue breaths. If you are unable to carry this out, check their circulation.

British Red Cross

The British Red Cross Society
9 Grosvenor Crescent
London
SW1X 7EJ

Tel: 020 7235 5454
www.redcross.org.uk

Circulation

Check for signs of circulation, such as breathing, movement and coughing, but for no longer than 10 seconds.

- If there are signs, continue giving rescue breaths at a rate of 20 per minute, checking circulation again after every minute. Once the casualty has started to breathe again, place them in the recovery position (*see* p428) and keep an eye on them until help arrives.

However, if you cannot give two effective rescue breaths and you know that the child has choked or there are no signs of circulation, then you should start CPR.

CPR (child)

- Find the child's lowermost rib with the middle finger of one hand. Go along this rib with your finger until it meets the breastbone. Position your index finger next to your middle finger on this point. Place the heel of your other hand next to your two fingers, on the lower half of the breastbone.
- Keeping the heel of your hand in position, remove your other hand. Lean over the child, with your arm straightened. Press down with the heel of your hand to roughly one third of the depth of the child's chest. Make sure your fingers do not press down onto the child's ribs. Repeat this five times at a rate of roughly 100 compressions per minute.
- After performing five chest compressions, tilt the head, lift the chin and give one rescue breath (*see* above). Continue this pattern – five chest compressions and one

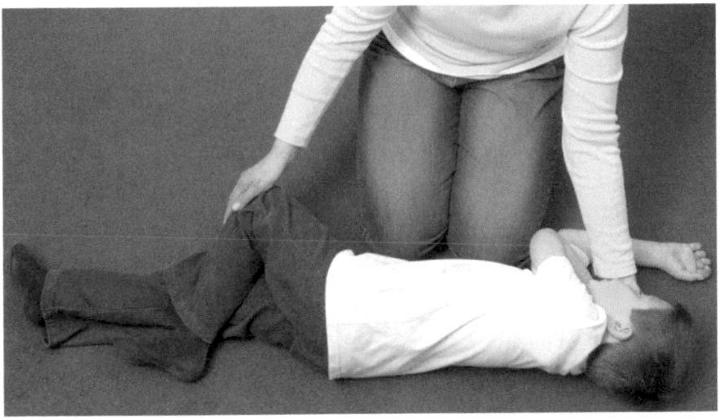

Use the recovery position for adults if the child is over a year old

rescue breath – at a rate of 100 compressions per minute for one minute.
- Carry on until medical help arrives or the casualty starts moving or breathing again. If breathing or circulation resumes, then place the child in the recovery position (*see* p428).

Response (infant)

This information is for an infant under the age of one. To check for consciousness, tap the sole of the infant's foot and try calling their name, if known.
- **If there is a response**, then take the infant with you to get the necessary medical support. Treat any injuries if you can.
- **If there is no response**, you need to check that the airway is open and that they are breathing.

Airway and breathing

- **To open the airway of an infant**, place one hand on their forehead and gently tilt their head back.
- Check for any obstructions and remove any obvious obstructions from the mouth using your thumb and forefinger.
- With one finger of your other hand, lift the infant's chin.
- **To check for breathing**, look along the chest for signs of movement, listen for sounds of breathing and place your cheek close to the infant's mouth for 10 seconds to try and feel for any breath.
- **If there are signs of breathing**, check for any life-threatening injuries and hold the infant in the recovery position (*see* below).
- **If the infant is not breathing**, then send someone else (if available) to phone for an ambulance while you carry out rescue breathing (*see* below).

Rescue breaths

To get oxygen into the lungs of an infant who is unconscious and not breathing, make sure the infant's head remains tilted back and the chin is lifted to keep the airway open (*see* above). You then need to give rescue breaths.
- Take a breath, but instead of pinching the infant's nose, as you would do with a child or an adult, place your lips around the infant's mouth and nose, forming an airtight seal. Breathe out gradually and firmly, looking to see the chest rise.

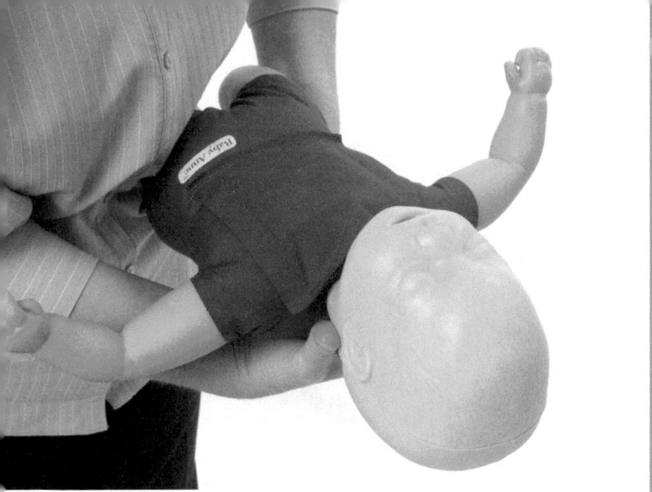

Hold the infant in the recovery position, with the head lower than the body

- Take your mouth away and watch to see if the infant's chest falls. If the chest visibly inflates as you blow and falls when you take your mouth away you have performed an effective rescue breath. If this does not happen, reposition the infant's head and try five more times to give two effective rescue breaths.

If you are unable to carry this out, check their circulation.

Circulation

Check for signs of circulation, such as breathing, movement and coughing, but for no longer than 10 seconds.

- If there are signs, continue

Recovery position (infant)

An unconscious infant who is still breathing should be put in the **recovery position** (*see* image above).

- Keeping the **head lower** than the body will allow vomit or fluids to drain from the mouth, keep the airway open and make sure that the neck and spine are aligned.
- While you are cradling the infant in the recovery position, if no helper is available to call for an ambulance, you can **take the infant with you** when you go and phone for emergency help.
- Keep a **close eye** on the infant while you wait for help to arrive and monitor any vital signs, such as response, pulse and breathing.

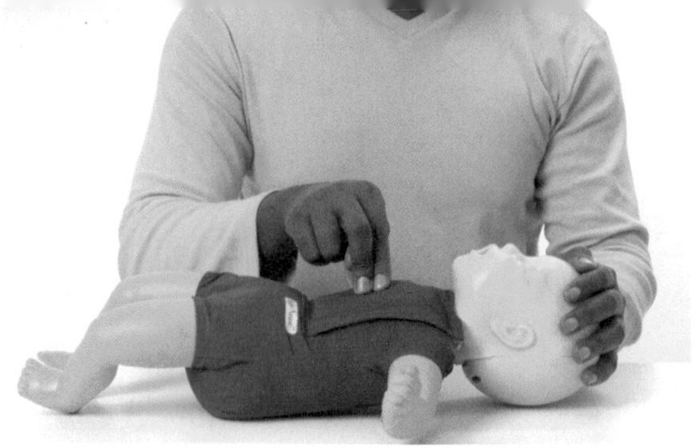

When performing chest compressions on an infant, use only two fingers

giving rescue breaths at a rate of 20 per minute, checking circulation again after every minute.

However, if you cannot give two effective rescue breaths and you know that the infant has choked or there are no signs of circulation, then you should start CPR.

CPR (infant)

- Place the infant on his back on a flat, firm surface, either at waist height or on the floor. From an imaginary line drawn between the infant's nipples, find the middle point and position the fingertips of your index and middle fingers about a finger's width below this point.
- Press down to roughly one third of the depth of the chest, then release the pressure, but keeping your fingers in contact with the infant's breastbone. Repeat this five times at a rate of roughly 100 compressions per minute.
- After giving five chest compressions, tilt the head, lift the chin and give one rescue breath (*see* above). Continue this pattern – five chest compressions and one rescue breath – at a rate of 100 compressions per minute for one minute.
- Carry on until medical help arrives or the infant starts moving or breathing again.

British Red Cross

The British Red Cross Society
9 Grosvenor Crescent
London
SW1X 7EJ

Tel: 020 7235 5454
www.redcross.org.uk

- If you are by yourself and there are no signs of circulation or breathing, perform CPR for one minute before taking the infant with you while you ring for an ambulance.

Choking

Choking occurs when an object, such as food or small objects (especially for children and infants), gets stuck at the back of the throat and blocks the windpipe. If the windpipe remains blocked for any length of time, there is a chance of the casualty losing consciousness, so prompt first aid is vital.

Standing behind the person who is choking, place your fist with your thumb facing in just over the upper abdomen, below the ribs

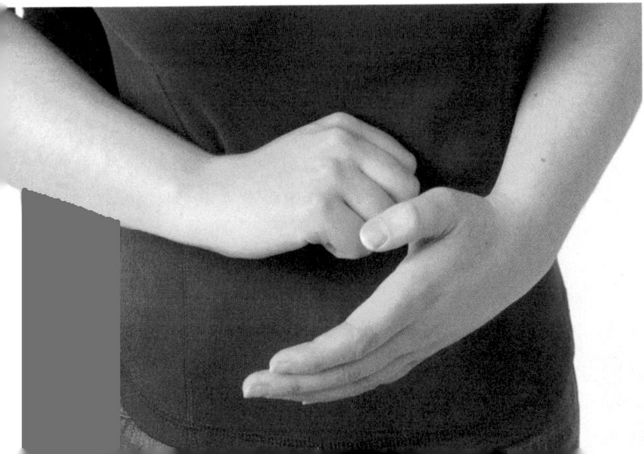

Adults

You'll first become aware that someone is choking if they have sudden difficulty in talking or breathing and start clutching their throat. They may also go very red in the face and cough.

- Encourage the casualty to carry on coughing. If breathing stops or they start to weaken, bend the casualty forward, stand behind and slap their back sharply between the shoulderblades – up to five times – with the flat of your hand. Hopefully the object will have become dislodged and you can remove it from their mouth.
- However, if this fails, stand behind again, clench your fist, and with the thumb against

their body, place it over the upper abdomen slightly below the ribs (*see* p440). This is the starting position for abdominal thrusts.

- Take hold of your fist with your other hand and pull inwards and upwards up to five times. Check to see if the object has become dislodged.
- Carry out up to three lots of back slaps and abdominal thrusts, but if the casualty is still choking, call an ambulance. Continue to alternate back slaps and abdominal thrusts until the ambulance arrives.
- If the casualty becomes unconscious, open the airway, check their breathing and carry out two rescue breaths. If you cannot give two effective rescue breaths, perform chest compressions to try and free the object.

Children

The choking symptoms will be the same as those of an adult.

- If the child is coughing, encourage them to carry on. If breathing stops or they start to weaken, bend the child forward, stand or kneel behind and slap their back sharply between the shoulderblades – up to five times – with the flat of your hand. Check in their mouth and pick out any visible objects.
- If back slaps fails, stand or kneel behind again, hold your fist against the lower part of the breastbone and press inwards up to five times. These are known as chest thrusts. Check to see if the object has become dislodged.
- If this doesn't work, hold your fist against the child's abdomen and press sharply inwards and upwards up to five times. Look again in the

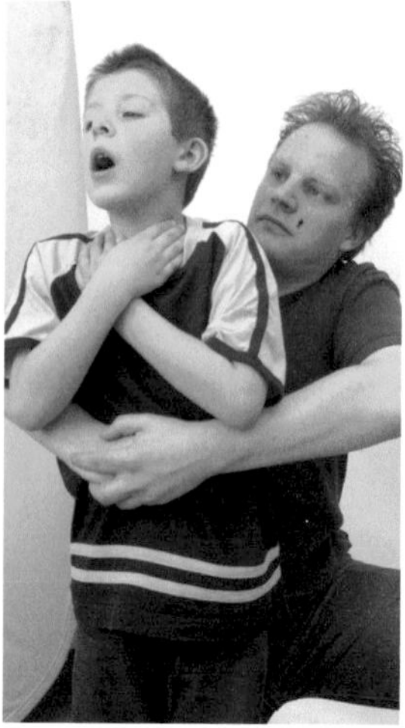

If back slaps haven't worked with a choking child, move to chest thrusts

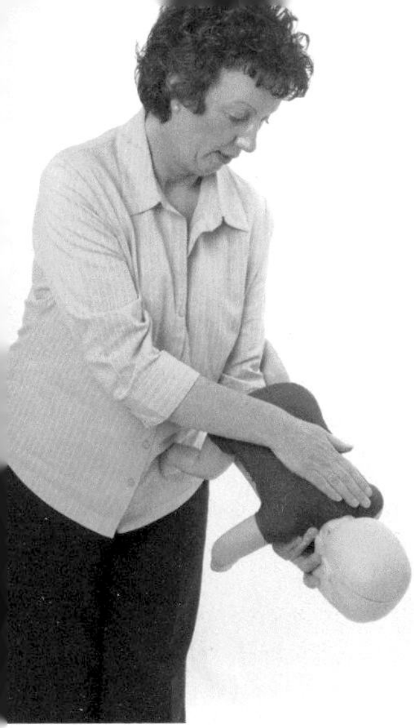

For a choking infant, give up to five sharp slaps on the back

mouth and remove any dislodged objects.
- After three lots of back slaps, chest thrusts and abdominal thrusts, if the child is still choking, call an ambulance. Continue with the three steps until help arrives.
- If the child becomes unconscious, open the airway, check their breathing and carry out two rescue breaths. If you cannot give two effective rescue breaths, perform chest compressions to try and free the object.

Infants

If an infant has trouble crying or making other noises, starts coughing, has difficulty breathing and generally looks in distress, then the airway may be partially blocked.

- Lay the infant along your forearm, face down, and give up to five sharp slaps on their back.
- Check the mouth to see if anything has become dislodged and remove any obstruction carefully with your fingertips.
- If this fails, lay the infant face up along your arm and, using two fingers, give up to five downward thrusts to the chest. Check the mouth again for any obstructions and remove if visible.
- After three lots of back slaps and chest thrusts, if the infant still appears to be choking, take them with you and call for an ambulance. Continue with the slaps and thrusts until help arrives.
- If the infant becomes unconscious, open the airway, check their breathing and carry out two rescue breaths. If you cannot give two effective rescue breaths, perform chest compressions to try and free the object.

Contact details

Useful websites and addresses about the information given in this chapter.

British Red Cross, 9 Grosvenor Crescent, London SW1X 7EJ
Tel: 020 7235 5454
www.redcross.org.uk/firstaid;
e-mail:
information@redcross.org.uk
The British Red Cross provides first aid training in the local community. To order a first aid kit or other learning materials, call 0845 601 7105.

Child Accident Prevention Trust (CAPT), 18-20 Farringdon Lane, London EC1R 3HA
Tel: 020 7608 3828
Fax: 020 7608 3674
e-mail: safe@capt.org.uk
www.capt.org.uk
A national charity committed to reducing the number of children and young people killed, disabled and seriously injured as a result of accidents.

Environment Agency
Floodline, Tel: 0845 988 1188
www.environment-agency.gov.uk
Offers advice on preparing for a flood and coping afterwards, as well as providing flood warning services and information on flood defence work.

Fire Kills
www.firekills.gov.uk
Home Office website on fire prevention.

FireNet International
www.fire.org.uk
Contains fire safety advice, including information about the different types of fire extinguisher.

Home Office, Public Enquiry Team, Home Office, 7th Floor, 50, Queen Anne's Gate, London SW1H 9AT
Tel: 0870 000 1585
Fax: 020 7273 2065
Textphone: 020 7273 3476
e-mail: public.enquiries@homeoffice.gsi.gov.uk
Click on the Crime & Policing button, then down to the 'What can you do' section for burglary prevention tips.

Home Safety Network
www.dti.gov.uk/homesafetynetwork/index.htm

Run by the government's DTI, the Home Safety Network has various advice pages, including information on home safety, carbon monoxide, drowning, fireworks and gardens.

Immunisation Programme, Department of Health, Room 602A, Skipton House, 80 London Road, London SE1 6LH
Tel: 020 7972 3807
Fax: 020 7972 5758
www.immunisation.org.uk
Information on immunisation from the National Health Service.

Informed Parent, PO Box 870, Harrow, Middlesex HA3 7UW
Tel: 020 8861 1022
www.informedparent.co.uk
Publishes a bulletin with information on the arguments against vaccination.

National Asthma Campaign, Providence House, Providence Place, London N1 0NT
Asthma Helpline: 0845 7 01 02 03; head office: 020 7226 2260
Fax: 020 7704 0740
www.asthma.org.uk
Research and other information for asthma sufferers.

NHS Direct
Tel: 0845 46 47
www.nhsdirect.nhs.uk
Extensive resource from the National Health Service (NHS). On the website you can search the NHS A–Z database for access to medical information.

Royal Society for the Prevention of Accidents (ROSPA), Edgbaston Park, 353 Bristol Road, Edgbaston, Birmingham B5 7ST
Tel: 0121 248 2000
Fax: 0121 248 2001
e-mail: help@rospa.co.uk
www.rospa.com/CMS
Gives general safety advice to prevent DIY accidents.

St. Andrew's Ambulance Association is one of Scotland's leading charities and the country's premier provider of first aid training and services.
Aberdeen, Tel: 01224 877271;
Fife, Tel: 01592 631758;
Glasgow, Tel: 0141 332 4031;
Edinburgh, Tel: 0131 229 5419;
Dundee, Tel: 01382 322 389
For all St Andrews Ambulance Association enquiries, e-mail firstaid@staaa.org.uk

St John Ambulance, National Headquarters, 27 St John's Lane, London EC1M 4BU
Tel: 020 7324 4000
Fax: 020 7324 4001
www.sja.org.uk

Index

Acknowledgements

The publishers would like to thank the following for producing the materials from which this book was derived:

Illustrators: Andrew Green, Antbits Illustration, Nick Pearson, Lorraine Hodghton

Writers: Anthony Bailey, Lynn Brittney, Paul Butt, Will Garside, David Holloway, Mike Lawrence, John McGowan, Joe McShane, Elizabeth Martyn, Ann Maurice, Rachel Parma, Mark Ramuz, Jane Sheard, Linda Sonntag, Toby Wallis, Virginia Wallis

Crown copyright material (pp281–8, 416–17) is reproduced with the permission of the Controller of HMSO and the Queen's Printer for Scotland.

Flooding text (pp426–7) copyright Environment Agency.

'Small children and their movements' text (p421) by kind permission of the Royal Society for the Prevention of Accidents (ROSPA).

IKEA Image House for the use of its images on pages 51, 56, 57, 82–3, 87, 96, 101, 104, 191, 201, 203, 204, 277, 329, 330, 332 and 342.

The British Red Cross for the first aid advice on pages 428–39 and the use of images on pages 406, 410, 420, 429, 431, 432, 435, 436, 437 and 439.